405 Woodworking Patterns

By the Editors of FC&A

FC&A Publishing
103 Clover Green
Peachtree City, GA 30269

Publisher: FC&A Publishing
Editors: Diane Dunn, Deborah Williams, Lydia Schulze, Kris Rose
Production: Art Department
Cover Design: Diane Dunn
Printed and bound by Banta Company

Twenty-fourth printing August 2002

ISBN 0-915099-84-5

We have made every effort to ensure the accuracy and completeness of these patterns and drawings. We cannot, however, be responsible for human error, typographical mistakes, or variations in measurements and individual work.

— TABLE OF CONTENTS —

METRIC CONVERSION CHART

Measurements: Simply apply metric units to most of the pattern grids instead of the inches and feet suggested in the text.

In the U.S.A., lumber generally is measured in inches, such as 2 inches by 4 inches, 1 inch by 2 inches, etc. For example, what you know as a 100 x 50mm (4 inches by 2 inches) stud would be called a 2 x 4 throughout the pattern book. A 2440 x 1220mm sheet of plywood would be a 4 x 8 sheet in this book.

Most building and decorating materials in the UK are sold in metric units, but you may find both metric and Imperial units like inches and feet being used side-by-side in some retail establishments. Here is a table you may use to convert from Imperial to metric units:

To Convert	Into	Multiply by
inches	millimetres	25.4
feet	metres	0.305
yards	metres	0.914
millimetres	inches	0.394
metres	feet	3.28
metres	yards	1.094

— INTRODUCTION —

CONGRATULATIONS! You made a valuable investment in the art of woodcrafting when you purchased ***405 Woodworking Patterns***! This book combines small and large patterns into one useful and informative book that will give you a pattern for every mood and a project for every skill level.

If you've ever been frustrated because the range and type of patterns in a book or pattern collection was too narrow, you won't be disappointed with this purchase. You can get down to the fun part of woodworking -- making beautiful, unique crafts AND larger, more useful projects such as furniture and outdoor garden decorations. If you weren't holding this book in your hands, you wouldn't believe the number of pretty and practical patterns we've included.

These 405 patterns come in a wide range of sizes designed to suit any taste or decor. Easy-to-follow instructions ensure that you'll finish with a great looking product every time.

Our patterns include old-time favourites and delightful new creations. Beginning and advanced woodworkers will find designs to challenge and charm them. We've included helpful tips on painting and finishing your products and occasional alternative suggestions for making patterns different.

The feeling of pride and satisfaction you get from creating quality crafts will be well worth the time you invest. The fun doesn't stop until you do. We guarantee you won't be bored.

RULES FOR SAFETY

- Wear goggles or glasses with shatterproof lenses.
- Wear tight-fitting clothes. Loose clothing can be easily pulled into machinery. If you're wearing a long sleeved shirt, keep the sleeves firmly rolled up or buttoned around the wrist to keep material from being pulled into the saw blade.
- Secure all machinery to a workbench or other sturdy stand. Vibrations can cause unsecured saws and other equipment to fall.
- Turn off equipment not in use.
- Position electrical cords so that they cannot be tripped over.
- Keep your workspace organized. Constantly hunting for a tool can cause undue stress and take the enjoyment out of a project.

EQUIPPING YOUR WORKSHOP

- Hammer
- Tape measure. A good tape measure has the first few inches broken down into 32nds for extremely precise measurements.
- Supply of sharpened pencils
- Sandpaper
- Sanding block
- Hand drill and an assortment of bits
- Screwdriver set
- Assorted screws and nails, especially small finishing nails
- Clamps
- Saw

A router and heavy-duty shop vacuum cleaner are optional items. A router will give your projects a finished look. The heavy-duty shop vacuum cleaner will make quick work of cleaning up.

COMMON SENSE FOR SAWS

The saw is the most important tool in your workshop. There are four basic types of saws that we suggest for use with these patterns: a scroll saw, a bandsaw, a table saw and a jigsaw. Three of these saws can be used to cut the patterns in this book. A table saw is necessary for the large woodworking projects and is almost essential when making shelves. Even though the scroll saw is probably the safest and easiest to work with, always use the one that is most comfortable for you. Here are a few simple tips to help you get the most efficient use from your saw.

- Follow all directions and safety procedures in the owner's manual that came with your saw.
- Use both hands and maintain a steady pressure when feeding wood into a saw blade. Forcing the wood may cause the blade to break or push the wood off course. Pushing wood into the side of the blade, or trying to turn a radius too small for the blade, can also break the blade or push it off its course. Breaking blades is dangerous and expensive.
- Keep plenty of extra saw blades on hand. When cutting intricate designs, especially on a scroll saw, the blade could break if too much pressure is applied.
- Keep your blade sharp. The sharper the blade, the finer the cut, which in the end means less sanding time.

TIPS FOR TOOL CARE

The tools you use will help determine how the finished product looks. High-quality tools will perform better and last longer than low-quality tools.

If you don't have the necessary tools to begin woodworking, you can hire them from HSS hire shops. Check the Yellow Pages under Tool and Equipment Hire to find a shop near you.

Remember to keep all tools oiled and clean. Grime and dust buildup impair machine function.

PURCHASING WOOD AND TIMBER

The types of wood are broadly divided into two categories: hard and soft. Generally, the harder the wood, the higher the price. Wood comes in different grades, as joinery fifths or unsorted.

Hardwood is sturdier and more durable than softwood. It does not scar easily, is very heavy and has a tight grain. It is preferred for use in fine furniture and cabinets. The most common types of hardwood are ash, basswood, butternut, beech, birch, cherry, mahogany, maple, oak and walnut.

Some woods, such as basswood, do not stain well but are perfect for painting and have few knots. Most others, such as oak, stain beautifully.

Some types of hardwood are more readily available in certain areas than others. Since hardwood is expensive, you may want to practice with the less expensive woods before putting too much money into a hardwood project.

People often select hardwoods with a specific project in mind. Ash is a flexible wood and is often used for projects that will be subjected to shock and vibration. For projects that will be exposed to water, greenheart and elm work well.

Soft woods work well for projects made for a wall or table display. These woods usually come from the pine or fir families and are usually less expensive than hardwoods.

The cheaper softwoods are more commonly known as deal. You will find pines, firs, cedars and larches among those softwoods commonly stocked at timber supply stores.

White pine is a very good general purpose wood. Many other types of pine are available and are useful for various projects. Pine wins out over all other softwoods because it is plentiful, easy to work with and usually more affordable. Yellow pine is relatively free from warping, shrinking and knots.

Cedar, which often has a reddish colour in the grain, is frequently used for outdoor furniture. Cedar is used to construct wardrobes and chests because of its aromatic smell, which is highly prized as a moth deterrent.

TIMBER SELECTION

Choose smooth wood with consistent colour and grain markings.

- Buy heart wood whenever possible. This wood is cut from the centre of the tree and is stronger and more durable than wood cut from the outside of a tree.
- Check for splits, shakes, knots and pitch pockets that would affect the display quality of your project. Buying wood with knots can be good or bad, depending on the situation. If the knots are not in a stress area of wood from which the patterns will be cut, they could lend character and beauty to the finished piece. If the knots are very tightly bound into the wood, the wood will probably be strong enough to withhold stress. However, if the knot has a black ring around it and is loose or has any movement or "give," the board or wooden piece could be too weak to withstand stress and should not be purchased. Use wood like this only when cutting out small objects that will allow you to work around the knots.
- Position patterns so that any flaws are outside the pattern area.
- Beware of warped timber! You can work around knots and splits, but warp is almost impossible to overcome.

When buying pine or soft timber, remember that in certain areas, dealers are giving you the size of timber before it was planed (smoothed and evened up). For example a 1"x 4" actually measures 3/4" x 3-1/2". The actual size of hardwood, however, is only 1/8" smaller than the nominal dimension, but there is no standard as there is in softwood. Therefore, a hardwood 1" x 4" measures approximately 7/8" x 3-7/8". This is very important when cutting out wood for a pattern where pieces must be joined because the thickness of the wood determines the outcome of the finished product.

Plywood may be used for some of the projects. It's better to use larger pieces that require no joining. Plywood is usually sold up to a maximum size of 4' x 8' sheets. Be sure to check for smaller sheets and miss-cuts if you only need small quantities. Plywood may also be purchased pre-sanded, so that only light sanding is necessary.

Particleboard (a pressed wood) can also be used but it does not finish well. It is better to use this type of wood only in areas where it will not show.

Luan plywood is inexpensive and finishes well. For most of the patterns that call for 1/4" or thin wood, luan would probably be the best choice. Luan would work well for Christmas ornaments, for example.

Most small patterns may be cut from either 1/2" or 3/4" wood. You can cut thinner items from plywood or particle board and stack them together to create a 3-D effect. Remember that if you cut a pattern from 3/4" wood when it calls for 1/2" wood, it will not fit together correctly. Make sure you check your wood sizes and make all necessary adjustments to the patterns before you begin.

SIZING PATTERNS

Many of the patterns included here are full-sized; however, there may be times when you need to enlarge or reduce a pattern. There are several ways you can do this. Experiment to find the method you prefer.

Photocopying is the easiest and most popular method of pattern sizing. Many available copiers can reduce or enlarge patterns from 50 to 160 percent. Photocopiers are located in many public places, including libraries, and copying is relatively inexpensive. The most obvious advantage of photocopying is that it may be used for exact pattern transfer as well as for enlargements.

You may also transfer patterns by the "grid" method. Graph paper may be purchased and the pattern traced directly onto a grid. Each grid square should then be enlarged to the size needed.

Measure the size of the grid on your grid paper. If

the grid size is 1/2 inch square, and you want your finished project to be twice the size of the pattern, lay down grid lines that are one inch square. If you want the item to be three times the size shown, lay down grid lines that are 1-1/2 inches square.

Determine where the pattern lines cross each grid line and mark your grid in the corresponding spot. Repeat this process grid by grid. After putting a dot where the pattern line intersects each grid line, it's simply a process of connecting the dots with curved lines where necessary.

Curved lines are simple to do by hand. Use a pencil to draw your patterns so that corrections will be easy to make. Any pattern that is to be the same size can be traced onto opaque or transparent paper.

Another way to enlarge or reduce your pattern is with a pantograph. An architectural tool, the pantograph looks like four long rulers joined in a zigzag design. This tool can be difficult to work with, but it is very reliable. You can find these useful instruments in craft and hobby shops, craft catalogues and woodworking magazine advertisements.

You may also want to consider using photography for pattern enlargement although this method can become expensive. Photograph your pattern using a 35 mm camera with slide film. Take the developed slide and project the image directly onto a piece of wood or paper and then trace it. This method has the advantage of an infinite enlargement range, however, its main drawback is the cost of film and developing.

TRANSFERRING PATTERNS TO WOOD

When transferring a pattern to a piece of wood, use tracing, carbon or graphite paper. Graphite paper is preferred as carbon transfers are difficult to remove from wood and the tracing lines are hard to conceal during the finishing process.

Any marks from graphite paper are easy to erase or sand away. Since this transfer paper is available in white colours as well as dark, it's ideal for transferring patterns to darker woods, such as walnut and cherry. You can find graphite paper at most office supply and graphic arts shops.

All of these tracing papers work in essentially the same way. Place the pattern on top of the transfer paper with the pattern facing up and the transfer medium side of the transfer paper down. Then, place the two together directly on top of the wood with the transfer medium against the wood. Trace the pattern, and remove the paper. The image is now transferred to the wood.

If you plan to make a pattern many times, consider making a template. You can make templates using scissors or a knife or saw them out when you saw the pattern. A template can easily be made from lightweight cardboard. If the pattern is to be used many times, the template can be made of thin plastic. Favourite patterns can be reproduced hundreds of times from a sturdy template.

When half patterns are shown (e.g., a heart shape, where each half is exactly the same), fold a piece of paper in half. Draw or trace the half pattern on the paper with the centre touching the fold. Cut the pattern on the folded paper. When the paper is opened, the pattern will be perfectly symmetrical.

HOW TO CUT YOUR PATTERN

Don't let a complex pattern discourage you. Most of these cuts only need a steady hand and a little patience.

Examine each pattern before you make any cuts. Use a smaller blade to cut curves and corners if there is no way to change the position of your saw and no waste stock (extra wood around the pattern) to cut into.

Break complicated cuts into simpler curves and lines. Don't be afraid to move your saw to a different position on the wood and approach the line from a different angle.

If your design calls for sharp corners where two lines intersect, cut the first line and keep going past the corner. Cut a loop around in the waste stock and cut the second line. You can also cut the first line and continue cutting to the edge of the wood. Take off the waste and turn the piece, then continue cutting from the edge to the second line.

When cutting sharp interior corners, you can cut the first line up to the corner, then back the blade out of the wood and cut the second line. Another method is to cut the first line up to the corner and back up a few blade widths. Turn into the waste area, leaving the first line, and get into position to cut the second. Cut the second line and take off the waste. Then go back and cut the last part of the second line up to the corner.

Today, with the new constant-tension scroll saws, you can quickly change direction, make right-angle turns or complete a 360° turn without making extra cuts or breaking a blade. Often the cuts are so smooth that you do not even have to sand after finishing a project.

When cutting small pieces or very thin veneers, tape your wood to heavy poster board or smooth cardboard. If the pieces are very thin, you can sandwich the wood between the two pieces of poster board. This will prevent the pieces from breaking or getting lost.

It is also helpful to cut more than one thin piece at a time. This method is called pad sawing. Stack up the wood pieces and tape them together. The stack should not be thicker than the saw's cutting capability. Saw the whole stack and remove the tape. The pieces will be identical.

JOINERY METHODS

Using a nail and hammer to join two wooden pieces is probably the most common joining method and certainly the easiest. Beginners often find that nails bend and wood splits with unbelievable frequency. If you are having nailing problems, here are some helpful hints.

Ask at the nearest hardware

or DIY shop what nail is best for the wood type and wood thickness that you are using. Your problem may be solved by buying a nail of the correct size or type for the job.

Use finishing nails with care when joining a corner piece that will show. They have a tendency to bend very easily when they are longer than needed. Try buying shorter nails or cutting the point with heavy wire cutters. Punch the nail down below the wood with a nail set so that it doesn't show, and plug the hole with wood putty. Sand the area flush with the wood, and the hole will be unnoticeable.

Hold nails firmly between your thumb and forefinger when hammering. This will keep the nails from going astray or bending so often.

Consider using old-fashioned cut nails when making furniture. These nails, if driven in parallel to the grain, will help to prevent splitting because of their construction and strength.

When hammering into small sections of end grain or side grain, drill small pilot holes before nailing. This will decrease the tendency of the wood to split. Take care not to drill your pilot holes too big. Excessively large pilot holes may weaken the joined area.

Have a helper hold loose ends of the boards while nailing. If you are working alone, use clamps or another device to hold the wood steady. This will help prevent misalignment and the need to remove the nails and begin again.

Screws are very often used in joining. Frequently, screws can be driven into wood more easily and with a greater degree of accuracy than nails. Screws are also less likely to split wood. It is important to use the correct screw type and size for the job.

Many woodworkers use screws in the majority of their joinery projects because they can be power driven. If you decide to use this method of driving screws, buy a power screwdriver or use a drill attachment. Most drills are equipped with a screw bit and are very easy to use.

Be sure that all visible screw holes are counter-sunk (set at or below the surface of the wood). Plug the holes with wood putty or small lengths of dowel. Milled plugs may also be purchased and glued in place.

JOINING WITH GLUE

Glues have been used with great success in wood joinery for a very long time. Many antiques that you see today that are still in very good condition were made from wood veneers (overlays) glued together.

There are many types of glue on the market. Animal glue is a natural glue derived from the by-products of the meat packing industry. This glue, widely used for veneers since the 17th century, is not recommended for outdoor use. One of its chief advantages is that the bond can be broken without damage to the wood when heat and moisture are applied.

Animal glue is available in a cake or granular form. The granular type is preferred by traditional woodworkers, but it is very messy and hard to use because it must be dissolved and warmed in a jacketed glue pot.

For pieces that are used indoors, most woodworkers use a high-quality white wood glue or a yellow aliphatic resin. These synthetic glues form a chemical bond that actually seep into the wood. In some cases, the bond is stronger than the wood itself. The yellow glues are stronger and more resistant to water but still should be used indoors.

Outdoor projects require a waterproof glue such as resorcinol or epoxy. This glue is highly water-resistant and is very good for outside projects, but there are a couple of drawbacks with using resorcinol. It must be used quickly because the drying time is very short and the joints are very noticeable.

Contact cement is widely used when laminating or veneering. Be careful when using contact cement because once a bond is made, it's impossible to break. Therefore, take care not to make mistakes when using this glue. It is also very toxic. Always use in a well-ventilated workshop.

Super glue works well on very small items. It dries very quickly and holds well but is quite expensive. Super-glue has also been known to bond skin but is very easy to remove with acetone or nail polish remover.

Urea or plastic resins are widely used for general purpose woodworking. Plastic resins are highly water-resistant and durable. The joints are not very noticeable, and they sand and finish well. Hardwoods do not bond quite as well with plastic resin as softwoods, such as fir, pine or cedar. This type of glue is very popular in England, as well as Canada and the United States. Like contact cement, it is very toxic so use only in a well-ventilated workshop.

There are many other glues on the market, especially those formulated for special purposes that are very good. For best results, follow label directions carefully.

Before gluing, make sure the surfaces to be glued are smooth, dry and free from oil or grease. Clean surfaces take glue much easier than dirty ones.

Apply the glue, then clamp the wood together tightly. Metal or strap clamps can be used. When using metal clamps, be sure to place a wood block between the clamp and the wood to prevent marring. Allow plenty of time for the glue to set and dry completely. Manufacturers usually specify drying times on the glue container.

Make certain that all glue is cleaned from the outer surface of pieces that you are going to stain. Stain will not absorb into any glue spots on your project.

"PICTURE PERFECT" FINISHING

How you finish any project is what will place your individual signature on a piece. So decide how you want the piece to look and get to work.

The first and most important step in finishing is sanding. Sand the piece with a rough grade of sandpaper (100-200 grit) to knock off all large bumps and splinters. Sand again with finer paper or emery cloth (up to 500 grit) until the piece is completely smooth. Steel wool (0000 or 4-0) is best for the final sanding and for smoothing bubbles between coats of finish or polyurethane. This is the secret to all those beautifully-finished pieces you find in expensive shops.

If you have any visible knots in your project, you can apply a soft wood filler over the knots before you sand.

There are several different ways to decorate your piece once you've finished sanding. You may paint, stain, stencil or finish with tung oil.

When painting a project, make sure you use top quality paint brushes made of camel hair or other natural fibres. These do not lose bristles and spoil the effect as cheaply made brushes do. Applicators on wooden handles are better because they don't leave brush marks. A power sprayer also gives a clean, finished surface. Keep several lint-free rags at hand for clean up as well as for applying stains and sealers.

The most popular type of painting for wooden pieces is tole painting. This is an easy method of applying paint in layers with common designs and shading techniques. Tole painting is probably simpler for a beginner than any other type of painting, and with practice, patience and proper instructions, anyone can master this technique. You'll find that a large variety of tole painting books are available in craft and hobby shops everywhere. In fact, many of the patterns included already have designs suitable for tole painting.

Acrylic (water-based) paints are easy to use and easy to clean with soap and water. You can use a brush cleaner that contains a conditioner to keep your brushes more supple and make them last longer. Acrylic paints, once dried on the wooden surface, become permanently waterproof. A coat of clear acrylic sprayed or brushed on the painted items acts as a sealer and completes the project.

Stenciling is another very popular finishing technique. Stenciling is the art of dabbing paint, ink or dye through openings in a piece of plastic or cardboard, leaving an impression behind. A great variety of patterns -- from flowers and animals to country designs -- is available.

Once you have chosen your stencil pattern, tape the pattern down to the wood surface. You may want to practice stenciling on paper before you attempt painting on the wooden piece, just to make sure it's going to turn out the way you're hoping it will.

The "dry brush" method of stenciling works best. Too much paint on your brush will run or drip. Use brushes, sponges or spray paint to stencil.

A new stenciling product on the market is stick paint. Stick paints resemble large children's crayons. You "colour" with these stick paints the same way you would with crayons. The stick application is very easy, and it involves less mess than other methods. It is rapidly becoming the favourite method of many first time stencilers.

Staining is another popular finish for wood crafts. Colour variety is an added advantage of wood stain. Just so you won't be surprised or disappointed, make sure you test your stain on a piece of scrap wood to check the colour before applying to the wood.

Stain is easy to apply. Brush or wipe it on with a lint-free soft cloth. Always apply the stain with the grain of the wood, then against the grain. Wipe off excess with the grain.

After staining, rub the piece with 0000 grit sand paper. Brush on a coat of polyurethane over the dried stain, brushing along with the grain, forcing out the bubbles. After it has dried thoroughly, rub with steel wool to eliminate any bubbles that may have formed.

For best results, use a tack cloth (found at paint and DIY shops) to remove dust after each sanding. Polyurethane forms a hard, bright, waterproof finish. It comes in a high gloss or satin finish. Make sure you are in a well-ventilated, dust-free environment when applying polyurethane.

Tung oil is also a great finish. Tung oil is a thick, heavy liquid applied directly to the wood by hand or with a lint-free cloth. Apply several coats to form a stain and water-resistant finish.

USEFUL, DECORATIVE FINISHING ITEMS

Keep these additional items on hand to help you finish each project. Be sure to check the instructions with each pattern for items not listed.

- Twine or ribbon for enhancing certain patterns
- Dowel rods of various sizes, shaker pegs
- Polyurethane, used to protect most outdoor patterns and some indoor patterns
- Hot glue
- Door harp, lamp and whirligig assemblies. Ask at hardware or craft shops or order from woodworking supply shops and mail order companies.
- Hangers to display your finished pieces
- Cup hooks, L-hooks, screw eyes and coat hangers. Available at hardware shops
- Small pliers and cutters

TURNING WOODCRAFTING INTO A PROFITABLE HOBBY

Once you've completed a few projects, you may want to try making money from your woodcrafting projects. Here are ten easy steps to get you started.

1. Look for places to sell your products. This will help you decide if a woodcrafting business would be profitable in your area. Possible markets include craft shows, craft shops, boutiques, antique shops, frame shops, tourist attractions, convenience stores, club or church fêtes and markets. If you have trouble convincing people to buy your crafts and display them in their shops, ask them about working under consignment. This means that for a small percentage of your profits, a shop would let you display your crafts.

You may also want to consider selling your products through the mail or post. You can advertise in national or regional magazines. All publications have numbers you can call to get more information about advertising rates.

2. Identify best-selling woodcrafts by visiting shows or shops where such item are sold. Note current prices. Choose a handful of pieces you think will sell the best.

3. Set up shop in a well-ventilated and well-lit area. Make sure you have the proper tools and necessary woods on hand. You don't want to waste time gathering supplies. Buy a good grade of wood to make your projects. This will save you time in the long run, and you will be able to offer your customers a better quality product.

Buy materials in small quantities to help cut start up costs. As your business grows, you will be able to purchase materials in larger quantities, which will save you money. Lower expenses mean higher profits.

4. Keep records. Record every purchase you make for your woodworking venture. Enter supplies, rental fees, transportation, etc. These records will be a big asset when tax time comes around.

Once you start selling products, record each item sold and its selling price. This will help you determine your best-selling products.

5. Open a separate bank account for your crafts. Pay for everything by cheque and deposit all receipts into this account. It will be a good double-check against your records when calculating the year's net profit and estimating taxes.

6. Make only a few of each item at first. If you did not pick hot sellers, you won't be stuck with a huge inventory that won't move.

7. Check with local authorities and make sure you have the proper licenses and tax or V.A.T. numbers to fulfill legal requirements.

8. Decide on a selling price. Make sure your rates are competitive with other woodcrafters. Your expense records will help you determine a profitable price.

9. Display your crafts attractively whether you've set up a booth at a craft show or are marketing your products through the mail or post. When you display your products directly to the public, make sure you have enough in-ventory to fill your space.

10. Be friendly and courteous to your customers. You're more likely to make a sale and have repeat business. If you don't have exactly the product the customer is looking for, you may be able to suggest one of your items as an alternative that the customer would like just as much or better.

With a little preparation and practice, you should soon be able to carve out a profit from your woodcrafting.

CRAFT FAIRS: FUN AND PROFITABLE

Craft fairs and shows are a very popular way to display and sell woodwork creations. You can find craft shows by checking your local newspapers or by asking in local craft shops. Small, local shows are often free or only require a small fee to enter. With good quality products and our hints in hand, you'll be able to pocket a nice profit.

Make your display stand out from the rest. Keep your space open and well-lit. Use long, narrow folding tables to exhibit your wares. They take up less room than square card tables. Rent or borrow such tables before you purchase them. These tables are difficult to transport, and you may decide to stop selling woodcrafts quicker than you had planned.

Cover your tables with long cloths. Store extra items underneath. Don't use table coverings that clash with your products.

Take plenty of inventory. Use boxes or crates to display your items at various heights. This will make your display more appealing and encourage people to give attention to each individual product.

Use products to accentuate your products. Put candles in the candlesticks you designed or real fruit in the fruit bowl you crafted. Using your imagination, you will discover plenty of household items that will show the beauty and usefulness of your woodcrafts.

Take a small wood piece to work on when business is slow. Often people will stop near your display just to watch. You may even want to custom paint a piece to suit your customer's wishes.

Carry a thermos, cooler and some sandwiches. This will prevent you from eating up all your profits at the concession stands.

Be prepared for unusual weather if the show will be held outside. Take sunscreen, umbrellas, heavy-duty plastic to cover your products in case of rain and the proper clothing so that you will be comfortable.

Selling a quality product you feel good about is easy. What are you waiting for?

REMEMBER

It's a great big world of woodworking out there, so have fun!

— CHAPTER ONE —

BIRDHOUSES & BIRD FEEDERS

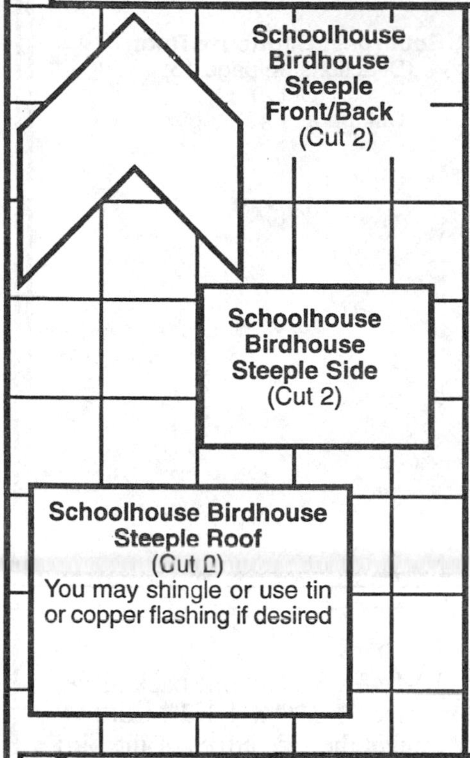

Schoolhouse Birdhouse Roof
(Cut 2)
See diagram to assemble. You may cover with shingles or tin or copper flashing, if desired.

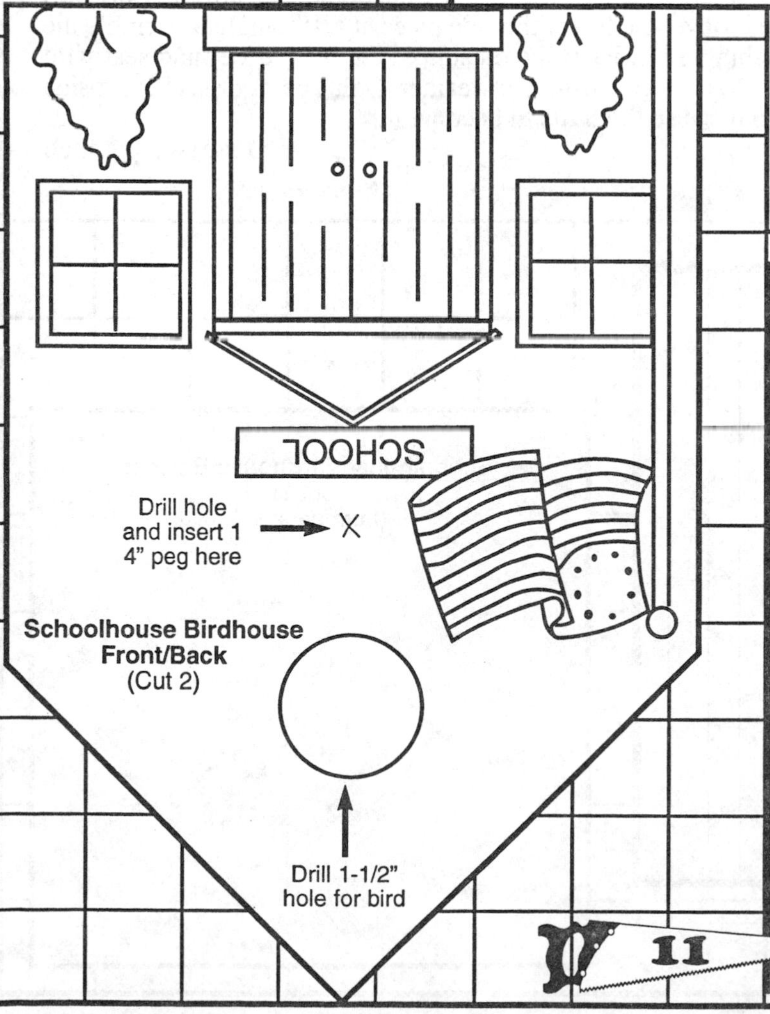

Schoolhouse Birdhouse

Cut pattern from 3/4" wood. Transfer designs onto pattern pieces using tracing or graphite paper. Paint with acrylics and finish with polyurethane to prevent weathering.

1 square = 1 inch

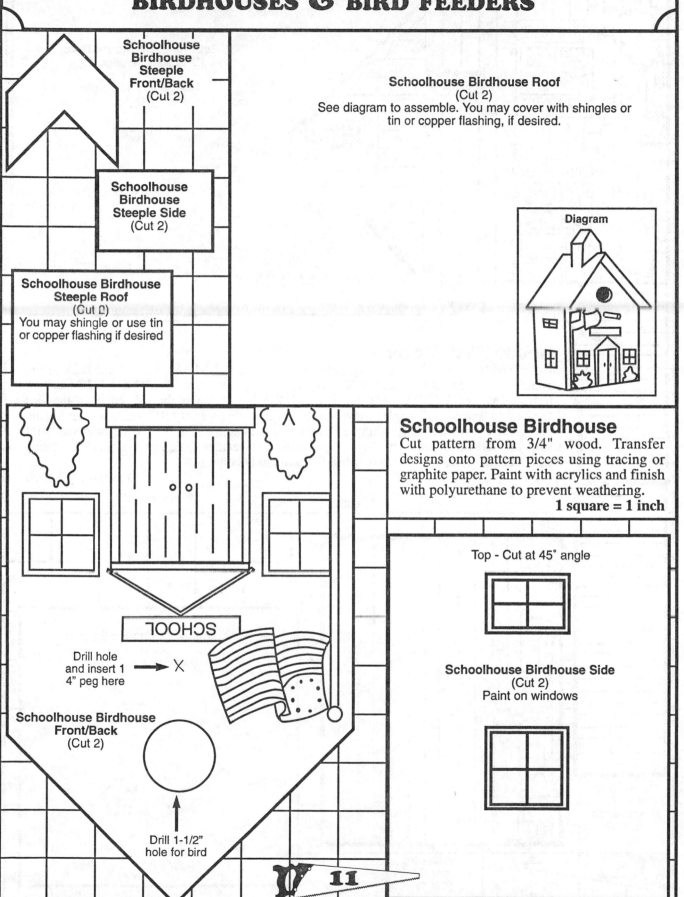

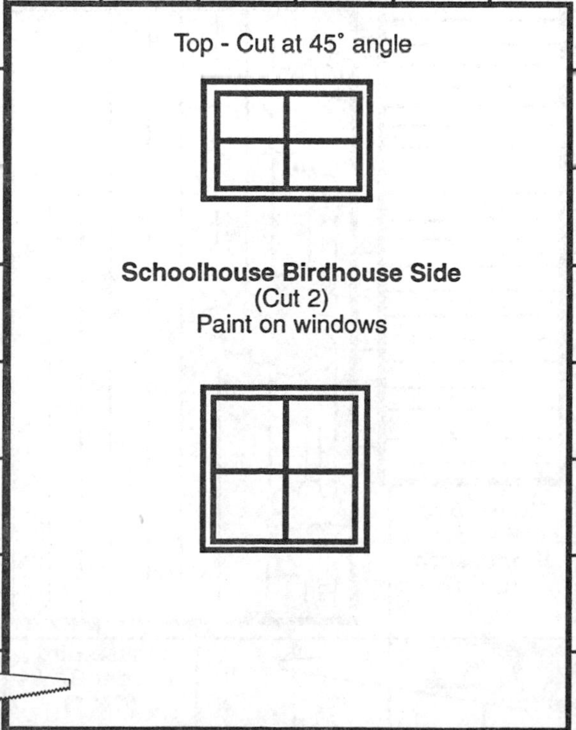

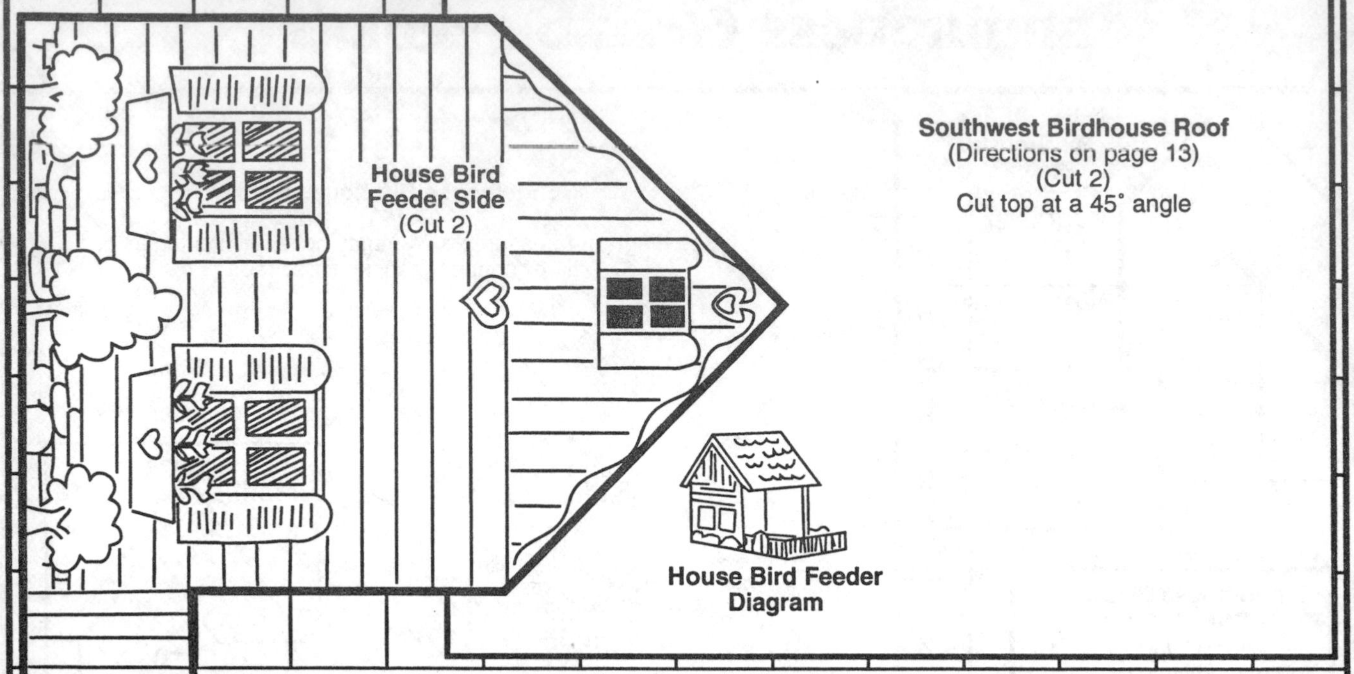

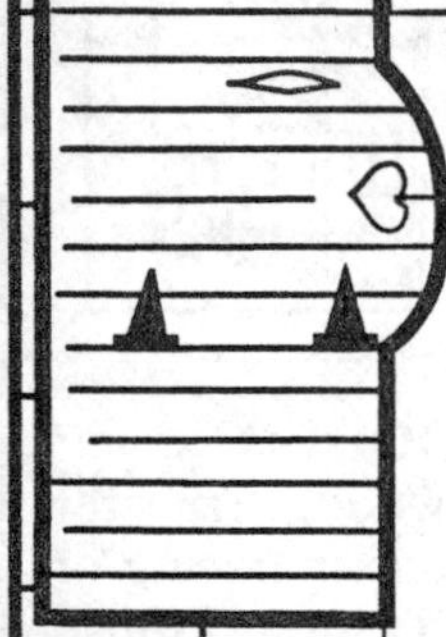

House Bird Feeder

Cut the pattern from 3/4" stock. Cut two sides as shown, 10-1/4" x 8". Cut one back piece, 5" tall x 6" wide. Cut one fence, 2" x 6". Cut one bottom piece 8-3/4" x 4-1/2". Cut two roof pieces; one 4-1/2" x 6-1/2" and one 5-1/4" x 6-1/2". Bevel the side edges of the bird feeder and fence at 45° angles. Bevel the top of the side piece at a 45° angle. Assemble the pieces with glue and #6 finishing nails. Paint the outside of the bird feeder and seal with several coats of polyurethane to protect it from the weather. Don't paint or seal the inside of the bird feeder, to do so may cause the birds to become ill.

1 square = 1 inch

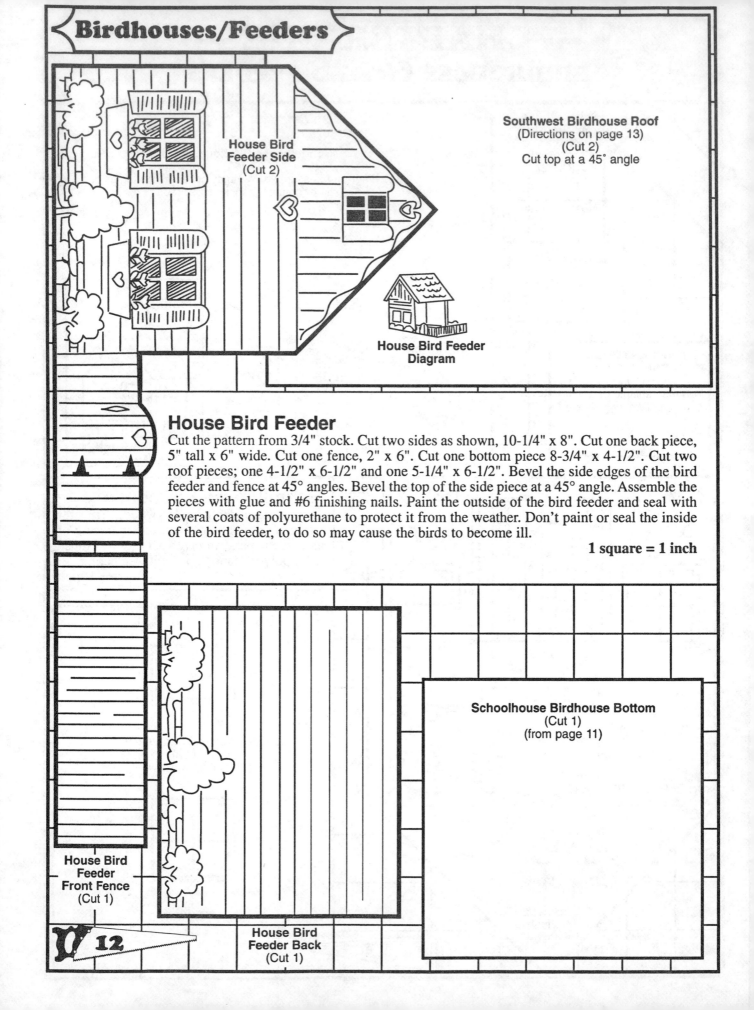

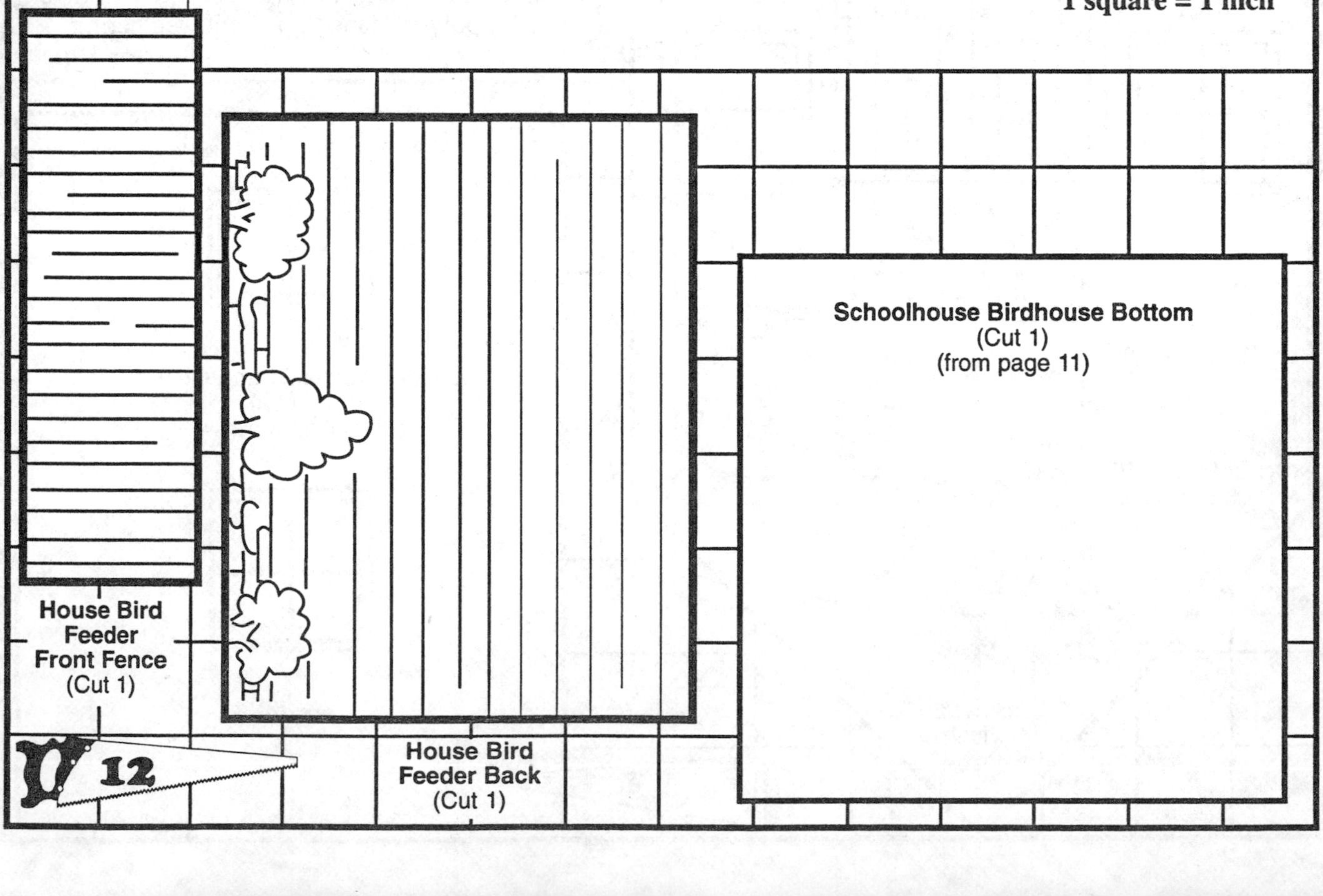

Southwest Birdhouse Bottom
(Cut 1)

Southwestern Birdhouse

Cut patterns using 3/4" wood. Cut one of the roof pieces 7/8" longer than the pattern (see diagram of birdhouse front). Drill several small holes through the bottom for drainage of rain water. Drill several small holes across the back piece for ventilation. Drill three 3/8" holes 1/2" deep for three 3/8" dowels 2-1/2" long. One will be used as a perch. Nail the sides, front, roof and bottom together as shown. Screw the back piece in place (this will serve as a door). The door will enable you to clean out the birdhouse as needed. Paint the outside of the birdhouse. Use several coats of polyurethane to protect it from the weather. Don't paint or seal the inside of the birdhouse. To do so may cause the birds to become ill.

1 square = 1 inch

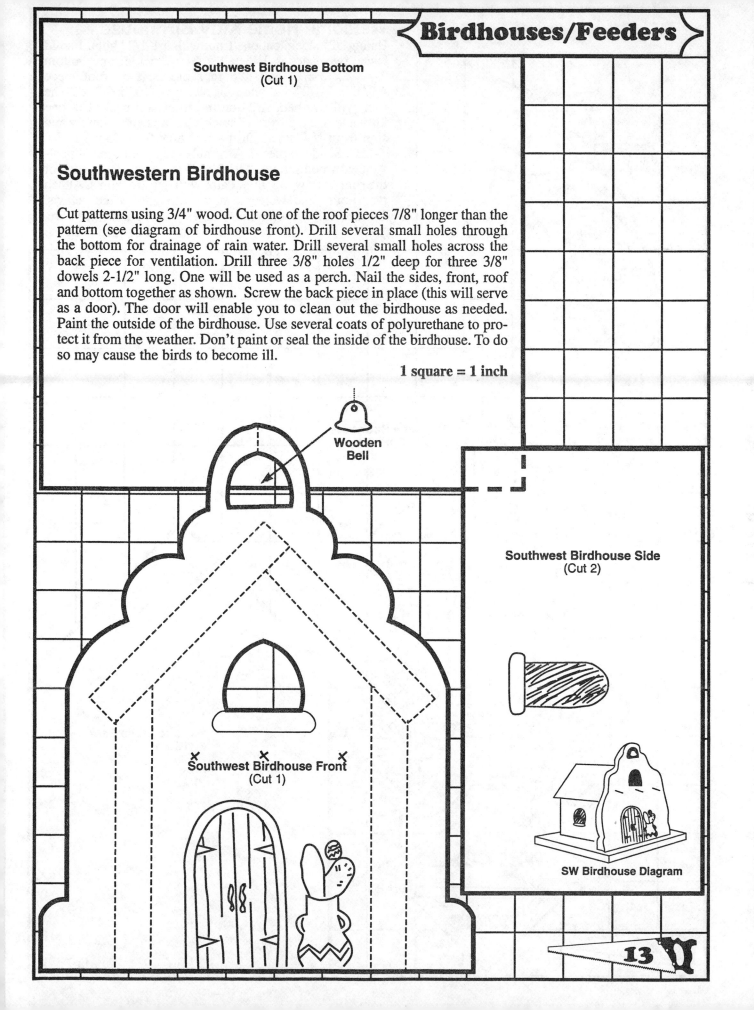

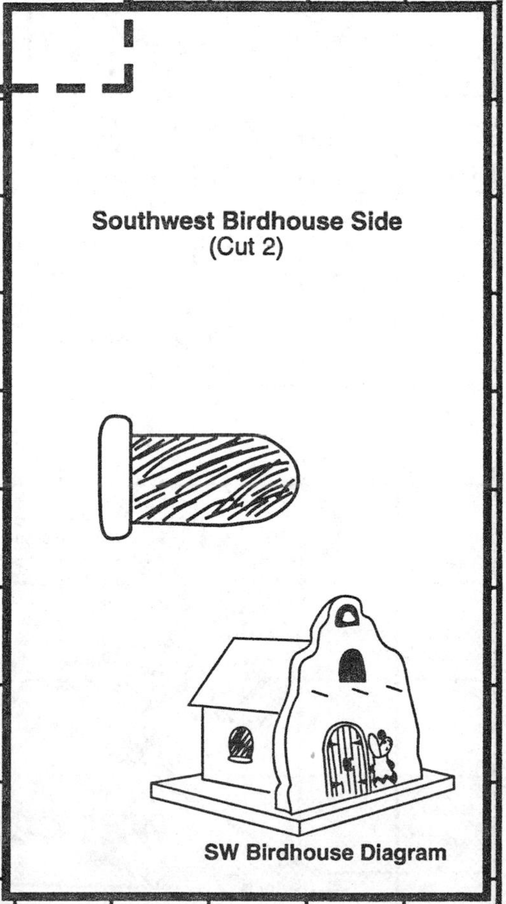

Welcome Home Kitty Birdhouse

Using 1/2" stock, cut one front with a 1-1/2" hole, 1 solid back, two sides 4-3/4" tall x 5-1/2" wide, one bottom 2-7/8" x 5-1/2" and two roof pieces. One roof piece 4-3/4" x 7-1/2" and one roof piece 4-3/16" x 7-1/2". The roof will overhang 1/2" on the front and back. Cut one kitty and one leg from 1" stock. Cut the heart, flowers and sign from 1/4" stock. Drill a 1/4" hole for a dowel 1/4" x 1-1/2". Sand the pieces. Assemble the birdhouse with galvanized wood screws. Attach the kitty to the front edge of the roof with wood glue. Paint with acrylic paints. Attach the flower and welcome sign with galvanized screws. Connect the welcome sign with 19 gauge galvanized wire.

1 square = 1 inch

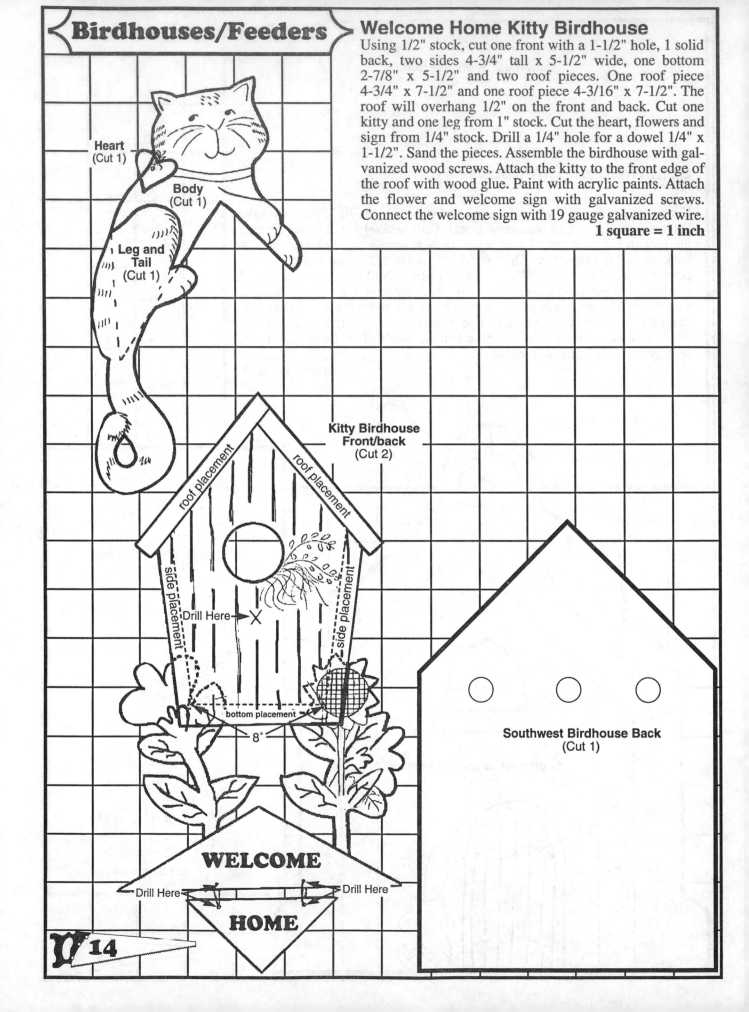

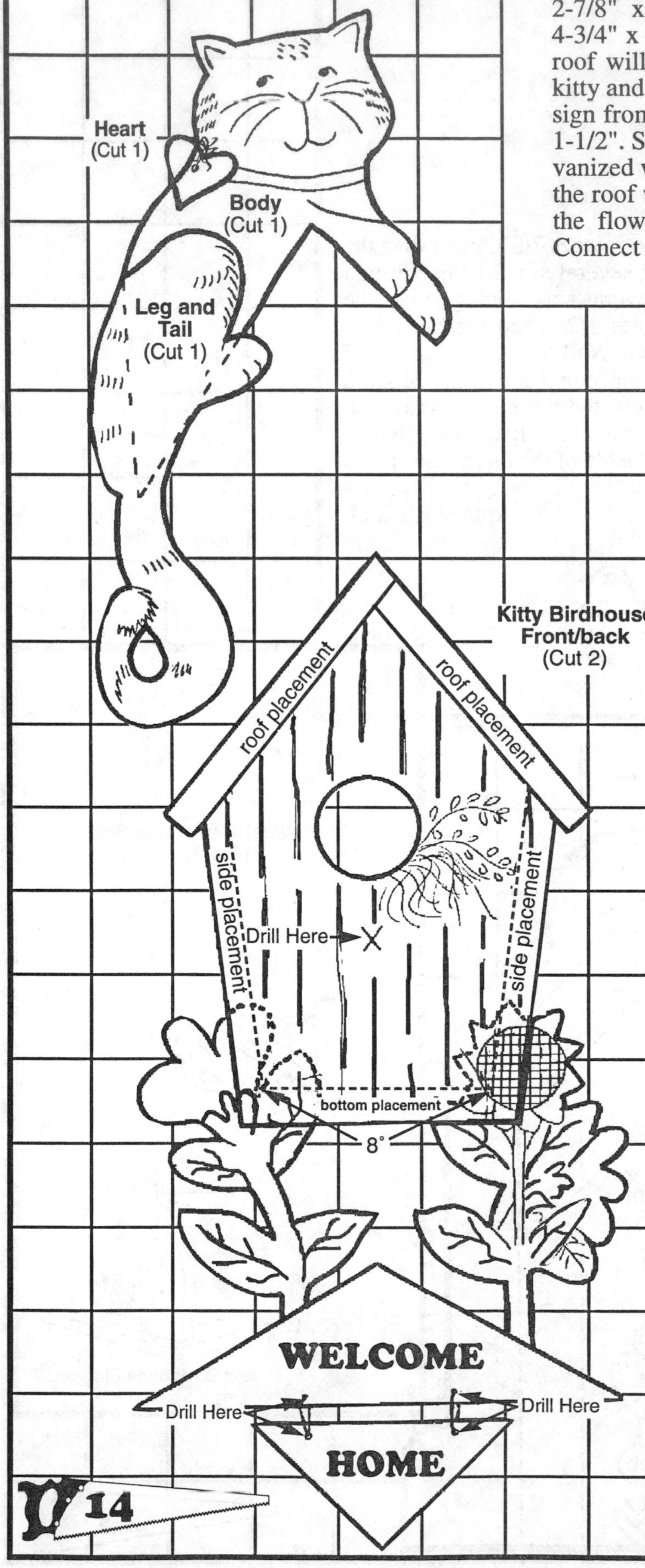

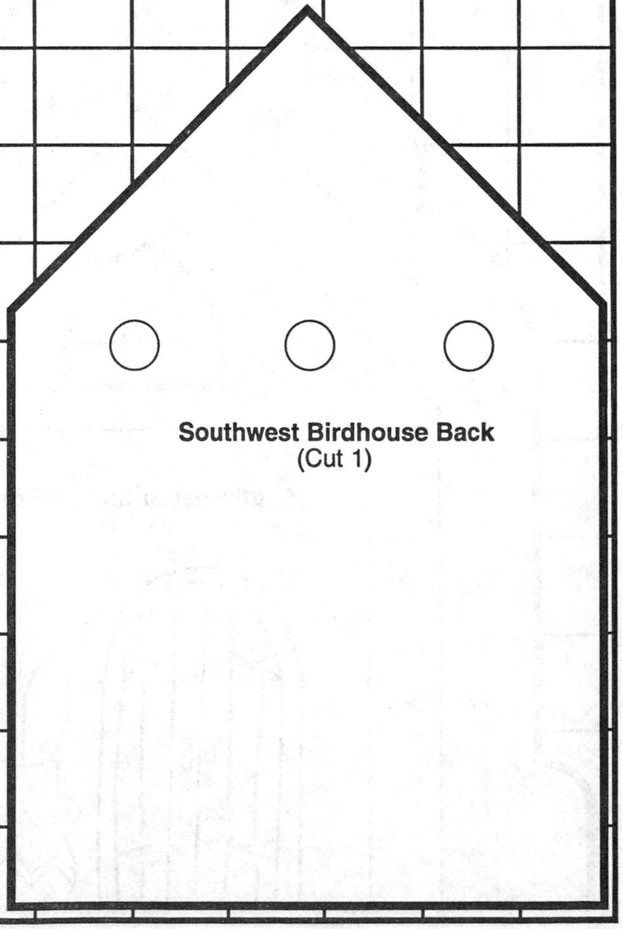

— CHAPTER TWO —
CLOCKS & LAMPS

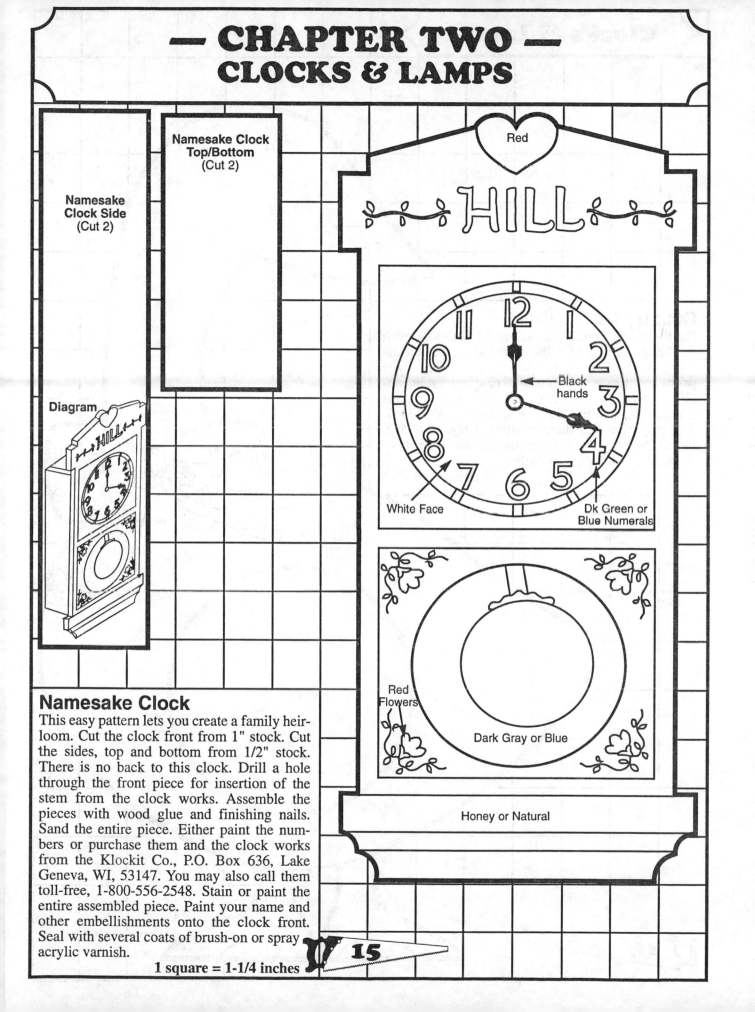

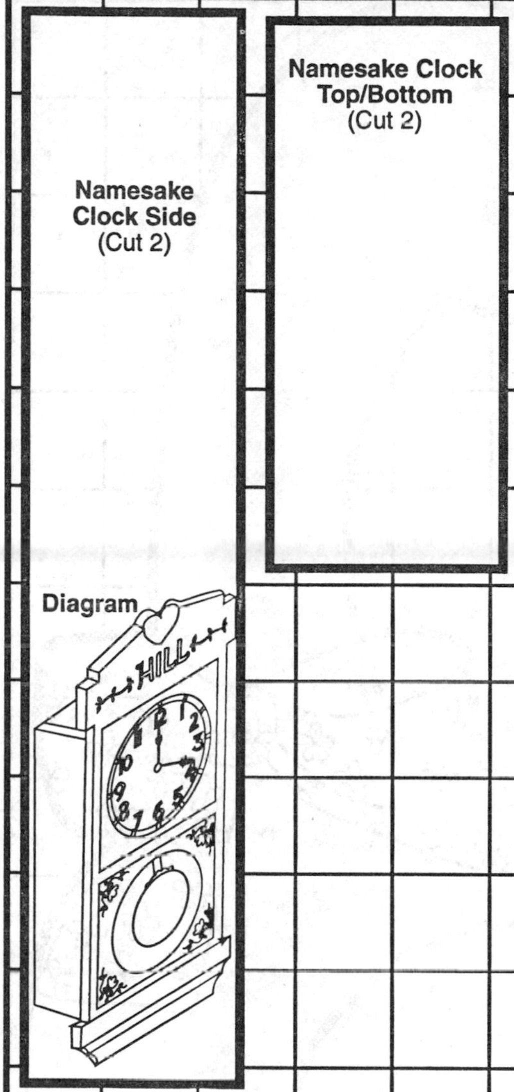

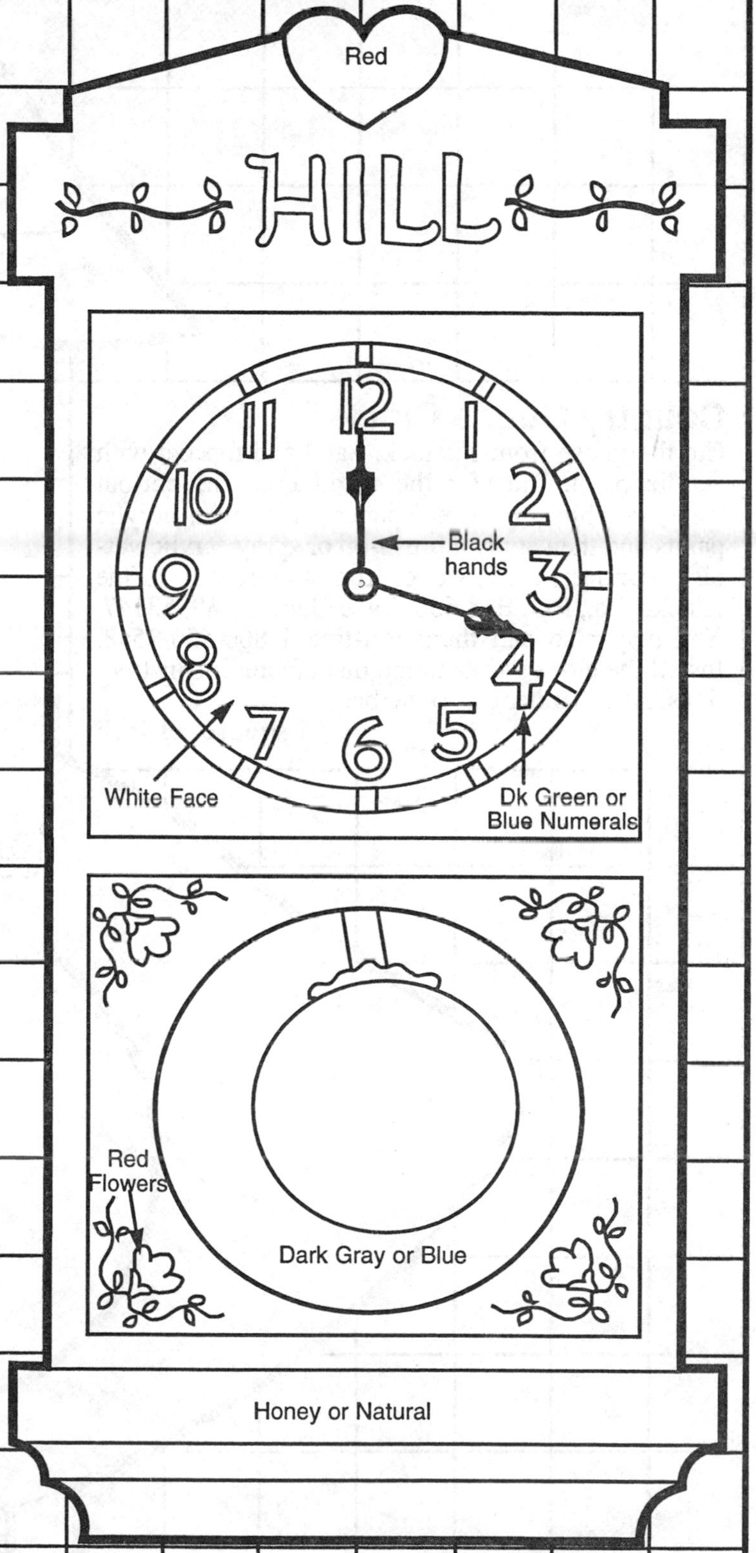

Namesake Clock

This easy pattern lets you create a family heirloom. Cut the clock front from 1" stock. Cut the sides, top and bottom from 1/2" stock. There is no back to this clock. Drill a hole through the front piece for insertion of the stem from the clock works. Assemble the pieces with wood glue and finishing nails. Sand the entire piece. Either paint the numbers or purchase them and the clock works from the Klockit Co., P.O. Box 636, Lake Geneva, WI, 53147. You may also call them toll-free, 1-800-556-2548. Stain or paint the entire assembled piece. Paint your name and other embellishments onto the clock front. Seal with several coats of brush-on or spray acrylic varnish.

1 square = 1-1/4 inches

Country Goose Clock

Cut the goose from 1" stock. Sand and topcoat with acrylic paint. Transfer the detail onto the cut-out using graphite or carbon paper. Paint with acrylic paints and then apply a brush-on or spray acrylic varnish. Purchase clock works from a craft shop or the Klockit Co., P.O. Box 636, Lake Geneva, WI, 53147. You may also call them toll-free 1-800-556-2548. Install the clock works to the manufacturer's instructions. Attach a hanger to the back.

1 square = 1 inch

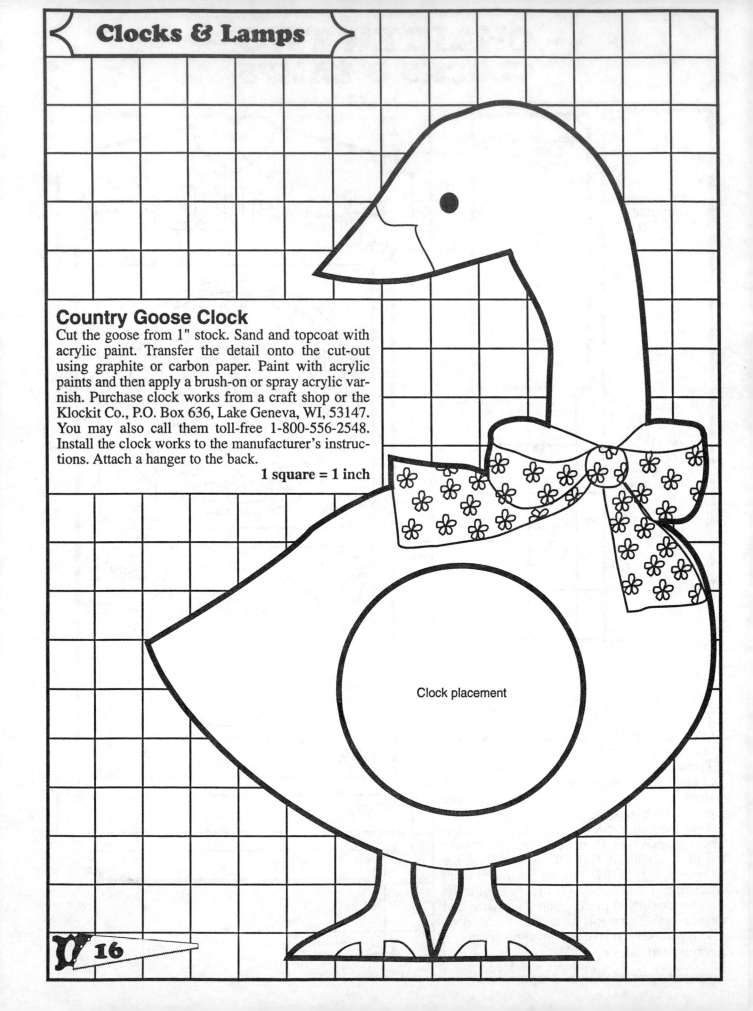

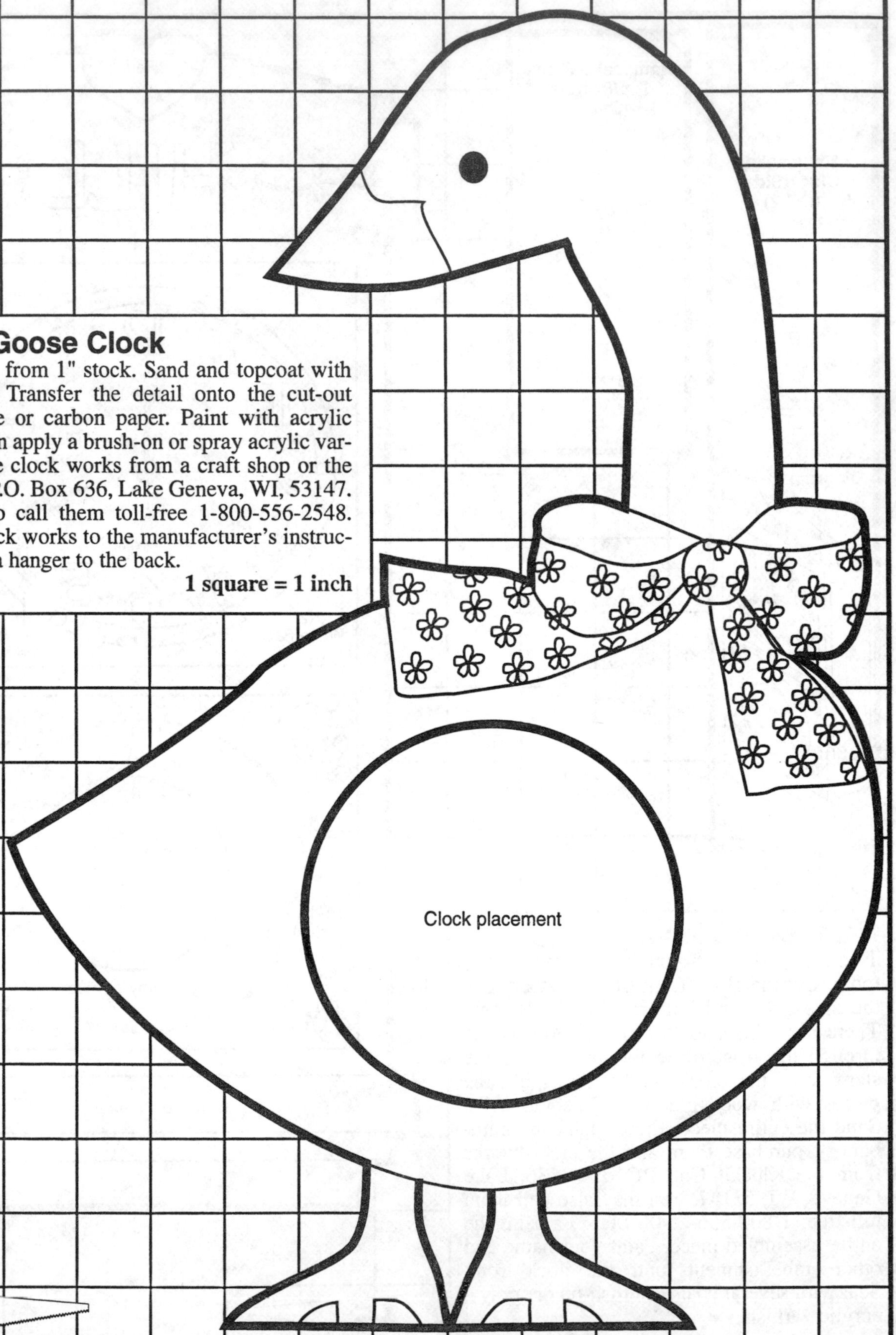

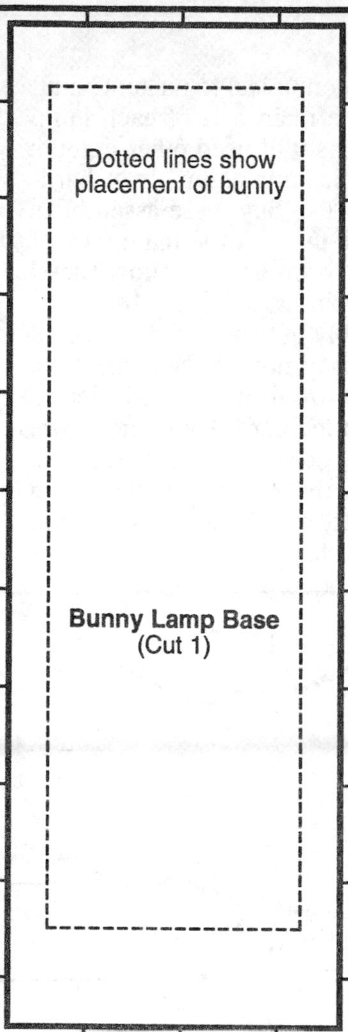

Bunny and Tulip Clock

Cut the bunny clock from 1" pine. Bore a 3-1/8" diameter hole, 1/2" deep in the centre of the back of the tulip for insertion of a mini quartz movement. Drill a 3/8" hole in the centre of the bored hole for insertion of the clock stem. Sand first with 150 grit and then 100 grit sandpaper. Topcoat using acrylic paint. Transfer the design with graphite paper. Paint the detail with acrylic paints. The numbers can be painted on or you may purchase the numbers from a craft, hobby shop or the Klockit Co. Seal with several coats of a spray or brush on acrylic varnish. The small quartz movement can be ordered in the U.S. from the Klockit Co., 1-800-556-2548, or send for a catalog for the proper dimensions: Klockit Co., P.O.Box 636, Lake Geneva, WI, 53147.

1 square = 1-1/2 inches

Bunny Lamp

Follow lamp directions. Cut bunny from 1-1/2" wood. Cut one heart from 1/4" wood. Cut one base from 3/4" wood. Assemble using the diagram as a guide. The dotted lines on the base show the placement of the bunny.

1 square = 1-3/4 inches

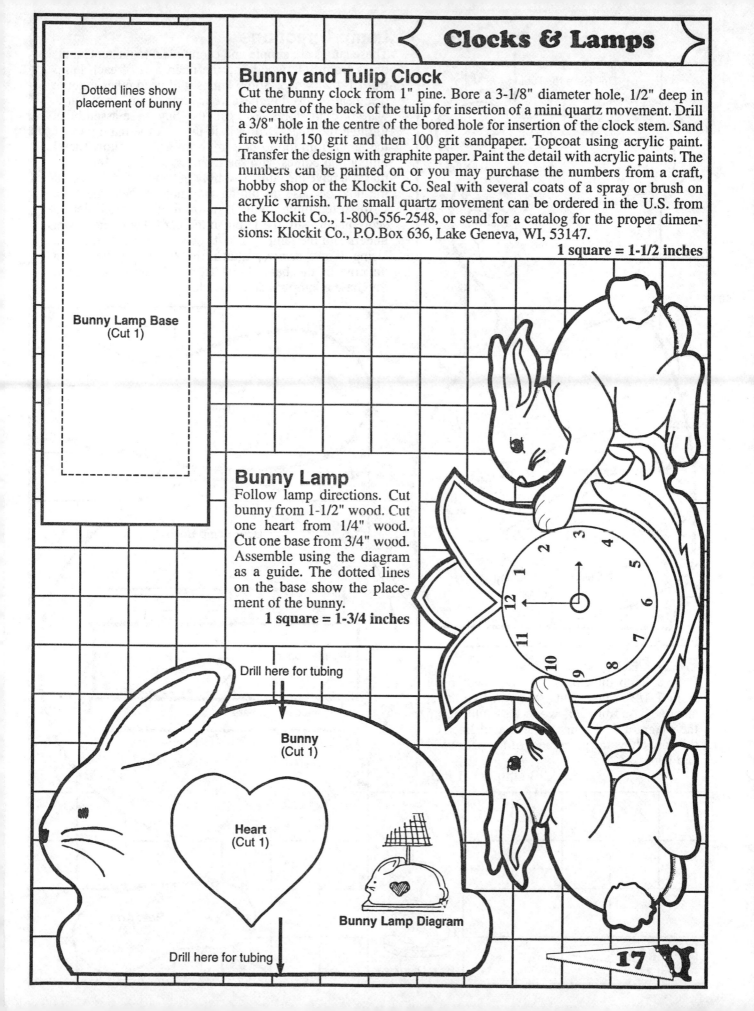

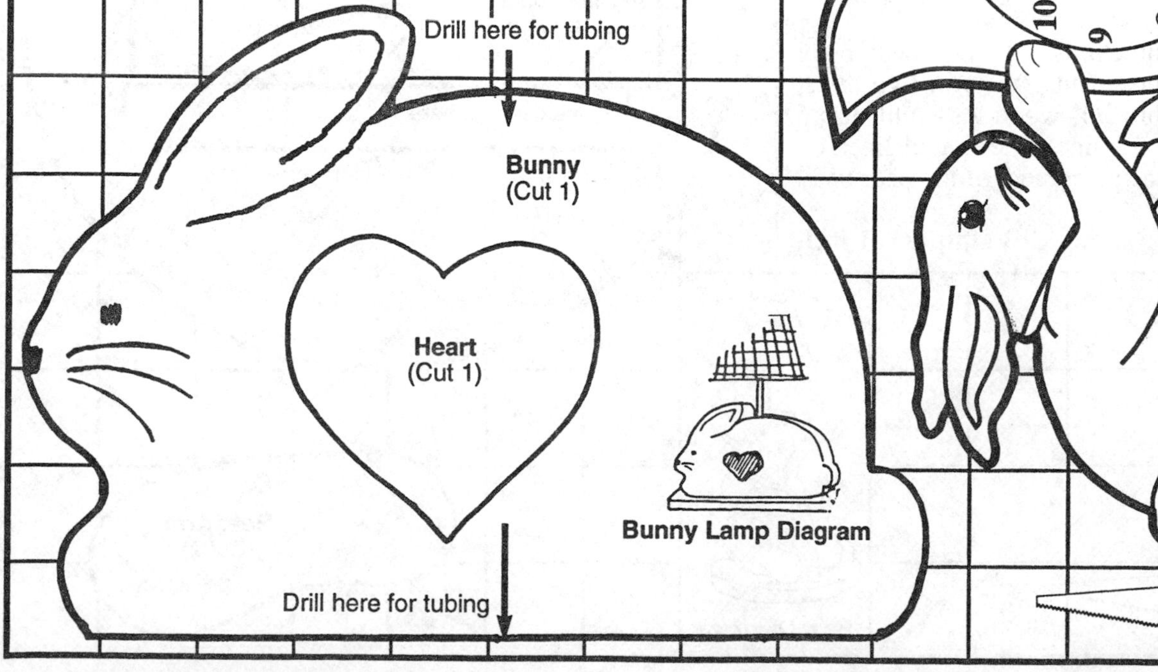

Clocks & Lamps

Lamp Directions

These lamps are simple and economical to make. Cut all bases from 3/4" wood and the main part of each lamp from 1-1/2" wood. Some lamps will need other cutouts (see bear lamp). Purchase your lamp assembly at hardware or craft stores. You can also buy these assemblies through the mail. Drill a hole through the main part of the lamp from top to bottom to insert the hollow metal tubing that comes with the lamp assemblies. Make sure that you have the lamp assembly in hand before you drill the hole because all tubing may not be the same size. Drill so the tubing will fit. It would be a good idea to score underneath the lamp so the cord that comes from underneath the lamp will not cause the lamp to wobble. Using wood screws, attach the lamp together from underneath the base. Paint to match the room decor. Purchase a lamp shade to match.

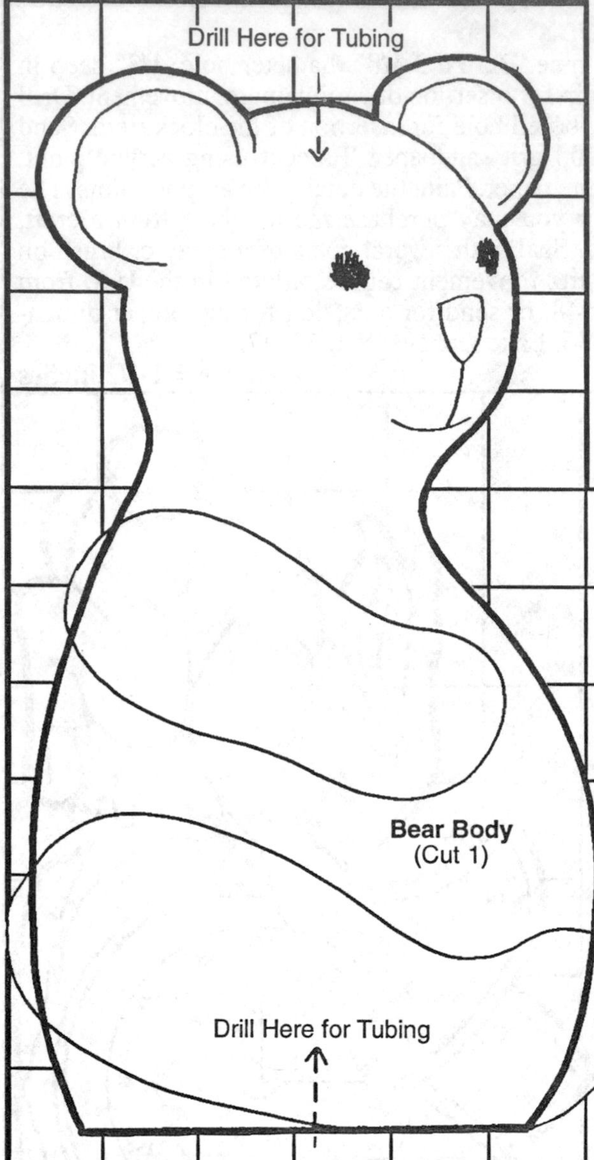

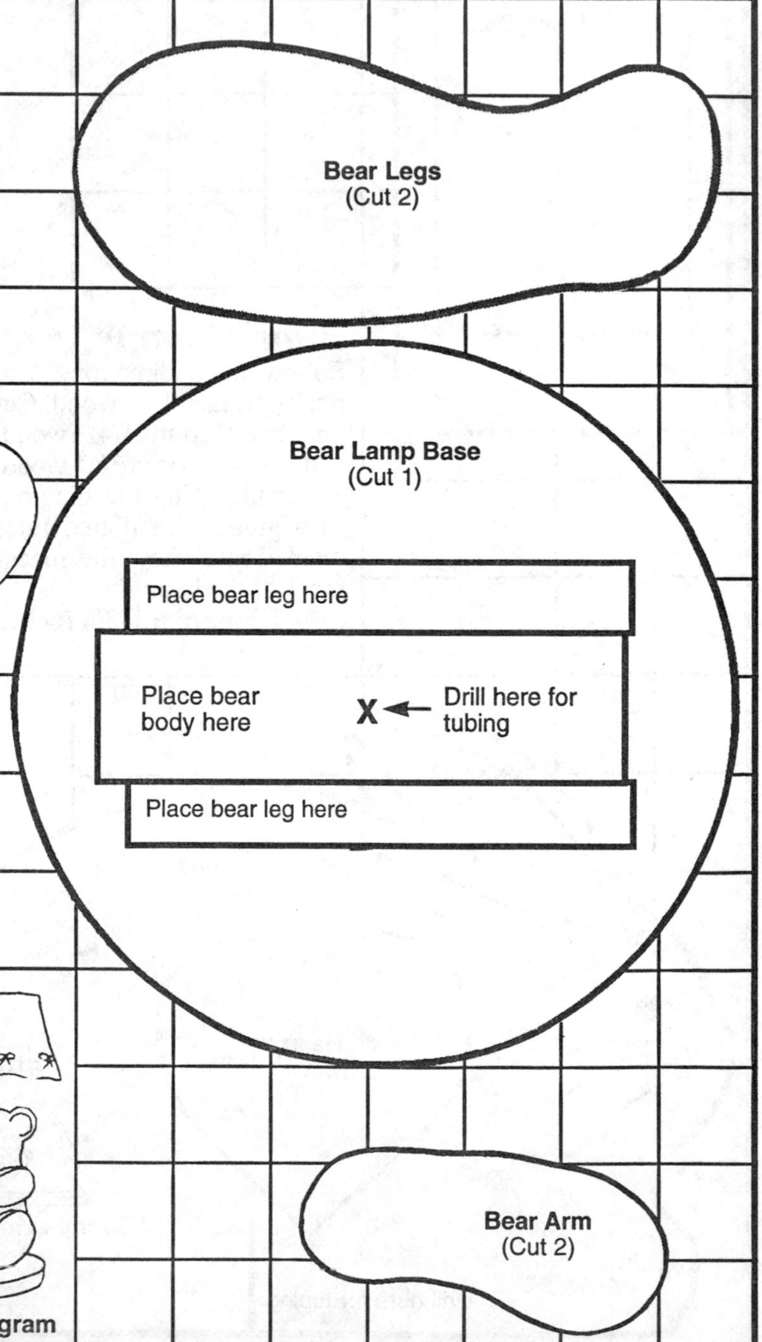

Bear Lamp

Follow lamp directions. Cut one bear body from 1-1/2" wood. Cut two legs, two arms, and one base from 3/4" wood. Assemble using the diagram as a guide. The dotted lines on the base show the placement of the bear body and legs.

1 square = 1 inch

Bear Diagram

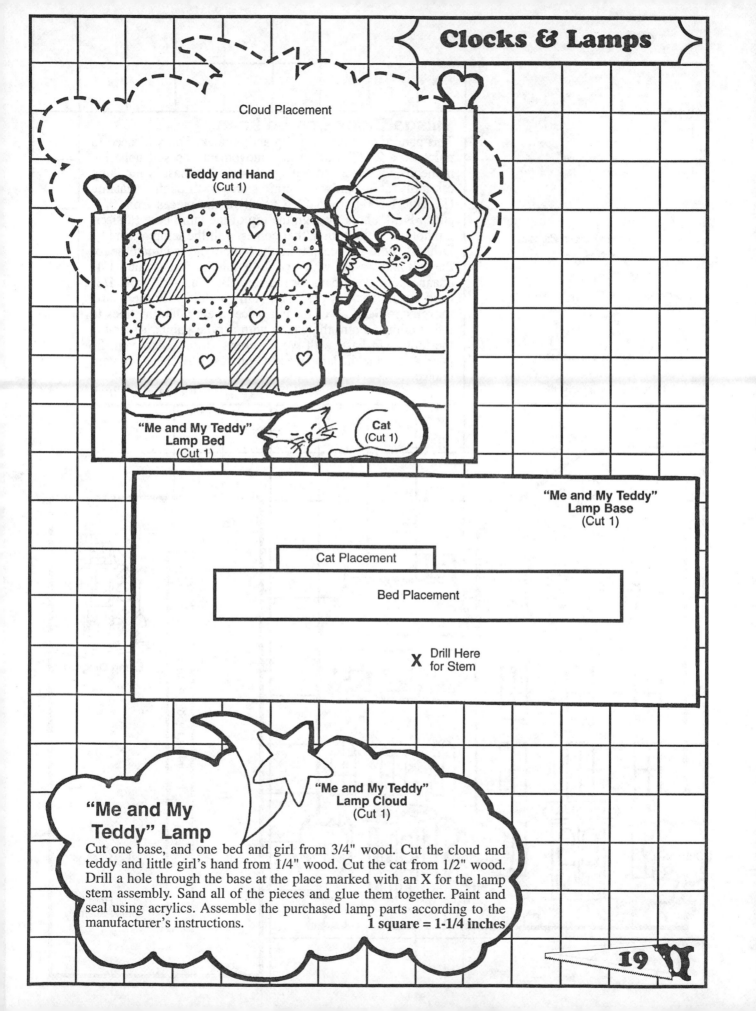

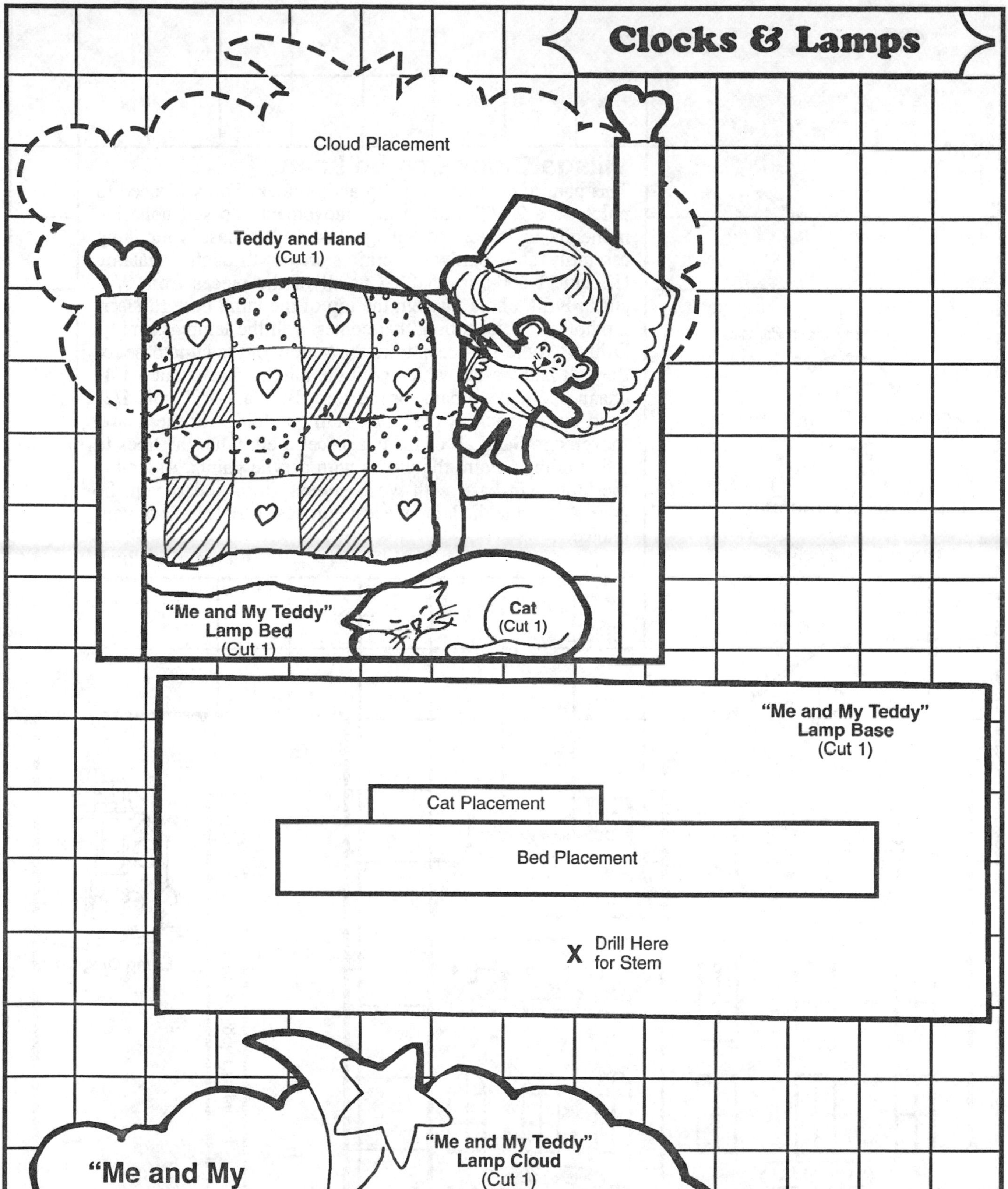

"Me and My Teddy" Lamp

Cut one base, and one bed and girl from 3/4" wood. Cut the cloud and teddy and little girl's hand from 1/4" wood. Cut the cat from 1/2" wood. Drill a hole through the base at the place marked with an X for the lamp stem assembly. Sand all of the pieces and glue them together. Paint and seal using acrylics. Assemble the purchased lamp parts according to the manufacturer's instructions.

1 square = 1-1/4 inches

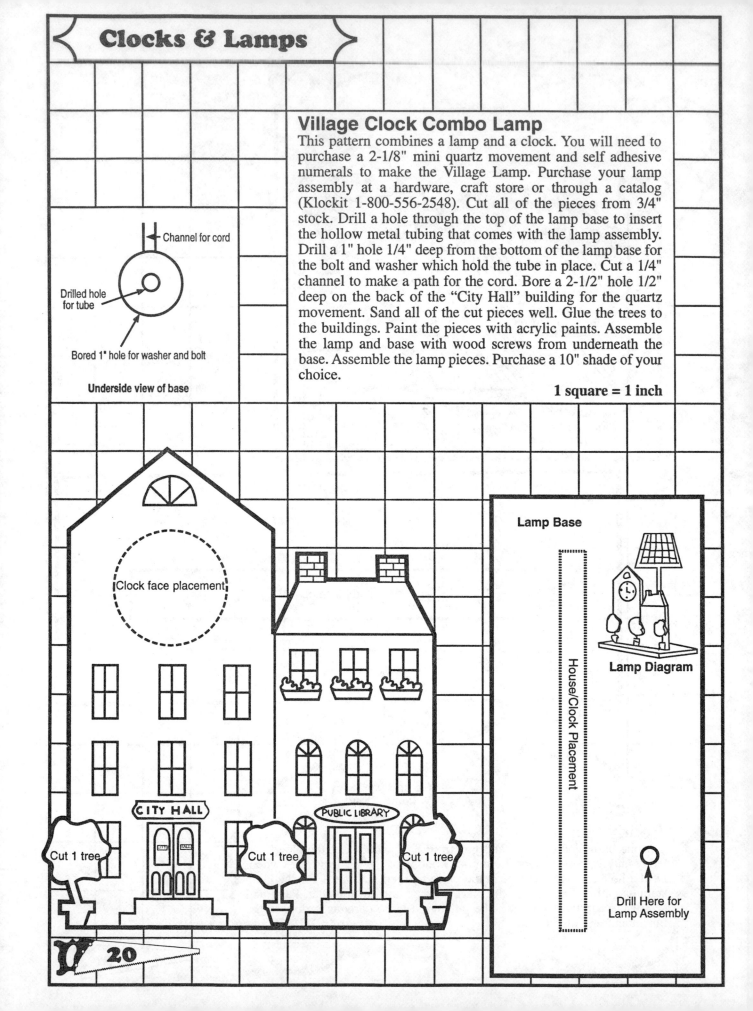

Village Clock Combo Lamp

This pattern combines a lamp and a clock. You will need to purchase a 2-1/8" mini quartz movement and self adhesive numerals to make the Village Lamp. Purchase your lamp assembly at a hardware, craft store or through a catalog (Klockit 1-800-556-2548). Cut all of the pieces from 3/4" stock. Drill a hole through the top of the lamp base to insert the hollow metal tubing that comes with the lamp assembly. Drill a 1" hole 1/4" deep from the bottom of the lamp base for the bolt and washer which hold the tube in place. Cut a 1/4" channel to make a path for the cord. Bore a 2-1/2" hole 1/2" deep on the back of the "City Hall" building for the quartz movement. Sand all of the cut pieces well. Glue the trees to the buildings. Paint the pieces with acrylic paints. Assemble the lamp and base with wood screws from underneath the base. Assemble the lamp pieces. Purchase a 10" shade of your choice.

1 square = 1 inch

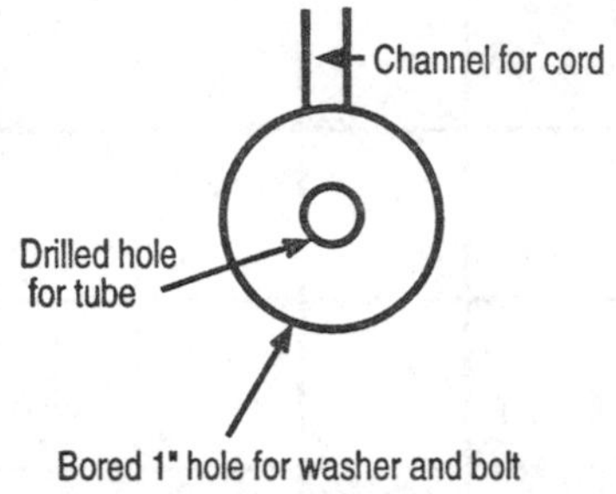

Underside view of base

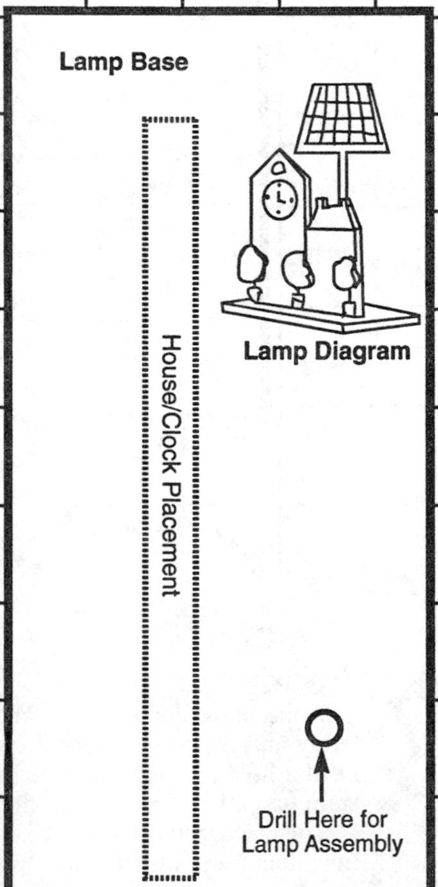

— CHAPTER THREE —
3-D DECORATIONS

3-D Bunnies
Cut patterns from 3/4" wood. Paint with acrylics and coat with polyurethane.
Actual size

Mr. and Mrs. Bunny
(Cut 1)

Flop-eared Bunny
(Cut 1)

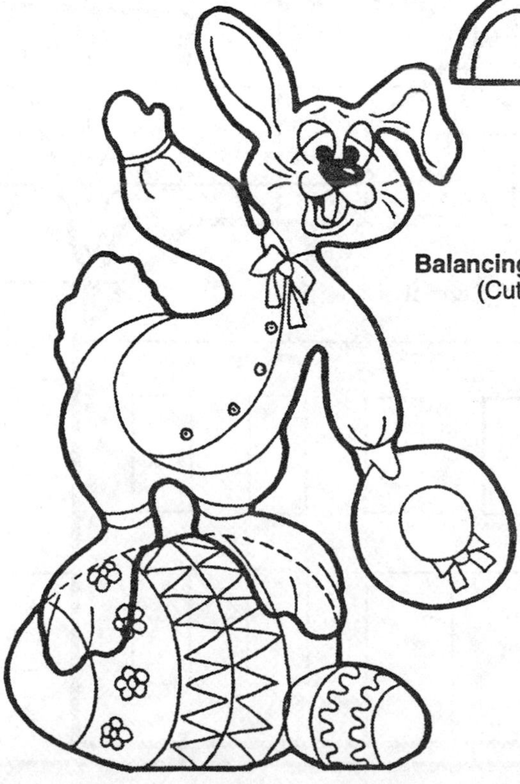

Balancing Bunny
(Cut 1)

Flop-eared Bunny's Tail
(Cut 1)

3-D Decorations

Sea Life on Stands

Cut patterns from 3/4" wood. Cut fins separately from 3/8" wood and glue in place. Drill hole as shown for 3/8" dowel rod. Make rectangular bases slightly larger than pattern length from 3/4" wood.

Actual size

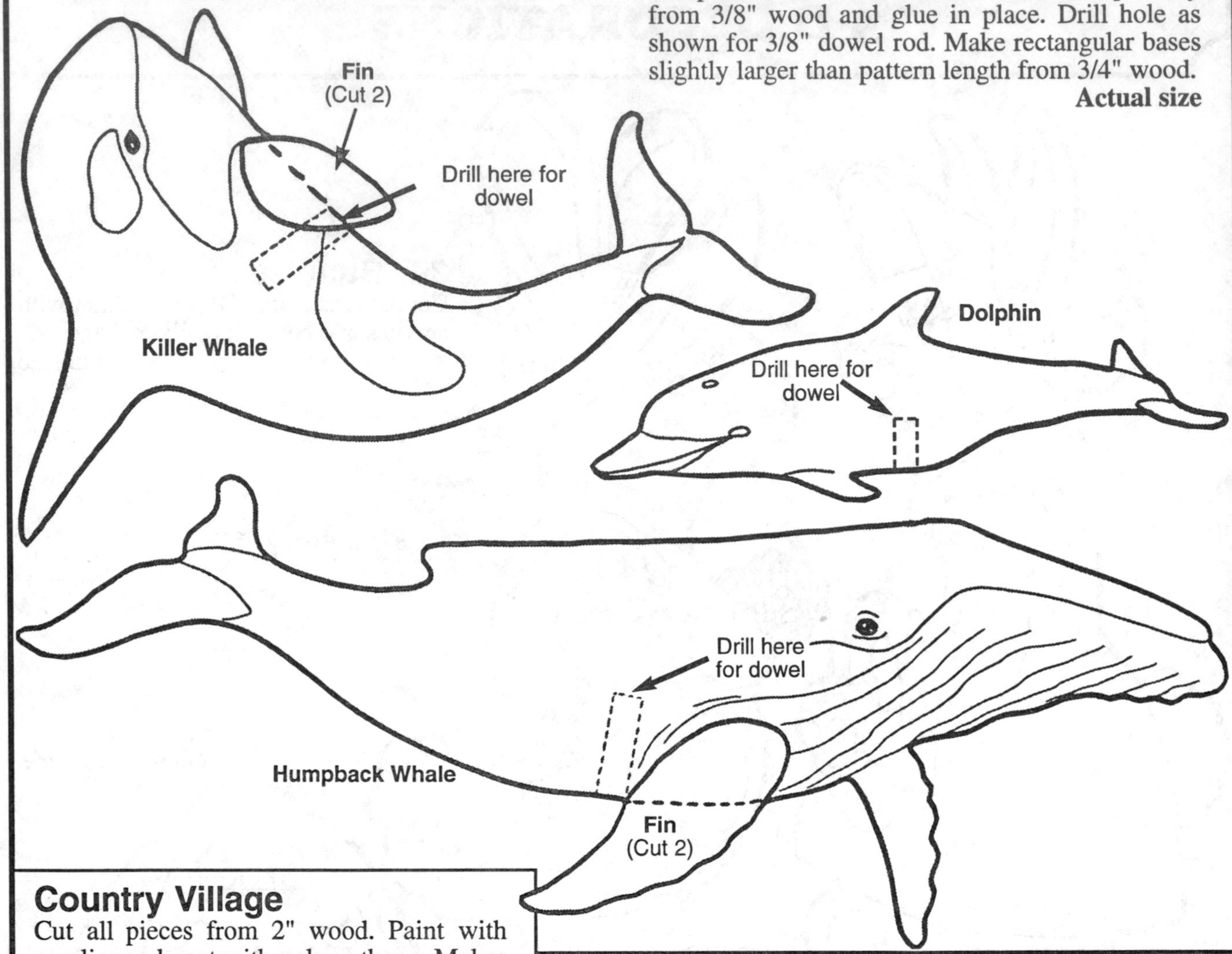

Country Village

Cut all pieces from 2" wood. Paint with acrylics and coat with polyurethane. Makes an adorable table top or bookcase display.

1 square = 1 inch

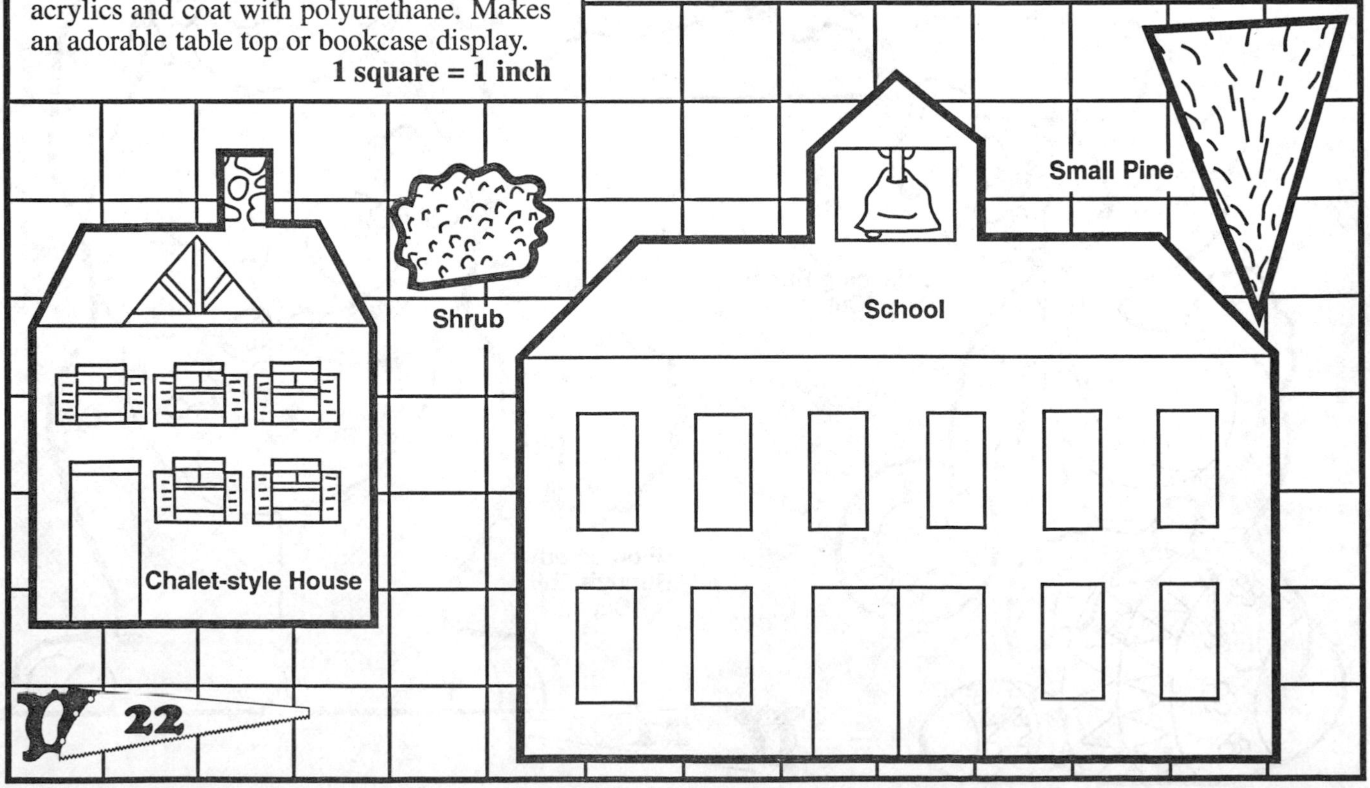

Country Village
continued from page 22

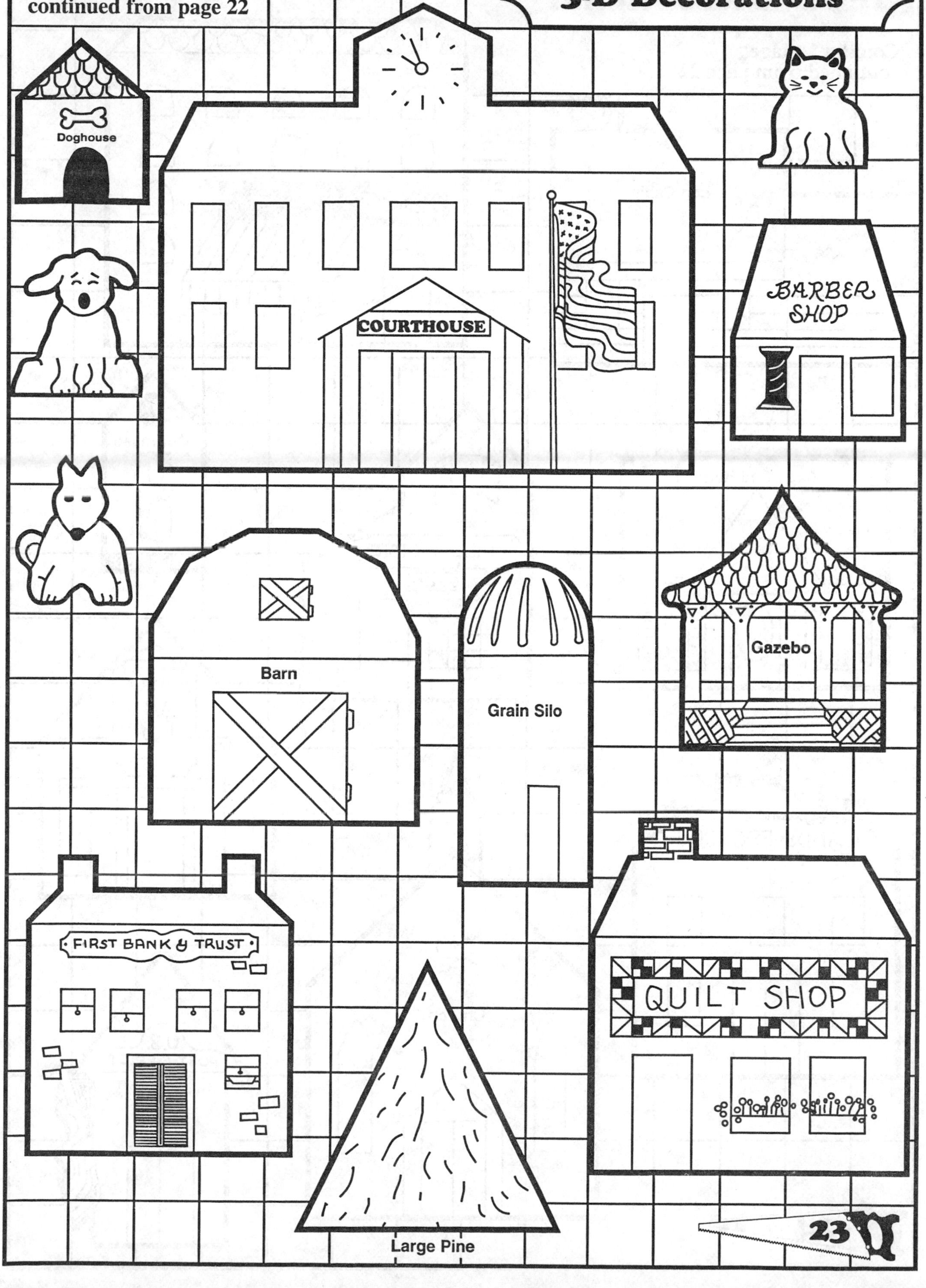

3-D Decorations

Country Village
continued from page 22

Cat and Bird Rockers

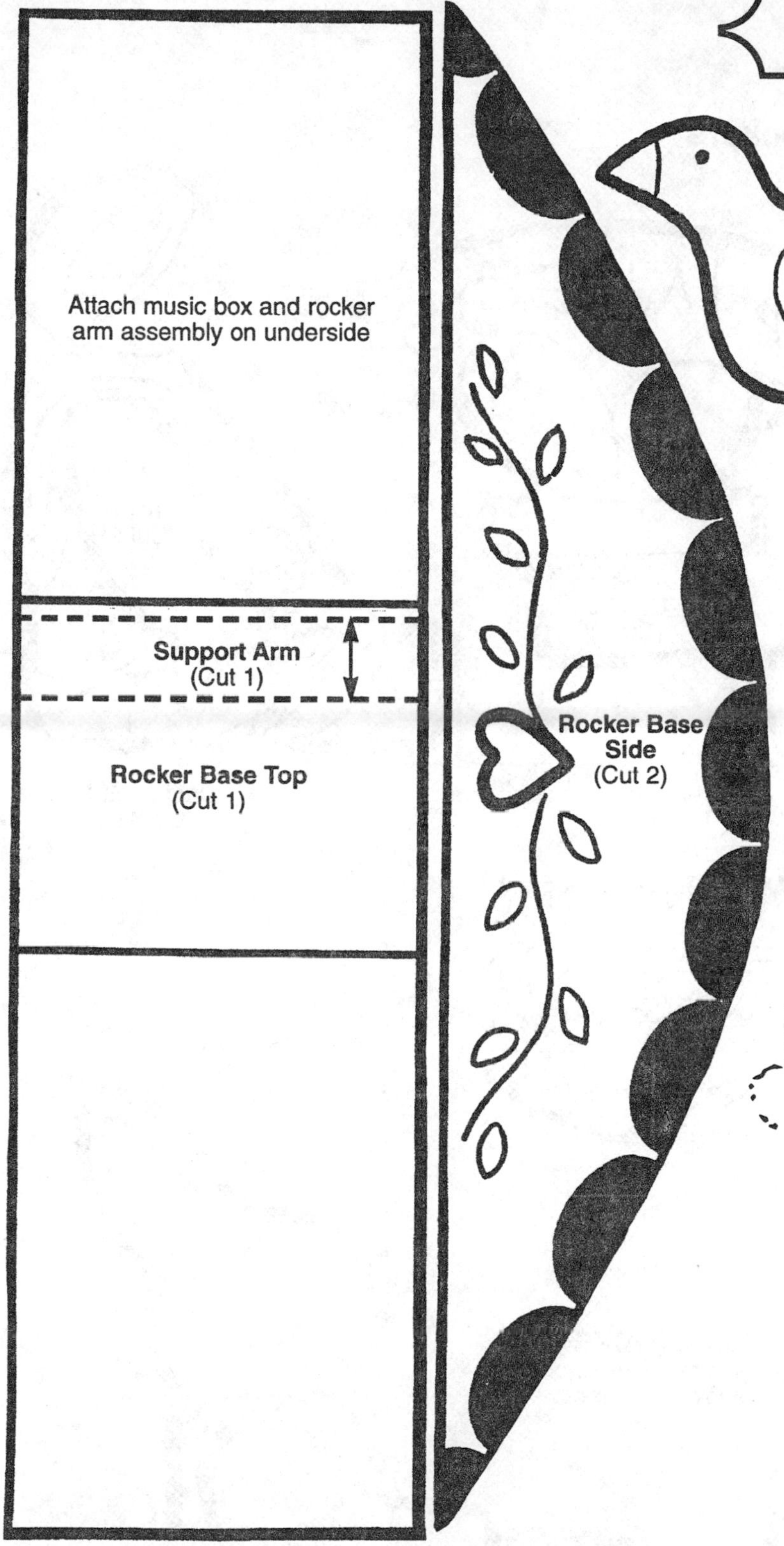

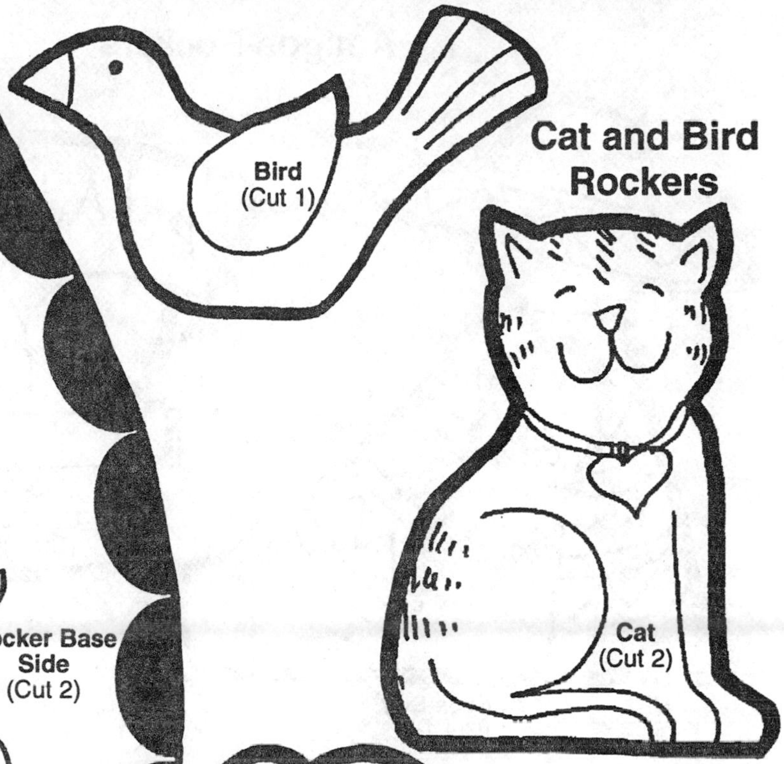

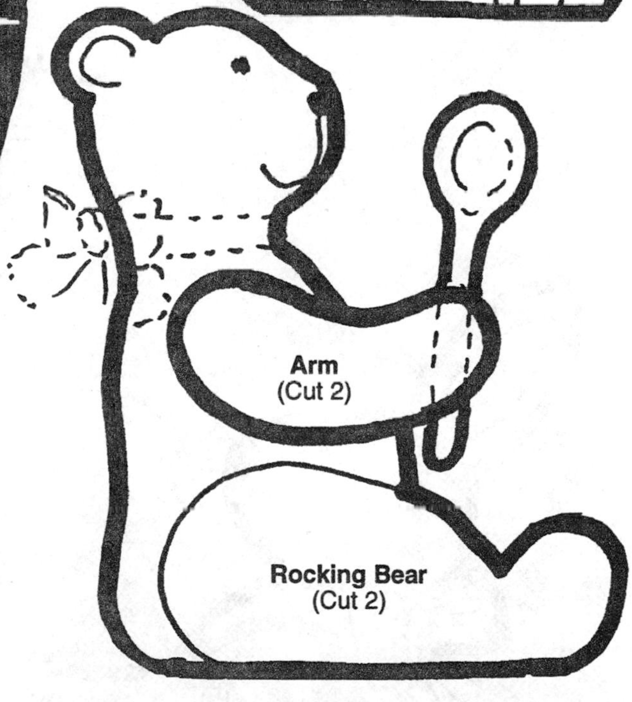

Rocking Bears

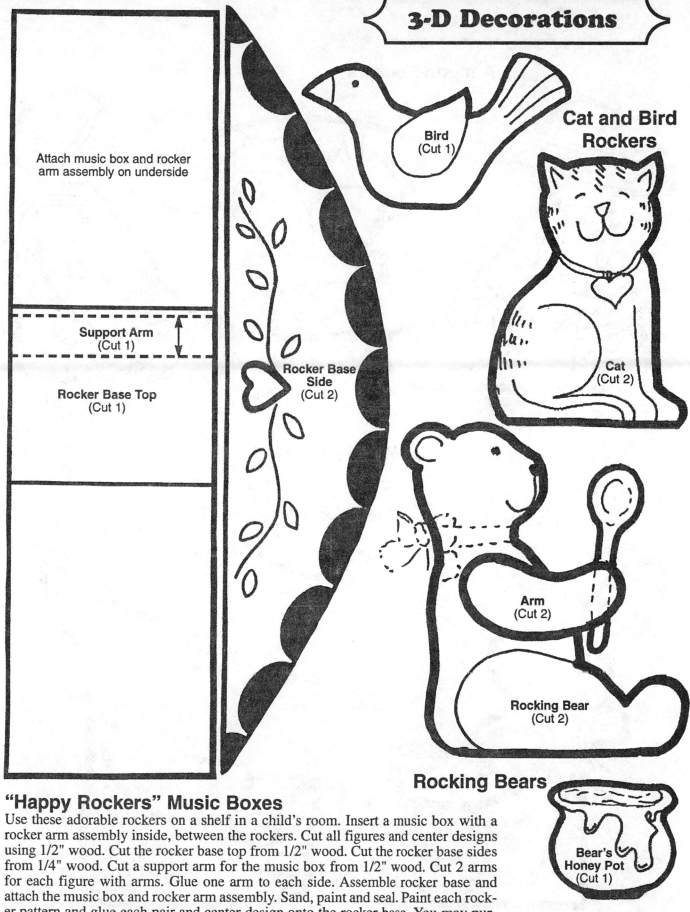

"Happy Rockers" Music Boxes

Use these adorable rockers on a shelf in a child's room. Insert a music box with a rocker arm assembly inside, between the rockers. Cut all figures and center designs using 1/2" wood. Cut the rocker base top from 1/2" wood. Cut the rocker base sides from 1/4" wood. Cut a support arm for the music box from 1/2" wood. Cut 2 arms for each figure with arms. Glue one arm to each side. Assemble rocker base and attach the music box and rocker arm assembly. Sand, paint and seal. Paint each rocker pattern and glue each pair and center design onto the rocker base. You may purchase the music box and rocker arm assembly from the Crafter's Mart, P.O. Box 2342, Greeley, CO 80632 (800)999-3445.

Actual size

Amigos Rockers

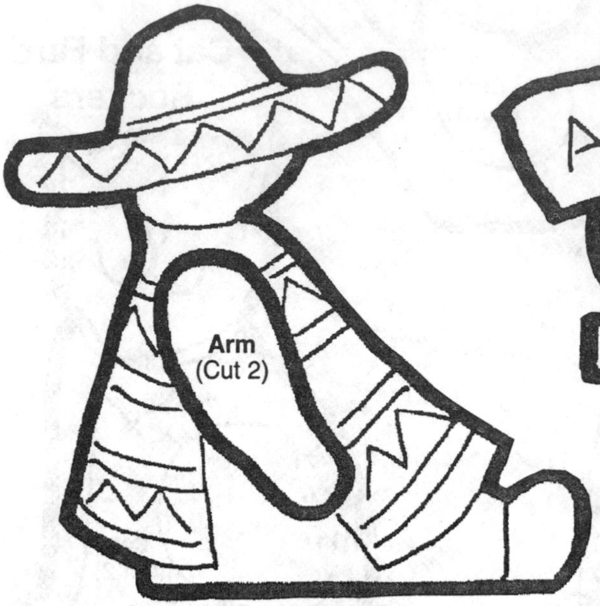

Amigos Boy
(Cut 1)

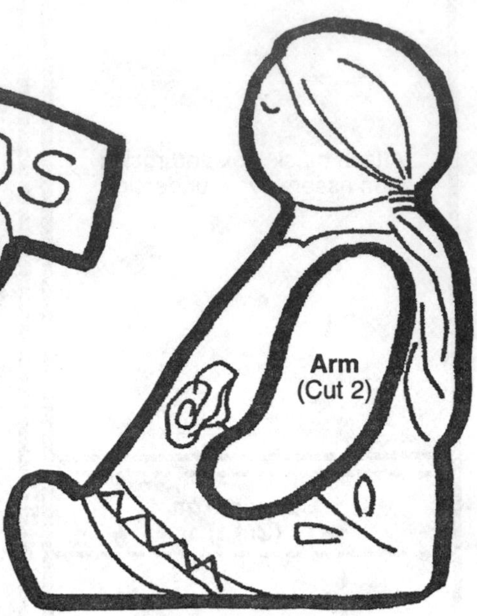

Amigos Girl
(Cut 1)

Amigos Rockers Diagram

Bunny Rockers

Hot glue mini carrots or other veggies to their paws.

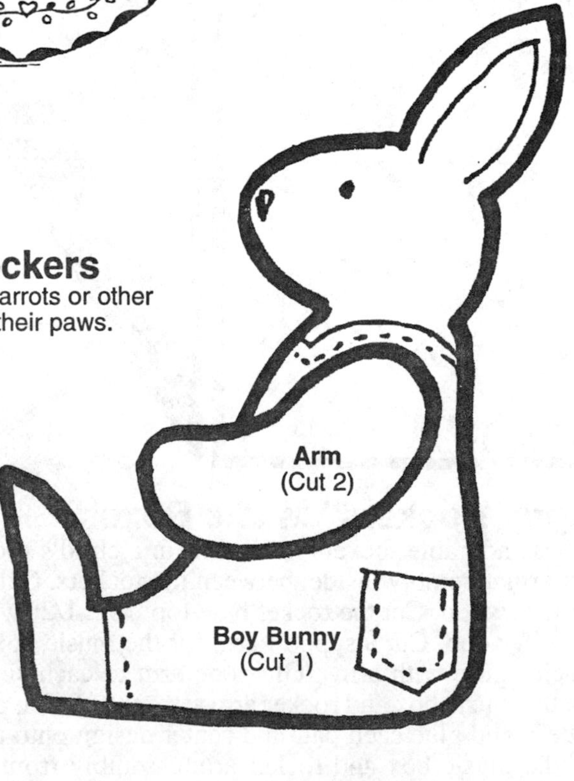

Amish Rockers

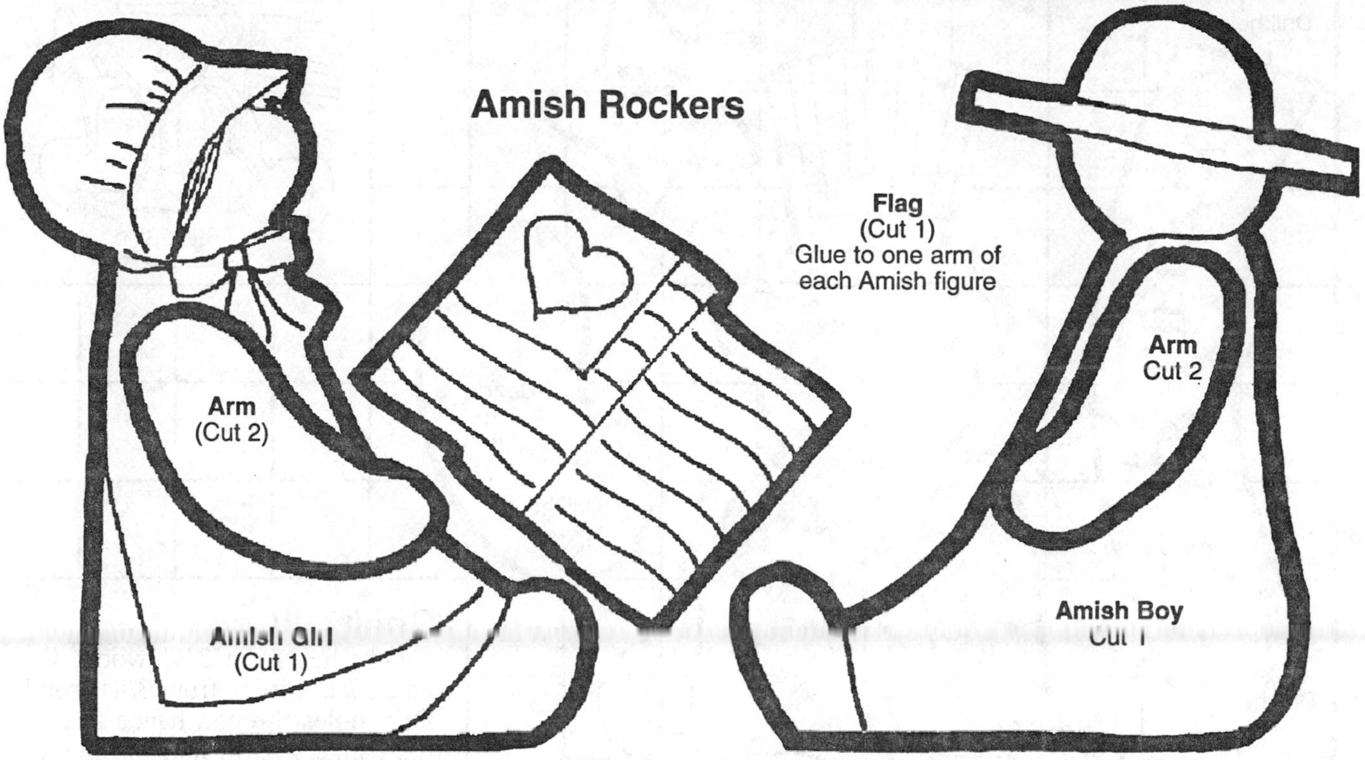

Goose Rockers

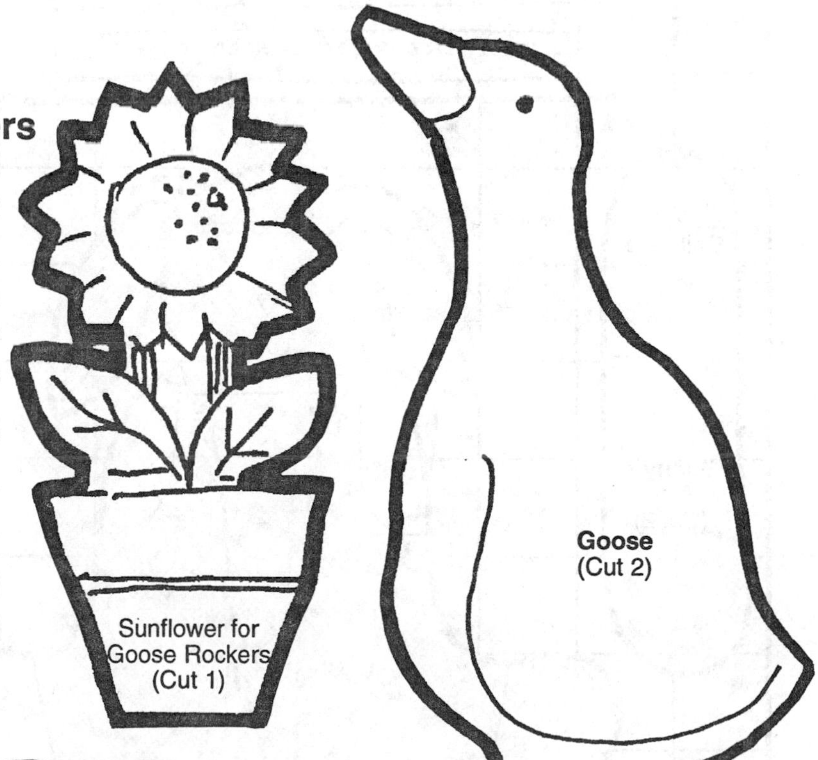

Best Friends Rockers

3-D Decorations

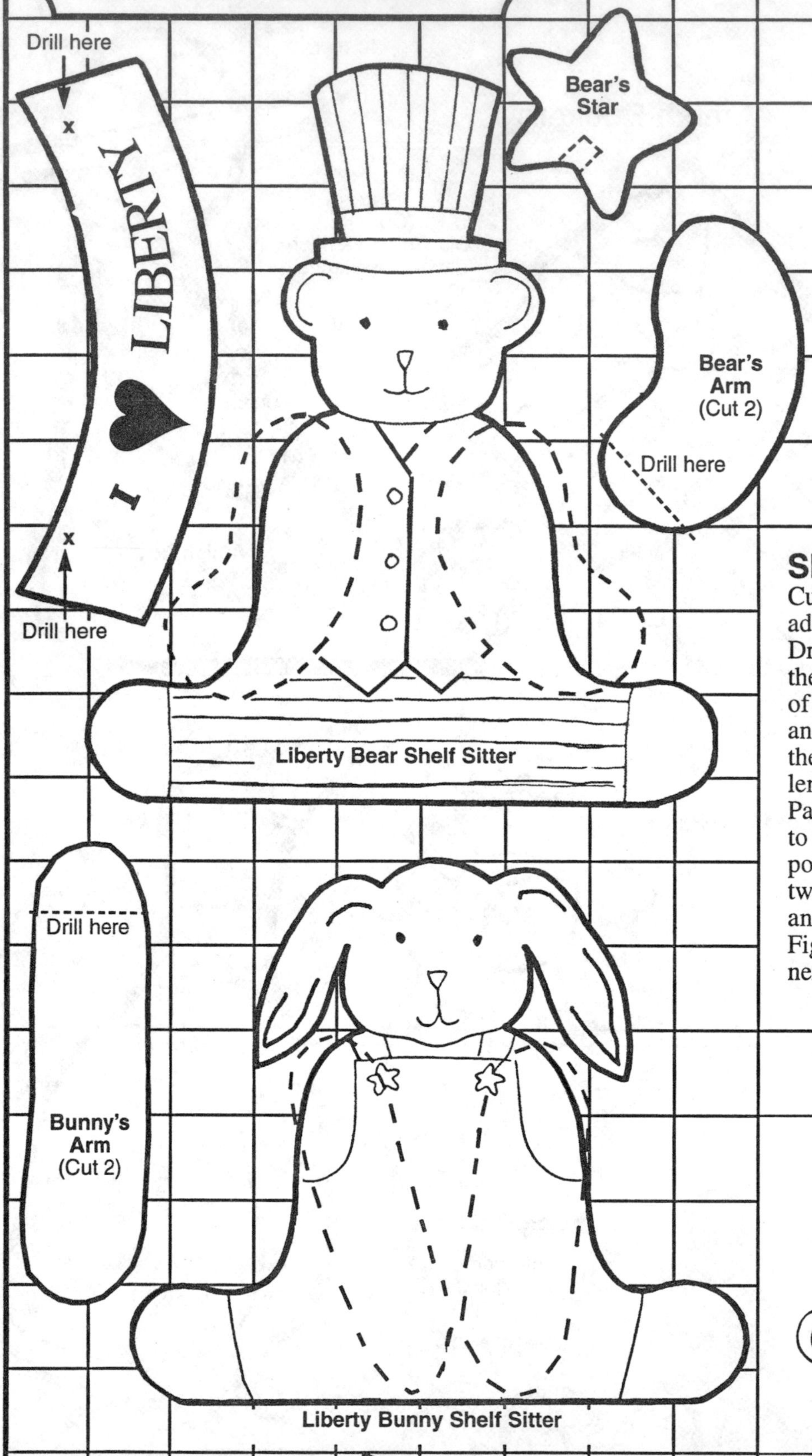

Shelf Sitters

Cut bodies from 3/4" wood. Cut additional pieces from 3/8" wood. Drill holes through hands to hold the banners. Drill holes in the top of the bear's arms to hold a flag and a 1/4" dowel for the star. Cut the dowel approximately the same length as the flag (see diagram). Paint with acrylic paint. Glue arms to bodies using hot glue. Coat with polyurethane. Thread wire or sisal twine through hands and banners and secure ends with knots. Figures will sit on shelf with banners hanging over the edge.

1 square = 1 inch

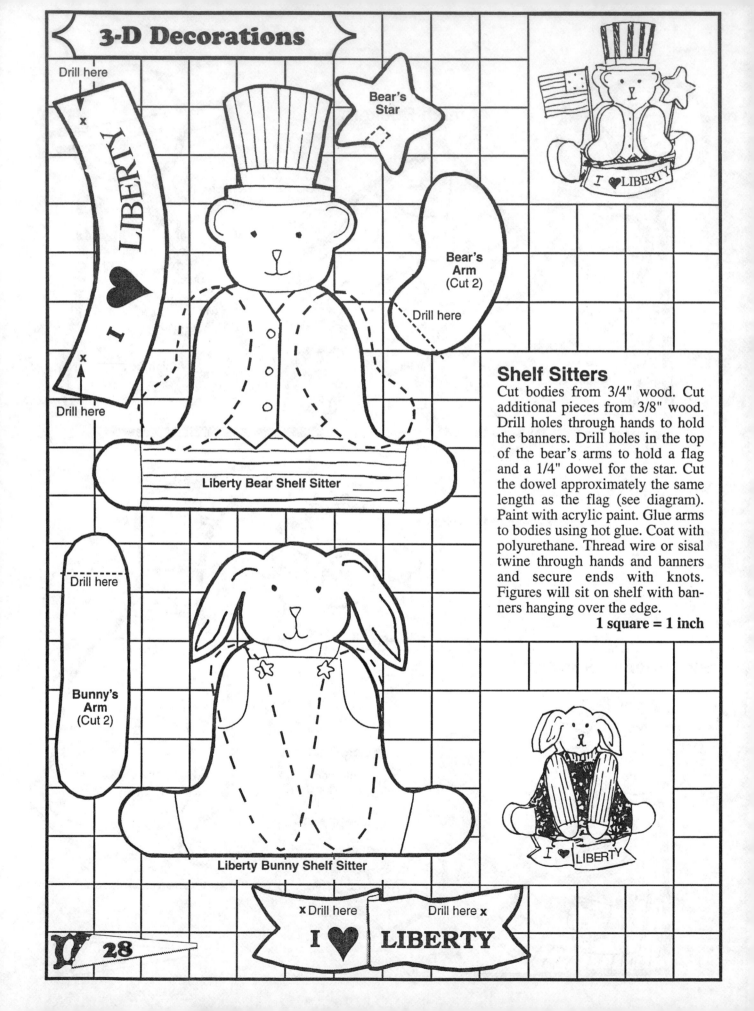

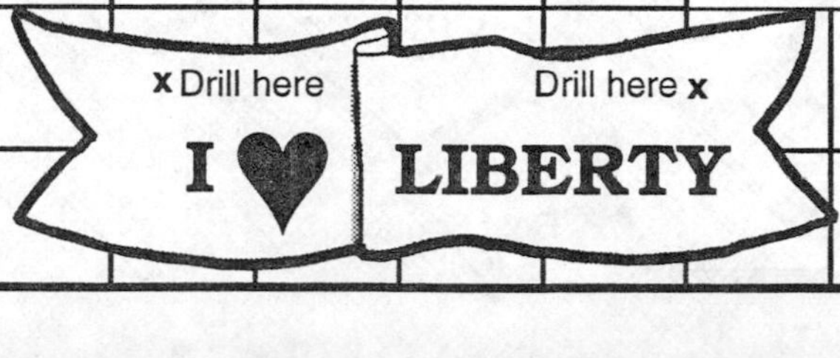

3-D Decorations

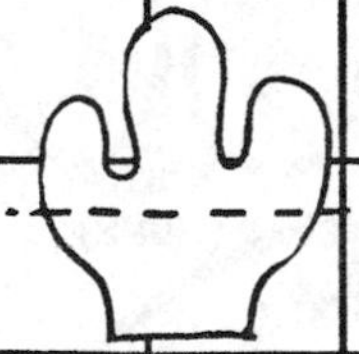

Amigo Cactus
(Cut 1)

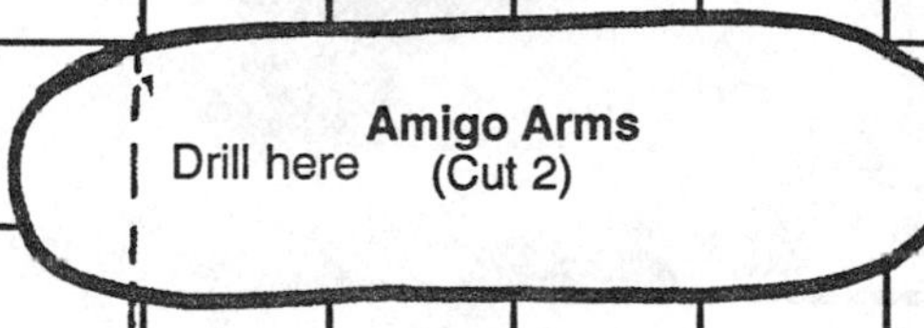

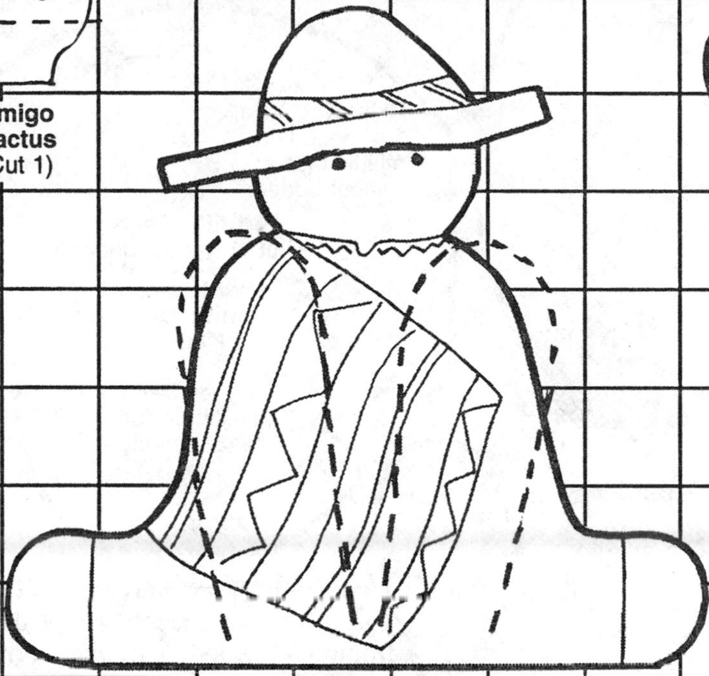

Amigo Diagram

Amigo Shelf Sitter

Humpty Dumpty Banner
(Cut 1)

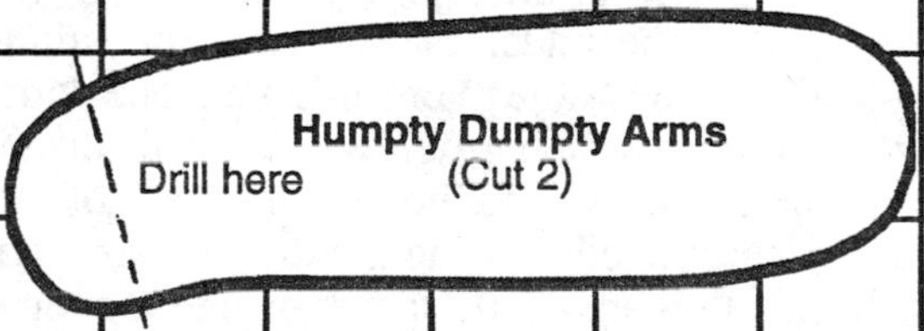

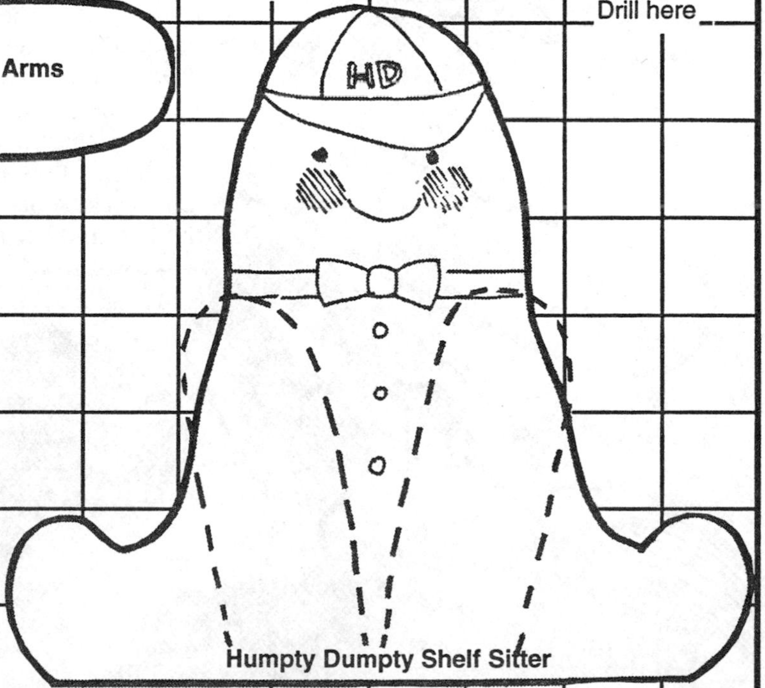

Humpty Dumpty Diagram

Humpty Dumpty Shelf Sitter

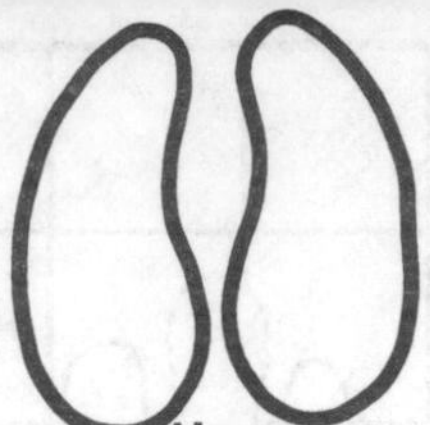

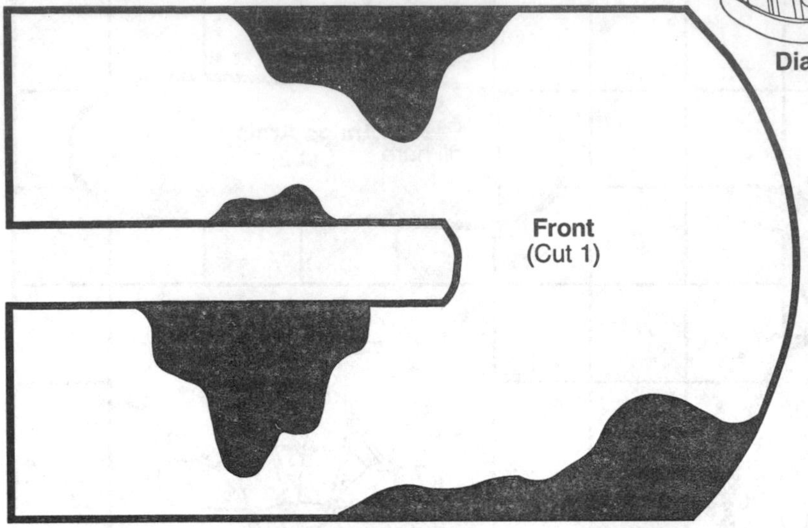

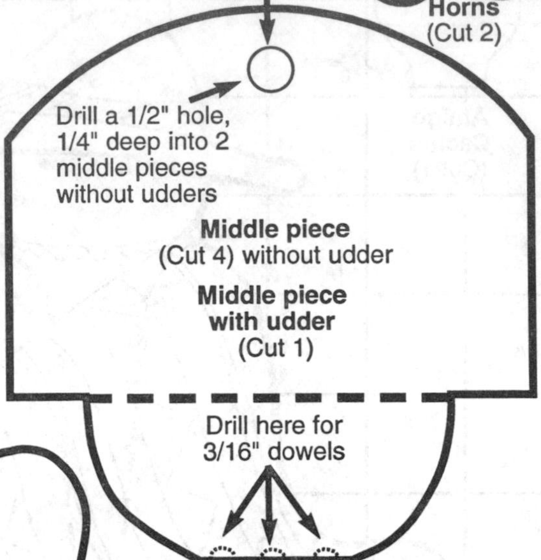

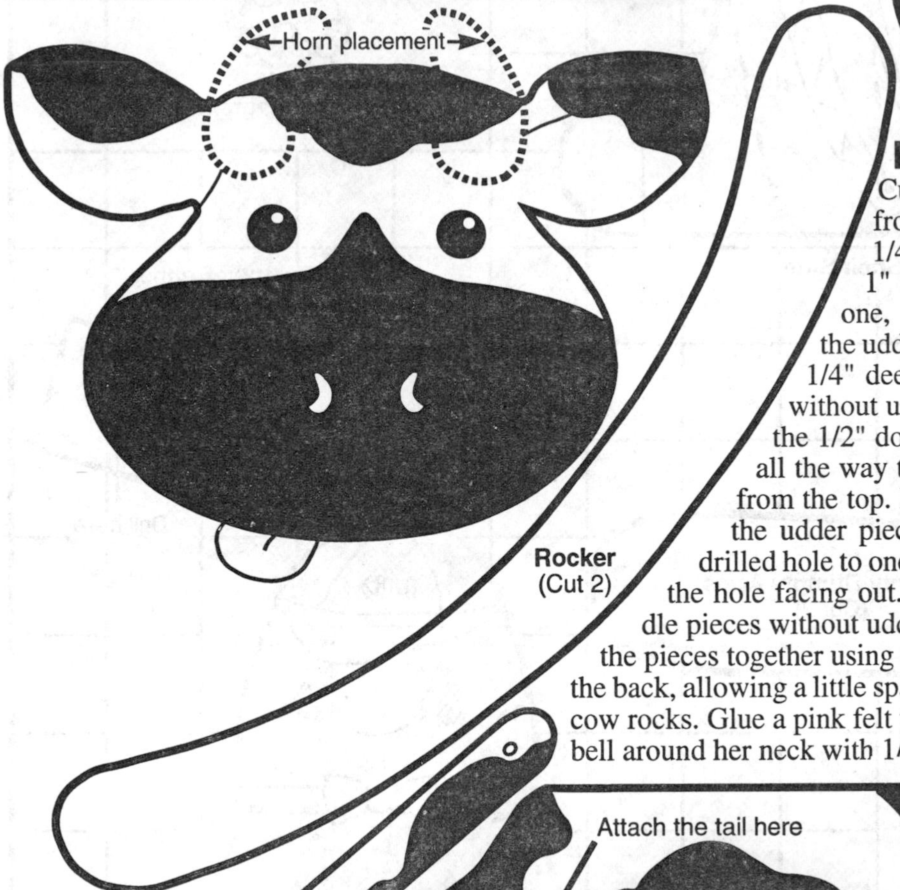

Rocking Holstein Cow

Cut all of the pieces except the horns from 3/4" wood. Cut the horns from 1/4" plywood. Cut three 3/16" dowels, 1" long, to be used with the udders. Cut one, 1/2" dowel, 1-1/2" long to support the udder section. Sand well. Drill a 1/2" hole 1/4" deep into two of the four middle pieces without udders, about 5/8" from the top to hold the 1/2" dowel with the udders. Drill a 1/2" hole all the way through the piece with the udder, 5/8" from the top. Drill three 3/16" holes, 1/4" deep into the udder piece. Glue one middle piece without a drilled hole to one middle piece with a drilled hole, with the hole facing out. Repeat with the two remaining middle pieces without udders. Paint all of the pieces. Nail all of the pieces together using the diagram as a guide. Nail the tail to the back, allowing a little space for free movement of the tail as the cow rocks. Glue a pink felt tongue in area shown. Tie a small cow bell around her neck with 1/8" red ribbon. **Actual Size**

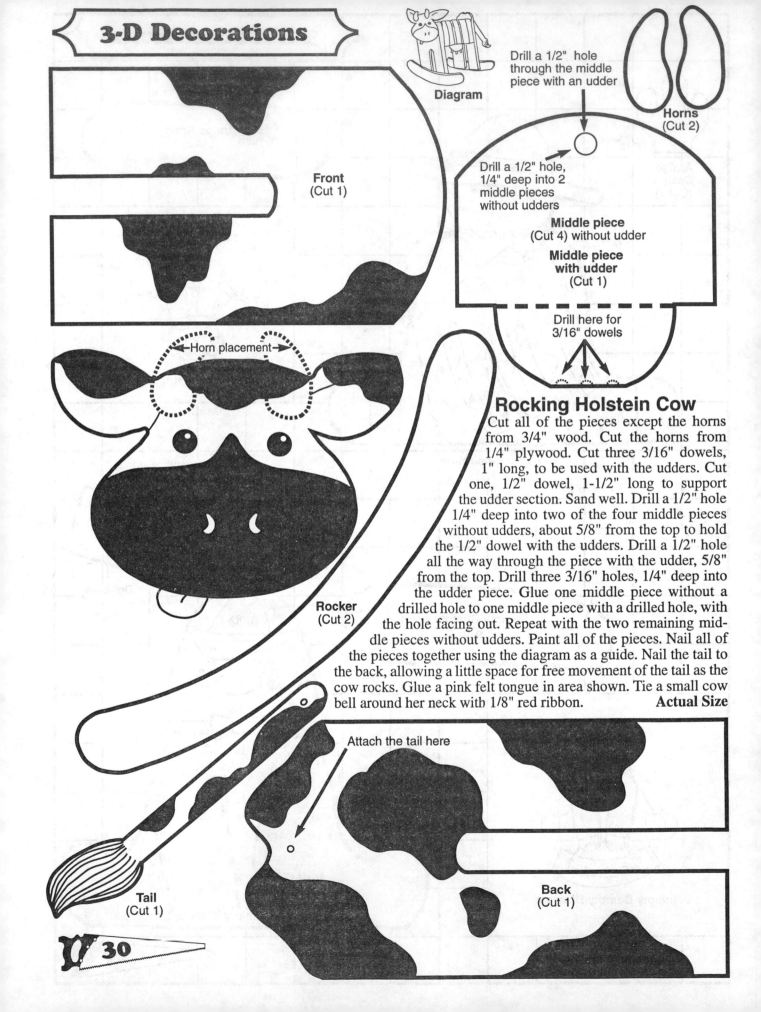

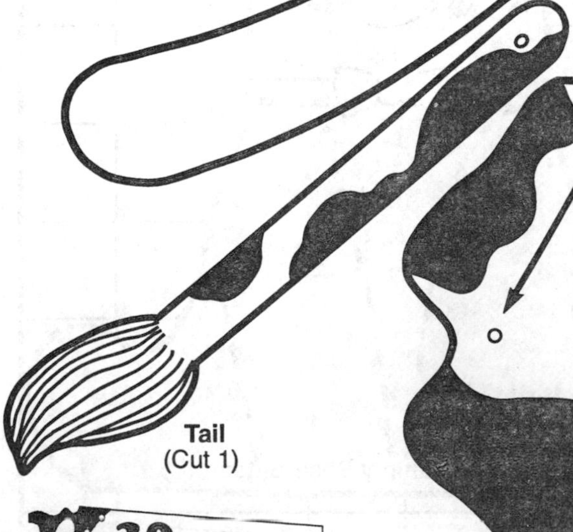

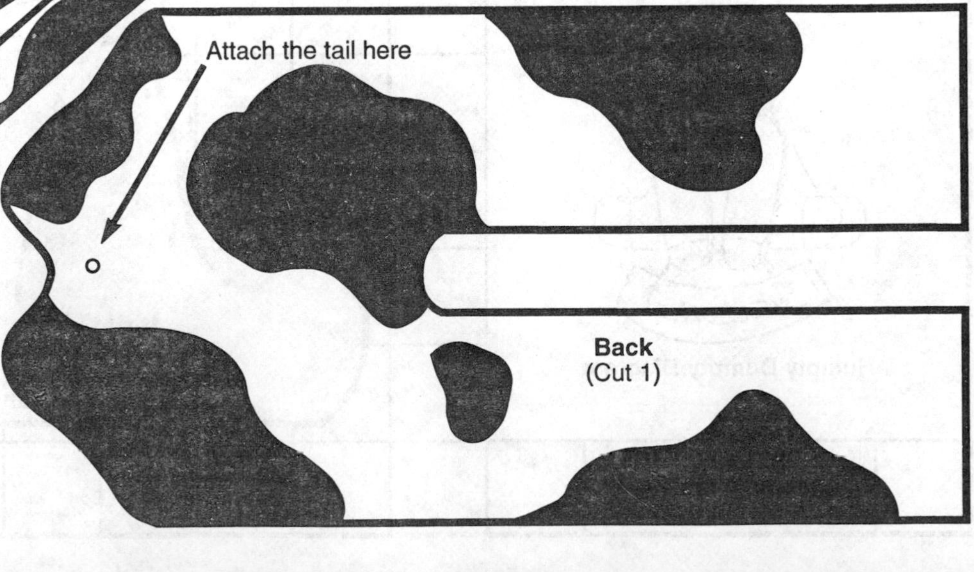

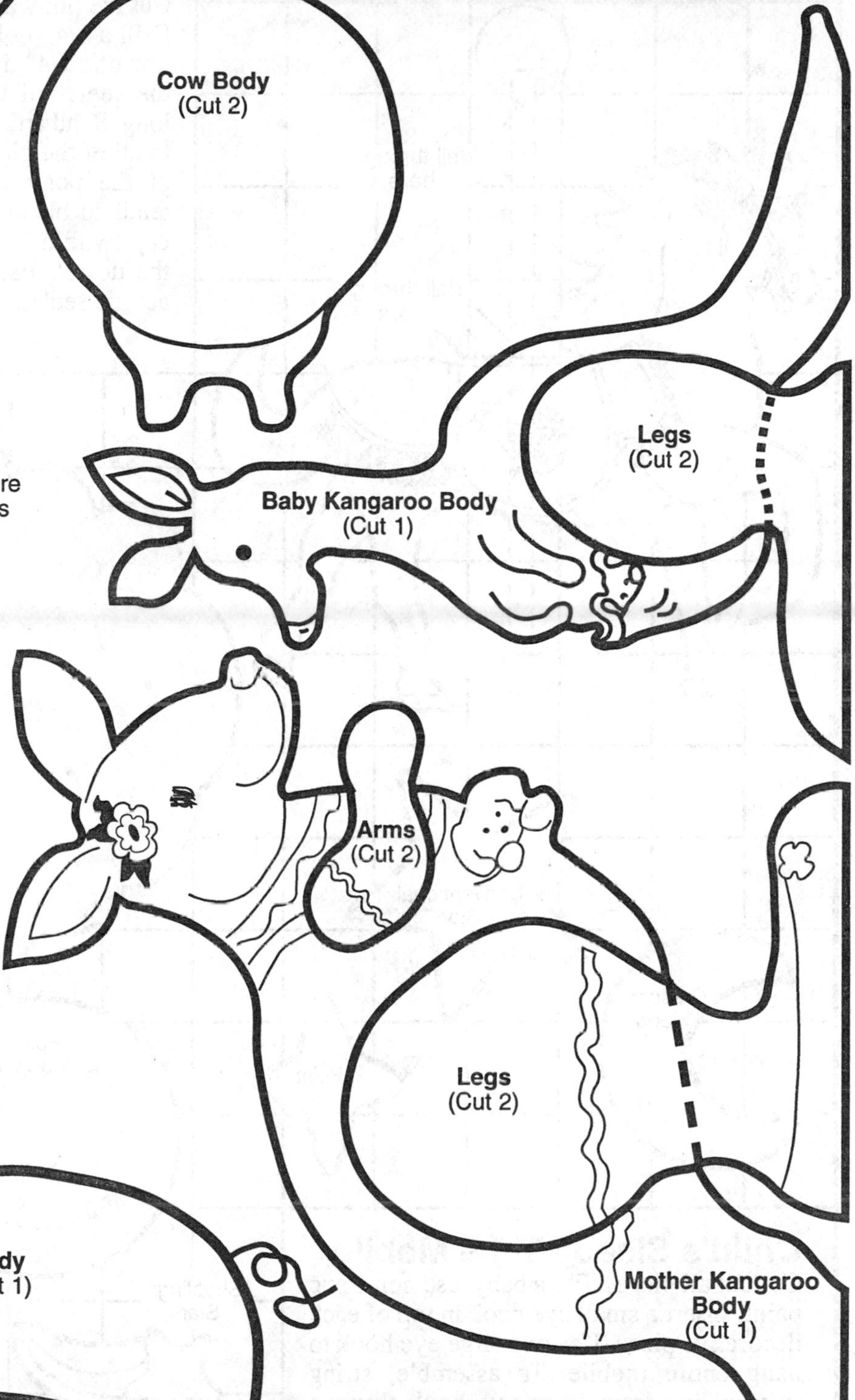

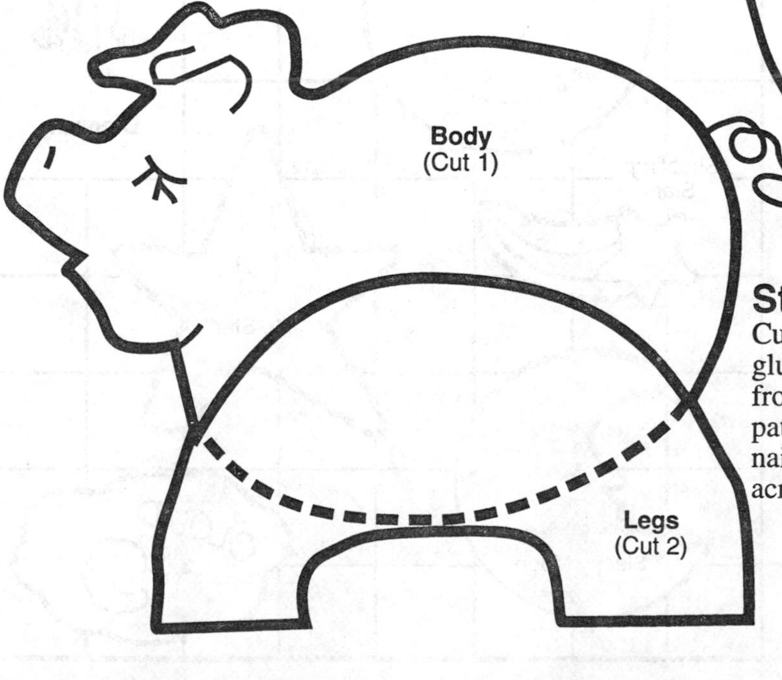

Stackable Animals

Cut each piece from 1/2" wood. Sand and glue the pieces together in order (i.e., head, front legs, middle, ...). Attach the tail, if the pattern calls for one, with a small finishing nail. Paint with acrylics. Seal using an acrylic spray sealer.

Actual size

3-D Decorations

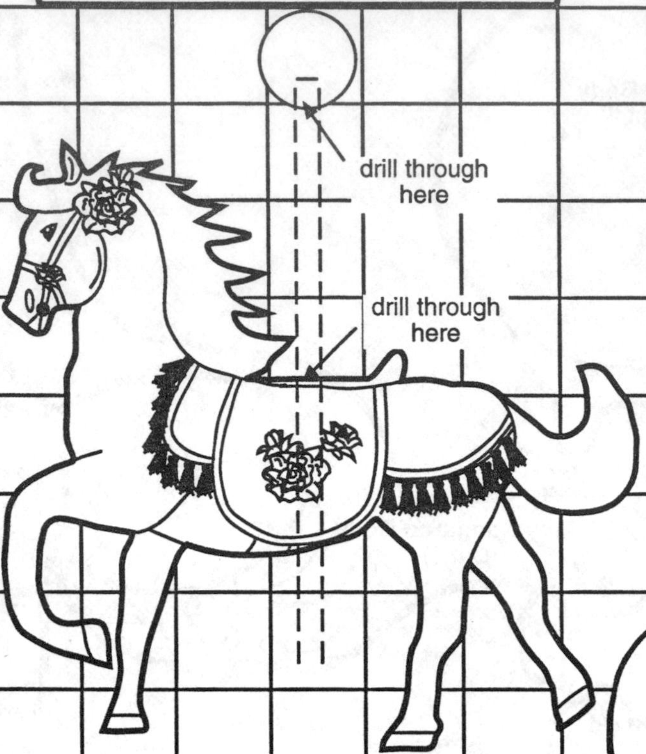

Prancing Pony on a Stand

Cut the pony and a 2" x 5-3/8" stand from 1" stock. Drill a 1/4" hole through the pony's body for insertion of a 1/4" dowel. Drill a 1/4" hole, 1/2" deep into the center of the stand. Cut a 1/4" dowel, 7-3/4" long. Sand and then apply a basecoat of acrylic paint to all of the pieces. Trace the details onto both sides of the pony using graphite paper. Carbon paper tends to bleed through paint. Glue a 1" dowel ball cap (with a 1/4" hole for insertion) onto the top of the dowel. Paint with acrylic paints. Seal with an acrylic sealer.

1 square = 1 inch

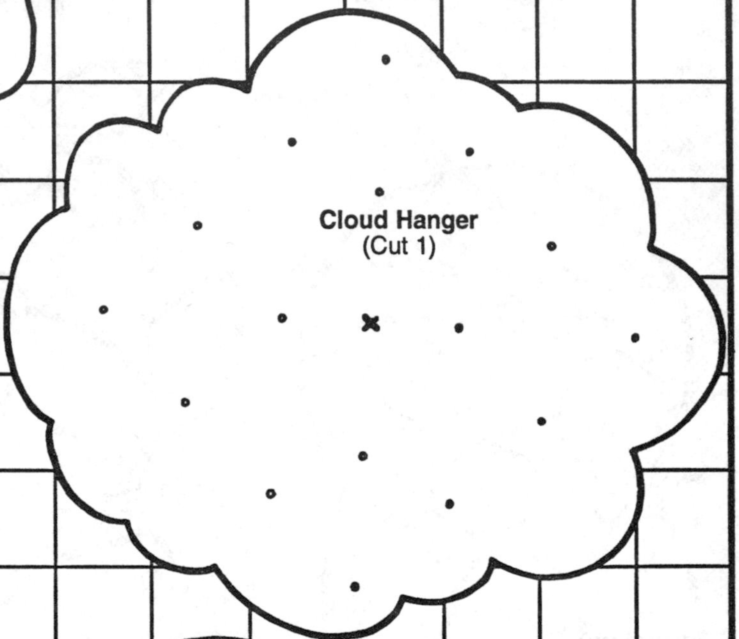

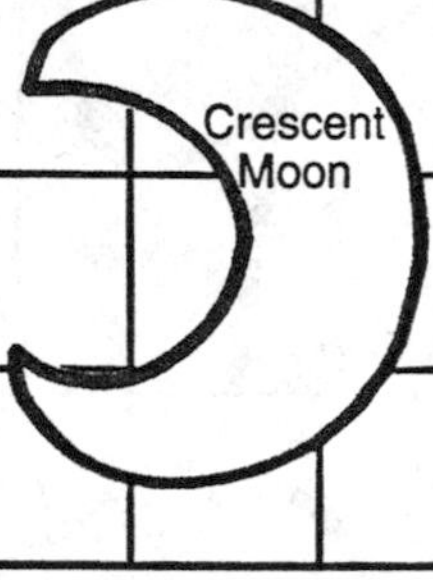

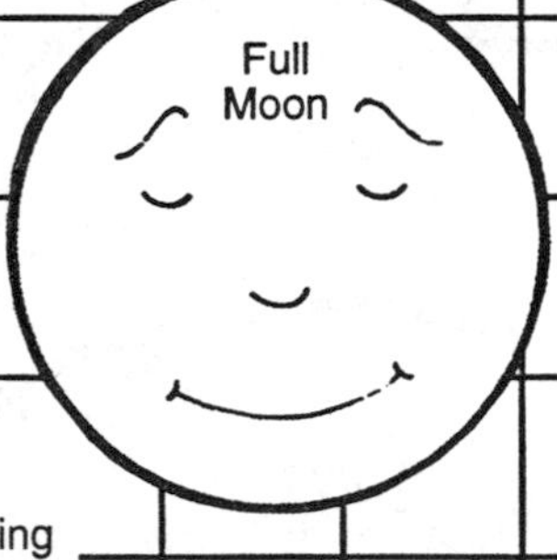

Diagram

Child's Sleepy-Time Mobile

Cut out all pieces. For a baby, use non-toxic paint. Insert a small eye hook in top of each decorative piece. Use one large eye hook to hang entire mobile. To assemble, string fishing line from large eye hook through base and attach each piece by small eye hooks (see diagram.) Hang objects at different lengths and use an odd number of mobile pieces (5,7,9). All pieces do not have to be used or just one piece may be cut out and used. It could be a mobile of happy stars.

1 square = 1-1/4 inches

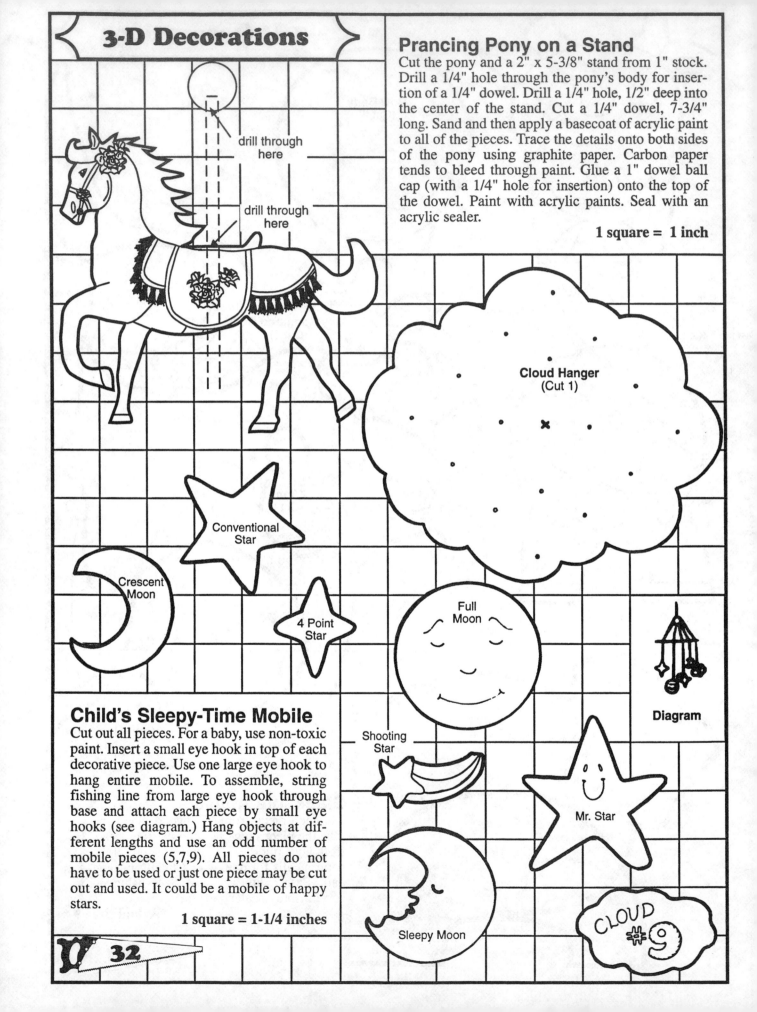

— CHAPTER FOUR —

FURNITURE

Adirondack Chair

This is a classic and so very comfortable. You will want to make at least two for the patio and two for the deck. You can make this project from any type of wood, but if you want it to last, use pressure treated lumber or heart-wood redwood.

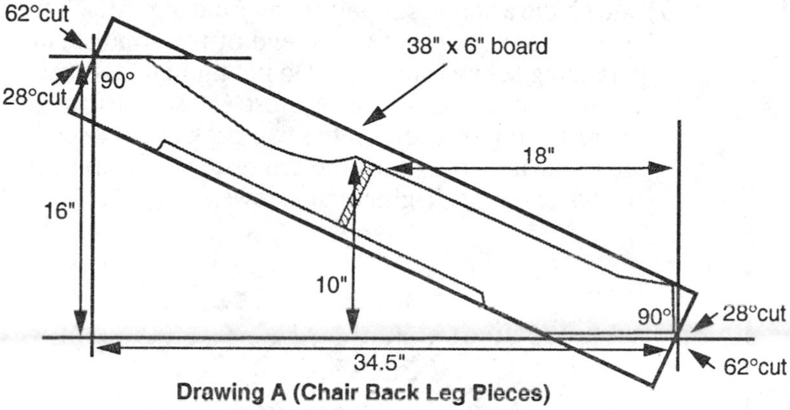

Drawing A (Chair Back Leg Pieces)

Bill-of-Materials

1' x 8' pressure treated lumber:
2 pieces 3-1/2" x 25" (front legs)
2 pieces 38" x 6" (back legs)
2 pieces 2" x 29" (armrest supports)
2 pieces 5" x 34" (armrests)
7 pieces 2-1/2" x 21-1/2" (seatboards)
2 pieces 2" x 6" (armrest stabilizer)
3 pieces 4" x 36" (center backrest)
2 pieces 3-1/2" x 29" (end pieces for backrest)
1 piece 2" x 23" (top bracket support)
1 piece 4" x 20" (lower back support)
1 piece 5-1/2" x 20" (front piece)

Hardware and Miscellaneous

Silicone glue
50 screws 1-1/4" Dacrotized
1 pint exterior stain

Tools Required

Circular saw
Saber saw
Drill with countersink bit
Screwdriver
Router with rounding-over bit
Flap wheel sander

Instructions for Chair

1) Measure and cut the leg pieces, the front piece and the lower back support.
2) Attach the front piece to the back legs as shown, using screws and glue. Attach the back support 18 inches from the end of the back legs. At this point only, put one screw in the top of the board on both sides. This will allow for minor adjustments later as the lower part of the back is attached.
3) Measure and cut the armrest, the armrest support and the armrest stabilizer.

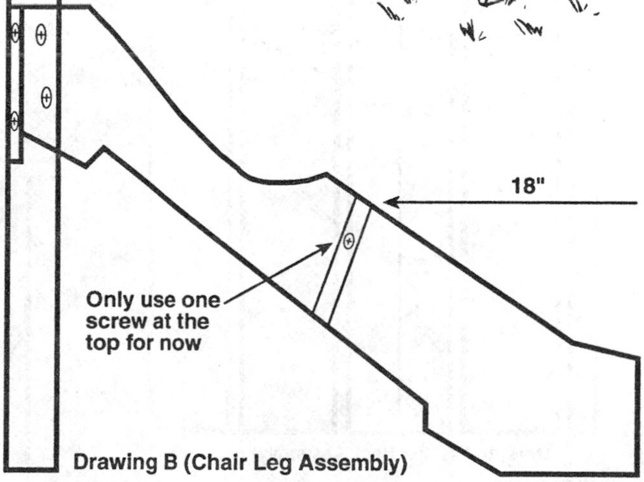

Drawing B (Chair Leg Assembly)

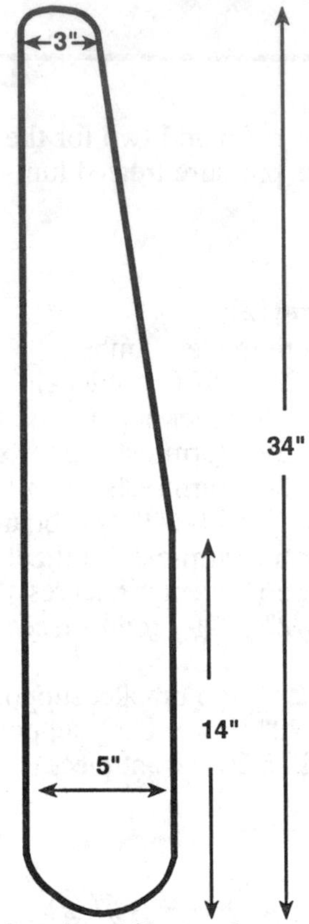

Drawing C (Armrest)

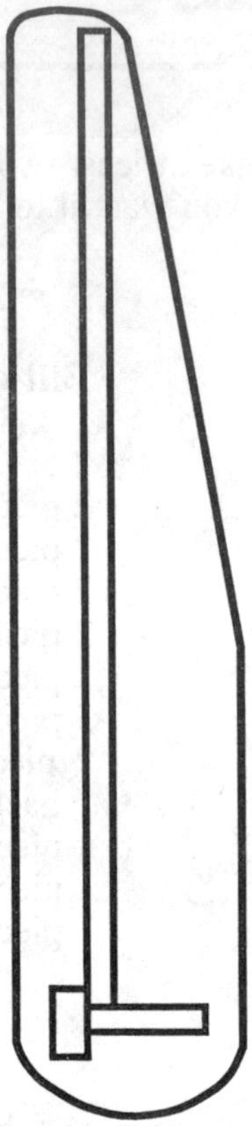
Drawing D (Armrest with Support)

4) Center the armrest stabilizer on the outside top of the front legs. Attach, using glue and screws from the inside of the leg. Remember to countersink the screws.
5) Measure and cut the back pieces and the upper back support piece.
6) Attach the two back end boards using only one screw (at this time) to the lower back support. They will hang loosely. You may need some help for these next few steps.
7) Attach the armrest support to the front leg. Attach the upper armrest support to the end of the armrest support using screws and glue. Do not tighten the screws at this point. Attach the armrest (as shown) to the armrest support. Position the two back end boards on the back support against the armrest and attach using screws and glue. Tighten all screws.

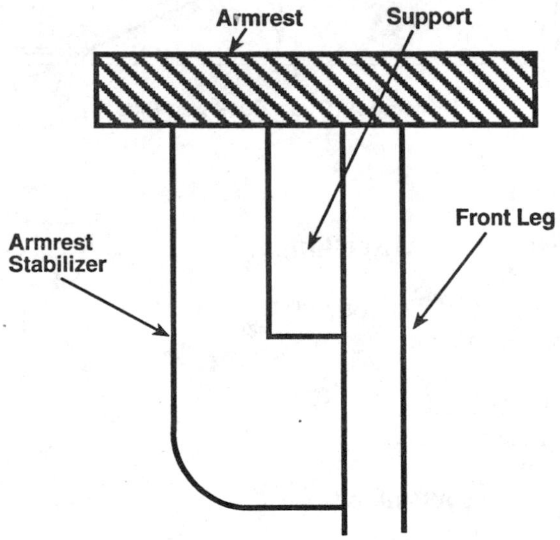

Drawing E (Armrest Stabilizer Assembly)

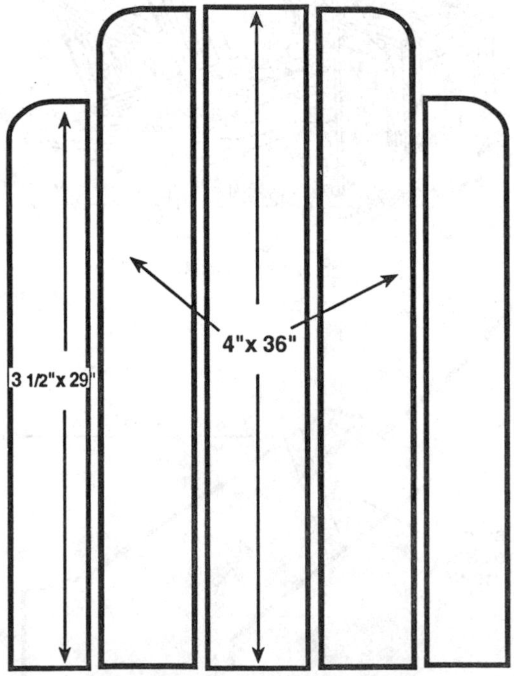

Drawing F (Chair Back Assembly)

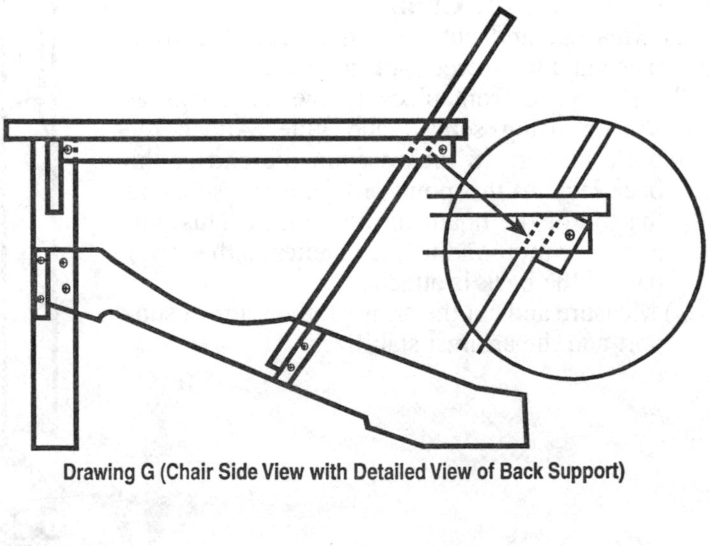
Drawing G (Chair Side View with Detailed View of Back Support)

8) Attach the remaining three back boards by evenly positioning them across the back. There should be a slight gap between the boards. Add all of the remaining screws and tighten.
9) Finish the project by routing the front seat area and the inner and outer sides of the armrest with a router and a rounding-over bit. If you want all sides of the armrest routed, do this before attaching it to the support. Rout the top of the back boards and continue down the sides as far as the router can reach.
10) Rout all of the top edges of the seat boards.
11) Evenly position the seat boards and attach using glue and screws.
12) Stain the project using an exterior-rated stain product. Sit back and enjoy the rewards of your labor.

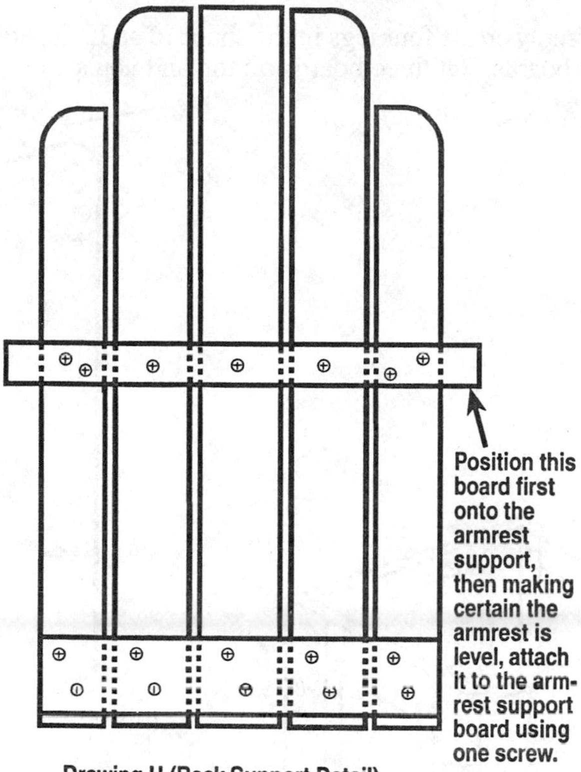
Position this board first onto the armrest support, then making certain the armrest is level, attach it to the armrest support board using one screw.
Drawing H (Back Support Detail)

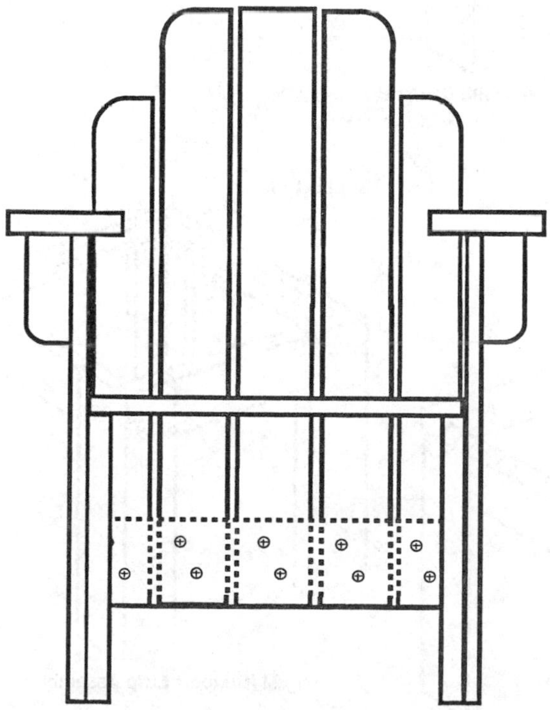
Drawing I (Front View of Chair)

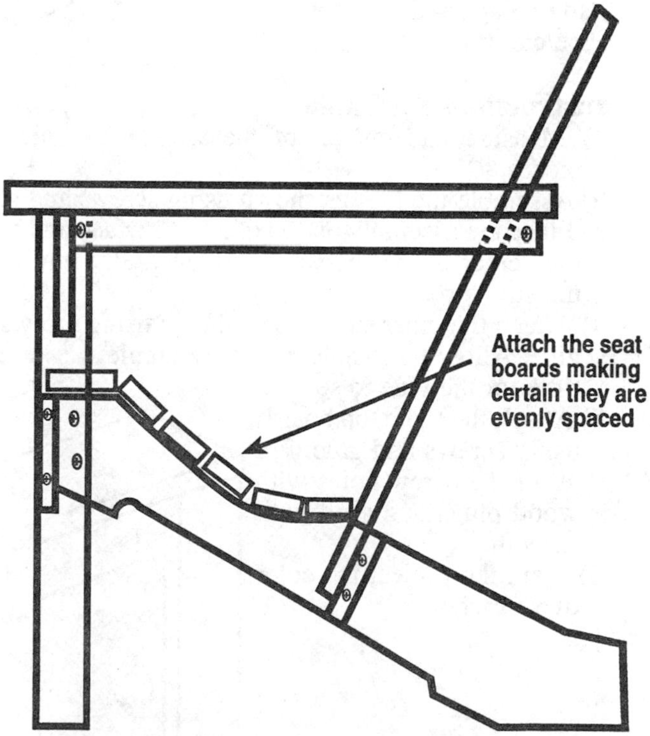
Attach the seat boards making certain they are evenly spaced
Drawing J (Chair Side View with Seat Boards)

Adirondack Table

This project is very easy to make, and quite functional. Simply create four legs in the shape of an L. Separate the legs by center boards. Attach inner support or spacer boards. Put three boards on top and you are done.

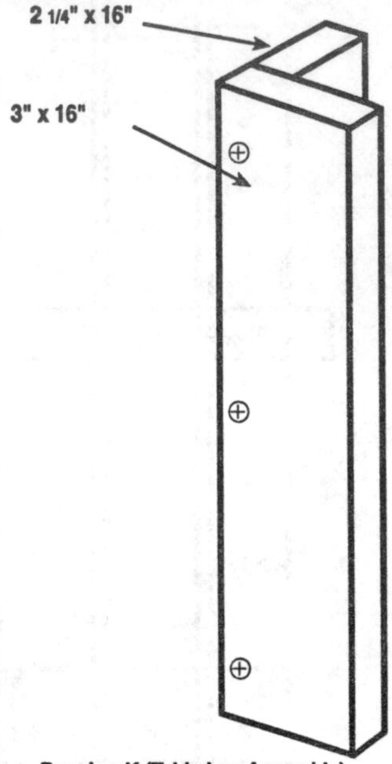

Drawing K (Table Leg Assembly)

Bill-of-Materials

1" x 4" pressure treated lumber:
4 pieces 3" x 16" (legs)
4 pieces 2-1/4" x 16" (legs)
4 pieces 3" x 6" (center pieces)
2 pieces 1" x 10-1/2" (inner support)
2 pieces 1" x 9" (inner support)
3 pieces 3-1/2" x 12" (top boards)

Hardware and Miscellaneous

Forty 1-1/2" woodscrews (Dacrotized or Galvanized)
Exterior grade glue or silicone glue
Stain of your choice
Wood plugs for 1/2" screw holes

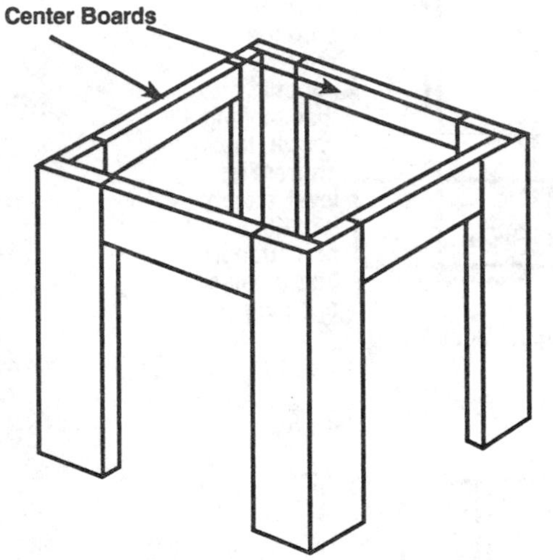

Drawing L (Table Legs with Center Boards)

Tools Required

Circular saw
Drill with countersink bit
Screwdriver
Router with rounding-over bit (optional)
Pad or flap sander
Pipe clamps

Instructions for Table

1) Measure and cut all of the wooden pieces.
2) Assemble the legs as shown using screws and glue.
3) Place the assembly on top of a flat surface and attach the center boards between the legs. Glue and clamp the structure.
4) Attach the inner supports as shown using screws and glue. Allow the whole assembly ample time for the glue to set.
5) Attach the three top boards using screws and glue. Fill all of the screw holes with wood plugs and sand until smooth.
6) Stain the project the color of your choice.

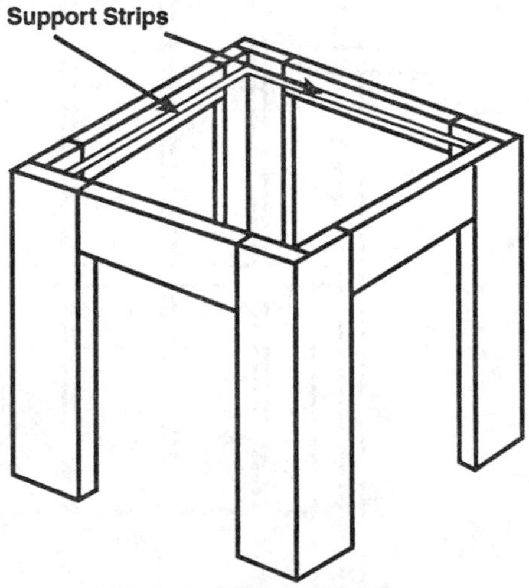

Drawing M (Support Strip Assembly)

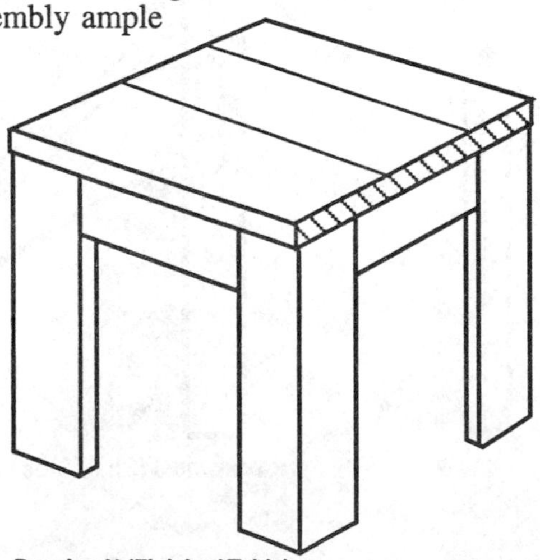
Drawing N (Finished Table)

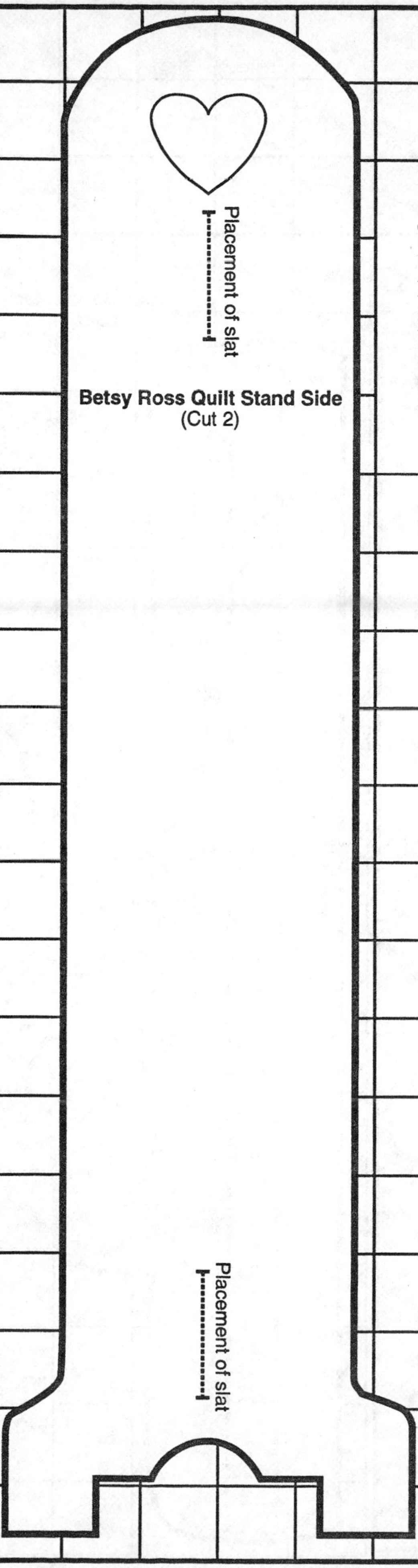

Betsy Ross Quilt Stand

This quilt stand is very easy to make and is a welcome addition to any home. Cut two side pieces from 3/4" stock and two slats from 3/4" stock. Assemble with wood glue and screws using a butt joint. Use the diagram as a guide. Stain or paint with acrylics. Seal with an acrylic spray or brush-on varnish. We finished the sides with country flowers.

1 square = 2 inches

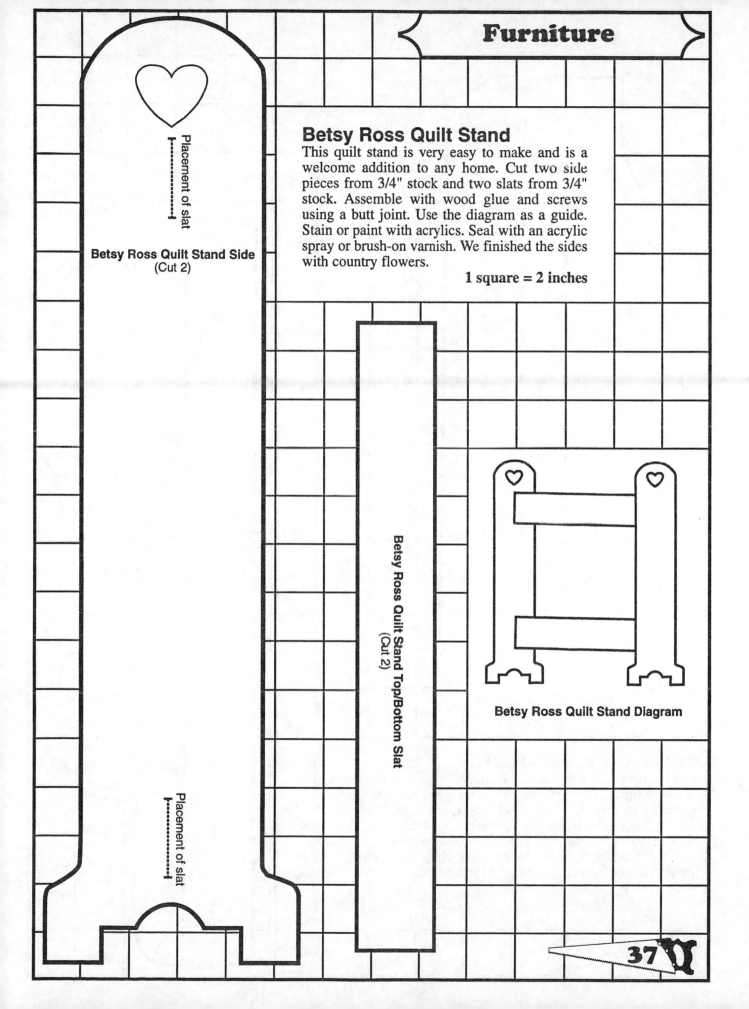

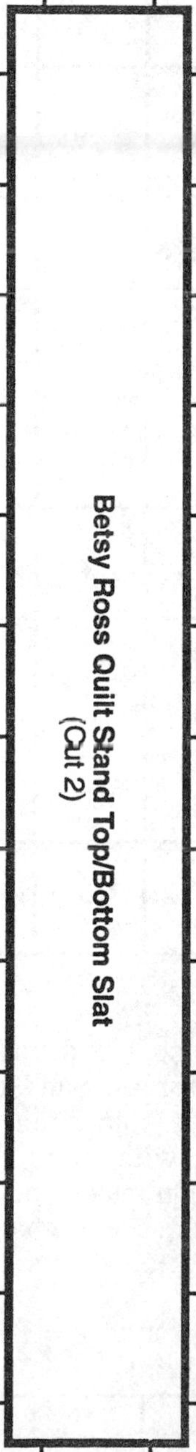

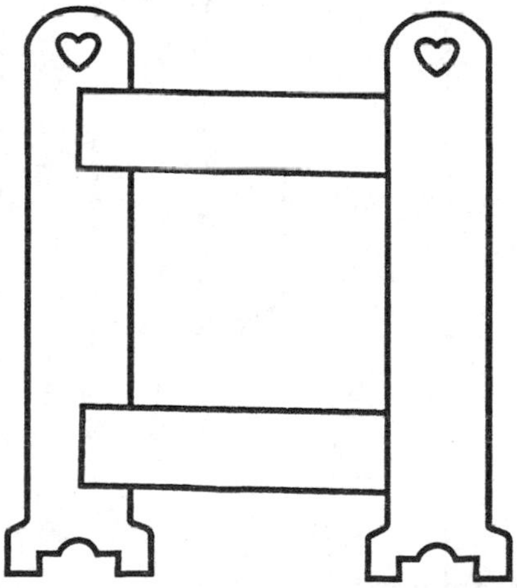

Betsy Ross Quilt Stand Diagram

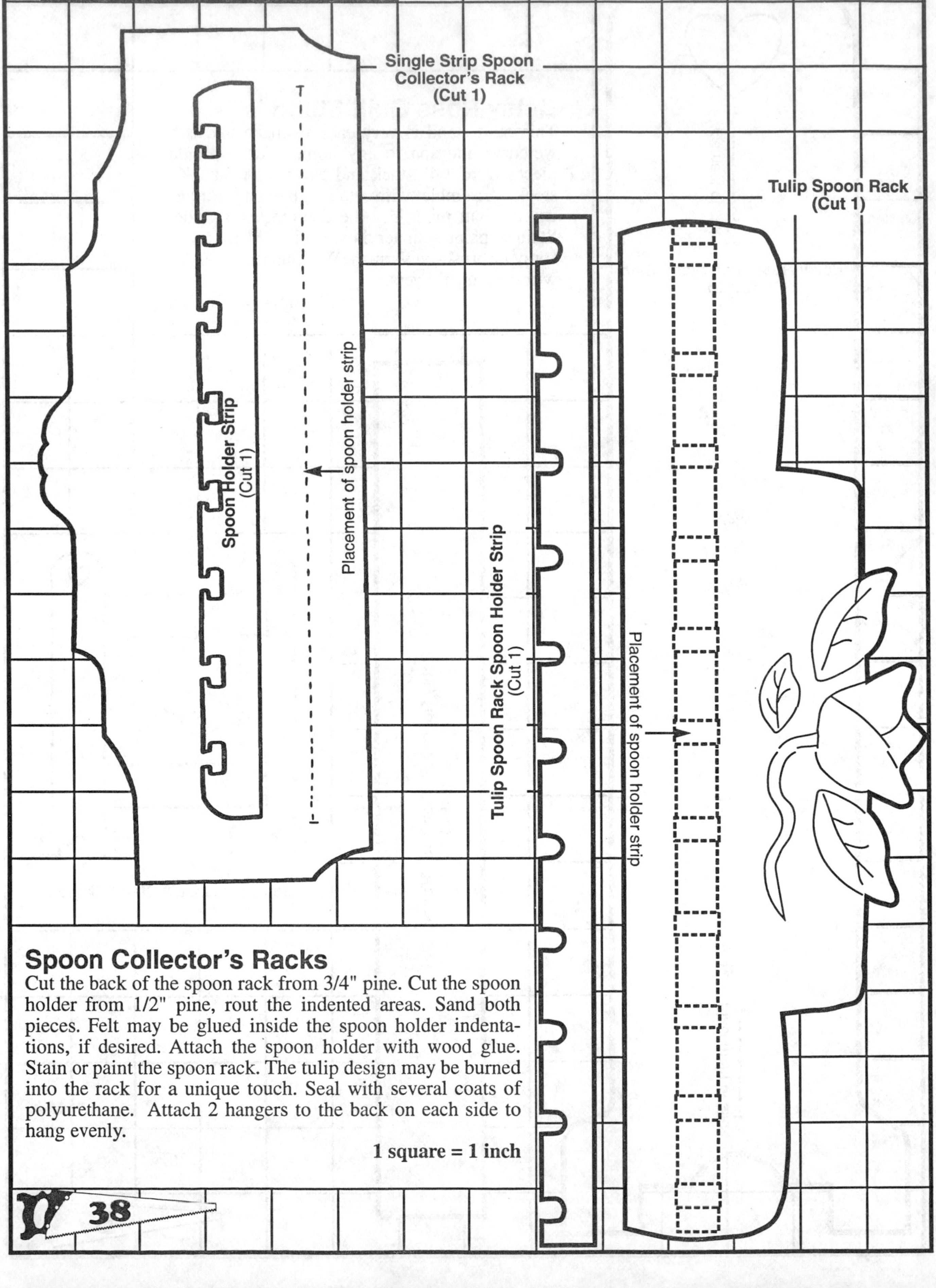

Spoon Collector's Racks

Cut the back of the spoon rack from 3/4" pine. Cut the spoon holder from 1/2" pine, rout the indented areas. Sand both pieces. Felt may be glued inside the spoon holder indentations, if desired. Attach the spoon holder with wood glue. Stain or paint the spoon rack. The tulip design may be burned into the rack for a unique touch. Seal with several coats of polyurethane. Attach 2 hangers to the back on each side to hang evenly.

1 square = 1 inch

Figure 1

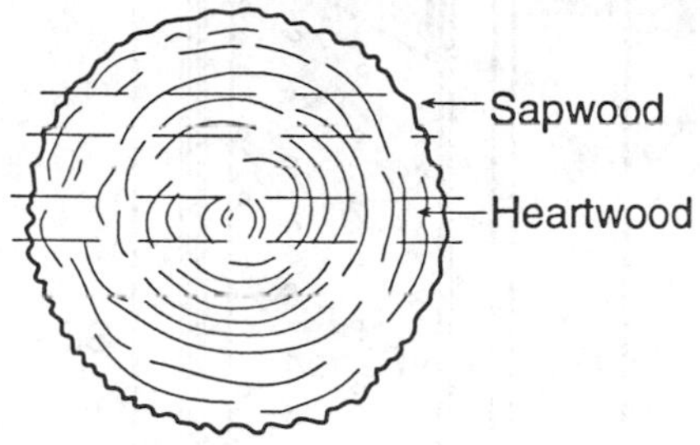

Figure 2

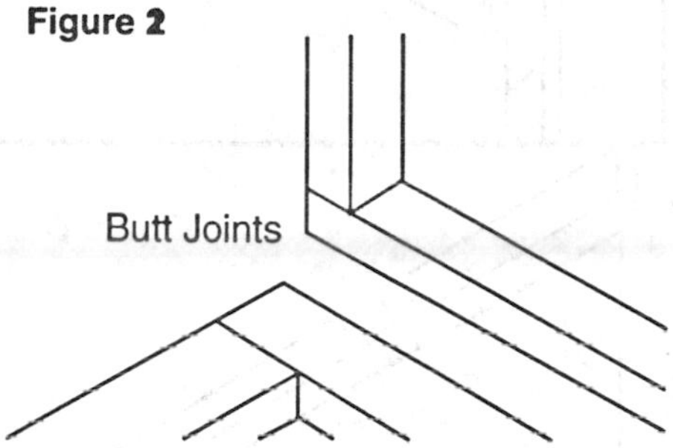

Figure 3

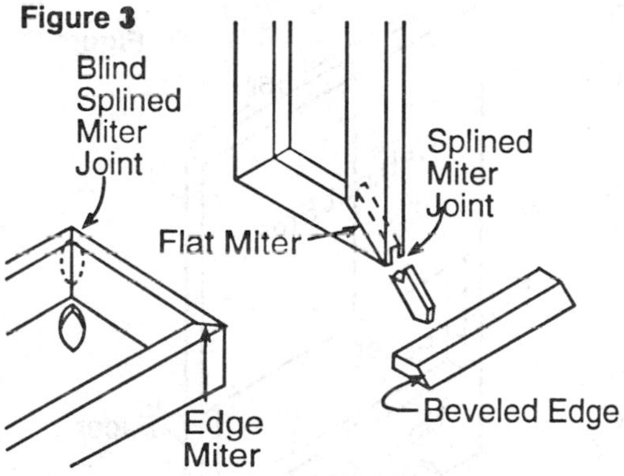

Figure 4

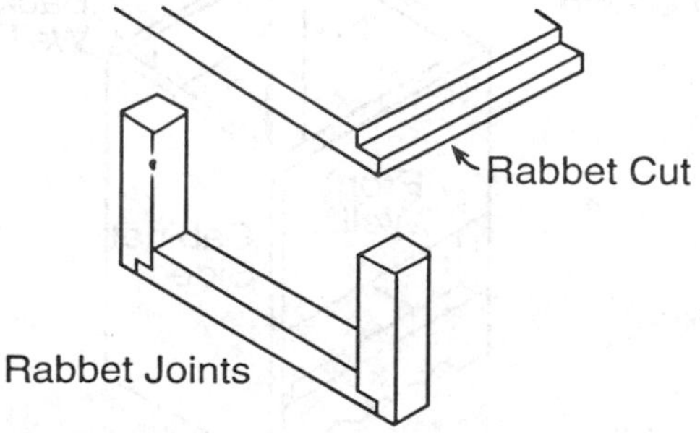

Potato Bin Trim
1/2 Section
(Cut 1)
Actual Size

Potato & Onion Bin

We doubt that any high-tech plastic invention could beat this little structure at doing the job it's meant to—keeping potatoes and onions edible for as long a time as Mother Nature will allow. It will hold twenty pounds of potatoes and five pounds of onions, yet takes up very little space! The bin is basically just a wooden box with a pegboard back (for ventilation). Inside, a pegboard floor separates the bin and drawer areas. We have divided the instructions into four sections: (1) cutting the parts, (2) assembling the cabinet. (3) assembling the drawer, and (4) finishing touches. You'll find lists of required materials under the appropriate sections.

Potato Bin Diagram

Cutting the Parts

Note: Some of the parts that are cut from pine will be wider than the stock you purchased, even if you purchased 1 x 12. To create a part that is wider than your stock, first cut two narrower boards to the specified length. Place them edge-to-edge, measure across them and trim one or both boards so that the total width is equal to the specified width of the part. To edge-join the two boards, you can simply glue and clamp them together, but a spline joint will be much stronger and will help prevent warpage and separation. To cut the dadoes for a spline joint, you can use a router with a 1/4 inch straight bit, or a table saw with a dado blade. When you have glued and assembled the joint, clamp it until the glue is completely dry.

1. Cut from 3/4" pine the parts listed in this step. Label each one for reference during assembly. For the Cabinet sides, refer to the cutting diagram provided in Figure A. For the Cabinet Trim, use the full-size pattern provided on page 39. For any part that is wider than the stock you purchased, spline two narrower boards together to achieve the width. In the parts list that follows, width is always listed as the first dimension for each part.

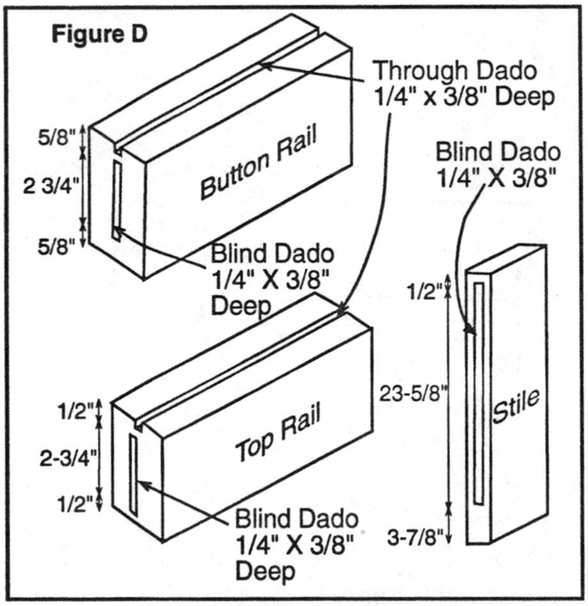

Figure D

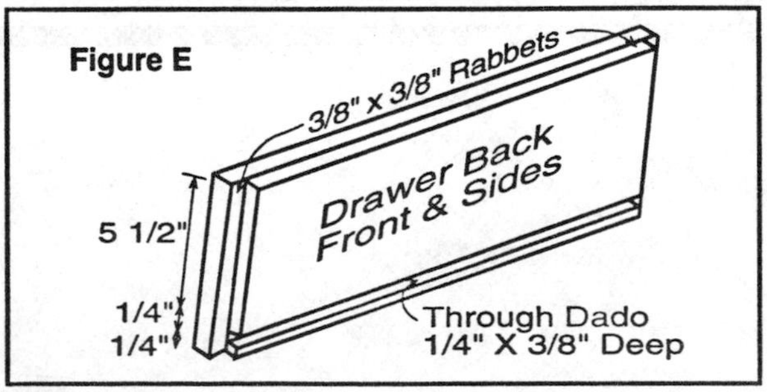

Figure E

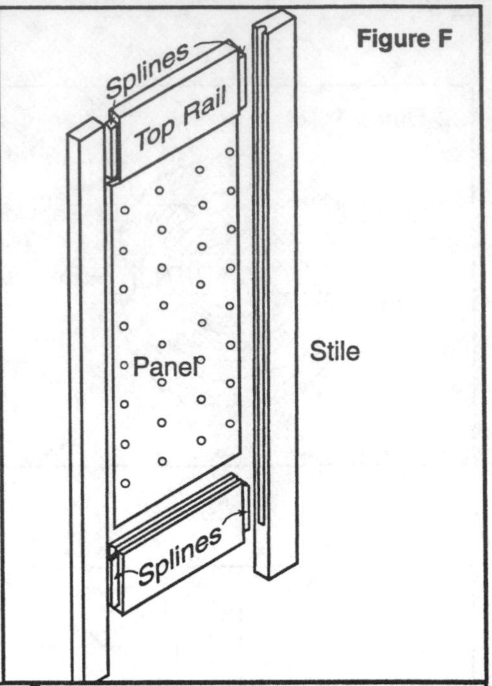

Figure F

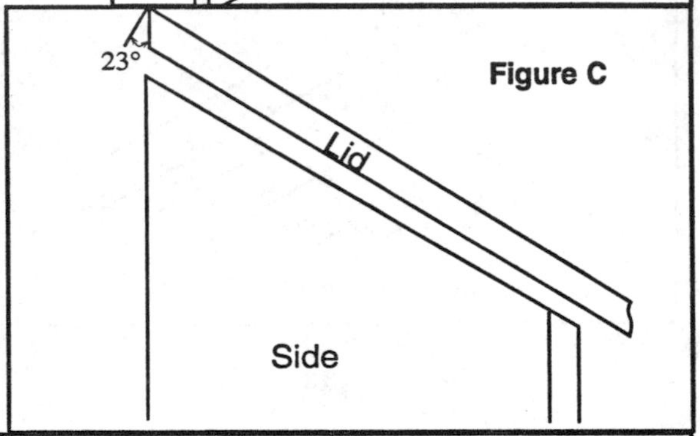

Figure C

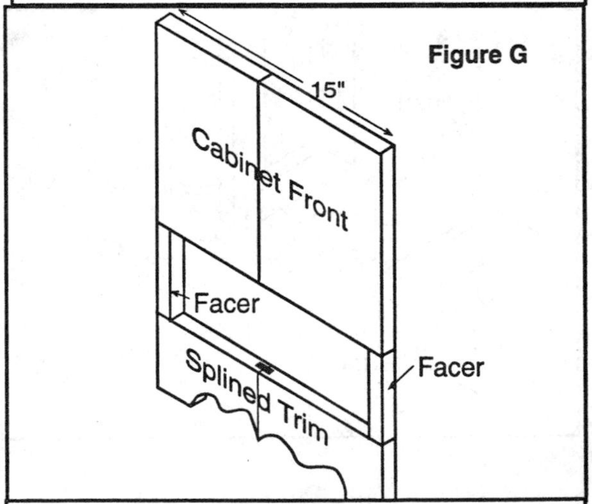

Figure G

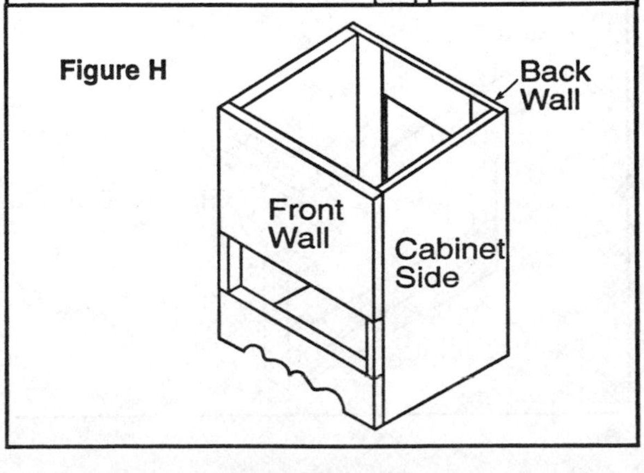

Figure H

Figure A, Figure B, Figure C

Part	Dimensions	Quantity
Cabinet Side	see Figure A	2
Cabinet Front	15" x 13-1/8"	1
Facer	3/4" x 6-1/8"	2
Cabinet Trim	use pattern	2
Lid	15" x 14-1/2"	1
Support	1" x 12-1/4"	5
Top Rail	3-3/4" x 10-1/2"	1
Bottom Rail	4" x 10-1/2"	1
Stile	1-1/2" x 28"	1
Drawer Parts:		
Side	6" x 9-3/4"	2
Front and Back	6" x 13-1/4"	2
Face	6-1/2" x 14-1/4"	1

2. Some of the parts that you cut in Step 1 must be modified. Bevel one 15-inch edge of the splined Cabinet Front at a 23-degree angle. This will be the upper edge.
3. Spline together the two Cabinet Trim pieces to create a single contoured Cabinet Trim, 15 inches long as shown in Figure B. Be sure that you match the proper edges for the spline joint, so the assembled Trim looks like the one shown. Clamp the Trim until the glue dries.
4. Bevel one 15-inch edge of the splined Lid at a 23-degree angle. This will be the rear edge. We routed a cove design along the three unbeveled edges — if you wish to do this, the decorative routing should be done on what will be the top surface of the Lid. Refer to Figure C which shows how the Lid will be attached to the Cabinet Sides. The bevel along the rear edge of the Lid determines which will be the top surface. Rout the

Figure J

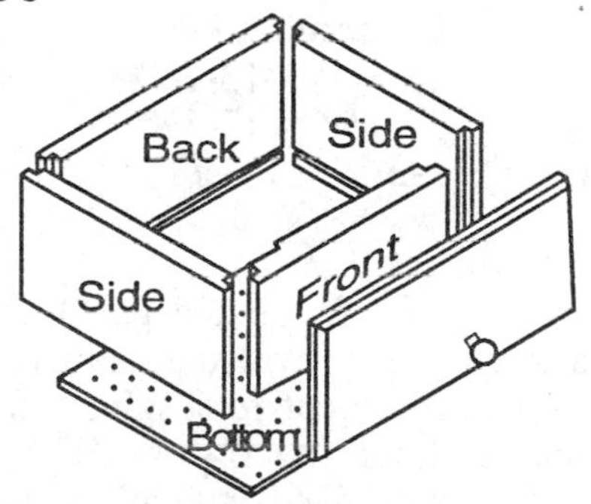

Figure I

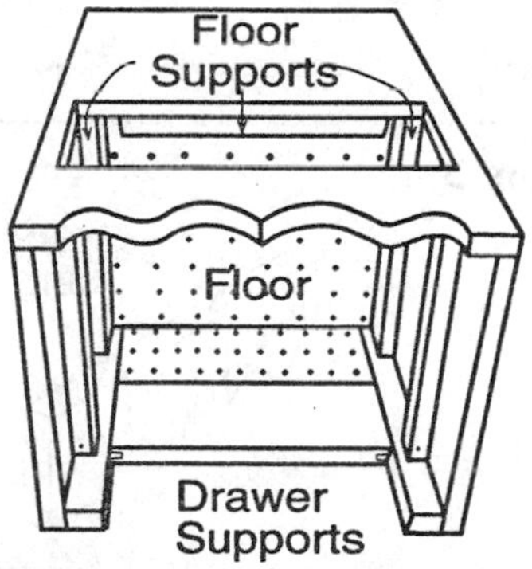

Figure 5

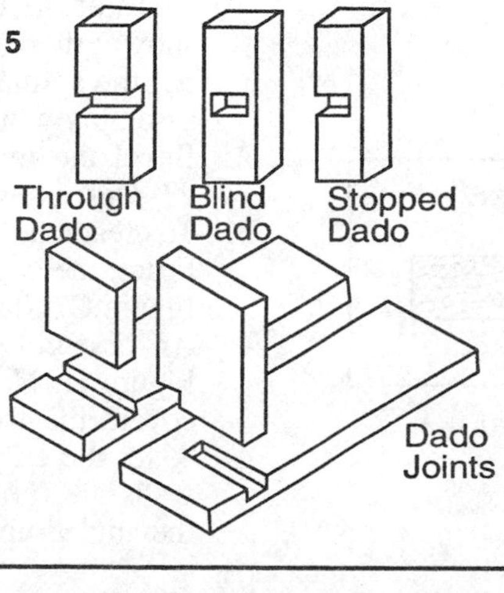

Figure 6

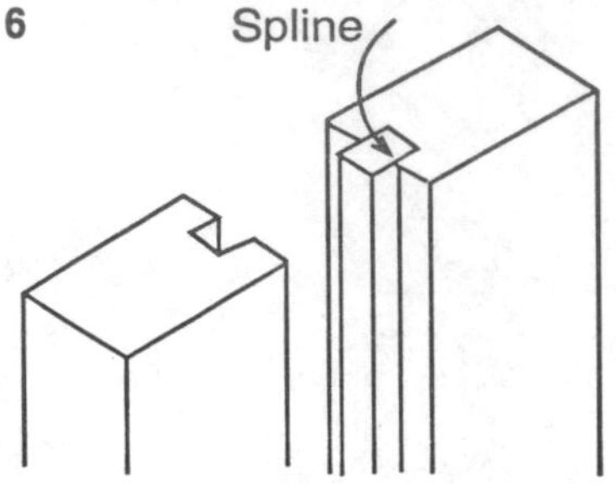

Figure 10

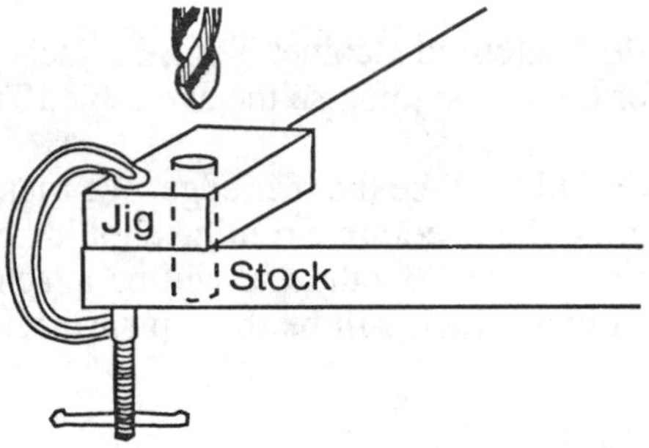

Figure B

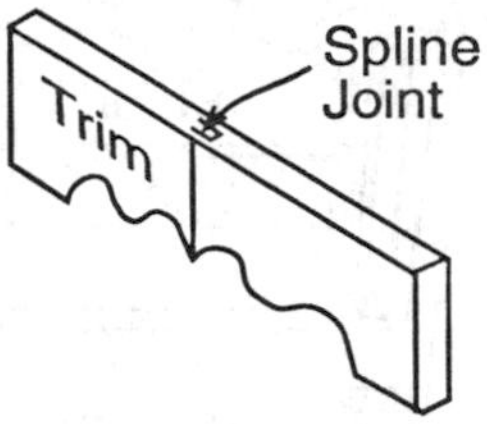

Figure 7

decorative design along the three unbeveled edges, on the top surface of the Lid.

5. The five Supports that you cut in Step 1 will be used for different purposes. Label two of them as Drawer Support. Label two more as Side Floor Supports. Trim the fifth one to a length of 11-3/4" and label it as the Front Floor Support.
6. The back wall of the cabinet is a standard frame-and-panel assembly (refer to Figure F if you are not familiar with frame-and-panel assemblies). A pegboard piece will serve as the panel, and the Rails and Stiles that you cut in Step 1 will serve as the frame members. The Rails and Stiles are modified as shown in Figure D. Note that all dadoes are 1/4" wide by 3/8" deep. For the Top Rail, cut a 2-3/4" long blind dado along the center of each end, as shown for the visible end in Figure D. In addition, cut a through dado along the center of one long edge. Cut identical dadoes into the bottom Rail, as shown. For each Stile, cut a 23-5/8" long blind dado along the center of one long edge — it should be stopped 1/2" short of the upper end, and 3-7/8" short of the lower end, as shown.
7. The Drawer Front, Back, and Sides will be assembled using rabbet joints, and a pegboard drawer bottom will fit into dadoes cut into these pieces. The Drawer Front, Back, and Sides are modified as shown in Figure E: Cut a 3/8" x 3/8" rabbet along both ends; and cut a through dado 1/4" wide by 3/8" deep, 1/4" from the long lower edge. Note that the rabbets and dado are cut into the same side.
8. the Drawer Face is routed to match the design on the Lid. We routed a cove design along both edges and ends, on one side of the Drawer Face.
9. Cut from pegboard the parts listed in this step, and label each one.

Part	Dimensions	Quantity
Floor	12-1/4" x 13-1/4"	1
Panel	11-1/4" x 17-3/4"	1
Drawer Bottom	9-3/8" x 12-3/8"	1

Assembling the Cabinet

1. A diagram showing the frame-and panel assembly that forms the back wall is provided in Figure F. For this assembly, you'll need to cut four splines for the frame joints; each spline should be 1/4" x 3/4" x 2-3/4". The splines are used in the Rail-to-Stile joints, as shown, and the pegboard Panel fits into the dadoes along the inner edges of the frame pieces. Assemble the cabinet back as shown; there's no need to glue the Panel into the frame, but the splined frame joints should be glued. Clamp the assembly while the glue dries.
2. Bevel the upper end of the assembled back wall at a 23-degree angle.
3. To create the front cabinet wall, glue together the Cabinet Front, the two Facers, and the splined Trim as shown in Figure G. Clamp while the glue dries.
4. An assembly diagram for the cabinet is provided in Figure H. Note the following things: (a) the front wall covers the front edges of the two Sides, but the Sides cover the edges of the back wall; (b) the front and back walls are turned so that the beveled upper edges match the angled upper edges of the Sides; and (c) all parts are

flush at the bottom. It may be necessary to trim some of the upper edges slightly, to get a good match between the parts. Glue together the parts as shown, and secure using finishing nails. Recess the nails and cover with wood filler.

5. Refer to Figure I as you install the Supports inside the cabinet. The two Side Floor Supports are attached to the Cabinet Sides just above the drawer opening in the front wall. The Front Floor Support is attached to the Cabinet Front in the same manner. The two Drawer Supports are attached to the Cabinet Sides, so that the upper edge of each Support is flush with the bottom of the drawer opening in the front wall. Glue the Supports in place and secure using finishing nails.
6. Place the pegboard Floor inside the Cabinet, on top of the Floor Supports. The Floor may be glued in place, but it is not necessary.
7. Hinge the Cabinet Lid to the top of the back wall, adjusting it so that the side edges are flush with the Cabinet Sides. Be sure it is turned the right way (see Figure C). The front of the Lid will overhang the Cabinet Front Wall.

Assembling the Drawer

1. An assembly diagram for the drawer is provided in Figure J. Assemble the Front, Back, and Sides around the pegboard Drawer Bottom, inserting the Bottom into the dadoes that were cut near the lower edges of the drawer-box pieces. Note that the parts will fit together only if the Front and Back cover the ends of the Sides, and if the Bottom is turned as shown. Glue the corner joints (there's no need to glue the Bottom into the dadoes), and secure using finishing nails.
2. Center the Face over the front of the Drawer, so that it extends equally beyond the top and bottom edges, and equally beyond the Sides. Glue it in place and secure by driving a couple of nails through the Front into the Face. Measure and mark the center point on the front of the Face. Drill a hole all the way through the Face and Front at the marked center point, using a bit that matches the diameter of the drawer-pull mounting bolt. The pull will be installed after the drawer has been finished.

Finishing Touches

1. Sand and stain (or paint) the bin, and the front of the drawer Face. You may wish to seal the inner surfaces of the drawer and bin. When the finish is dry, install the drawer pull and insert the drawer.
2. A full-size pattern for the design we painted on the front of the bin is provided on the next page. You may prefer to use a design of your own — if so, we suggest that you draw it on paper first. When the stain has dried completely, use carbon paper to transfer the design to the center of the Cabinet Front. We painted the words and onions yellow, and added pale yellow highlights to the onions. The potatoes are brown with black details.

Figure 8

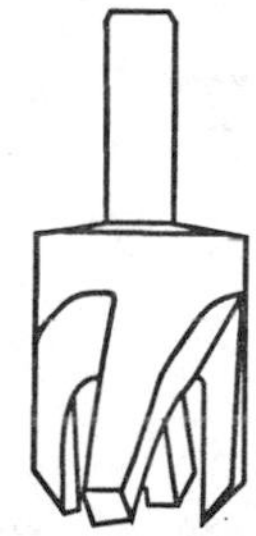

Figure 9

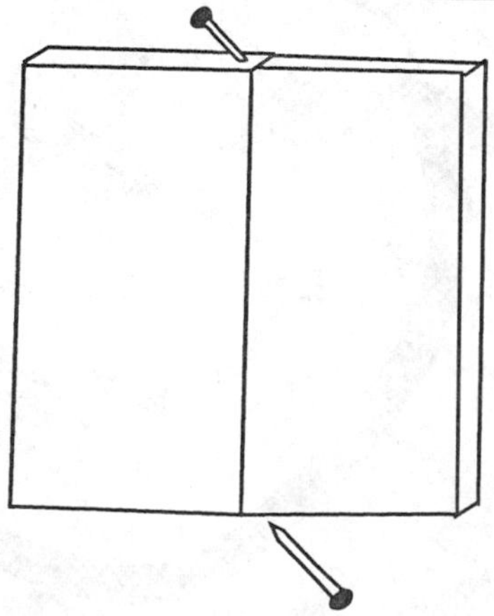

Figure A

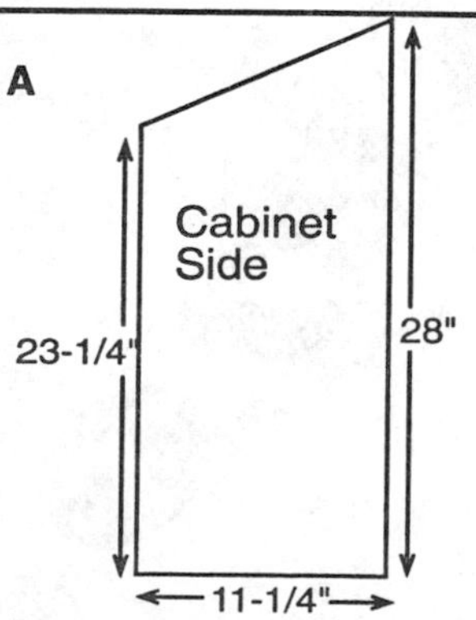

Potato Bin Front Decal

This pattern can be painted on or cut out, painted and glued on for a 3-dimensional design

Actual size

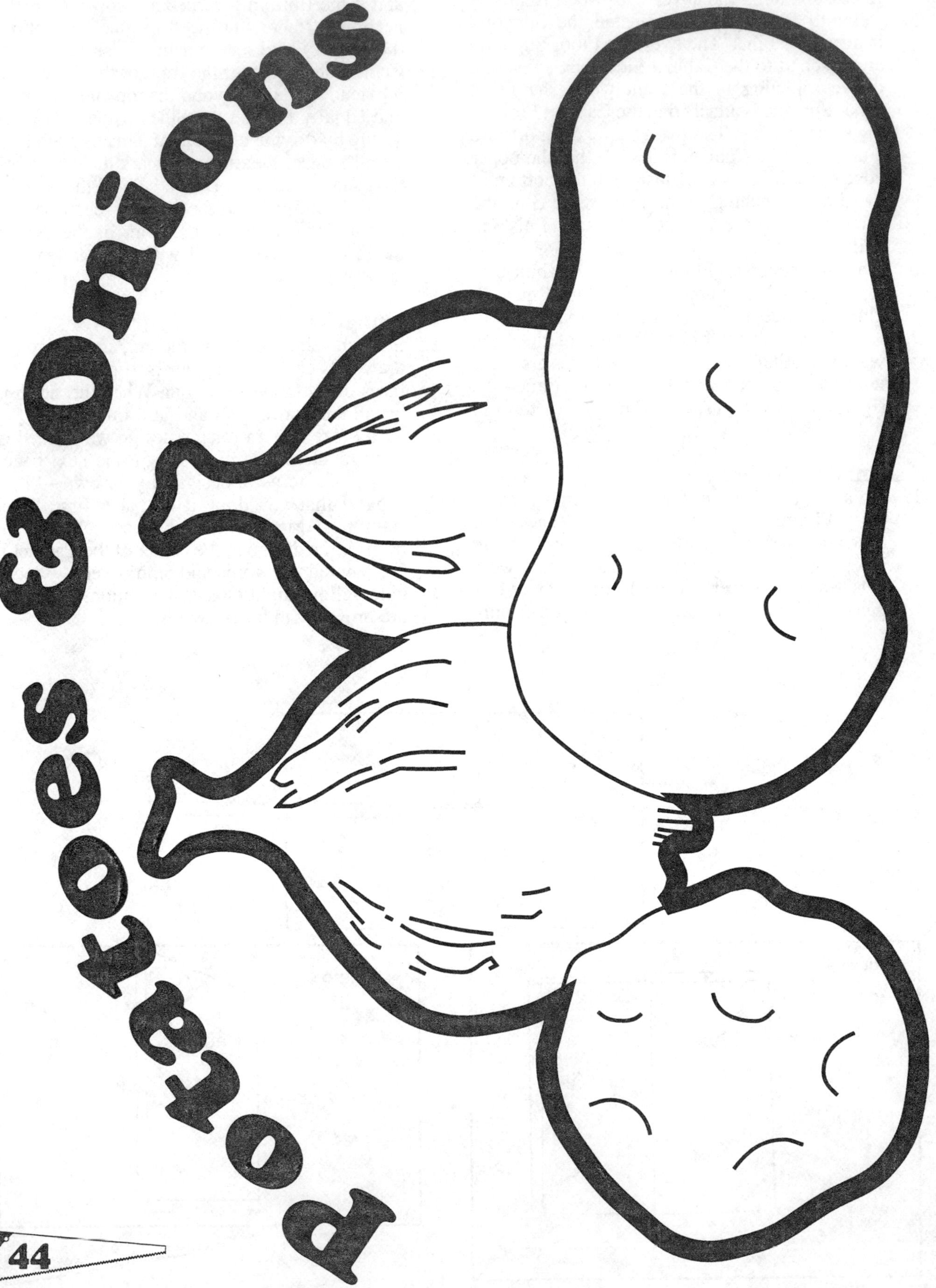

Carousel Horse Accent Table

Cut one middle piece and two side pieces from 2" stock. Cut one oval table base from 1" wood. Cut one round tabletop 13-1/4" in diameter from 3/4" wood and drill a 3/4" hole through the center. You'll need a 3/4" dowel cut 36" long for a carousel pole. Drill a hole large enough to insert the 3/4" dowel, into the middle piece as indicated. Sand all pieces. Connect the side pieces to the middle piece (as shown) using large wood screws and wood glue. Attach the the horse's legs to the oval base with wood screws drilled into the hooves from the underneath side of the table base. Use the same procedure to attach the carousel pole/dowel to the base. Lower the circular tabletop over the carousel pole and down onto the horse's back (see diagram), attach with wood glue and nails. Glue a predrilled 1-1/2" wooden ball onto the top end of the carousel pole. Basecoat all pieces. Transfer the design using graphite paper. Paint with acrylic paints. Seal with an acrylic spray or brush-on varnish.

1 square = 3 inches

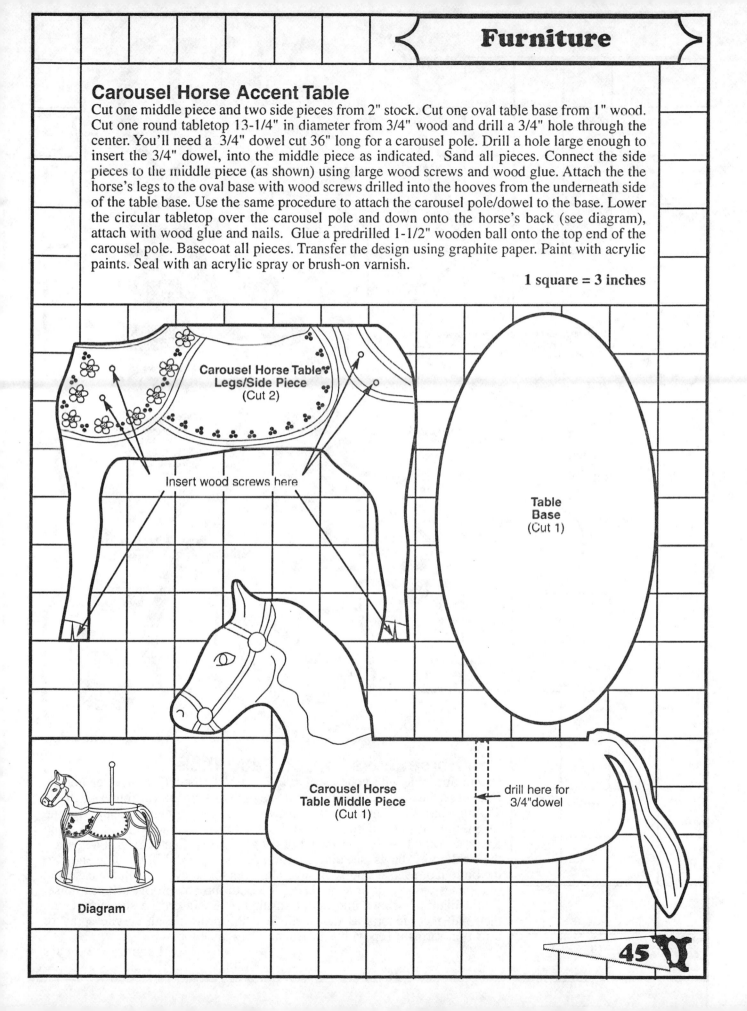

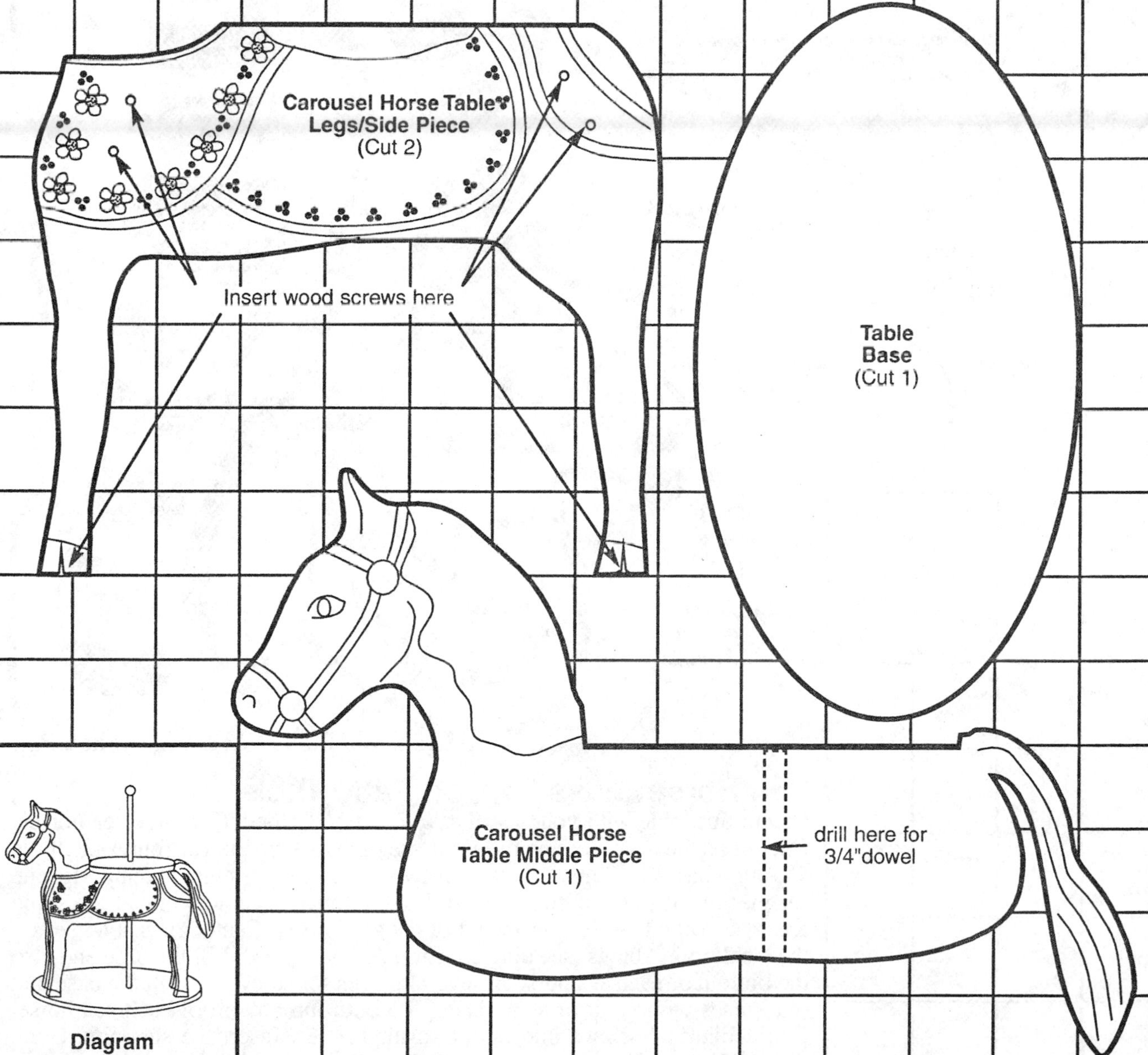

Diagram

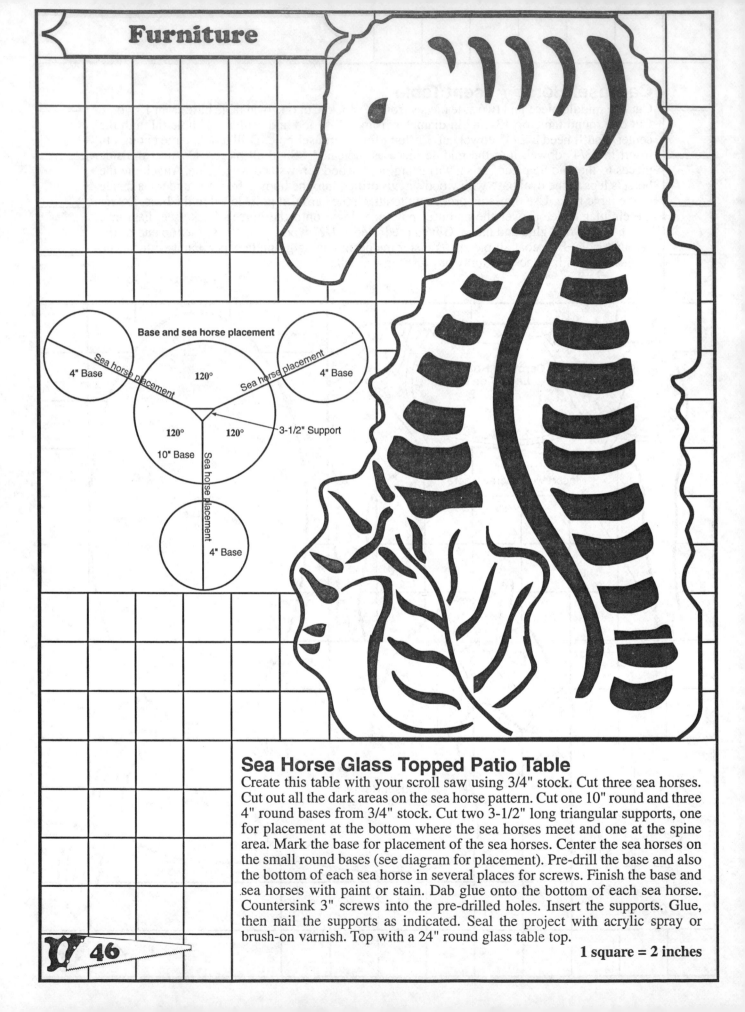

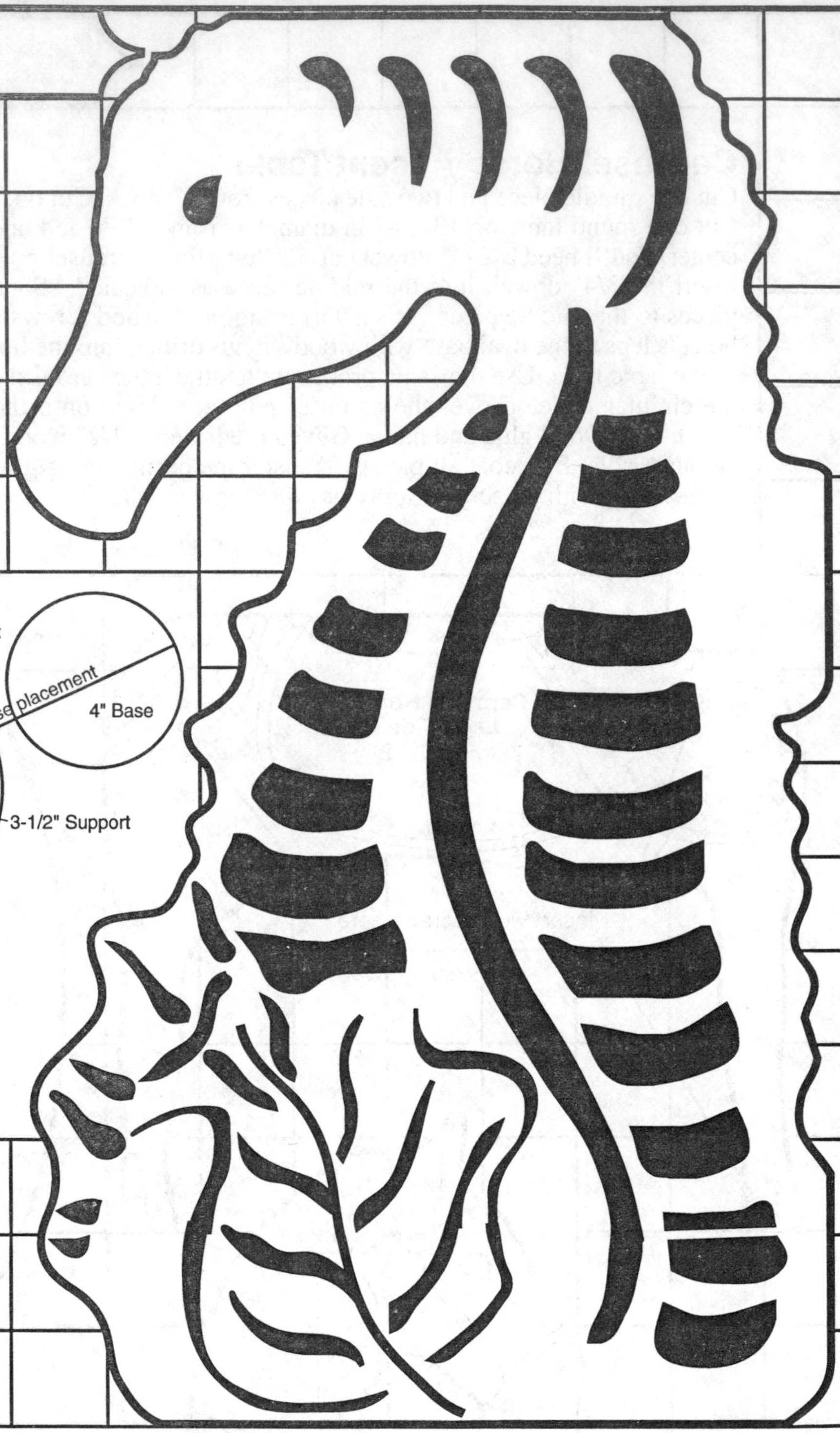

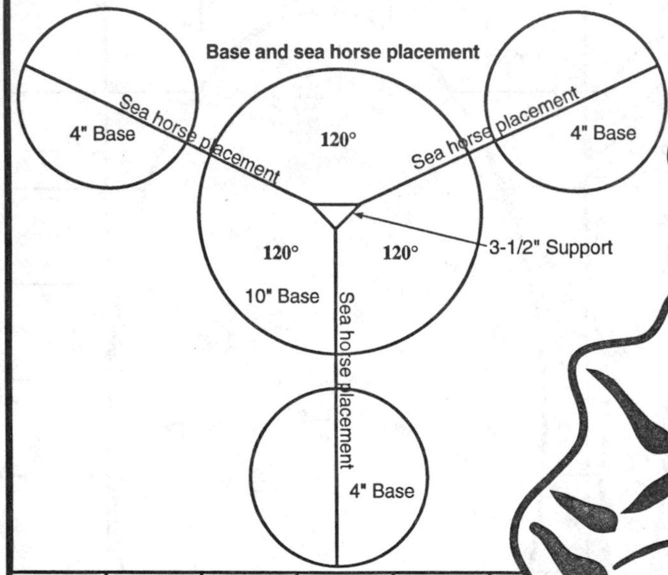

Sea Horse Glass Topped Patio Table

Create this table with your scroll saw using 3/4" stock. Cut three sea horses. Cut out all the dark areas on the sea horse pattern. Cut one 10" round and three 4" round bases from 3/4" stock. Cut two 3-1/2" long triangular supports, one for placement at the bottom where the sea horses meet and one at the spine area. Mark the base for placement of the sea horses. Center the sea horses on the small round bases (see diagram for placement). Pre-drill the base and also the bottom of each sea horse in several places for screws. Finish the base and sea horses with paint or stain. Dab glue onto the bottom of each sea horse. Countersink 3" screws into the pre-drilled holes. Insert the supports. Glue, then nail the supports as indicated. Seal the project with acrylic spray or brush-on varnish. Top with a 24" round glass table top.

1 square = 2 inches

— CHAPTER FIVE —
GARDEN ORNAMENTS

Gardening Grandparents

Grandma's putting together a sweet bouquet for grandpa. Cut each pattern from 3/8" exterior grade plywood. Cut a stake from 1" x 2" stock. Predrill the pattern and the stake where indicated for insertion of 1", #8 or #10 screws. Sand well. Base coat the cut-out pattern. Trace the lines onto the pattern using graphite or carbon paper. Paint with acrylic paints. Apply several coats of outdoor polyurethane. Insert the stake into the ground, then attach the pattern with screws.

1 square = 4 inches

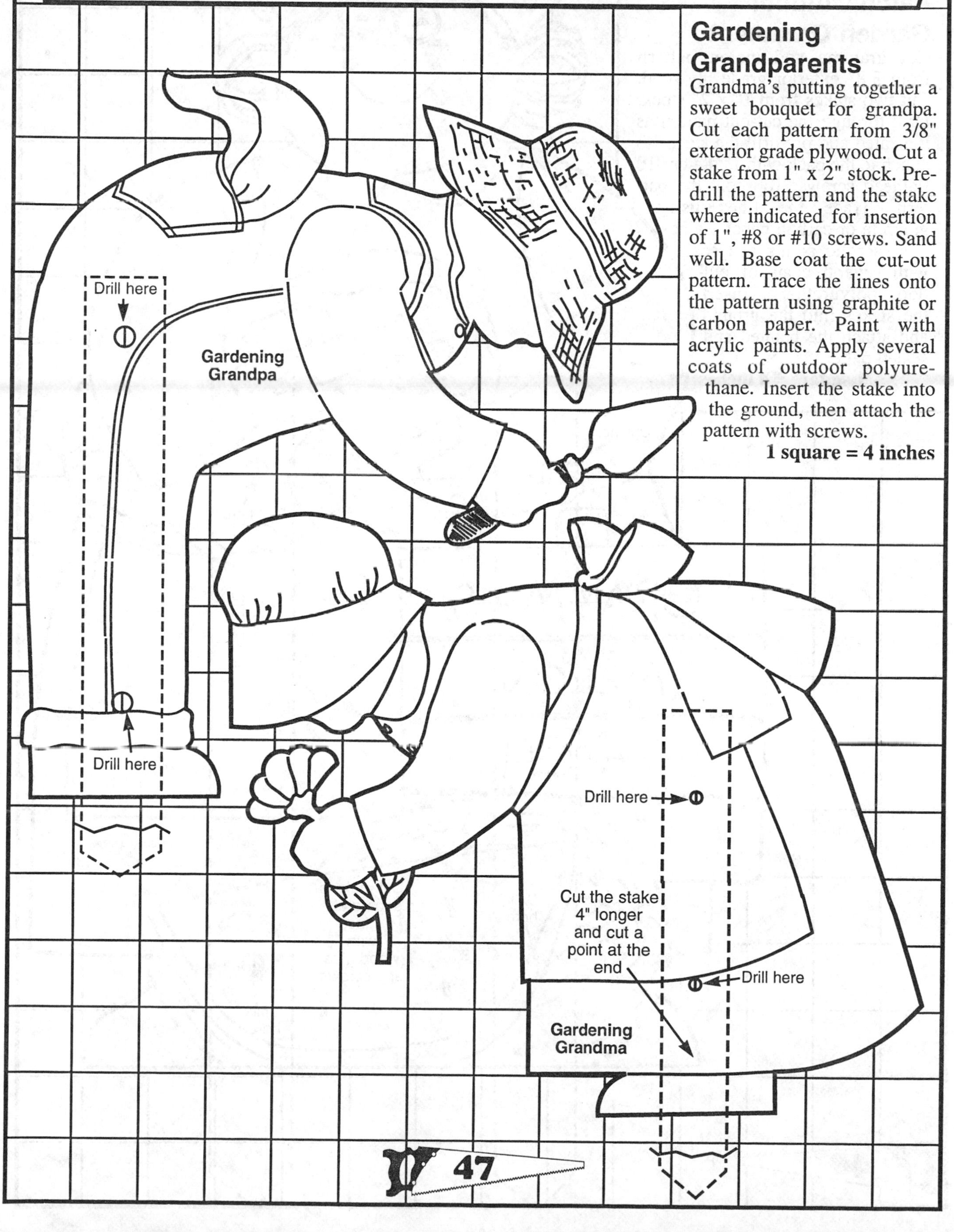

Gramma's Melon Patch Outdoor Garden Ornament

Cut gramma and melon pattern from 3/8" exterior grade plywood. Cut two stakes from 1" x 2" stock. Drill through the cut-out pattern as indicated and pre-drill the stakes to attach to the back with 1", #8 or #10 flathead screws. Top coat the pattern. Trace the lines using graphite or carbon paper. Paint with acrylic paints and seal with several coats of outdoor polyurethane. Insert the stakes into the ground and attach the painted and sealed pattern.

1 square = 4 inches

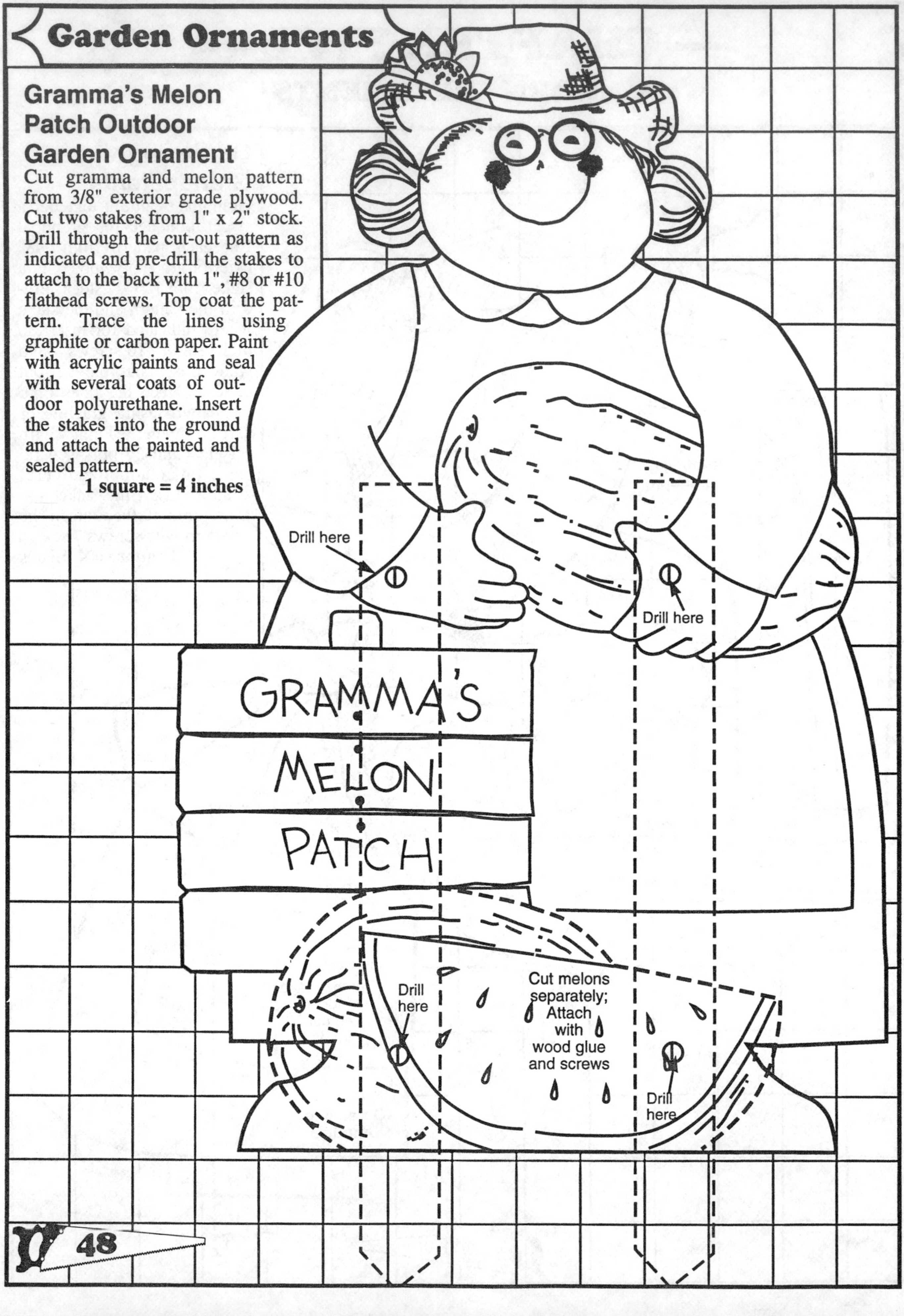

Swinging Scarecrow

Cut the body, two arms and two legs from 3/4" outdoor grade plywood. Drill holes where indicated. Sand and paint. Seal with polyurethane. Glue straw to the areas shown on the pattern. Tie the arms and legs to the body with raffia, cord or strips of frayed cloth. Drill a hole in the hat and suspend him from a screw eye and hook from a porch, barn or mailbox. Option: Drill a hole in his head and glue a straw hat or old felt hat on his head. Make a hole in the top of the hat for the rope hanger.

1 square = 3 inches

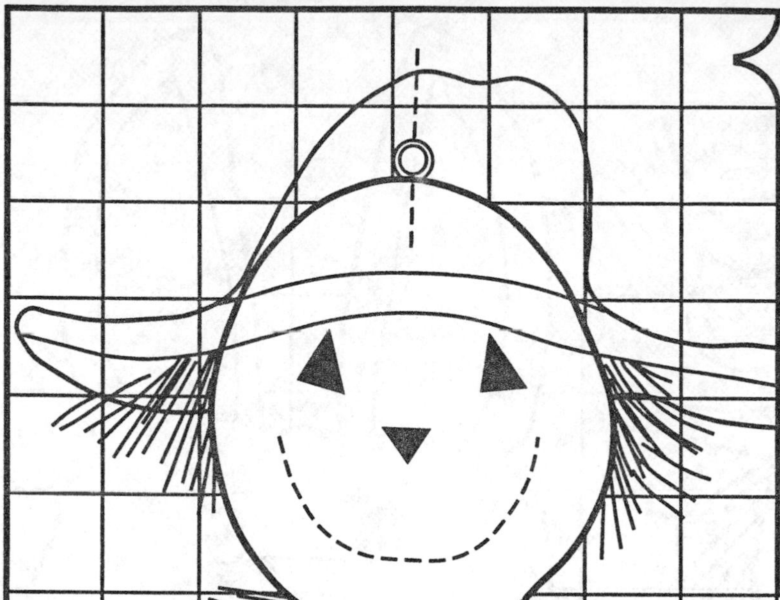

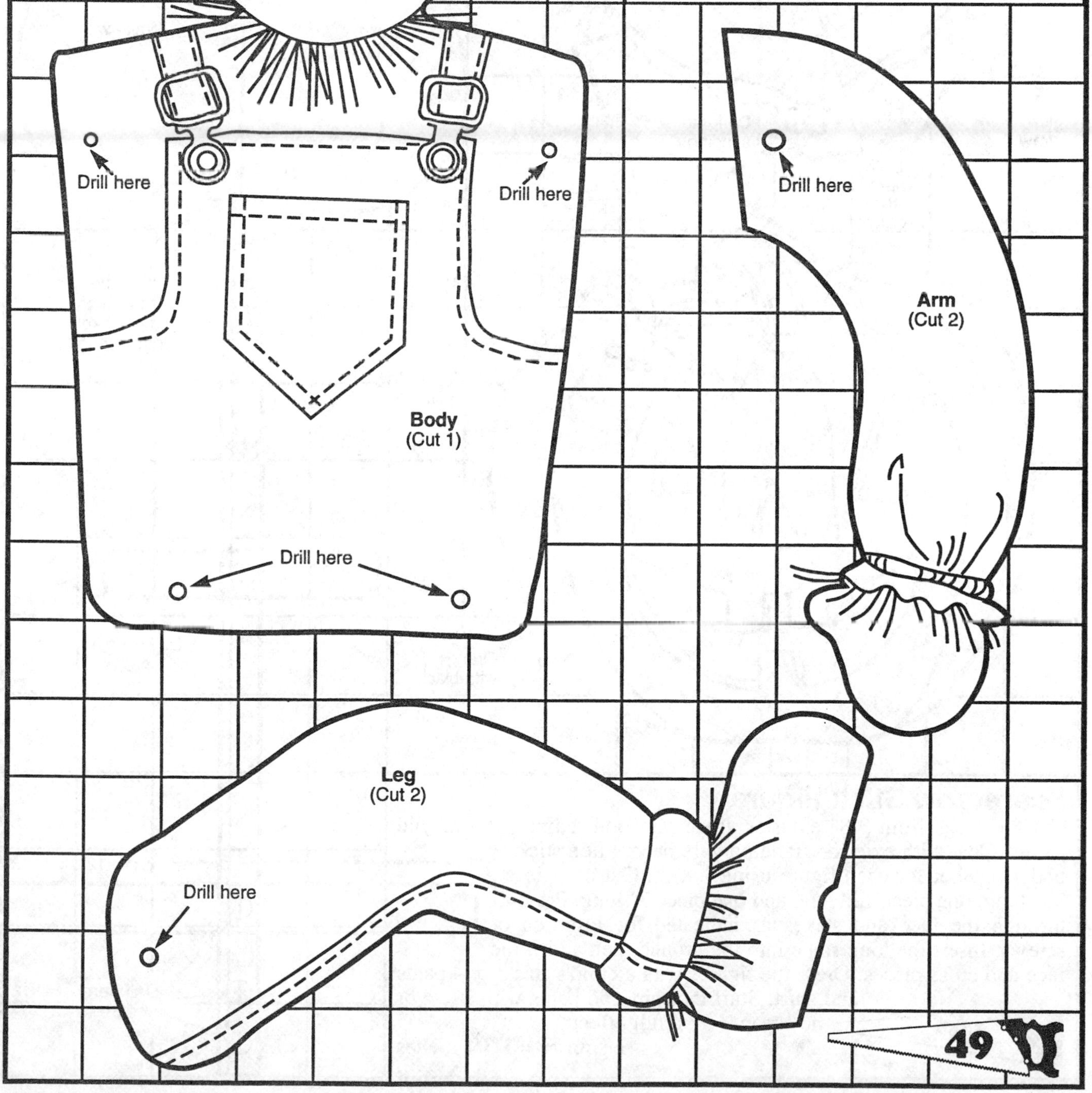

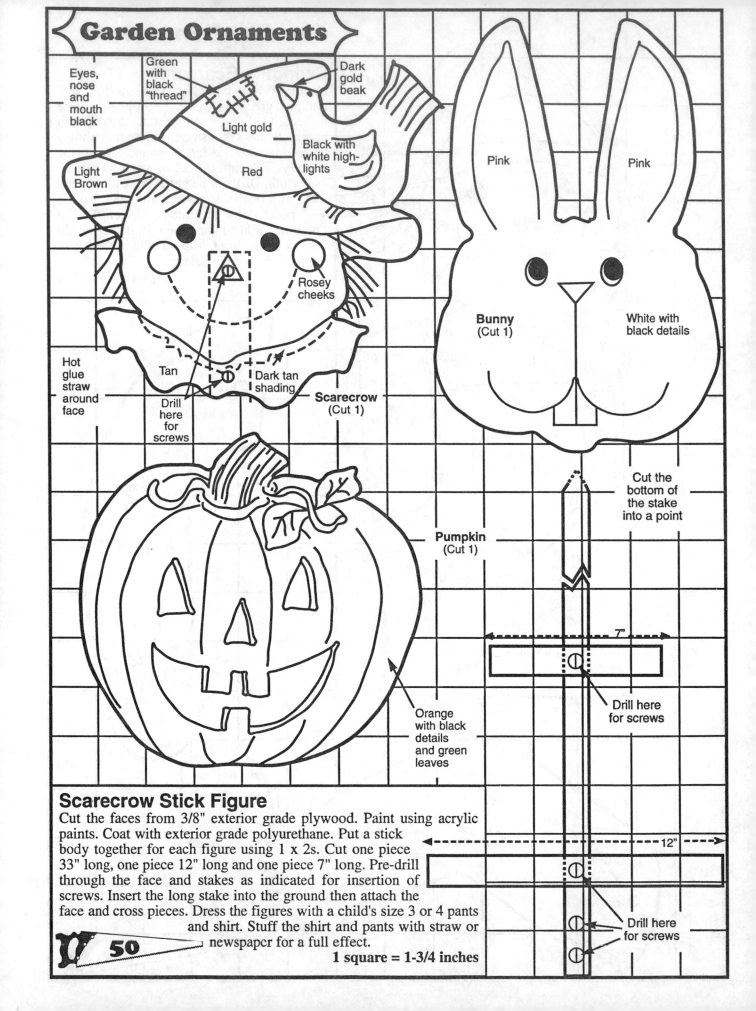

Garden Ornaments

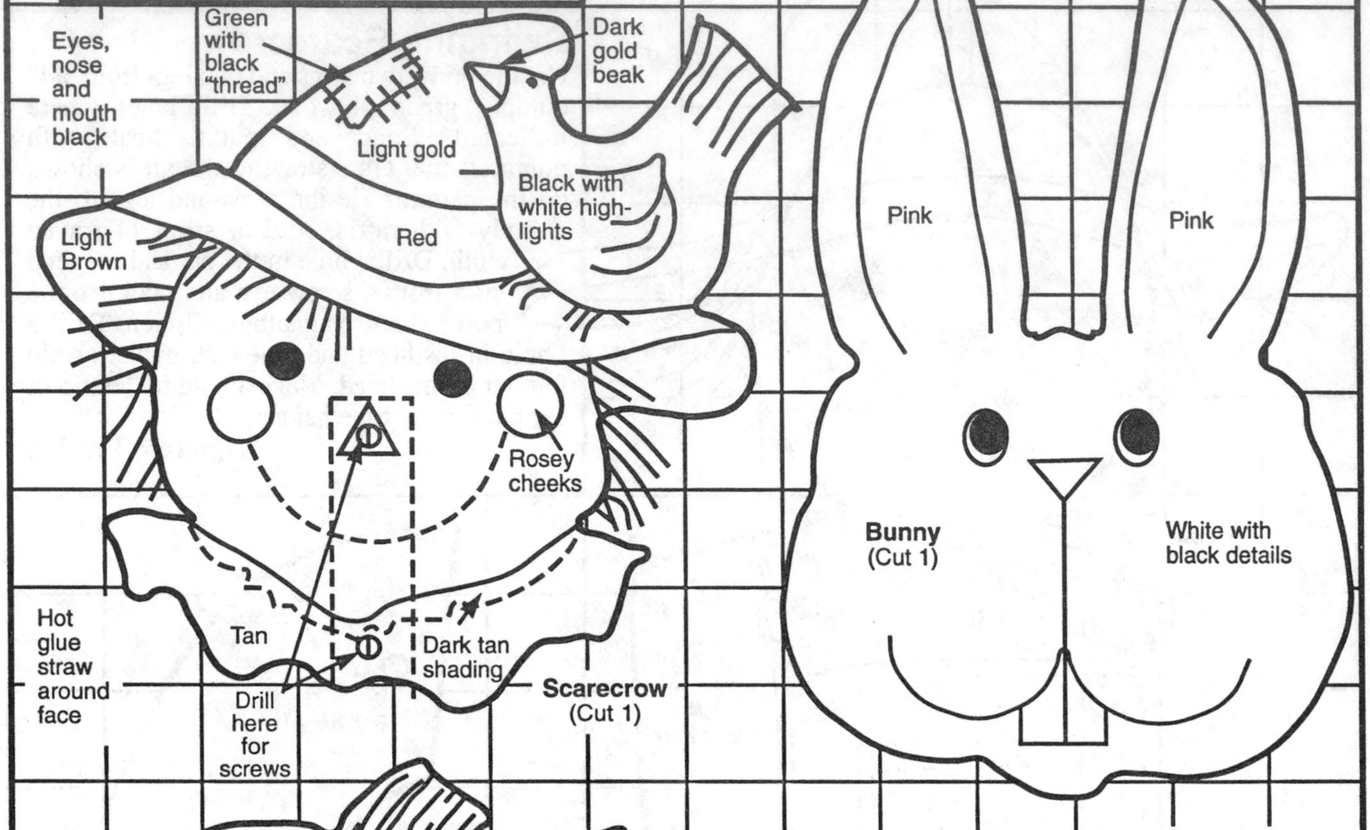

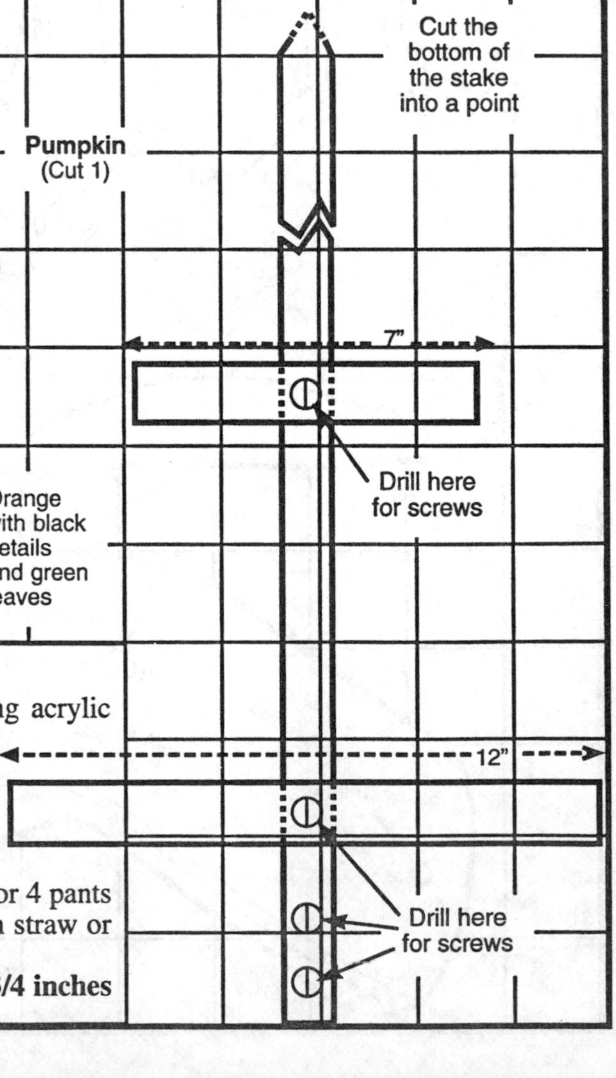

Scarecrow Stick Figure

Cut the faces from 3/8" exterior grade plywood. Paint using acrylic paints. Coat with exterior grade polyurethane. Put a stick body together for each figure using 1 x 2s. Cut one piece 33" long, one piece 12" long and one piece 7" long. Pre-drill through the face and stakes as indicated for insertion of screws. Insert the long stake into the ground then attach the face and cross pieces. Dress the figures with a child's size 3 or 4 pants and shirt. Stuff the shirt and pants with straw or newspaper for a full effect.

1 square = 1-3/4 inches

Bird Garden Ornaments

Cut bodies from treated wood at least 3/4" thick. Either extend wood and sharpen on the end to form a stake to insert into the ground or drill a hole and insert dowel on bottom.

Cut wings from thinner wood and attach with nails or screws.

1 square = 1-1/2 inches

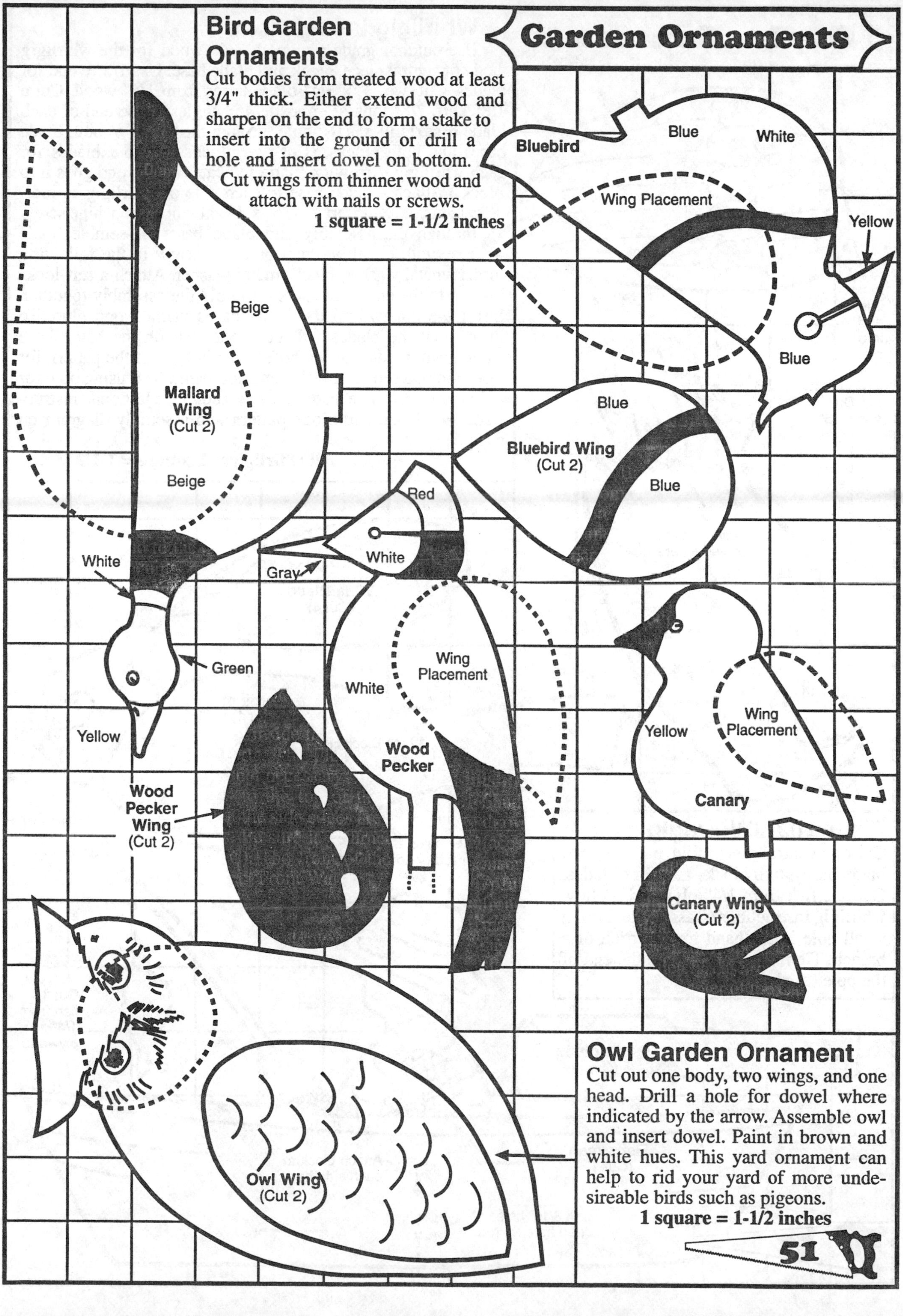

Owl Garden Ornament

Cut out one body, two wings, and one head. Drill a hole for dowel where indicated by the arrow. Assemble owl and insert dowel. Paint in brown and white hues. This yard ornament can help to rid your yard of more undesireable birds such as pigeons.

1 square = 1-1/2 inches

Whirligig Instructions

Use outdoor grade plywood, 3/4" wood for the whirligig body or central piece, block and blade base. Use 1/8" wood for blades. Cut two, 3" x 3/4" blade bases from 1/4" wood. Cut a 1/8" kerf, 7/8" long at opposite 45° angles in the end of each blade base. Drill a 3/16" hole through the center of both blade bases and both blocks. (Cut two blocks and four blades for each whirligig. Arrow on blade indicates which end goes into block.) Attach a blade base to each side of whirligig as indicated by an X. Insert a 3/16" x 3" galvanized machine screw through the assembly and blade bases. Assemble blade base with metal washers onto the screw in the following order: metal washer, block, metal washer. Attach a self-locking nut to the end of the screw to hold the assembly together. Insert the blades into the blade bases using wood glue. To insure that the blades will be secure, attach the blade base using small brads. Drill a hole at the bottom of the pattern for insertion of a rod or dowel. Sand and paint. Seal using outdoor polyurethane. Some patterns may require additional instructions. See blade and block pattern and assembly diagram on page 53.

All whirligigs: 1 square = 1-1/2 inches

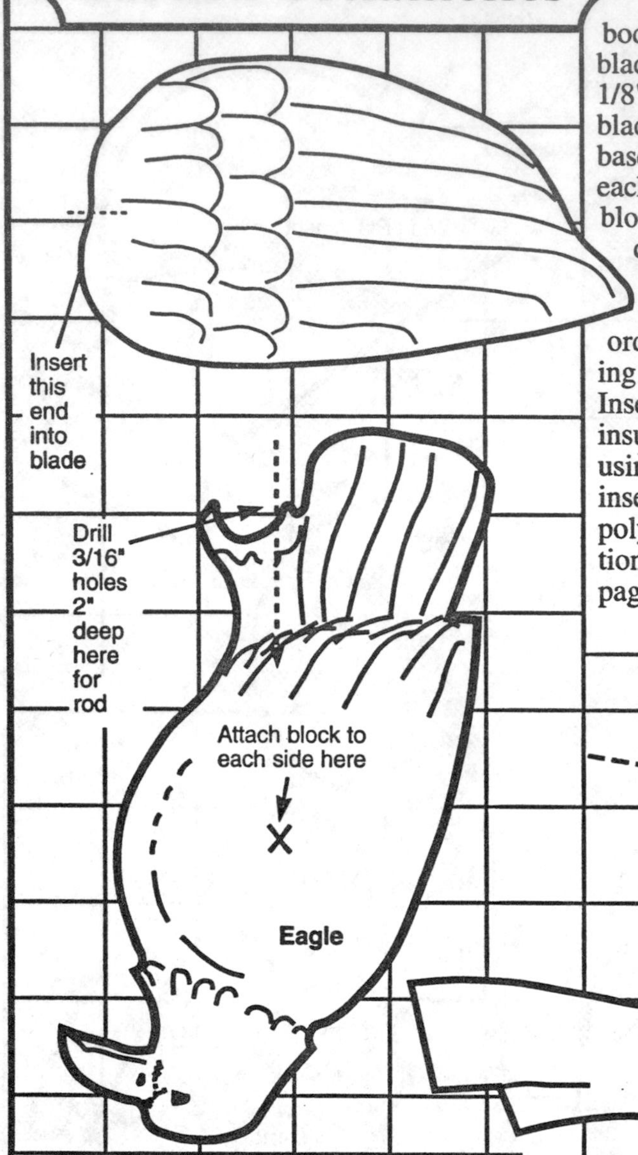

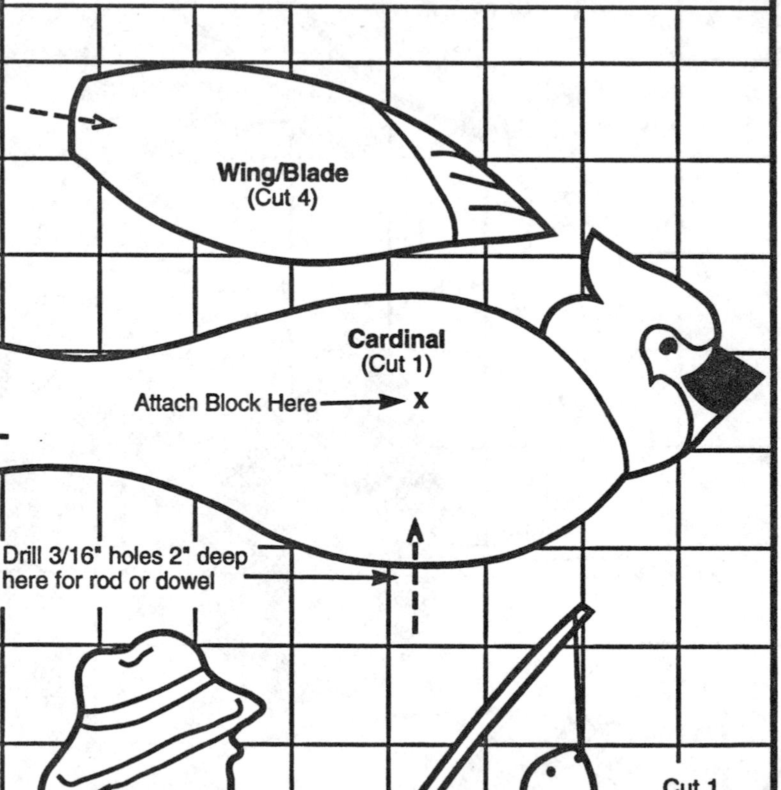

Fisherman Whirligig

Cut one central piece, four paddles, two blade bases, two blocks and four blades. Cut one fish from 1/4" plywood. Follow whirligig instructions to assemble. Drill a small hole in the hand for insertion of a branch. Tie fishing line and to the end of the pole (as shown).

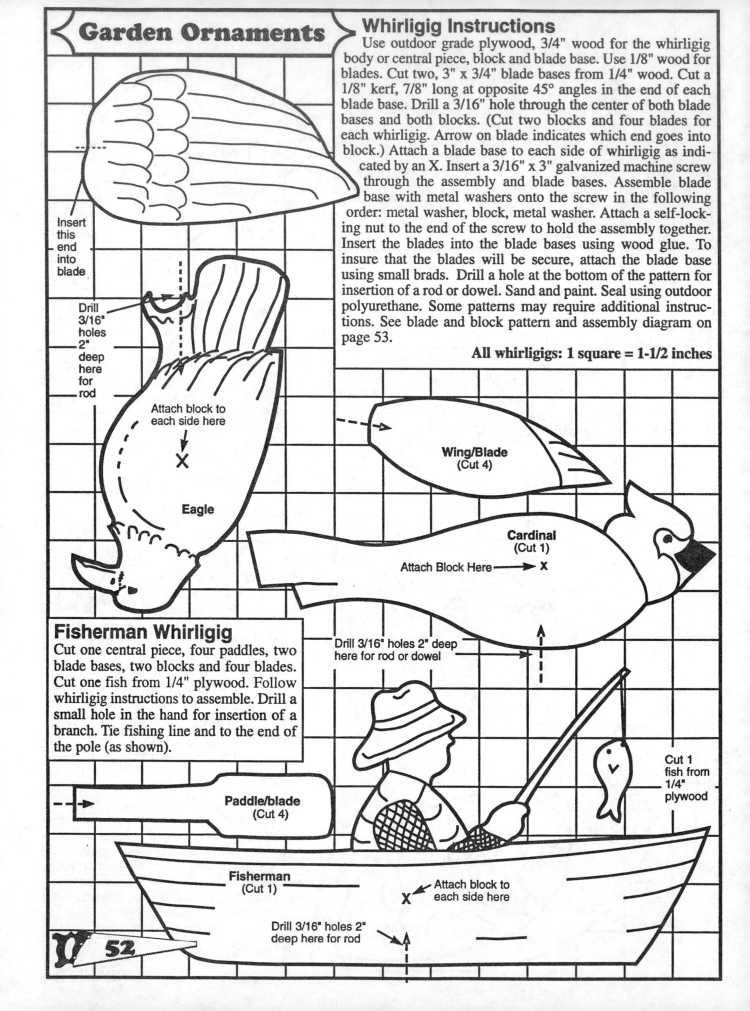

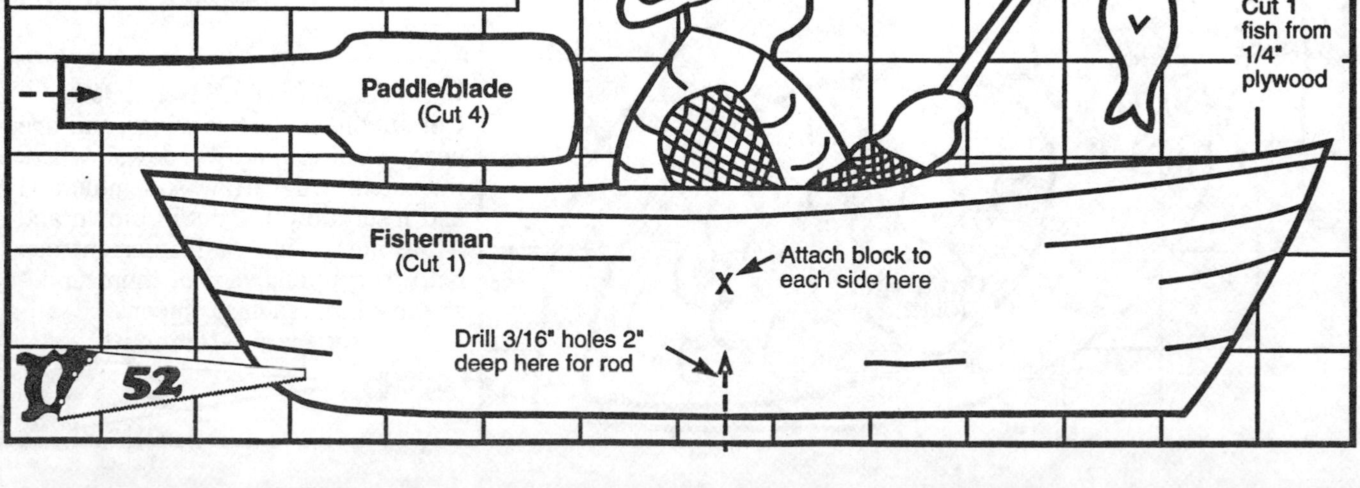

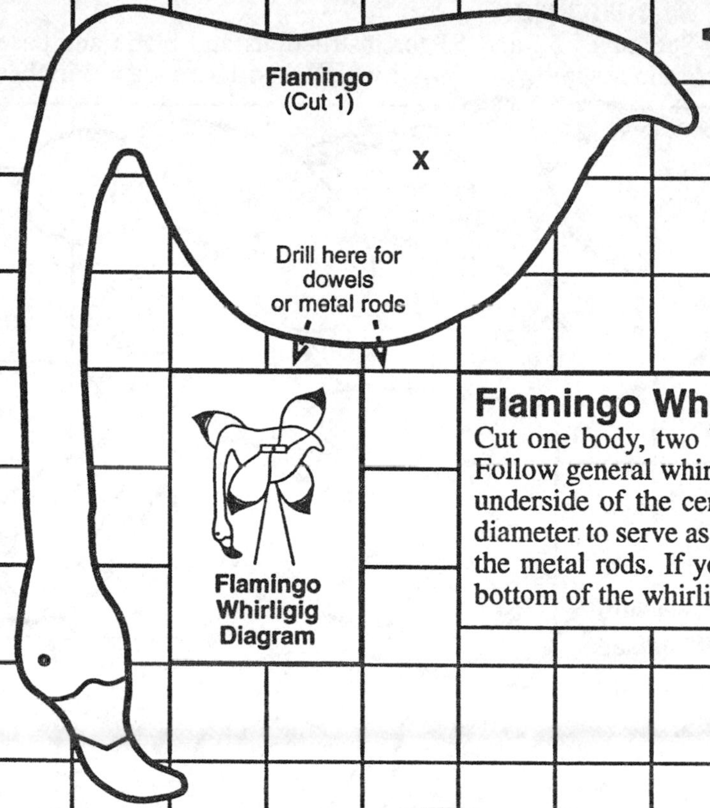

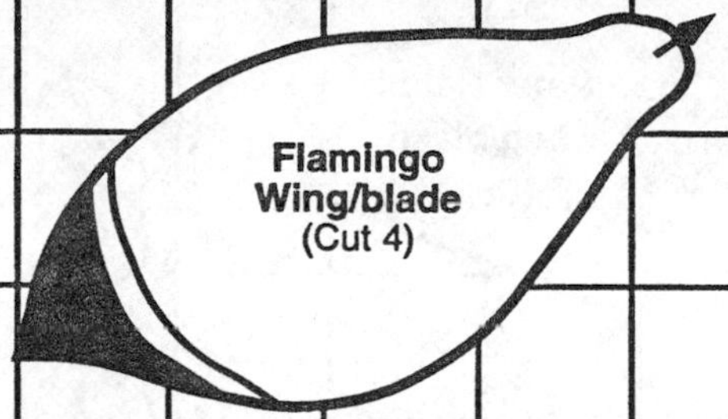

Flamingo Whirligig Diagram

Flamingo Whirligig

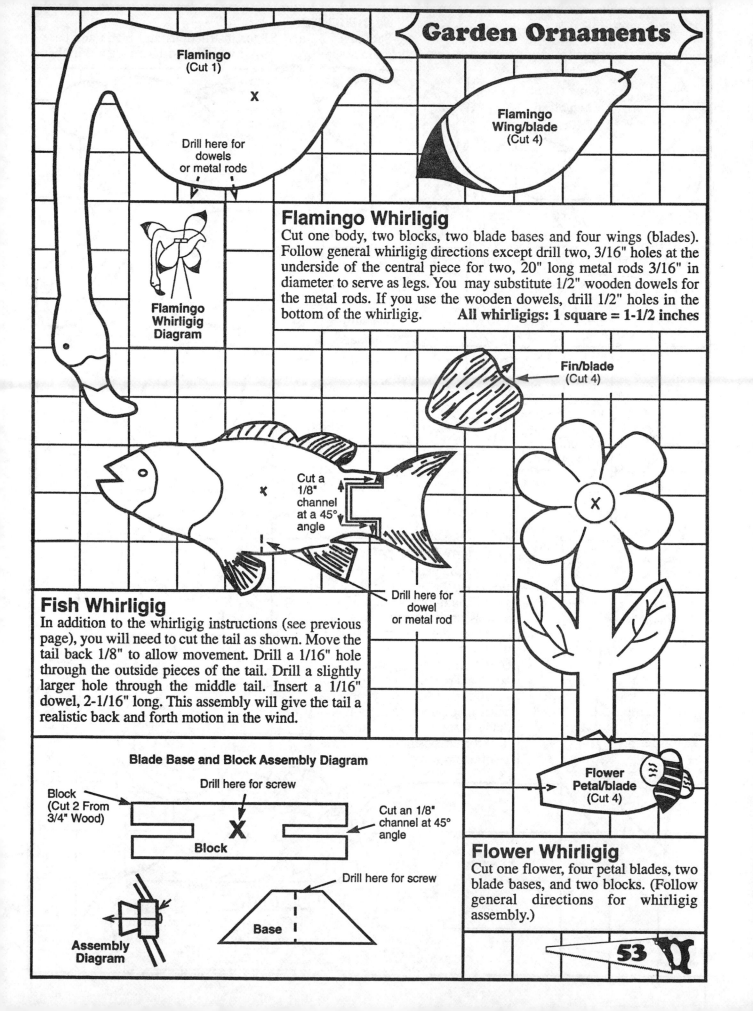

Cut one body, two blocks, two blade bases and four wings (blades). Follow general whirligig directions except drill two, 3/16" holes at the underside of the central piece for two, 20" long metal rods 3/16" in diameter to serve as legs. You may substitute 1/2" wooden dowels for the metal rods. If you use the wooden dowels, drill 1/2" holes in the bottom of the whirligig. **All whirligigs: 1 square = 1-1/2 inches**

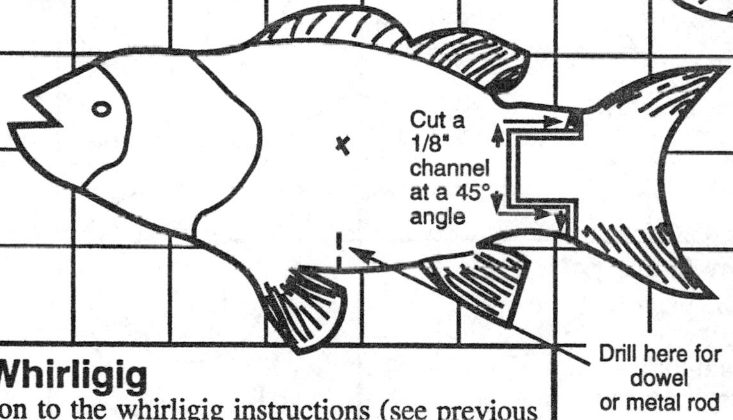

Fish Whirligig

In addition to the whirligig instructions (see previous page), you will need to cut the tail as shown. Move the tail back 1/8" to allow movement. Drill a 1/16" hole through the outside pieces of the tail. Drill a slightly larger hole through the middle tail. Insert a 1/16" dowel, 2-1/16" long. This assembly will give the tail a realistic back and forth motion in the wind.

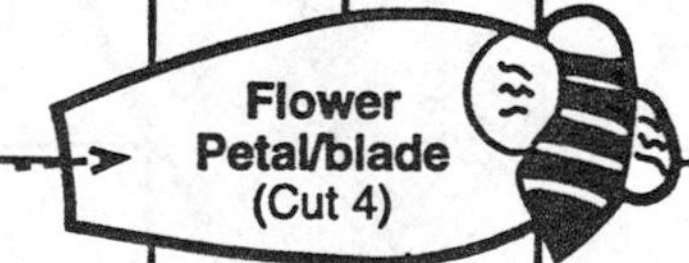

Blade Base and Block Assembly Diagram

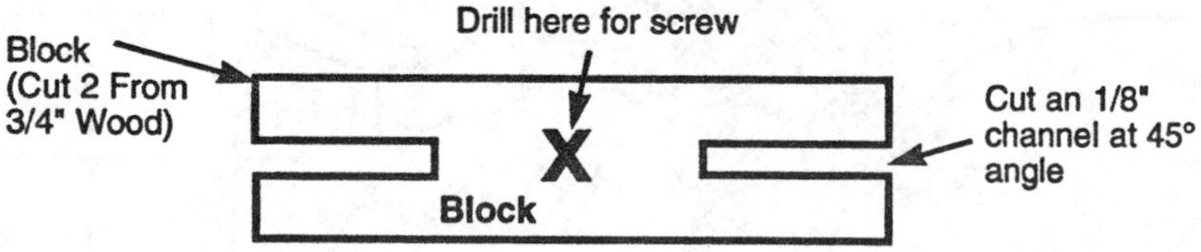

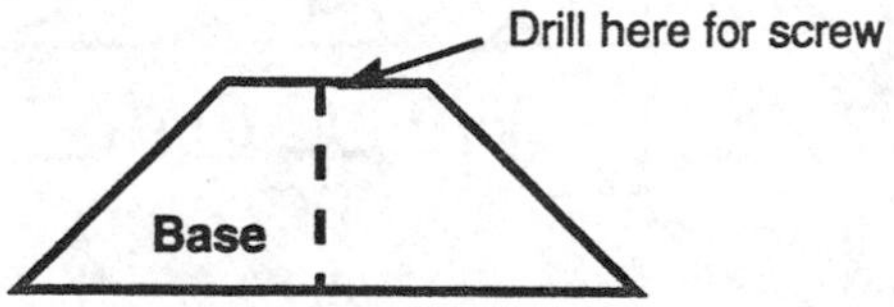

Assembly Diagram

Flower Whirligig

Cut one flower, four petal blades, two blade bases, and two blocks. (Follow general directions for whirligig assembly.)

Garden Ornaments

Whirligigs

See pages 52 and 53 for instructions and blade and base diagram assembly. **All whirligigs: 1 square = 2 inches**

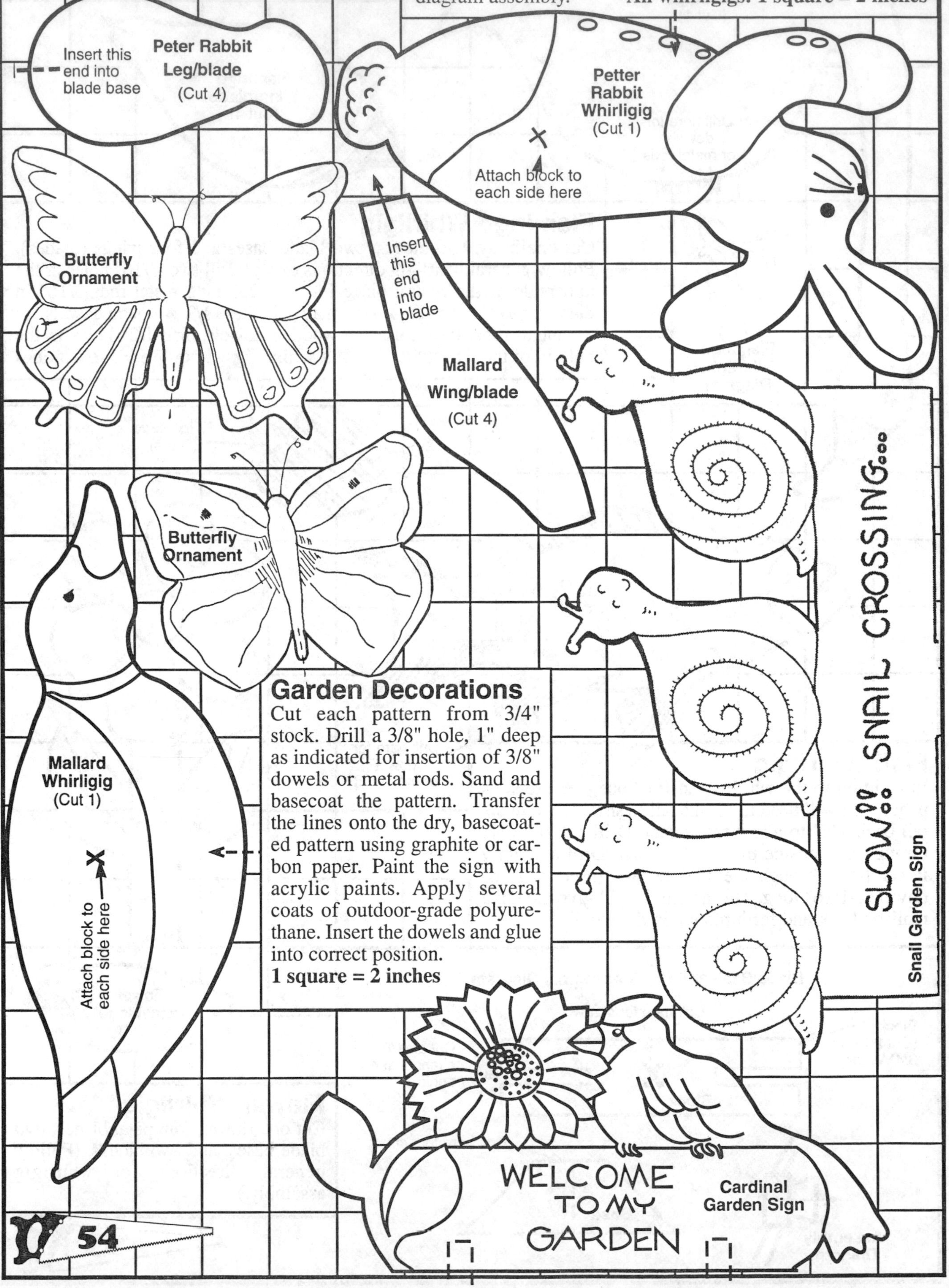

Garden Decorations

Cut each pattern from 3/4" stock. Drill a 3/8" hole, 1" deep as indicated for insertion of 3/8" dowels or metal rods. Sand and basecoat the pattern. Transfer the lines onto the dry, basecoated pattern using graphite or carbon paper. Paint the sign with acrylic paints. Apply several coats of outdoor-grade polyurethane. Insert the dowels and glue into correct position.

1 square = 2 inches

Christmas Blessings Grandparents' Wreath

Cut out all pieces. Finish and assemble wreath. Glue grandchildren's (or children's) photos on each star, along with the date of birth.

1 square = 3/4 inch

Christmas Ornaments

Cut each ornament from 1/2" wood. Sand well. Transfer the designs onto the wood with graphite or carbon paper. Drill a small hole at the top of each one for insertion of gold or silver cord for hanging. Paint and seal with acrylics.

Actual size

See Ornament instructions
on previous page.

Santa, Sleigh and Reindeer Garden Decoration

Cut the pieces from 1/2" exterior grade plywood. The sleigh and Santa measure 63" long x 45" high and the reindeer measures 25" long x 45" high. Cut two reindeer bodies for each deer you assemble. To secure the antlers to the deer's head, drill a 3/8" hole, 1" deep into the bottom of the antlers and 1" deep into the deer's head as indicated, for insertion of a 3/8" dowel. Using treated lumber, cut one 1" x 6" x 16" spacer for each deer. Assemble the reindeer with all weather glue and 1-1/4" galvanized wood screws. Attach the spacer between the two reindeer bodies and then attach the legs and antlers. Paint the assembled decoration with acrylic paints and then seal with several coats of exterior grade polyurethane. Attach two aluminum gutter bands to the back of the sleigh for insertion of two, 1" x 2" stakes. Insert a screw eye into each reindeer's neck. Tie heavy rope to Santa's hands and pull the rope through the screw eyes.

1 square = 5 inches

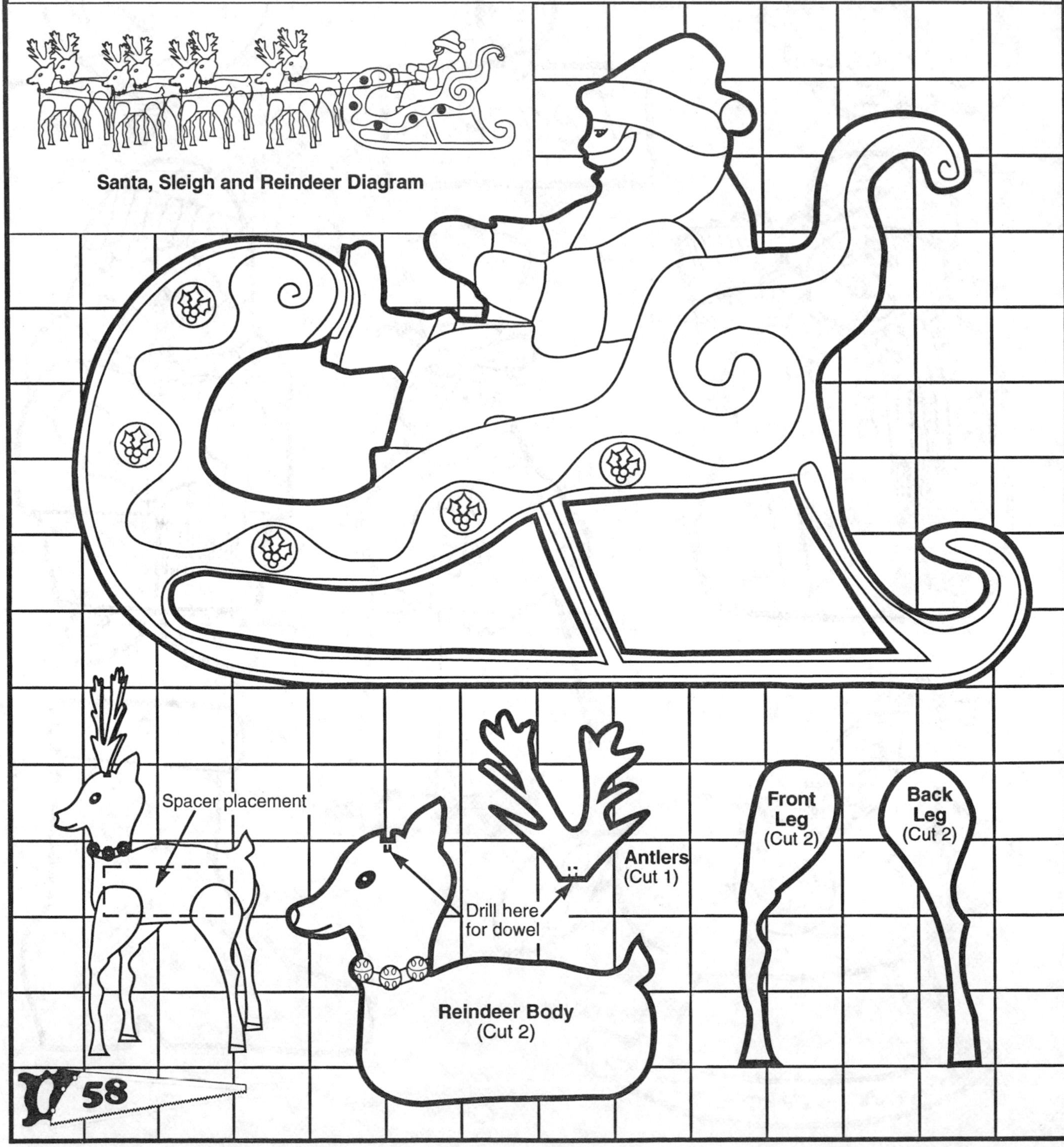

Olde English Carolers Garden Decorations

Cut the patterns from 3/8" exterior grade plywood. Trace the pattern onto the plywood using carbon or graphite paper. Sand edges lightly. Cut two stakes from 1" x 2" wood. Pre-drill the pattern and stakes for insertion of 1" #8 or #10 screws. Paint with acrylic paints. Seal with several coats of outdoor polyurethane. Insert the stakes into the ground, and then attach the pattern to the stakes with screws.

1 square = 5 inches

Southwest Nativity

Assemble using the adobe stable or use the pieces alone. When using the stable, cut the stable and base from 3/4" wood and assemble as shown, (see diagram). Cut one each of the three cacti, one star, one angel, one each of the three Magi, one shepherd and lamb and one Mary, Joseph and baby Jesus from 1/2" wood. Drill a hole in the star and angel as shown to insert a 1/4" dowel. Drill holes in the adobe stable as shown to insert the dowels of the star and angel. It would be easier to paint before assembly. Paint in southwestern colors rather than the traditional Christmas colors. Coat with clear acrylic spray. Attach figures using wood screws from the underside.

1 square = 1 inch

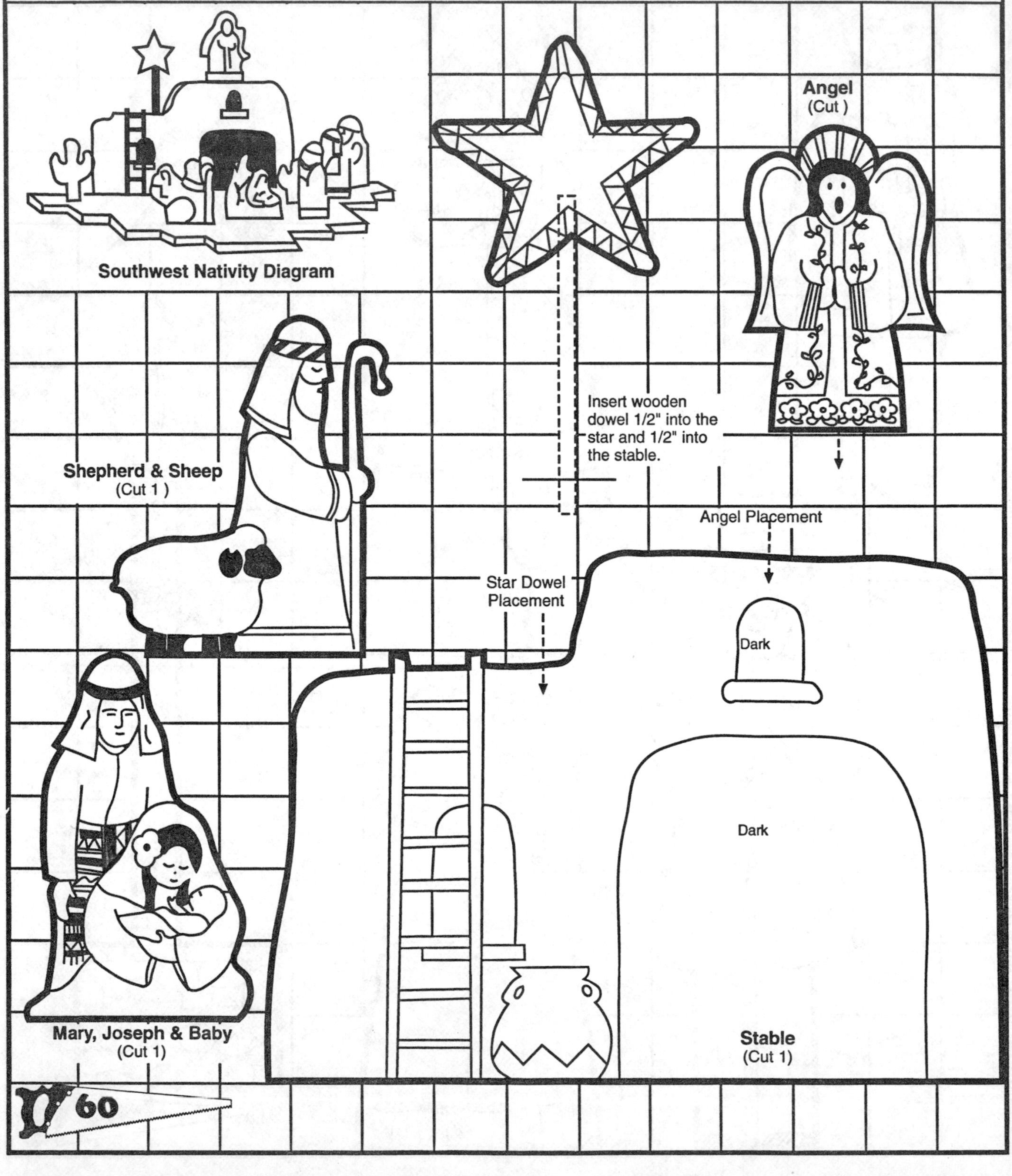

See SW Nativity instructions on previous page.

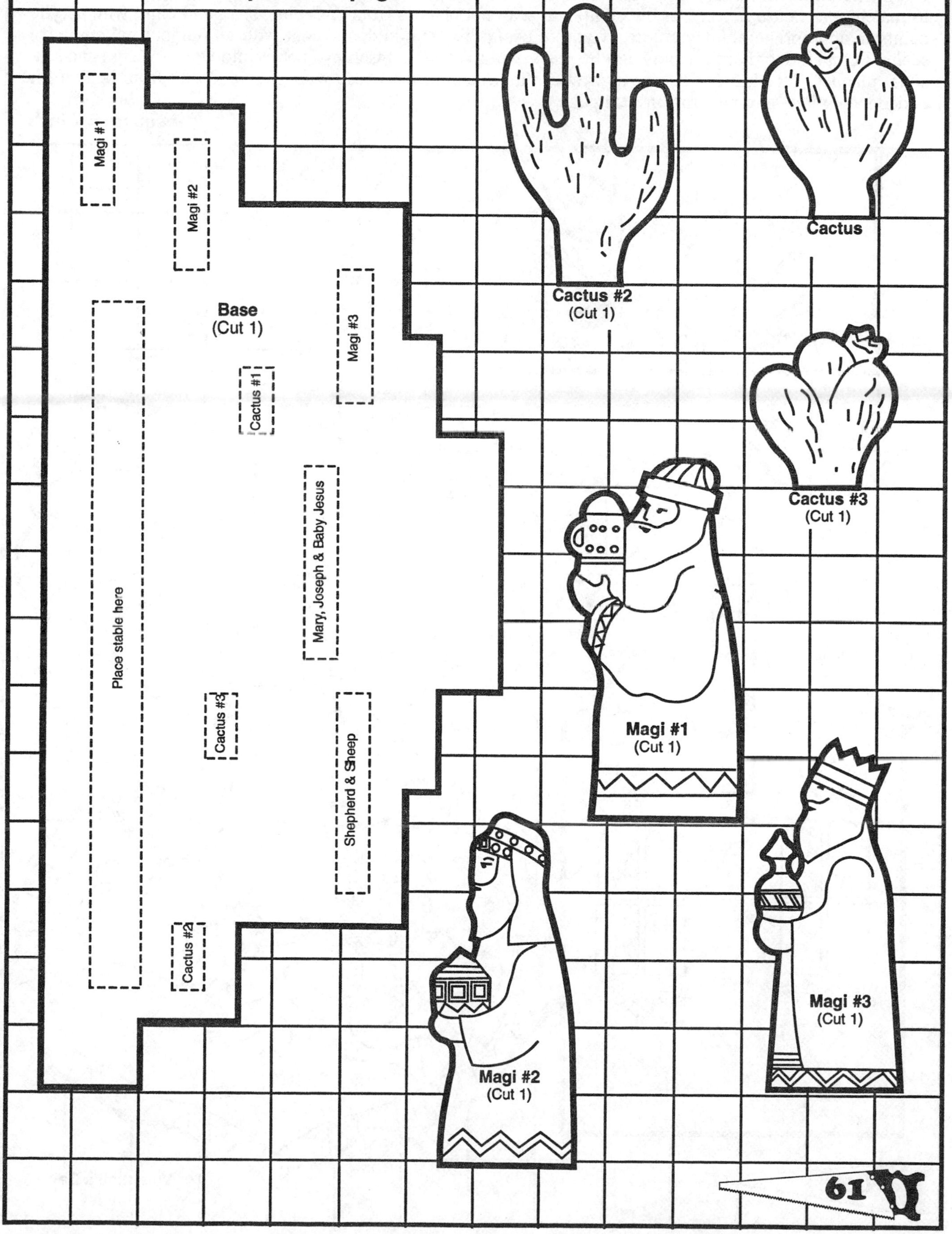

House Holiday Welcome Sign

Cut the house and welcome sign from 3/4" pine. Sand the house and welcome sign. Paint with acrylic paints to match your house decor. Cut the additional seasonal plaques from 3/4" pine, sand and paint with acrylic paints in appropriate holiday colors. If you're using this sign outdoors, coat with an outdoor polyurethane sealer. For an indoor hanger, spray acrylic sealer will work well. Insert eye hooks into welcome sign and seasonal plaques. Attach the welcome sign where indicated on the house with glue, and nail from behind for added strength. (More patterns on next page.)

1 square = 1 inch

Insert "S" Hook Here
Insert "S" Hook Here
St. Patrick's Day Hanger
Insert "S" Hook Here
Insert "S" Hook Here
HAPPY EASTER
Easter Hanger
Insert "S" Hook Here
Insert "S" Hook Here
Thanksgiving/Fall Hanger
Insert "S" Hook Here
Insert "S" Hook Here
Christmas Hanger
Insert "S" Hook Here
Insert "S" Hook Here
Insert "S" Hook Here
Anniversary Hanger

Santa's Christmas Train

Set this train on a mantle or under a tree. Cut the engine, caboose and two cars from 2" wood. Drill two, 3/8" holes through each side of each car for insertion of axle pegs or dowels. Drill a 3/8" hole, 5/8" deep into the top of the hood on the engine for insertion of a 3/8" dowel, 1-1/4" long to serve as a smokestack. Cut wheels from 1/2" wood or purchase the wheels and smokestack from "Woodworks", 1-800-722-0311, 4500 Anderson Blvd., Fort Worth, TX. 76117. Drill a 3/8" hole, 1/2" deep into the rooftop of the caboose for insertion of a 3/8" dowel, 1-1/4" long. Cut Santa's head and arms from 3/4" wood and the presents and Christmas trees from 1/2" wood. Sand and then paint all of the pieces using acrylics. Slip a wheel onto each axle. Dab a bit of glue into the drilled holes on each car. Insert one axle and wheel into each hole. Glue the presents onto one car and the trees onto another car. Glue Santa as shown. Insert a screw eye and cup hook as shown into each train. Glue the 3/8" dowel into the hole in the hood of the engine. Glue a 1/2" roundhead plug to the top of the dowel. Glue the other 3/8" dowel into the hole on top of the caboose. Glue a 1" flathead plug to the top of the dowel.

1 square = 1 inch

Bunny, Squirrel & Christmas Tree Garden Ornament

Cut all of the pattern pieces from 3/8" exterior grade plywood. Trace the pattern onto the wood with carbon or graphite paper. Lightly sand the edges of the cut patterns. Cut three stakes using 1" x 2" wood. Pre-drill the areas indicated. Cut a point at the bottom of each stake. Paint the patterns with acrylic paints then seal with several coats of polyurethane. Drive the stakes into the ground then attach the pattern to them with the screws.

1 square = 3 inches

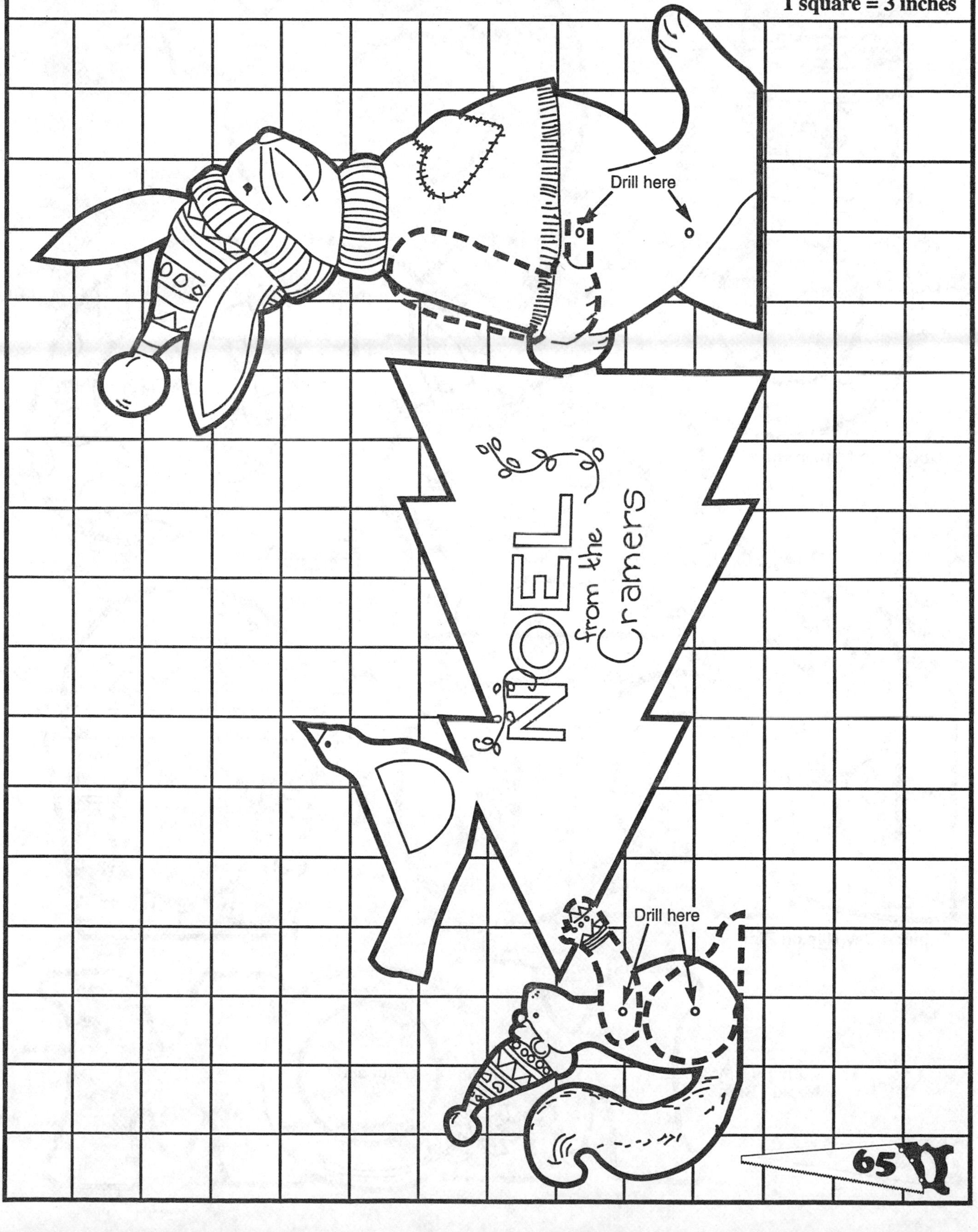

Napkin Rings

Cut out from 3/4" pine (don't forget to cut out holes) and finish on both sides, as shown. Coat with clear acrylic and enjoy on special and everyday occasions. **Actual size**

Snowman Napkin Ring

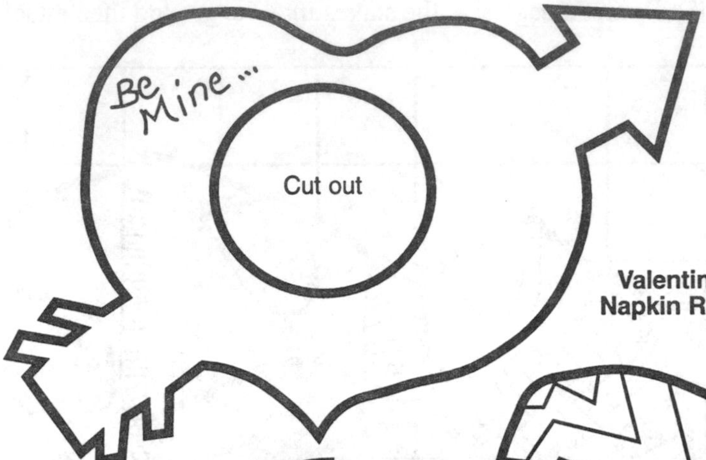

Valentine Napkin Ring

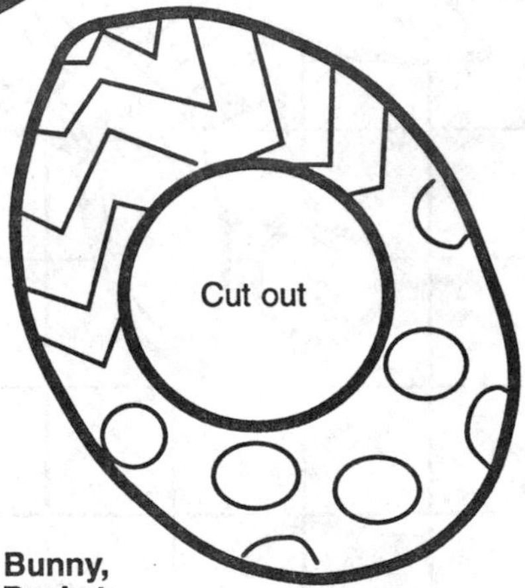

Easter Bunny, Egg & Basket Napkin Rings

Father's Day Napkin Ring

Mother's Day Napkin Ring

See instructions on previous page.

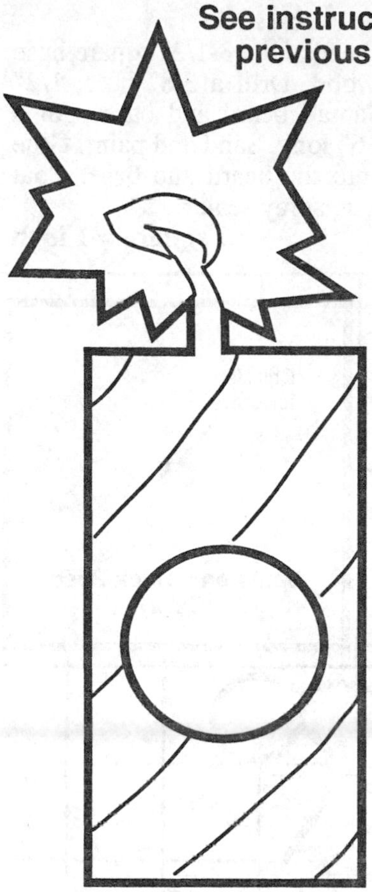

Firecracker Napkin Ring

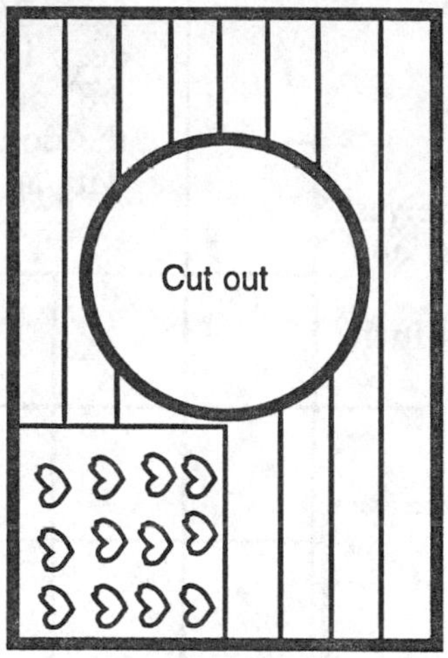

Flag Napkin Ring
(Paint your choice of flag)

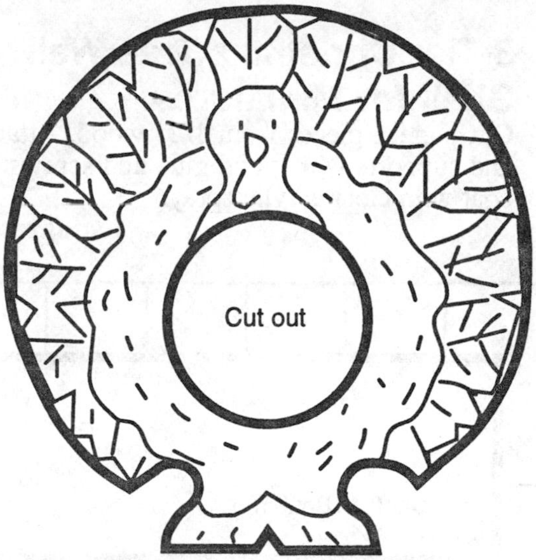

Thanksgiving Turkey Napkin Ring

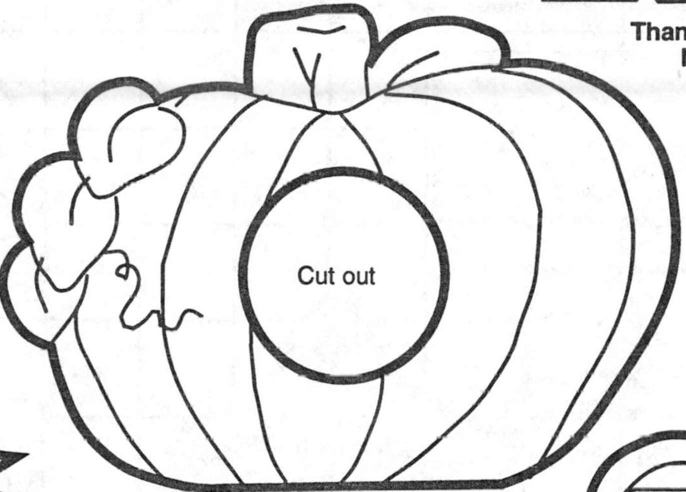

Pumpkin Napkin Ring

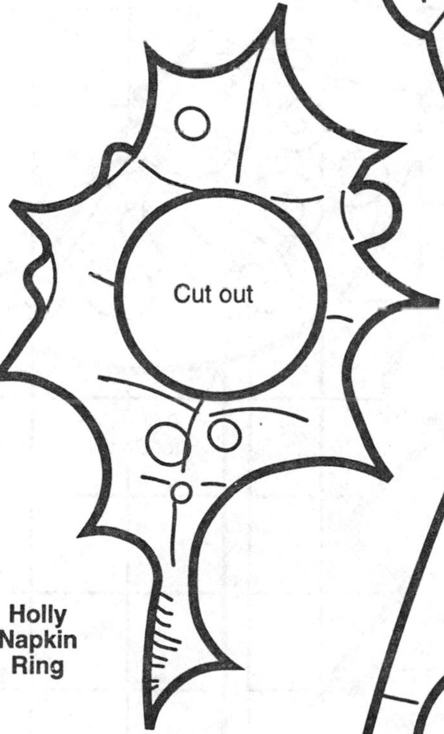

Holly Napkin Ring

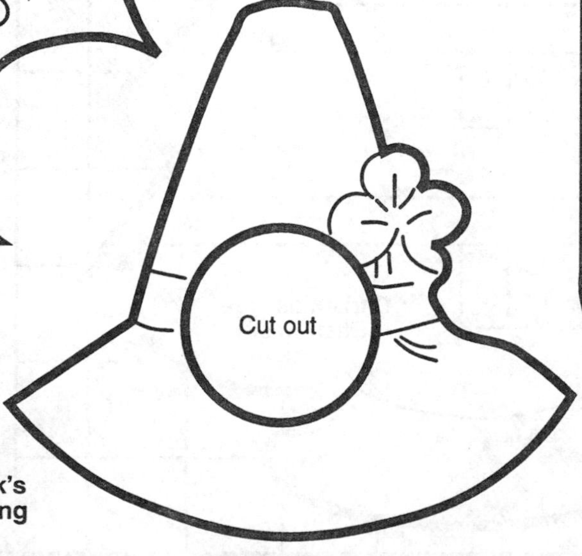

St. Patrick's Napkin Ring

Christmas Angel Napkin Ring

3-Tier Christmas Tree Wall Shelf for Miniatures

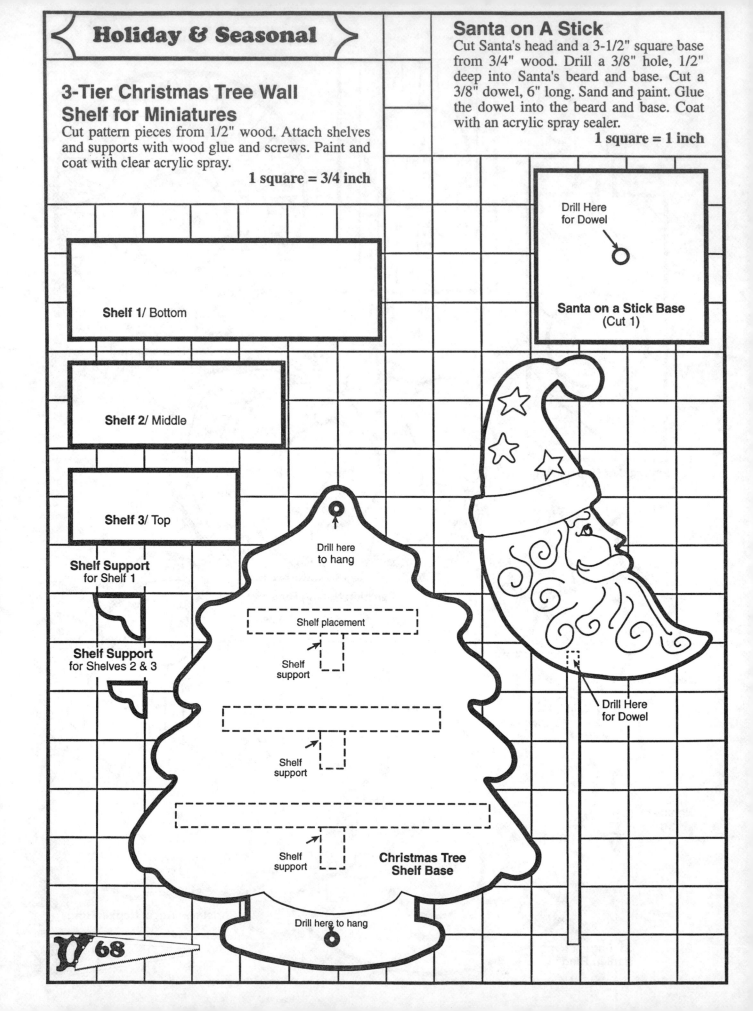

Cut pattern pieces from 1/2" wood. Attach shelves and supports with wood glue and screws. Paint and coat with clear acrylic spray.

1 square = 3/4 inch

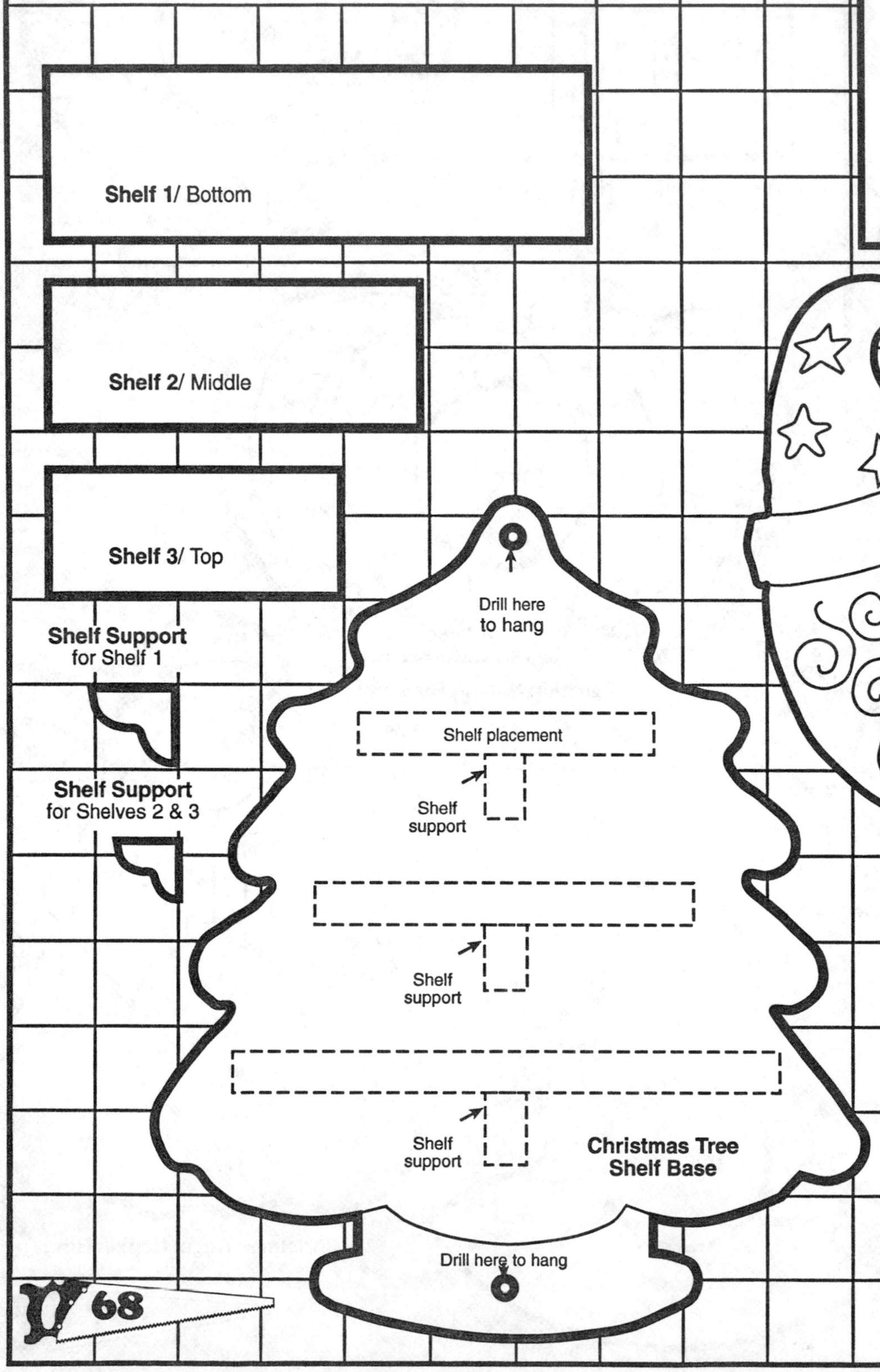

Santa on A Stick

Cut Santa's head and a 3-1/2" square base from 3/4" wood. Drill a 3/8" hole, 1/2" deep into Santa's beard and base. Cut a 3/8" dowel, 6" long. Sand and paint. Glue the dowel into the beard and base. Coat with an acrylic spray sealer.

1 square = 1 inch

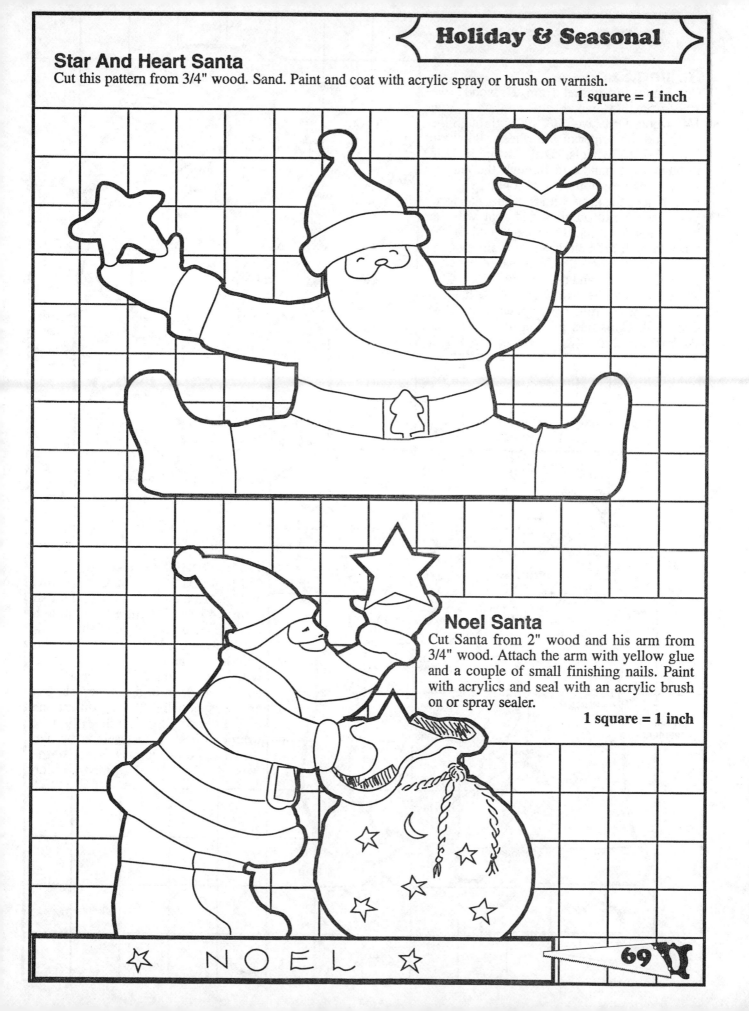

Star And Heart Santa

Cut this pattern from 3/4" wood. Sand. Paint and coat with acrylic spray or brush on varnish.

1 square = 1 inch

Noel Santa

Cut Santa from 2" wood and his arm from 3/4" wood. Attach the arm with yellow glue and a couple of small finishing nails. Paint with acrylics and seal with an acrylic brush on or spray sealer.

1 square = 1 inch

Rolling Santa

Cut Santa and basket from 2" wood, two arms from 3/4" wood, and two stars from 1/4" wood. Drill two, 3/8" holes through the body and the center of the wheels. Purchase four, 1-1/2" wheels. Drill a small hole through each hand and through the star as shown, for insertion of a 3" long, 18 gauge wire. Attach the arms with finishing nails and glue. Paint with acrylics and seal with an acrylic spray sealer. Thread one end of the wire through the hole in the star and twist it around itself. Insert the other end of the wire through the hand and twist it into a loop. Dab some glue into the drilled area of the hand to keep the wire from slipping through. Glue some silk Christmas greenery to the top of the basket. **1 square = 1 inch**

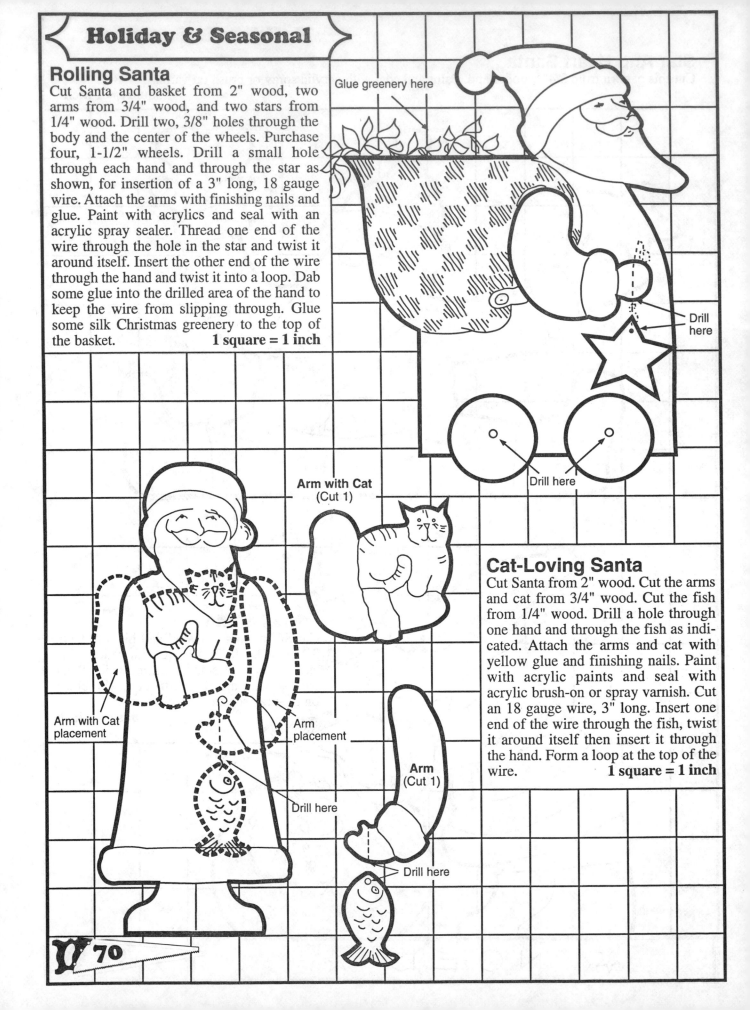

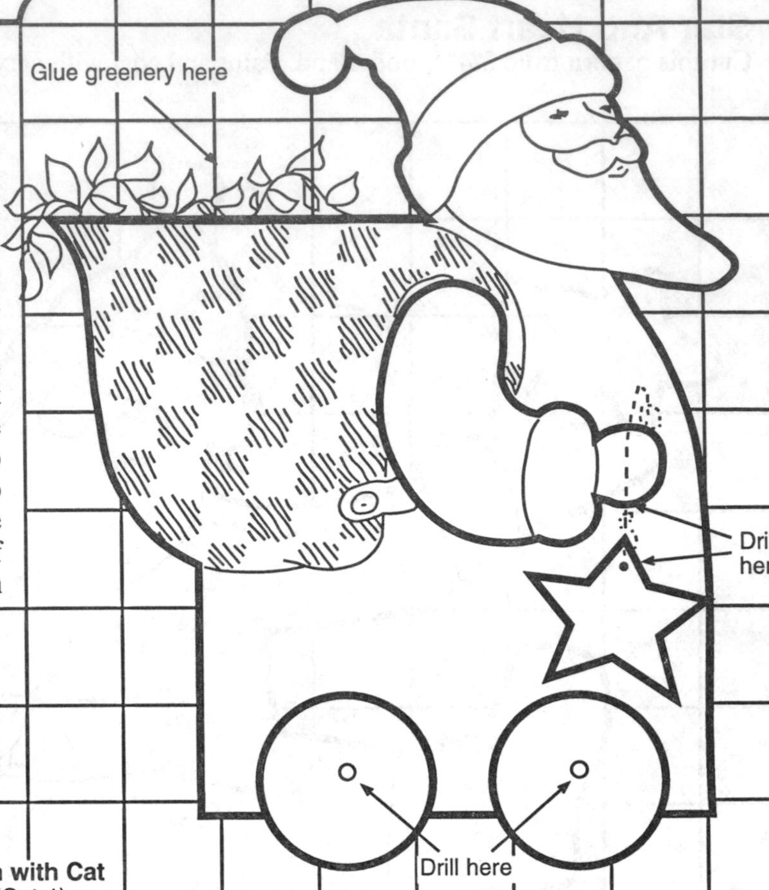

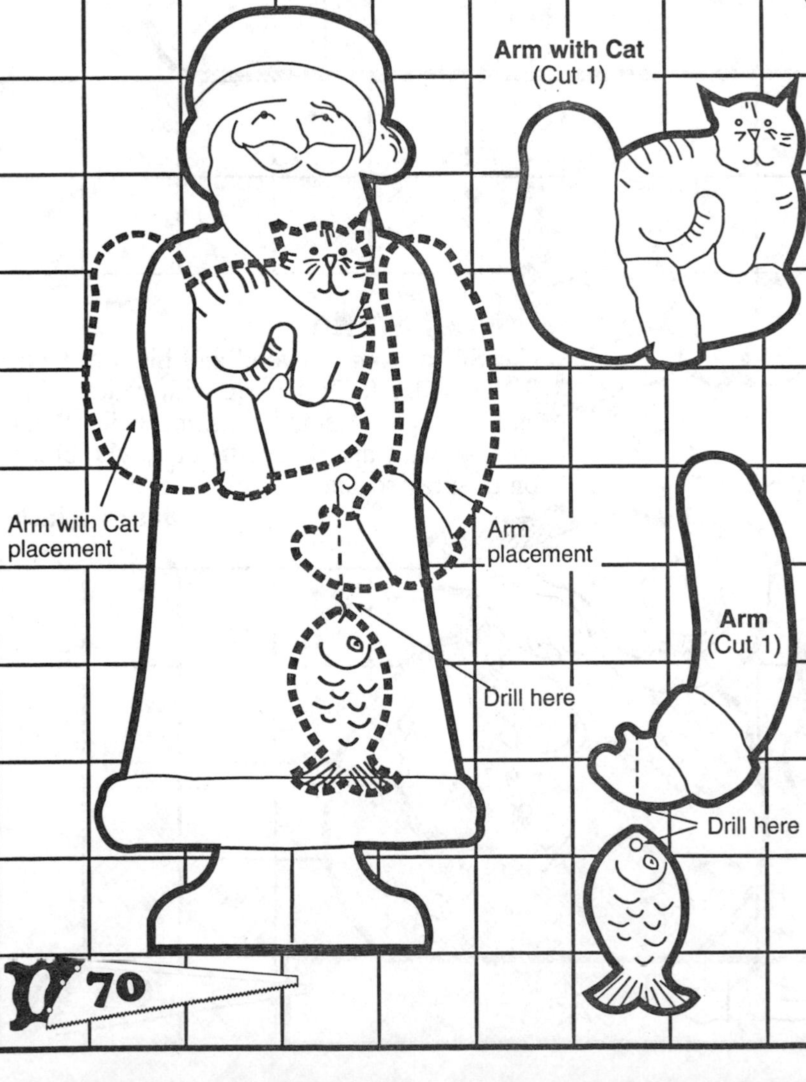

Cat-Loving Santa

Cut Santa from 2" wood. Cut the arms and cat from 3/4" wood. Cut the fish from 1/4" wood. Drill a hole through one hand and through the fish as indicated. Attach the arms and cat with yellow glue and finishing nails. Paint with acrylic paints and seal with acrylic brush-on or spray varnish. Cut an 18 gauge wire, 3" long. Insert one end of the wire through the fish, twist it around itself then insert it through the hand. Form a loop at the top of the wire. **1 square = 1 inch**

Tall Primitive Santa

Cut Santa from 2" wood. Drill a hole in each hand for insertion of star garland which may be purchased in a craft store. After the paint dries thoroughly, sand the entire cut out with fine grit sandpaper. Allow some of the wood to show through the paint, especially on the edges. This primitive Santa looks best if left unvarnished.

1 square = 1 inch

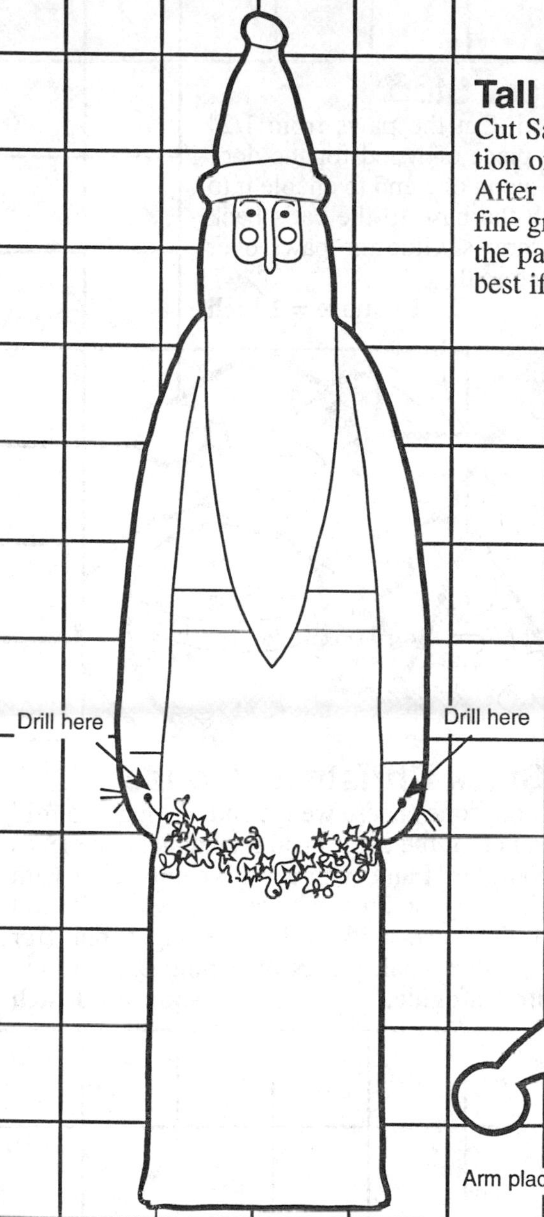

Blue Bird Santa

Cut Santa from 2" wood. Cut one arm and both blue birds from 3/4" wood. Cut the birdhouse from 1/4" wood. Drill a hole through one hand and through the roof of the birdhouse as indicated for insertion of an 18 gauge wire. Attach the blue birds with yellow glue. Attach the arm with yellow glue and finishing nails. Paint the pattern pieces with acrylic paints and seal with acrylic spray or brush on varnish. Cut a length of wire, insert it into the drilled hole in the birdhouse, pull it through and twist a short piece around itself. Push the other end through the hand and form a loop so that the wire doesn't pull through. Dab some wood glue into the hole in Santa's hand to secure the wire and keep it from slipping through.

1 square = 1-1/2 inches

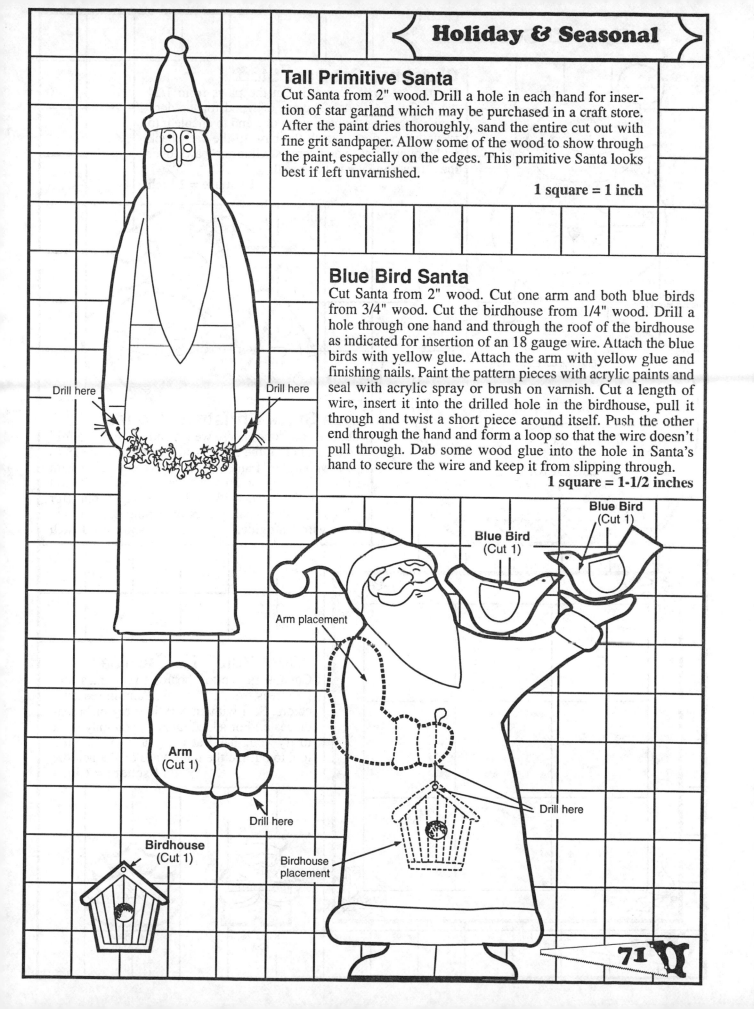

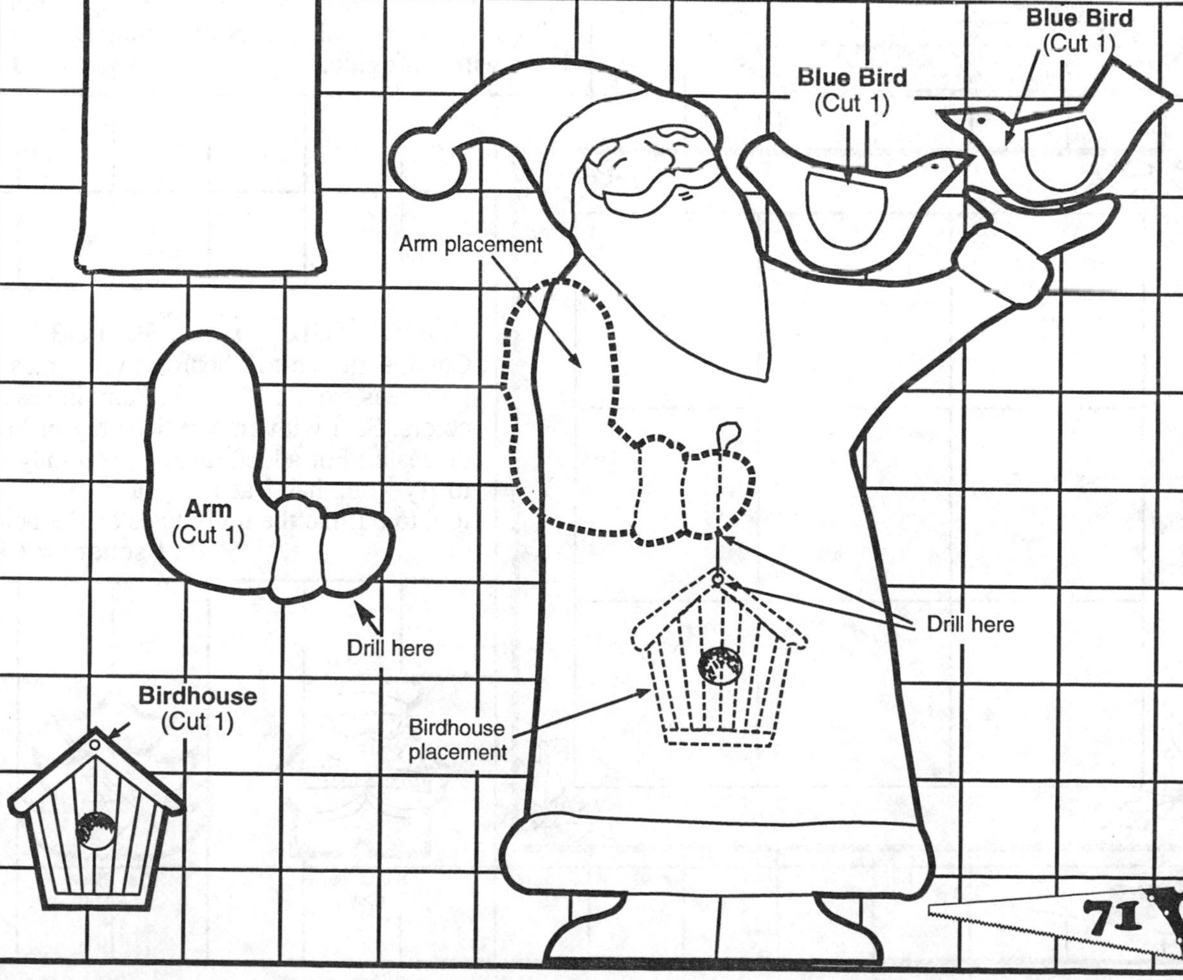

Christmas Cat Door Stop

Cut the cat from 1" wood. Cut the paws from 1/2" wood. Cut a 4" x 4-1/2" piece of wood for the door stop base. Taper the base along one end to enable it to fit under the door. Attach the base to the cat's back with countersunk wood screws. Glue the paws over the screws. Sand, paint and seal.

1 square = 1 inch

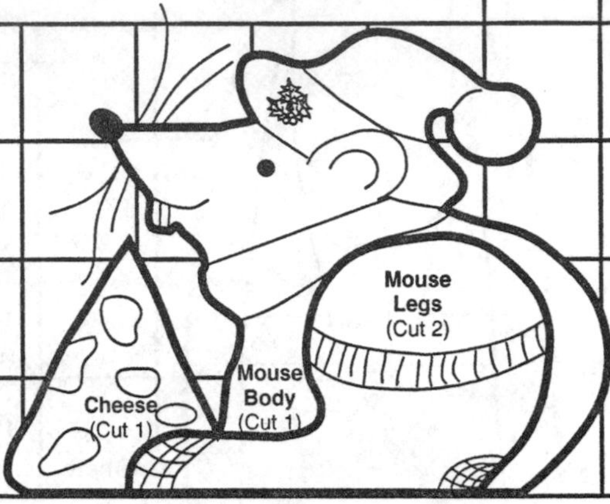

Side Stack Christmas Mouse

Cut one body, one cheese wedge and two legs from 1" pine. Sand all of the pieces and then attach the pieces with wood glue. Paint with acrylic paints. Seal with an acrylic spray or brush-on varnish. Make several holes in the nose with a large straight pin (for whiskers). Glue small pieces of fishing line into the holes with craft glue. **1 square = 1 inch**

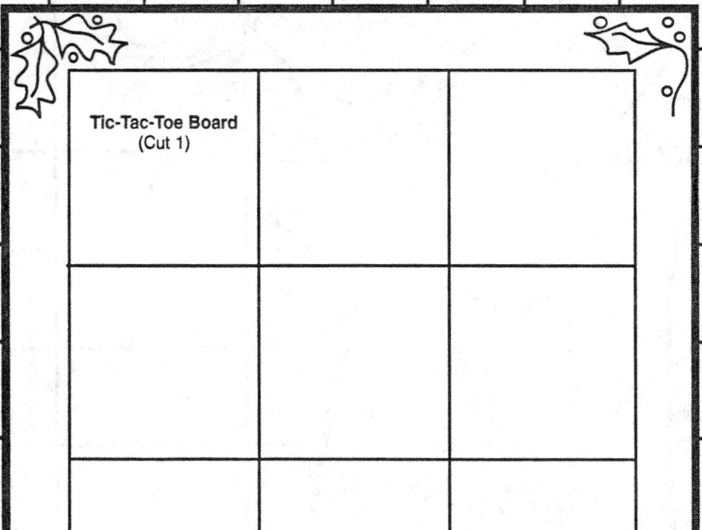

"Cool-Yule" Tic-Tac-Toe

Cut the tic-tac-toe board, five Santas and five trees from 1/2" stock. Paint in seasonal colors. Seal with an acrylic spray or brush-on sealer. For added interest, you may want to try your hand at using a wood-burning tool to outline the holly lines on the board.

1 square = 1 inch

Santa Piece
(Cut 5)

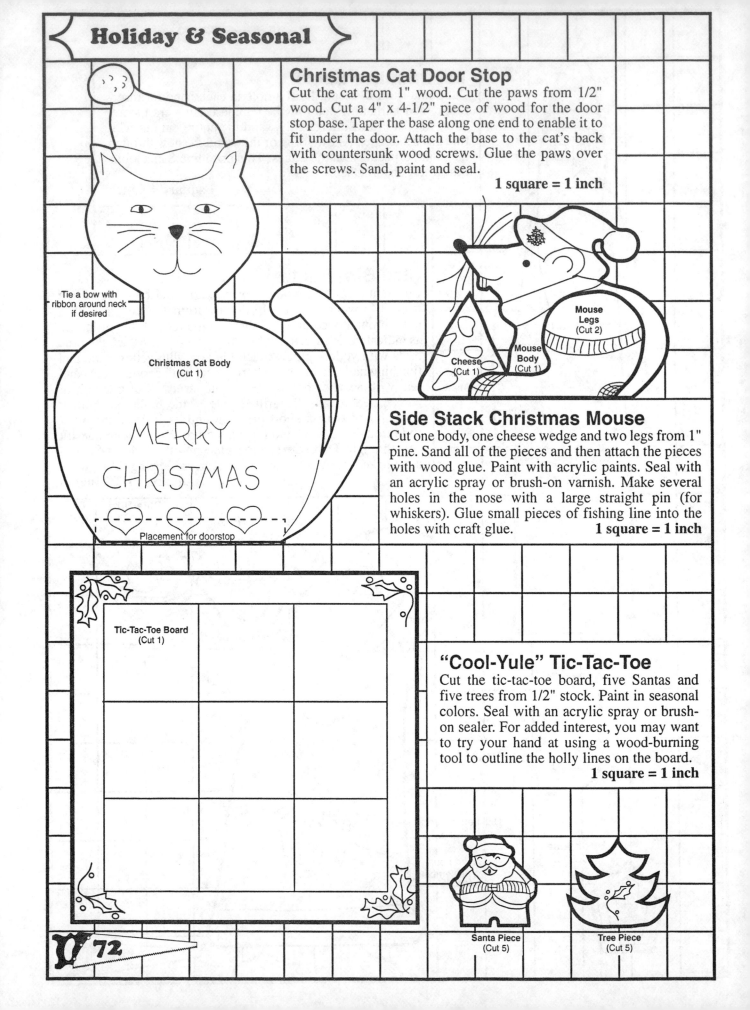

Tree Piece
(Cut 5)

— CHAPTER SEVEN —

HOUSEHOLD HELPERS

Collapsible Baskets

Cut the pattern(s) from 1" hardwood. Wood such as walnut is a good choice for the baskets because it has a rich, dark patina when oiled. Softwood such as pine or fir tend to split easily when cut thin. Trace the cutting line onto the cut-out pattern. Drill a small pilot hole where indicated for insertion of a 1/4" offset scroll saw blade; this will allow freer movement when forming a basket. Drill a hole where indicated on the bottom of the basket for insertion of a #6 countersunk flathead wood screw. (The screw placement is crucial for the basket to work properly.) Drill 3/8" holes in the sides for insertion of 3/8" dowels. Cut the base. Insert the scroll saw blade and cut on the dark lines. Sand the area around the outer diameter. The base, when turned, will allow the basket to stand. Tilt the cut area and gently push down to form the basket. If you intend to place food in the basket, a non-toxic oil sealer needs to be applied.

1 square = 1 inch

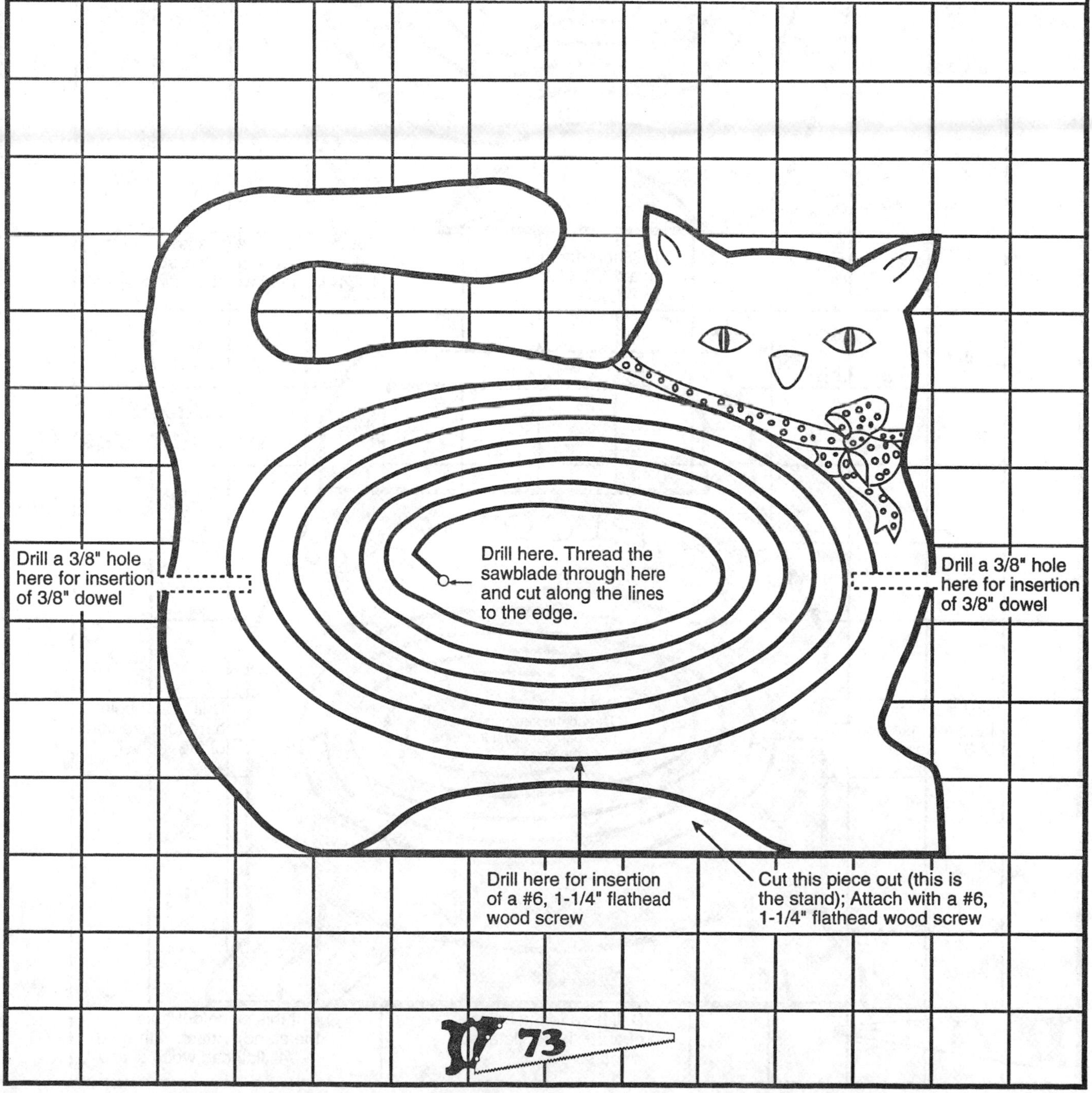

Drill a 3/8" hole here for insertion of 3/8" dowel
Drill here. Thread the sawblade through here and cut along the lines to the edge.
Drill a 3/8" hole here for insertion of 3/8" dowel
Drill here for insertion of a #6, 1-1/4" flathead wood screw
Cut this piece out (this is the stand); Attach with a #6, 1-1/4" flathead wood screw

Collapsible Apple Basket

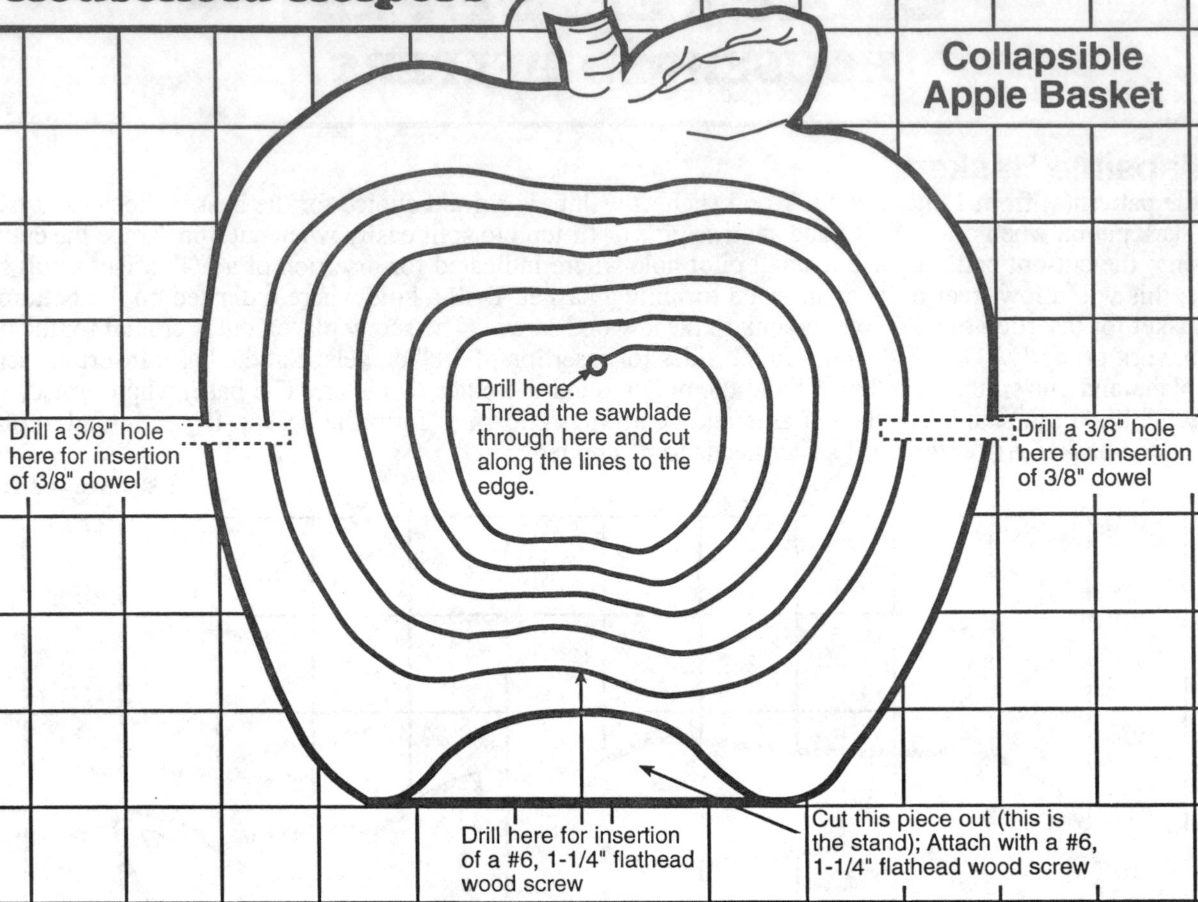
Drill here.
Thread the sawblade through here and cut along the lines to the edge.
Drill a 3/8" hole here for insertion of 3/8" dowel
Drill a 3/8" hole here for insertion of 3/8" dowel
Drill here for insertion of a #6, 1-1/4" flathead wood screw
Cut this piece out (this is the stand); Attach with a #6, 1-1/4" flathead wood screw

Collapsible Washtub Basket

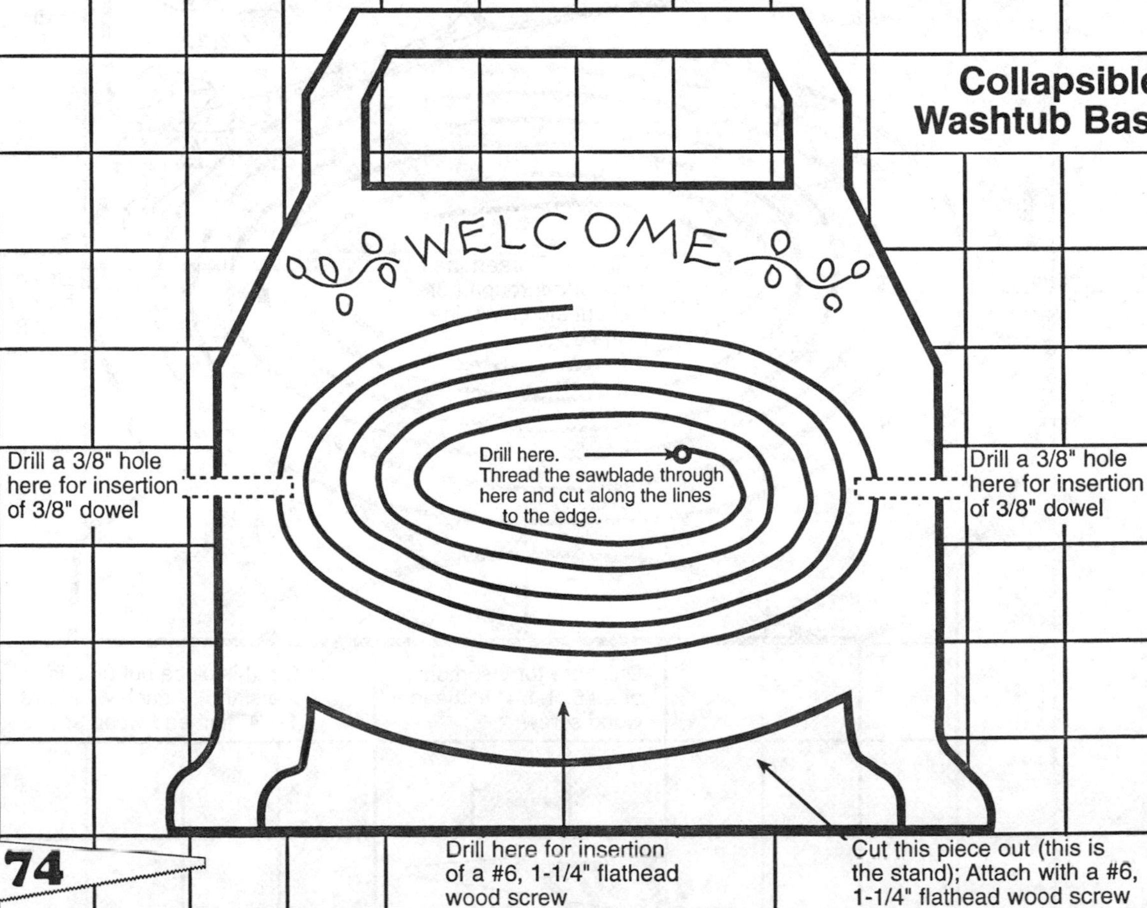
WELCOME
Drill here.
Thread the sawblade through here and cut along the lines to the edge.
Drill a 3/8" hole here for insertion of 3/8" dowel
Drill a 3/8" hole here for insertion of 3/8" dowel
Drill here for insertion of a #6, 1-1/4" flathead wood screw
Cut this piece out (this is the stand); Attach with a #6, 1-1/4" flathead wood screw

Four Seasons Perpetual Calendar

Cut one back from 1/2" plywood. Cut date and month tiles from 1/4" plywood. Cut six, 14" long tracking strips from 3/4" x 3/4" pine. Cut a 1/4" deep x 1/8" wide rabbet in the top and bottom tracking pieces. Cut a 1/8" wide by 1/4" deep rabbet on each side of the four remaining tracks. Sand all of the pieces. Attach the tracking pieces with yellow glue and 1" finishing nails. Countersink the nails. Fill the nail holes with wood filler. Allow the filler to dry and then sand smooth. Cut six month tiles and paint months on both sides if you want to save time and material. The holiday tiles may be painted on the back of the numbers that correspond with that holiday. However, this is not always possible since every holiday doesn't come on the same day each year. Some holiday tiles may be combined with others (Example: Mother's Day could be on the back of Father's Day because they come in different months). If you don't want to combine tiles, forty-eight pieces will need to be cut out, painted and varnished.

1 square = 1-1/2 inches

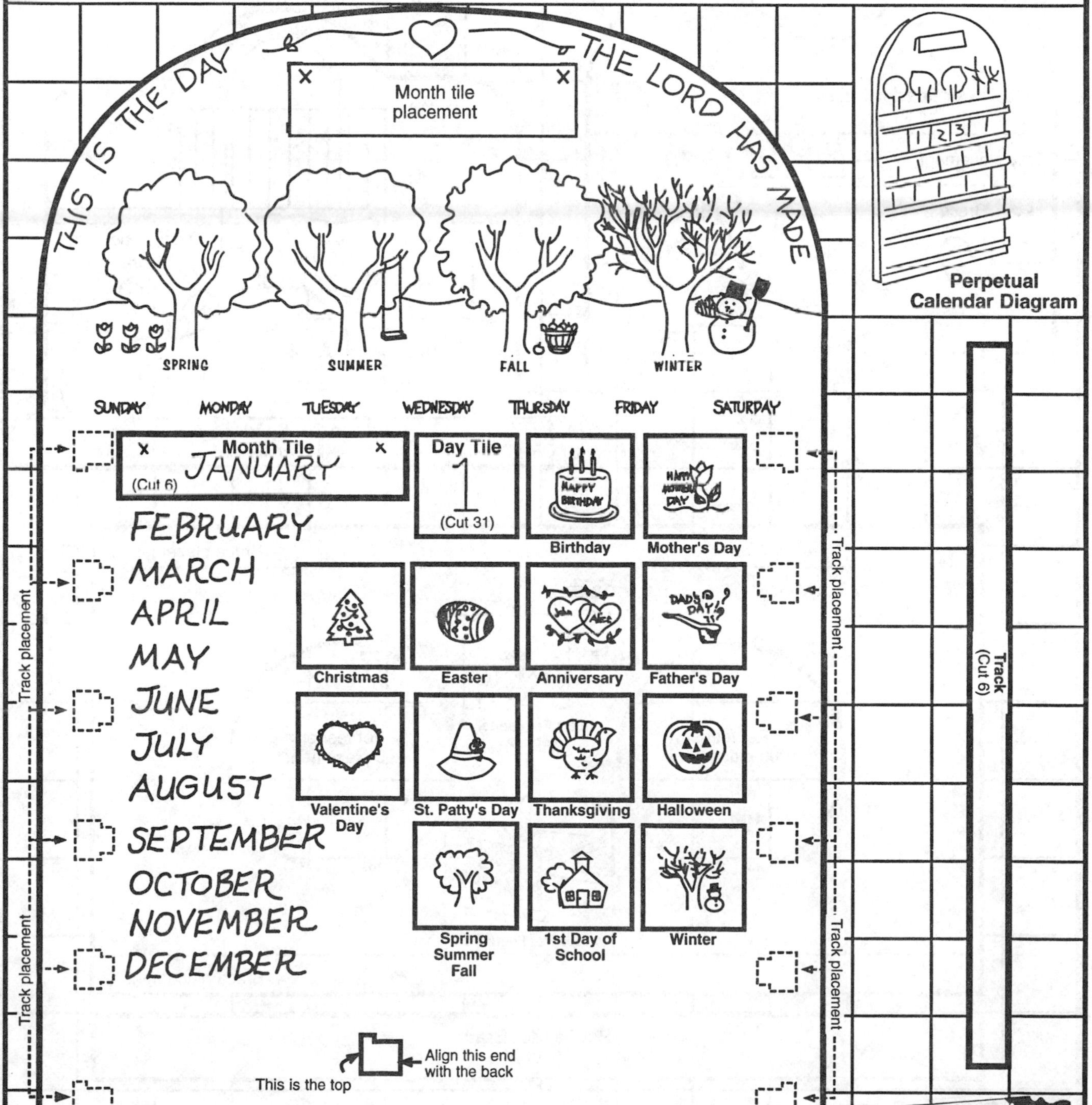

Pet Feeders

Cut all of the pieces from 3/4" pine. You will need to purchase food and water dishes. (Margarine tubs make very good dishes.) Center the dishes as shown on the feeder tray and cut a circle for each dish. (Be very careful when measuring the holes. It is very easy to make a circle too large so the dishes can be pushed through by your pet, creating a mess.) Make sure the dishes fit tightly into the holes. Assemble the tray between the side pieces and attach a brace to each side with wood glue and finishing nails. Sand well. Paint with acrylic paints. Seal with a brush-on or spray varnish.

1 square = 1-1/4 inches

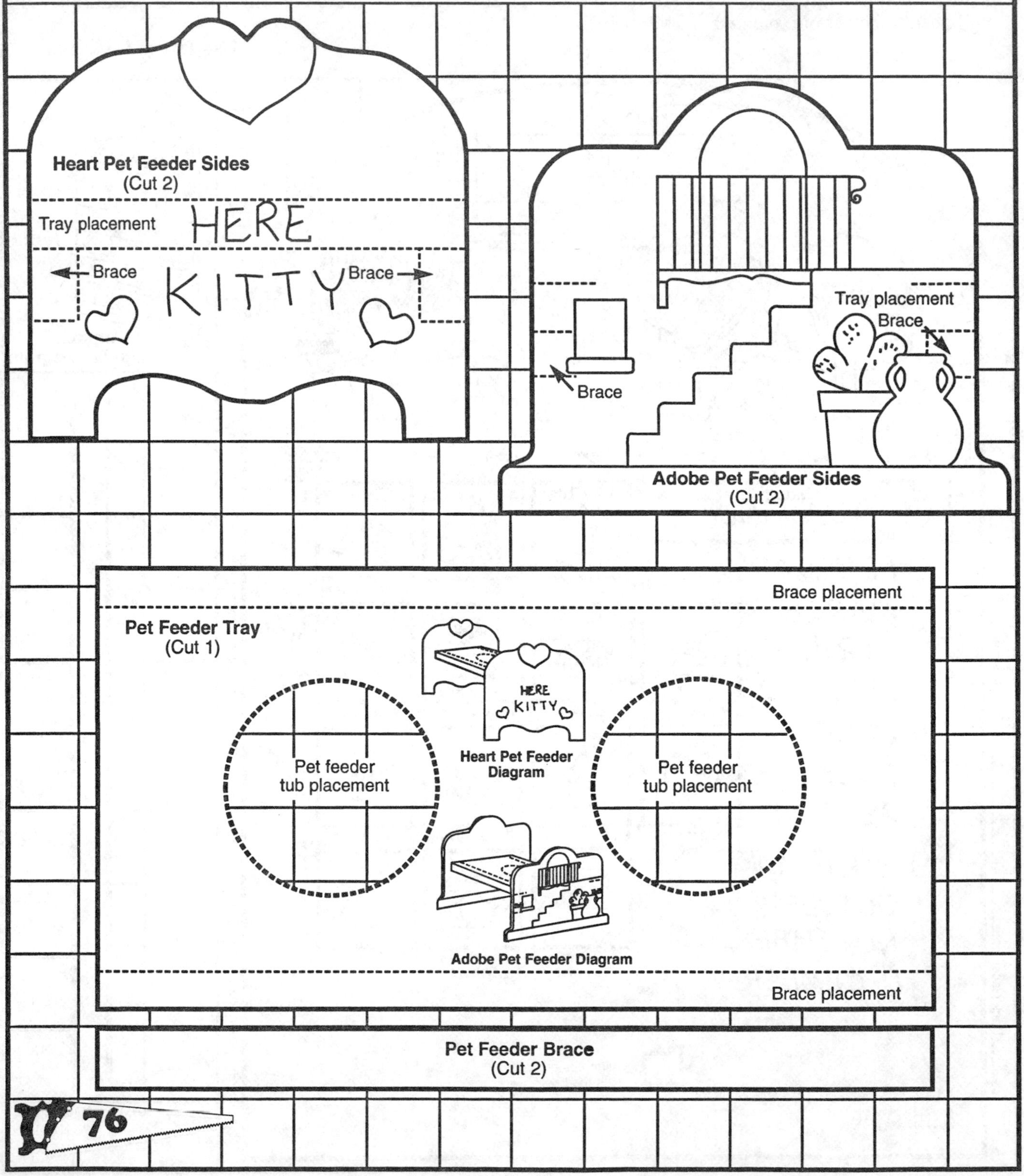

Kitty Pet Feeder Diagram

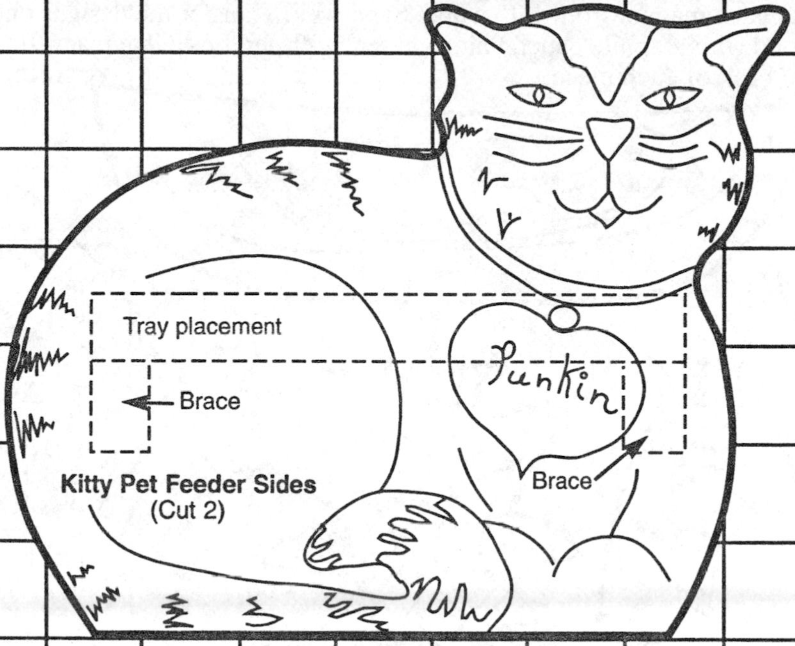

Puppy Pet Feeder Diagram

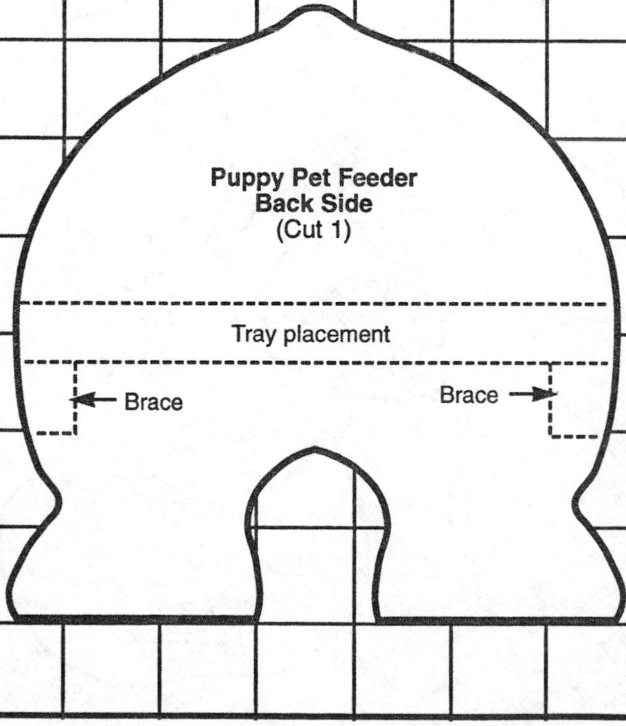

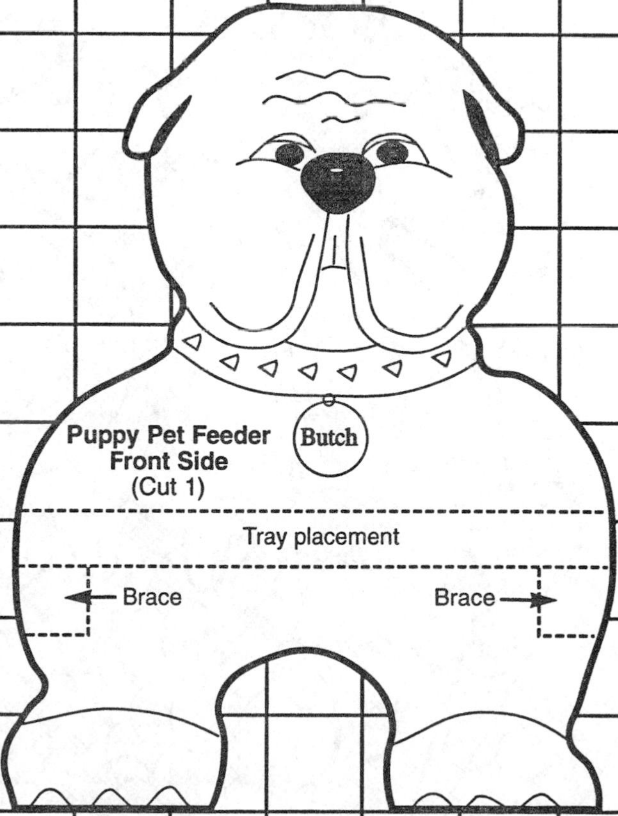

Funny Fruit & Veggie Refrigerator Magnets

Cut each magnet from 1/4" wood. Sand well. Transfer the designs onto the wood with graphite paper. Paint and seal with acrylics. Glue magnet(s) onto the back of each piece.

Actual size

Schoolhouse Photo Display

Cut out of 1/4" wood and finish as shown. This makes a wonderful keepsake.

1 square = 1-1/2 inches

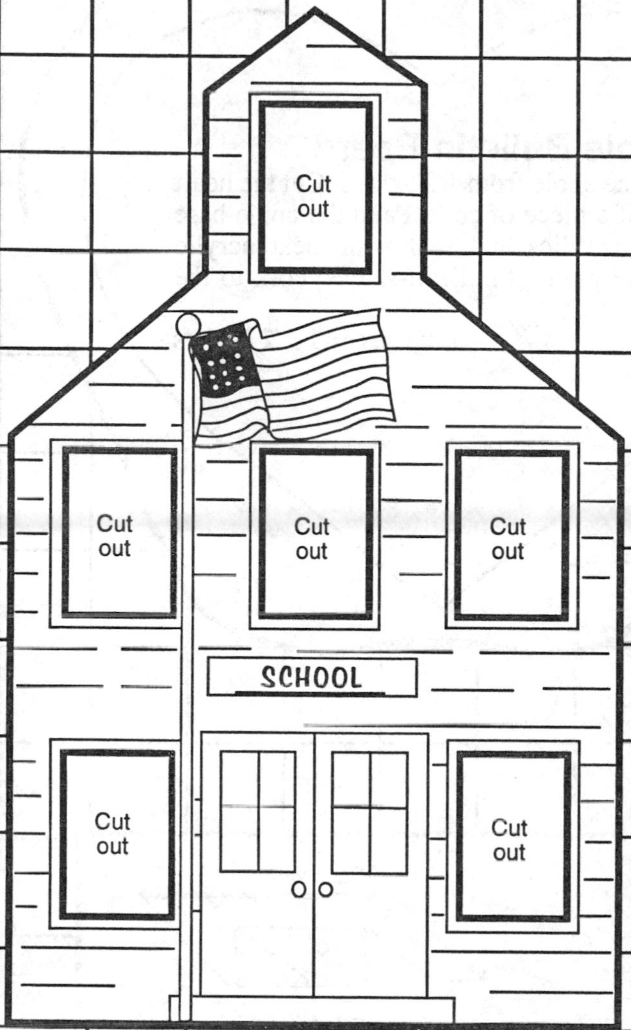

Schoolhouse Blackboard

Cut blackboard from 1/2" wood. Paint the rectangular area with blackboard paint. Glue strips on top, as shown, for a frame.

1 square = 1-1/2 inches

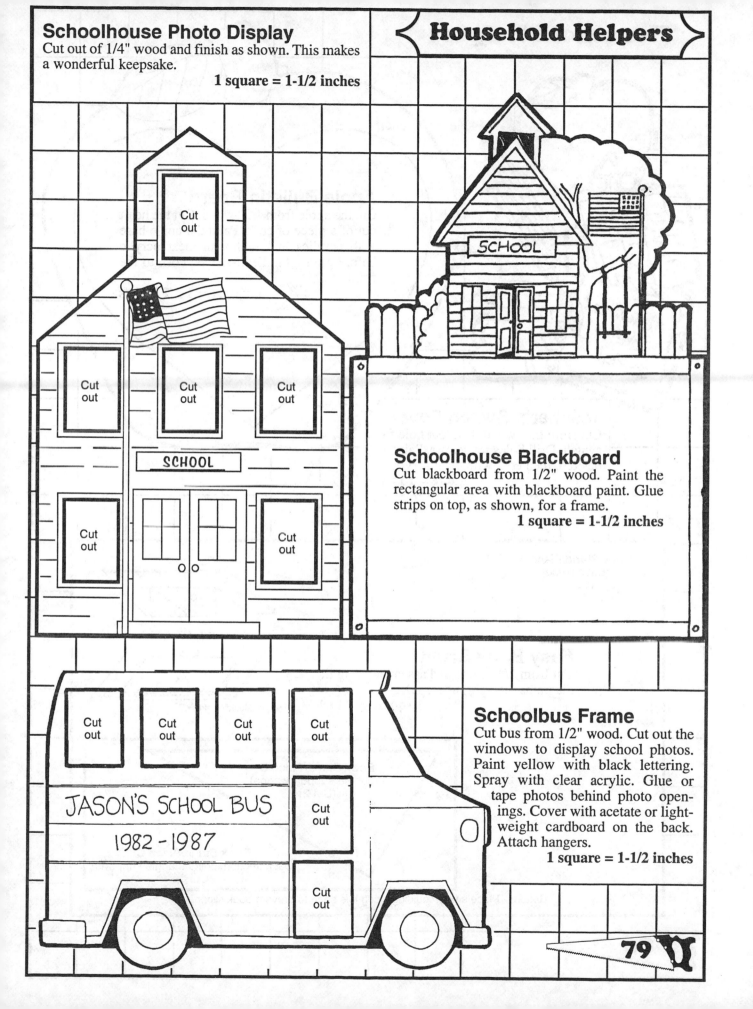

Schoolbus Frame

Cut bus from 1/2" wood. Cut out the windows to display school photos. Paint yellow with black lettering. Spray with clear acrylic. Glue or tape photos behind photo openings. Cover with acetate or lightweight cardboard on the back. Attach hangers.

1 square = 1-1/2 inches

Household Helpers

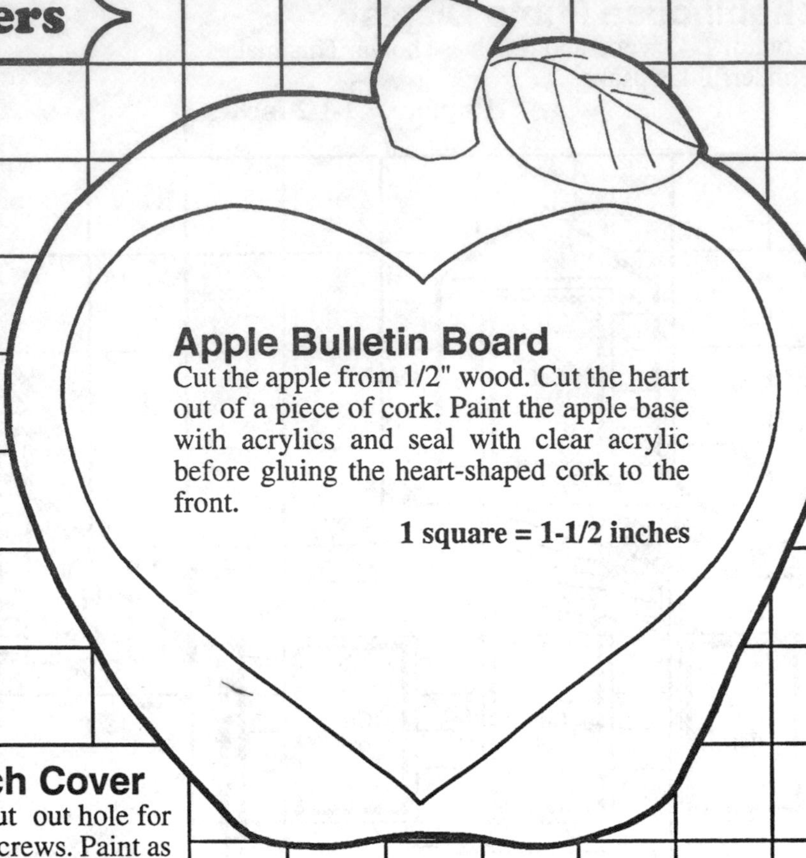

Apple Bulletin Board

Cut the apple from 1/2" wood. Cut the heart out of a piece of cork. Paint the apple base with acrylics and seal with clear acrylic before gluing the heart-shaped cork to the front.

1 square = 1-1/2 inches

Teacher's Switch Cover

Cut from thin wood. Cut out hole for switch. Drill holes for screws. Paint as desired, then coat with clear acrylic.

1 square = 1 inch

Book Stand/Piece A
(Base piece)
(Cut 1)

Back view

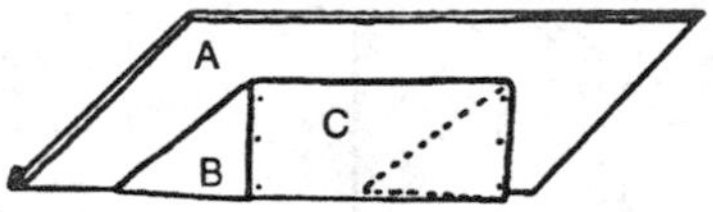

Front view

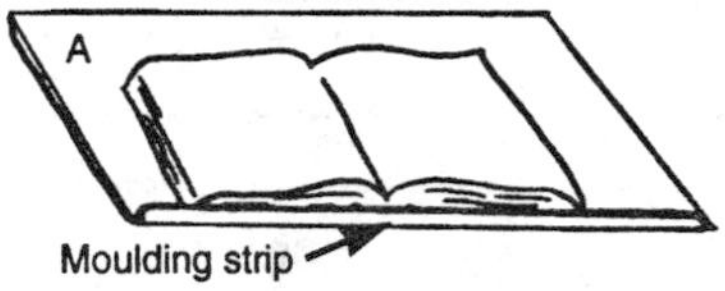

Easy Book Stand

Cut from 1/4" wood and assemble using the diagrams (at right) as a guide.

1 square = 1 inch

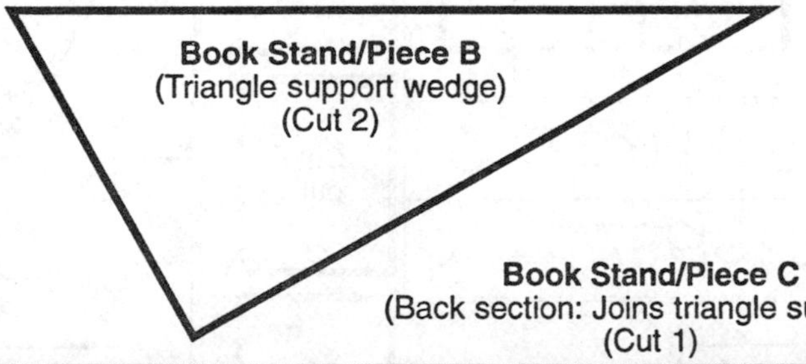

Book Stand/Piece B
(Triangle support wedge)
(Cut 2)

Book Stand/Piece C
(Back section: Joins triangle supports)
(Cut 1)

Bottom - Place small moulding along this edge to prevent book slippage.

Doorstops

Cut each doorstop and base from 1" wood. Cut each base to the width of individual doorstop pattern. Cut cottage, shrubs and step from 1/4" wood. Taper each base to fit under a door. Sand all of the pieces. Attach the cottage shrubs and step with wood glue. Attach the bases to the back of each pattern with wood glue and countersunk screws, then fill the holes with wood filler. Paint with acrylic paints. Seal with a brush-on or spray acrylic varnish.

1 square = 1-1/4 inches

Family Album Picture Frame

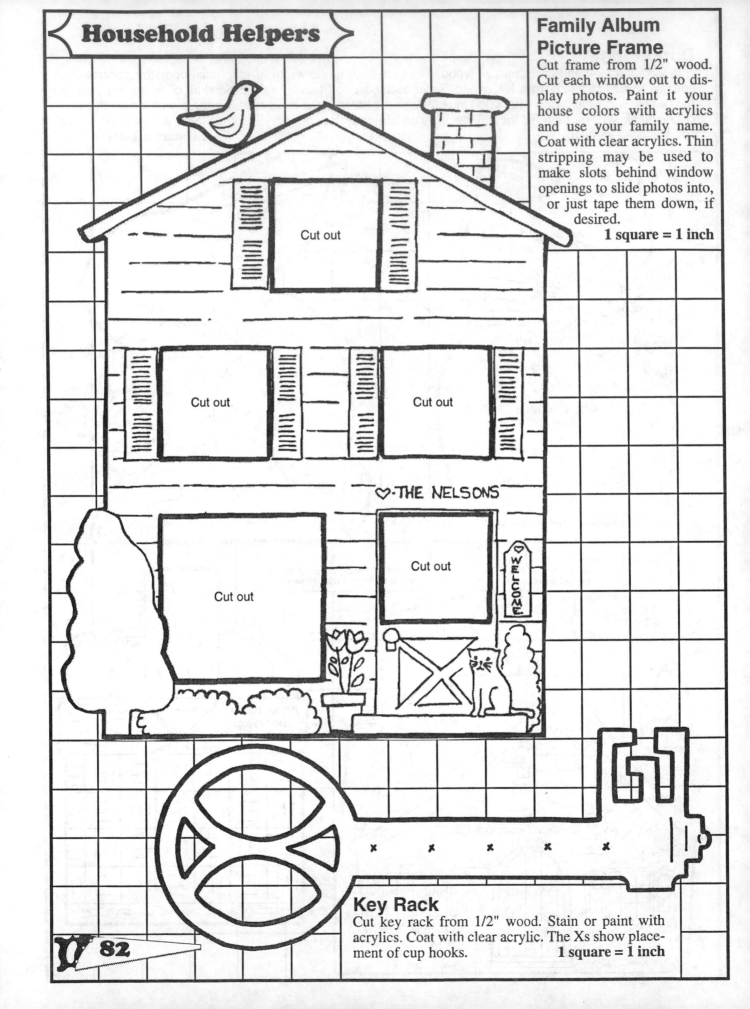

Cut frame from 1/2" wood. Cut each window out to display photos. Paint it your house colors with acrylics and use your family name. Coat with clear acrylics. Thin stripping may be used to make slots behind window openings to slide photos into, or just tape them down, if desired.

1 square = 1 inch

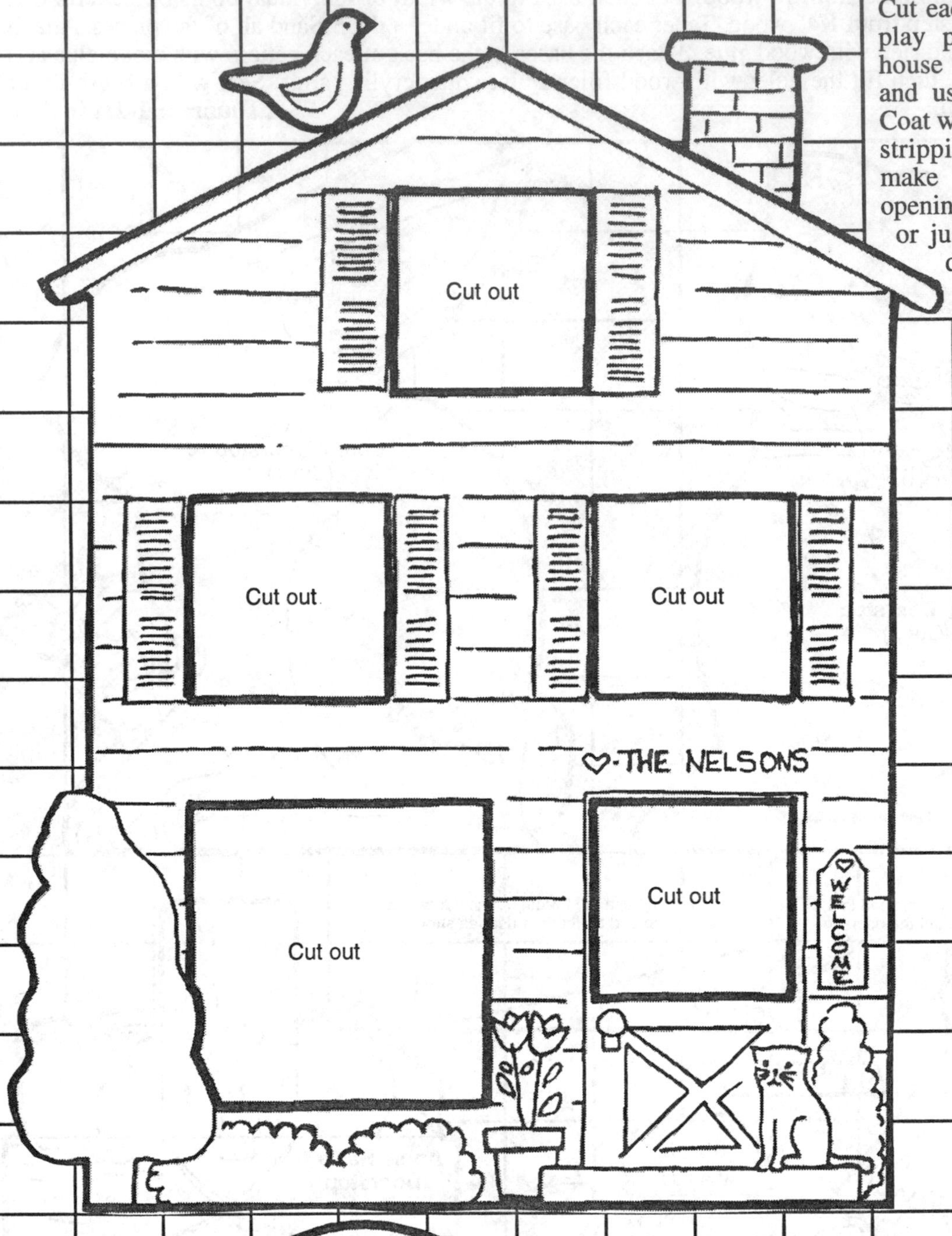

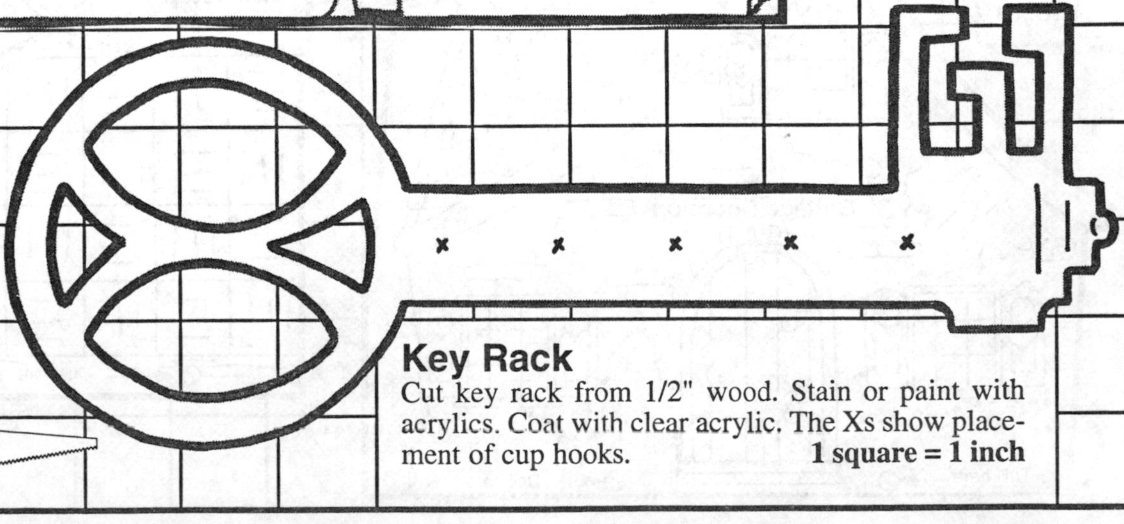

Key Rack

Cut key rack from 1/2" wood. Stain or paint with acrylics. Coat with clear acrylic. The Xs show placement of cup hooks.

1 square = 1 inch

Napkin Rings

Cut out from 3/4" pine (don't forget to cut out holes) and finish as shown on both sides. Coat with clear acrylic and enjoy on special and everyday occasions.

Actual size

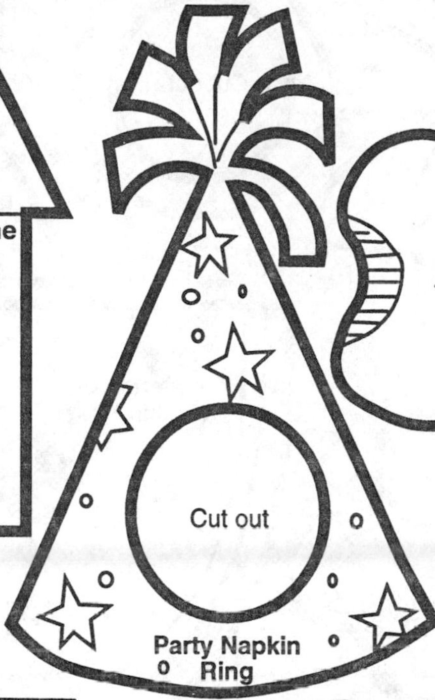

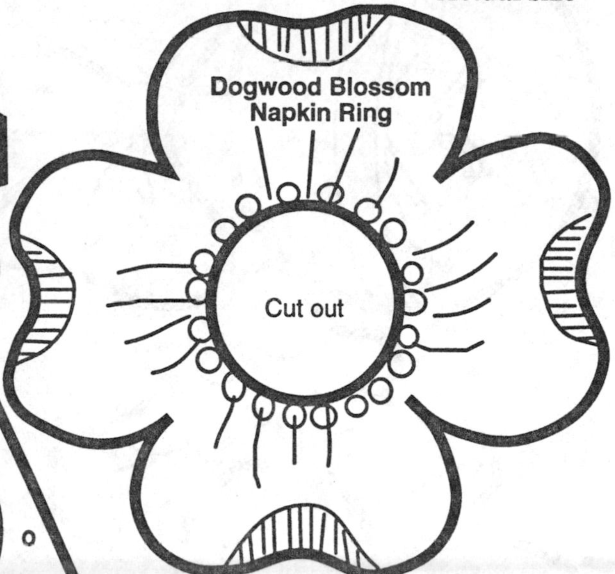

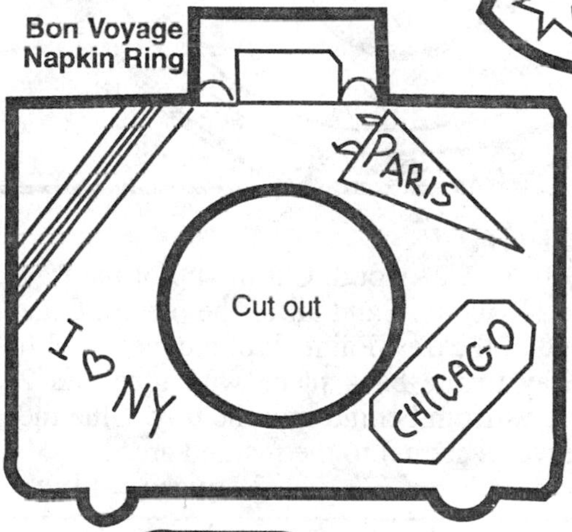

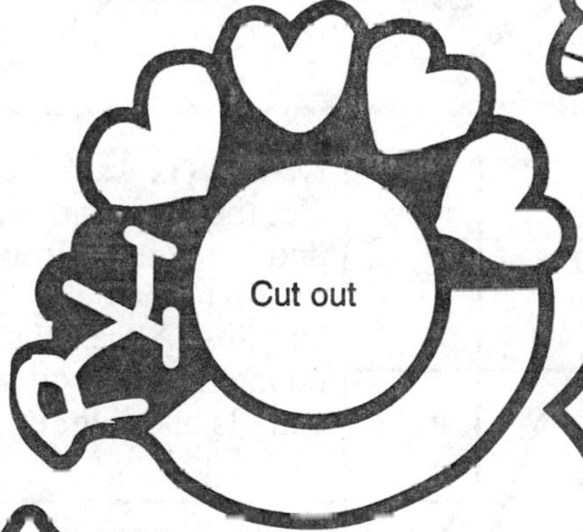

Get Well Napkin Ring

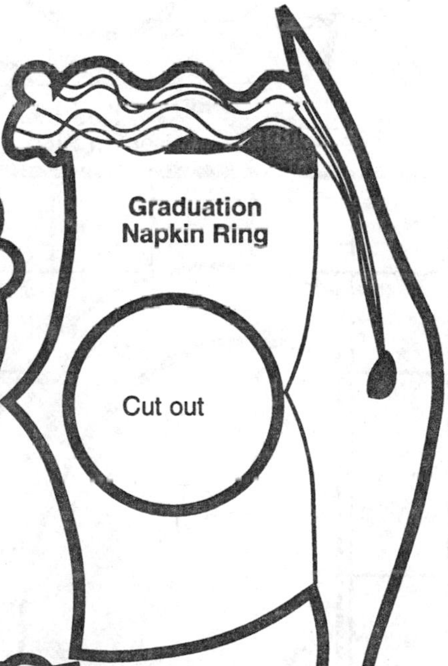

Spring Flower Napkin Ring

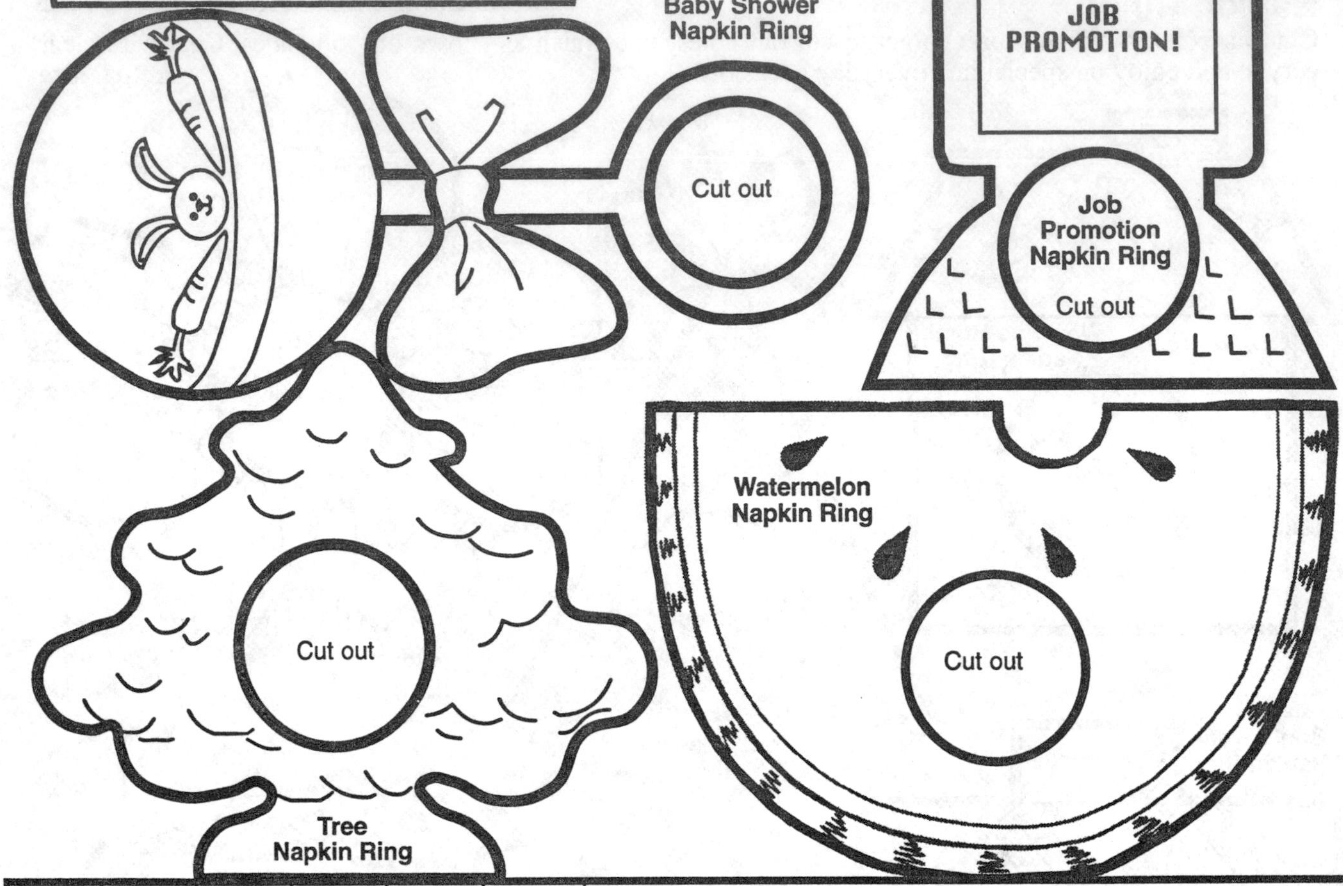

Mallard Dresser Tray

Cut the back and tray from 1/2" wood. Cut the lip of the tray and the cattails from 1/4" wood. Sand all of the pieces. Glue the lip to the outer edge of the tray. Paint all of the pieces with acrylics. Attach the tray to the back piece with glue and 2 countersunk wood screws from behind into the tray. Glue the cattails and jute (to serve as stems) to the marked areas.

1 square = 1 inch

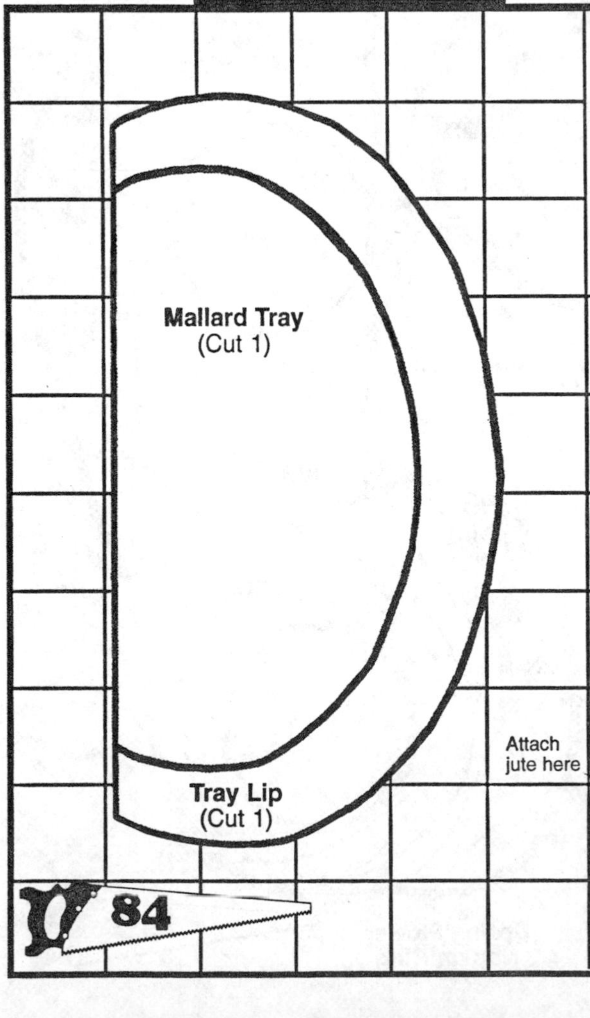

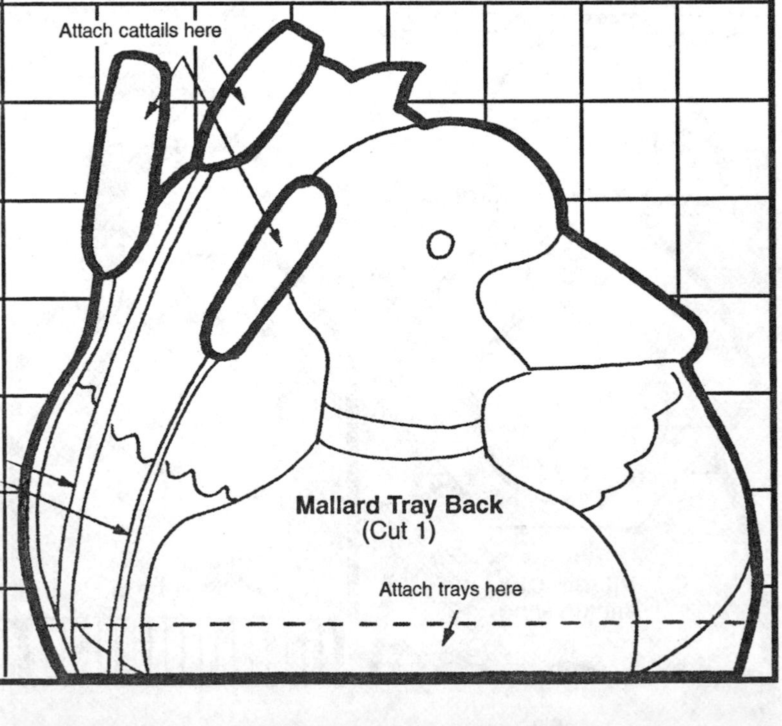

Wooden Slatted Baskets

Cut out two basket sides from 3/4" wood and nineteen slats from 1/2" or thinner wood for each basket. Slats are usually stained. Place slats on spaces marked with an "X". Use small finishing nails. Baskets may be made using wooden lathe, found at a lumber yard. Just cut the lathe the desired length, and space evenly around basket. See next page for more ways to "top off" your basket.

1 square = 1 inch

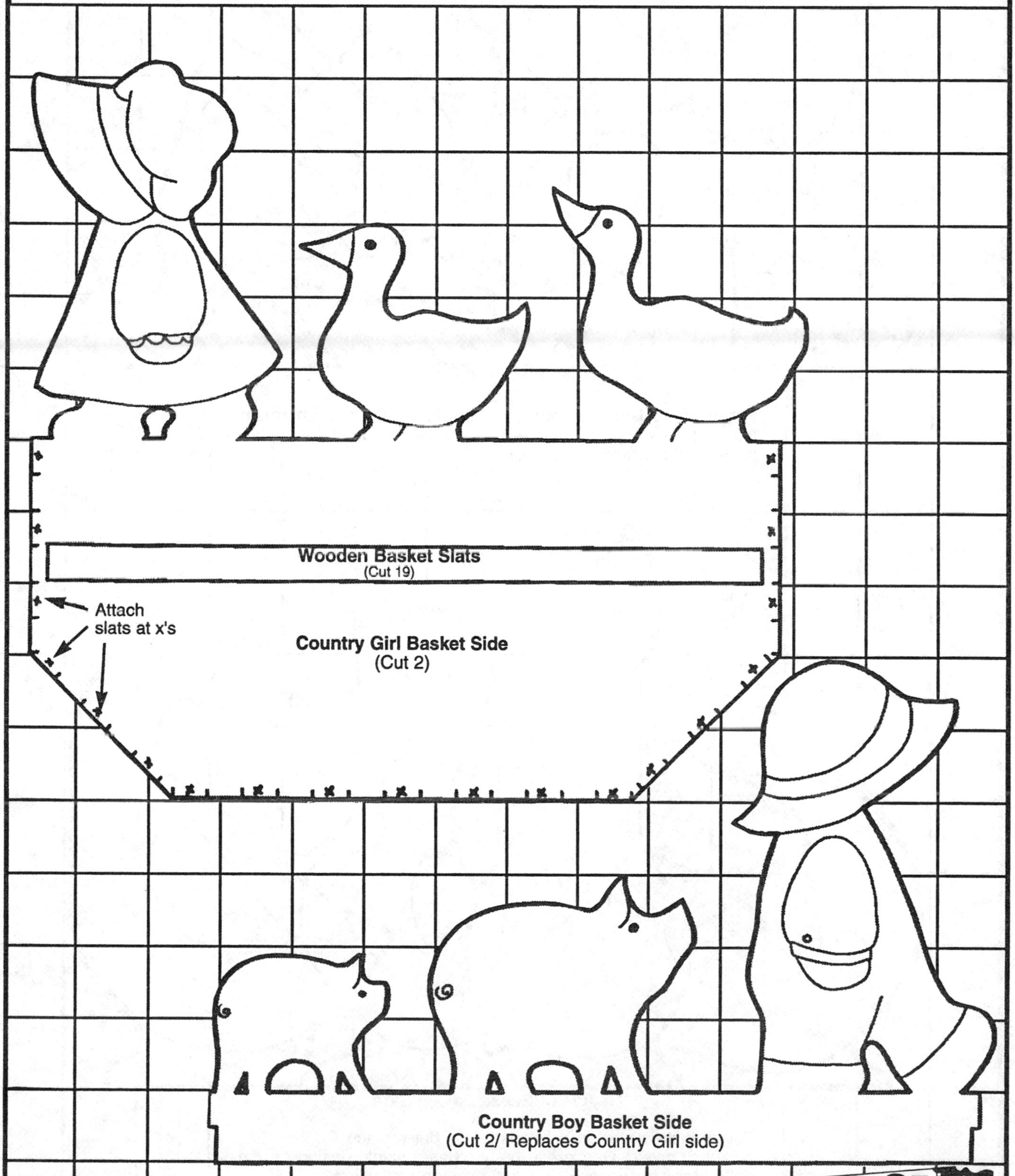

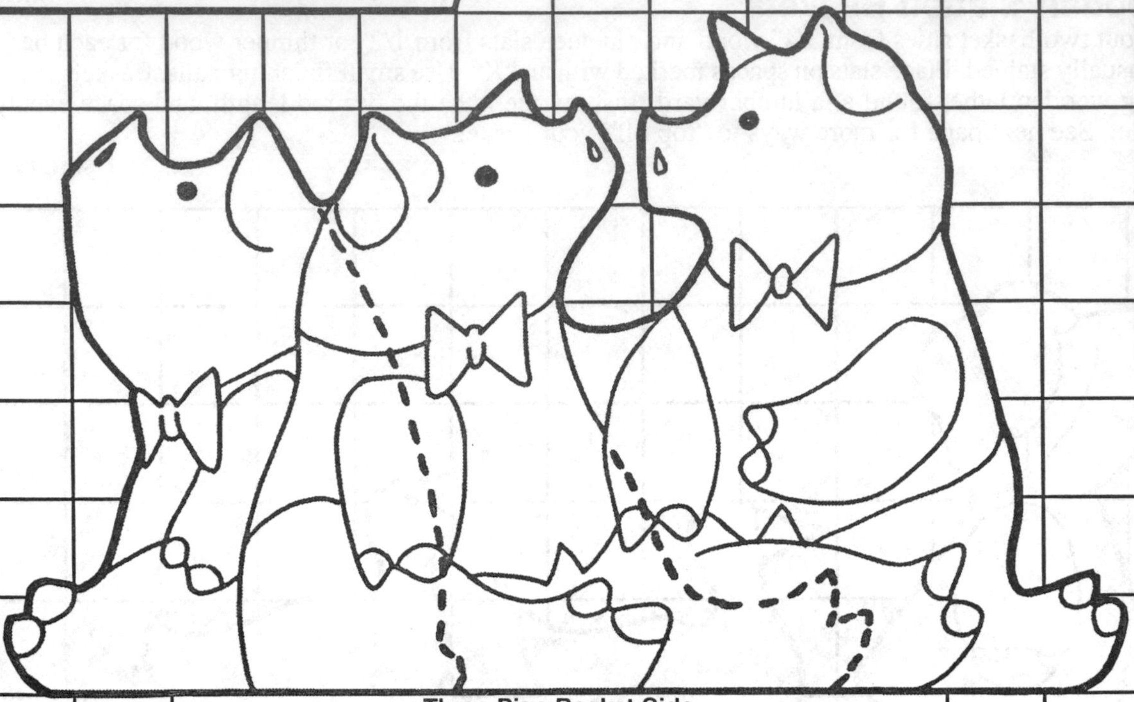

Three Pigs Basket Side
(Cut 2)
Follow instructions on previous page, but replace Country Girl side with pigs. Pigs can be used as a single design or use dotted lines to cut each pig separately for a grouping.

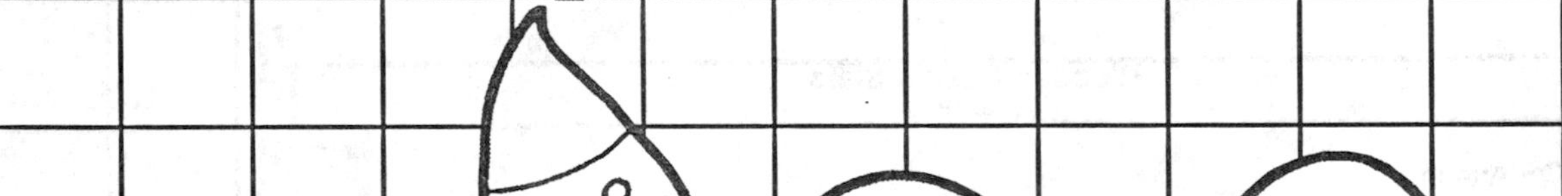

Gaggle of Geese Basket Side
(Cut 2)
Follow instructions on previous page, but replace Country Girl side with geese. Geese can be used as a single design or use dotted lines to cut each pig separately for a grouping.

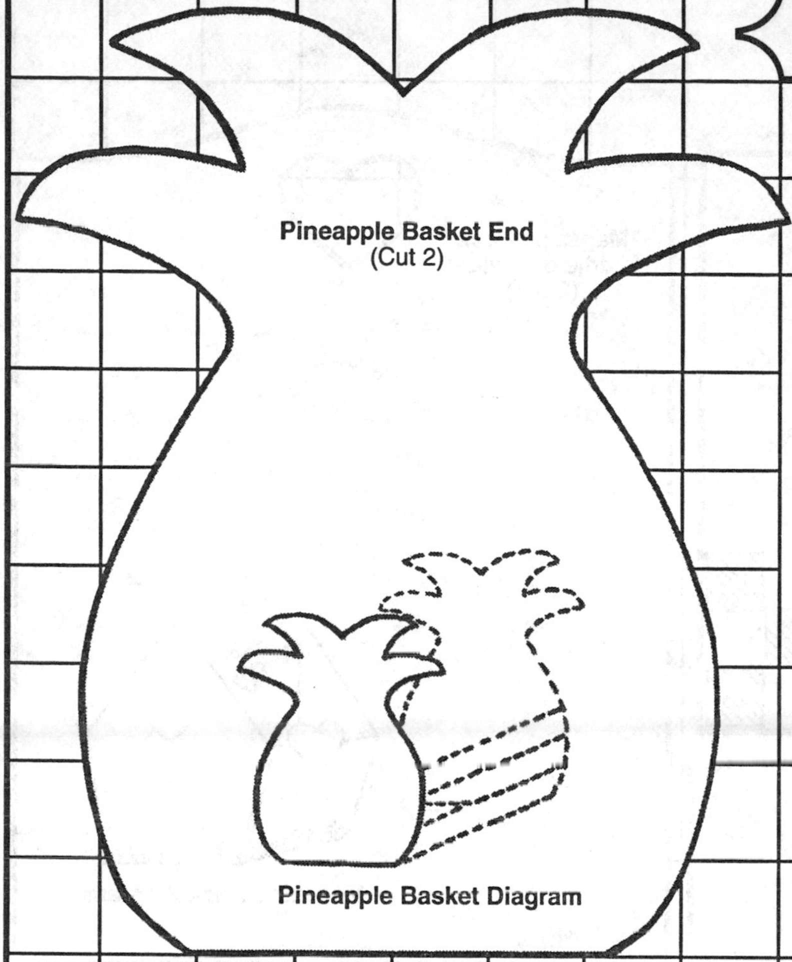

Pineapple Basket

Cut two basket sides from 3/4" wood. Cut seven slats (3 for the bottom and 2 on each side) from 1/4" wood. Sand edges well. Paint in pineapple colors or use wood stain. Seal with clear acrylic or varnish.

1 square = 1 inch

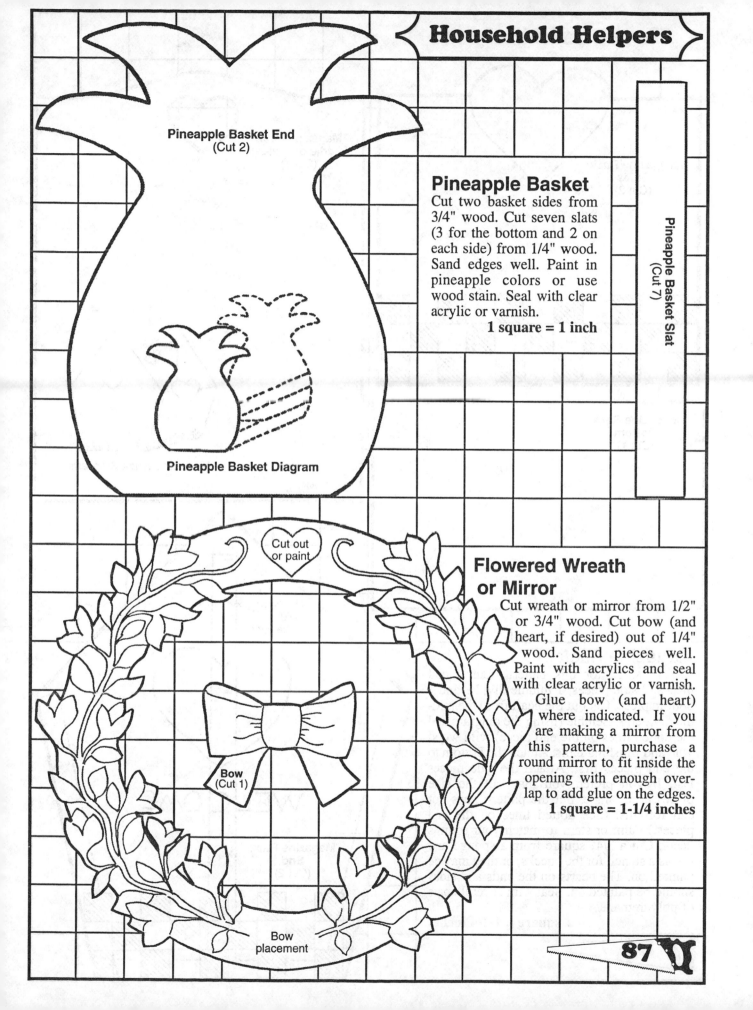

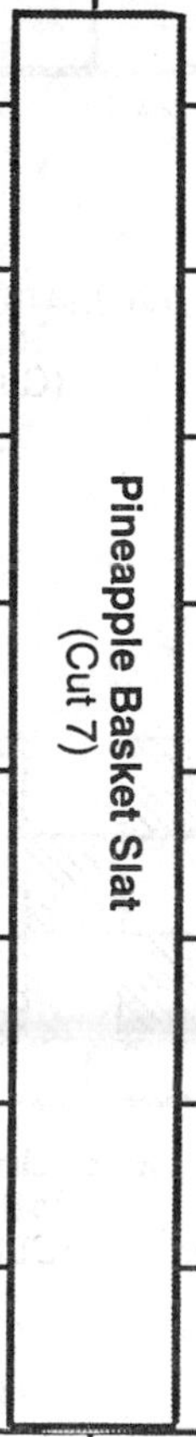

Flowered Wreath or Mirror

Cut wreath or mirror from 1/2" or 3/4" wood. Cut bow (and heart, if desired) out of 1/4" wood. Sand pieces well. Paint with acrylics and seal with clear acrylic or varnish. Glue bow (and heart) where indicated. If you are making a mirror from this pattern, purchase a round mirror to fit inside the opening with enough overlap to add glue on the edges.

1 square = 1-1/4 inches

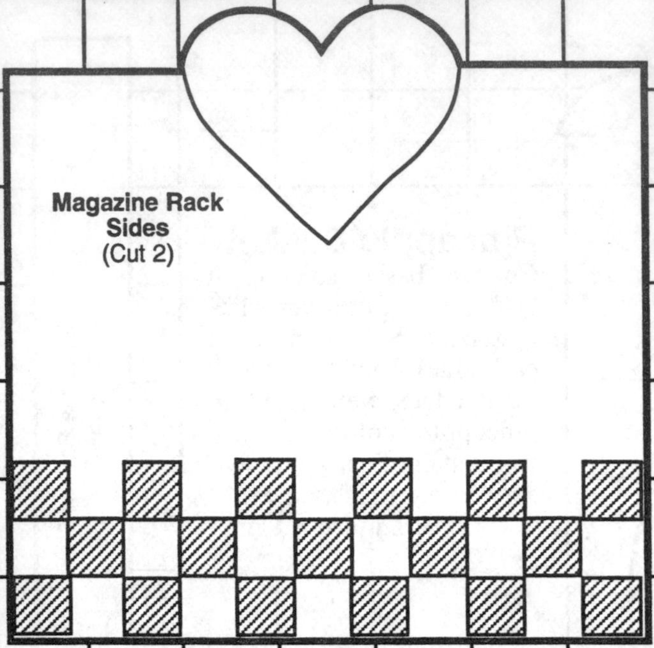

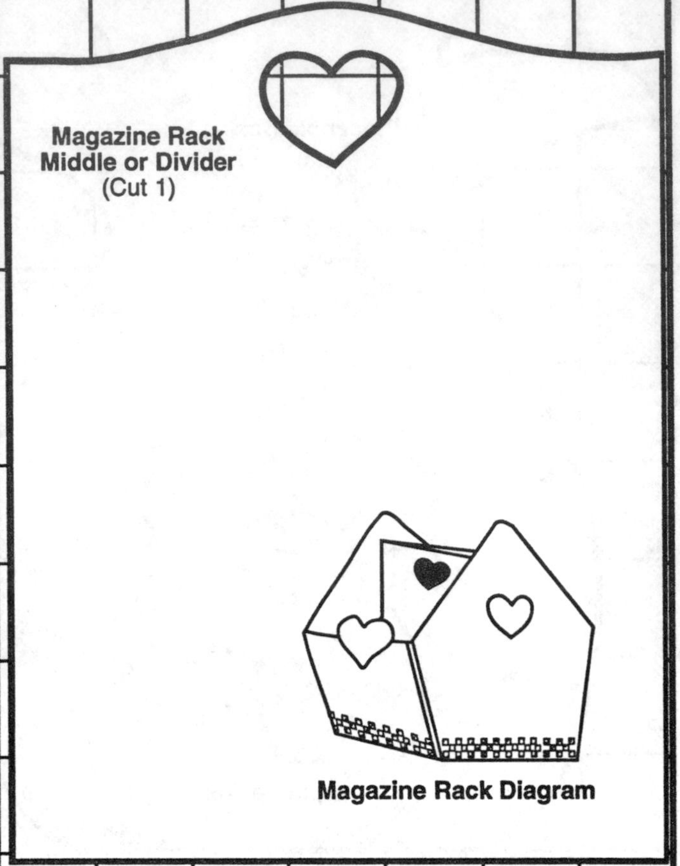

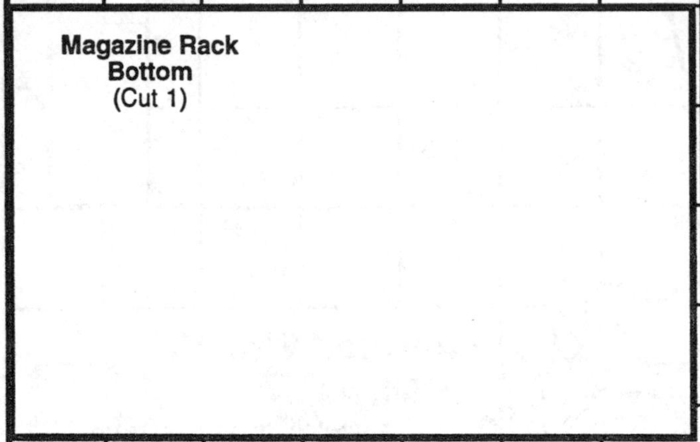

Magazine Rack

Use 1" stock for this pattern. Cut 2 end pieces, 2 side pieces, 1 middle divider and 1 bottom piece. Cut out the heart from the middle divider. Assemble (using the diagram and the dotted lines on the end piece) with wood glue and finishing nails. Attach the bottom to the end pieces first. Attach the side pieces last. If you prefer, you may cut the side pieces at an angle, but the pattern does not call for this. (See dotted lines on the end pieces.) Paint or stain to match your room's decor. Cut a 3/4" square from a sponge and use as a stencil for the checks, or they may be painted on. The hearts on the ends and sides should be painted on. Seal with several coats of polyurethane.

1 square = 1-1/4 inches

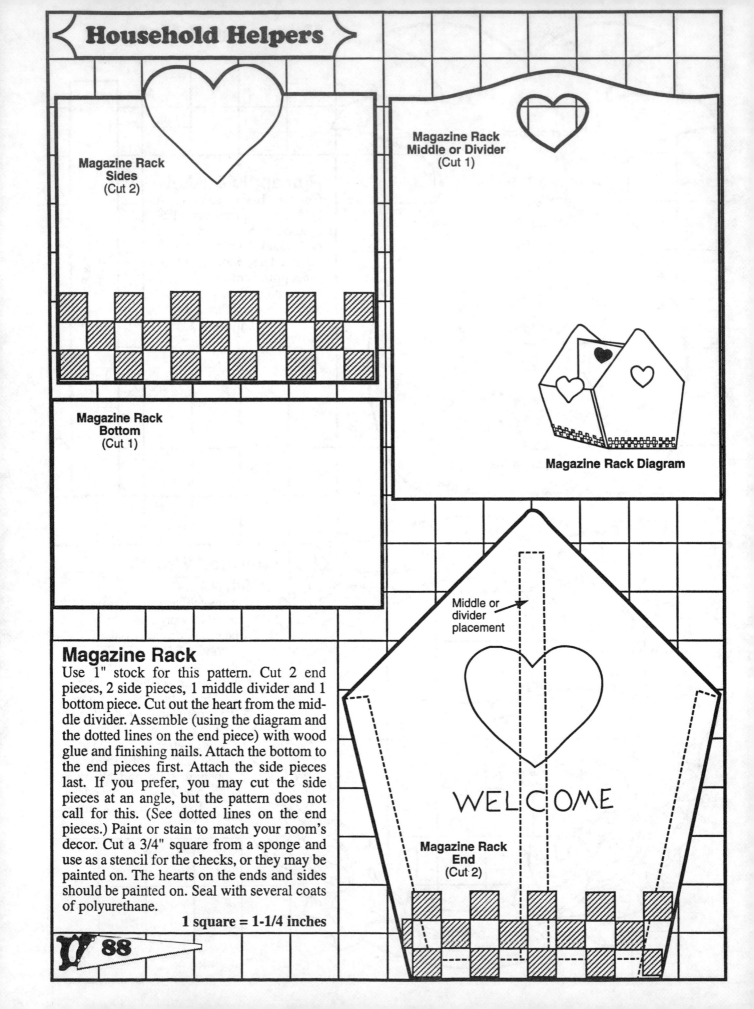

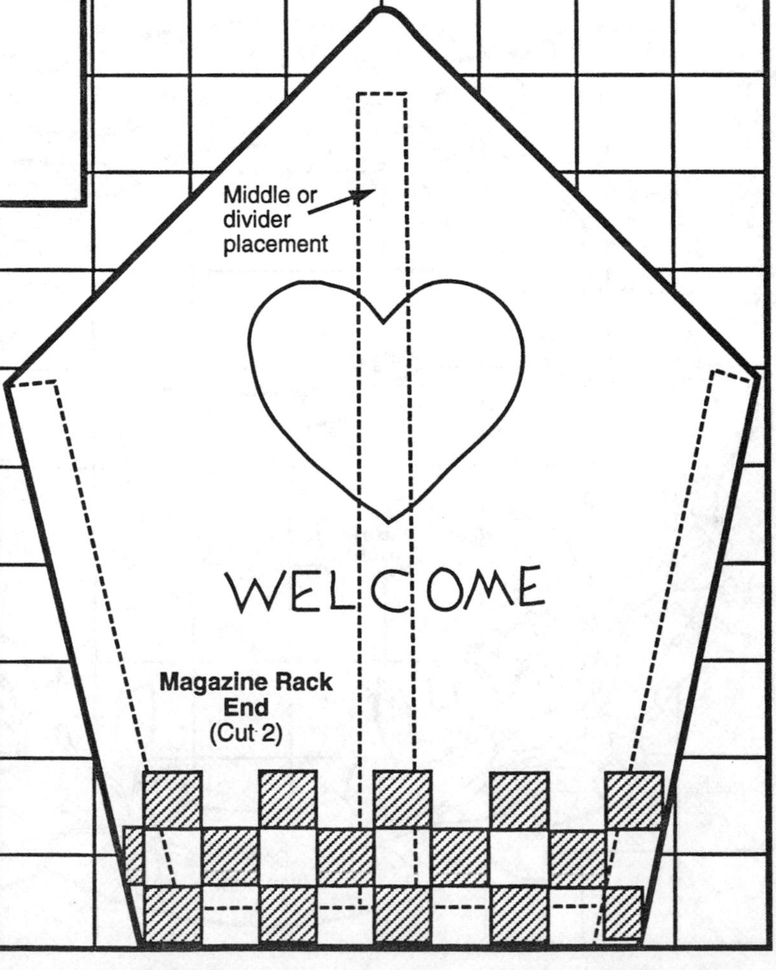

Wooden Kitchen Trivets

Cut out each trivet from 1" wood. Sand well. Cut four legs (1" in length) for each trivet from a 1/2" dowel. Drill 1/2" holes, 3/8" deep to fit dowels. Glue the legs in to stabilize them. Use a wood burner to etch in the designs. Stain, using a light wood stain and when dry, seal with butcher block oil. Note: You may want to glue some small felt circles on the bottoms of the legs to prevent scratching.

1 square = 1 inch

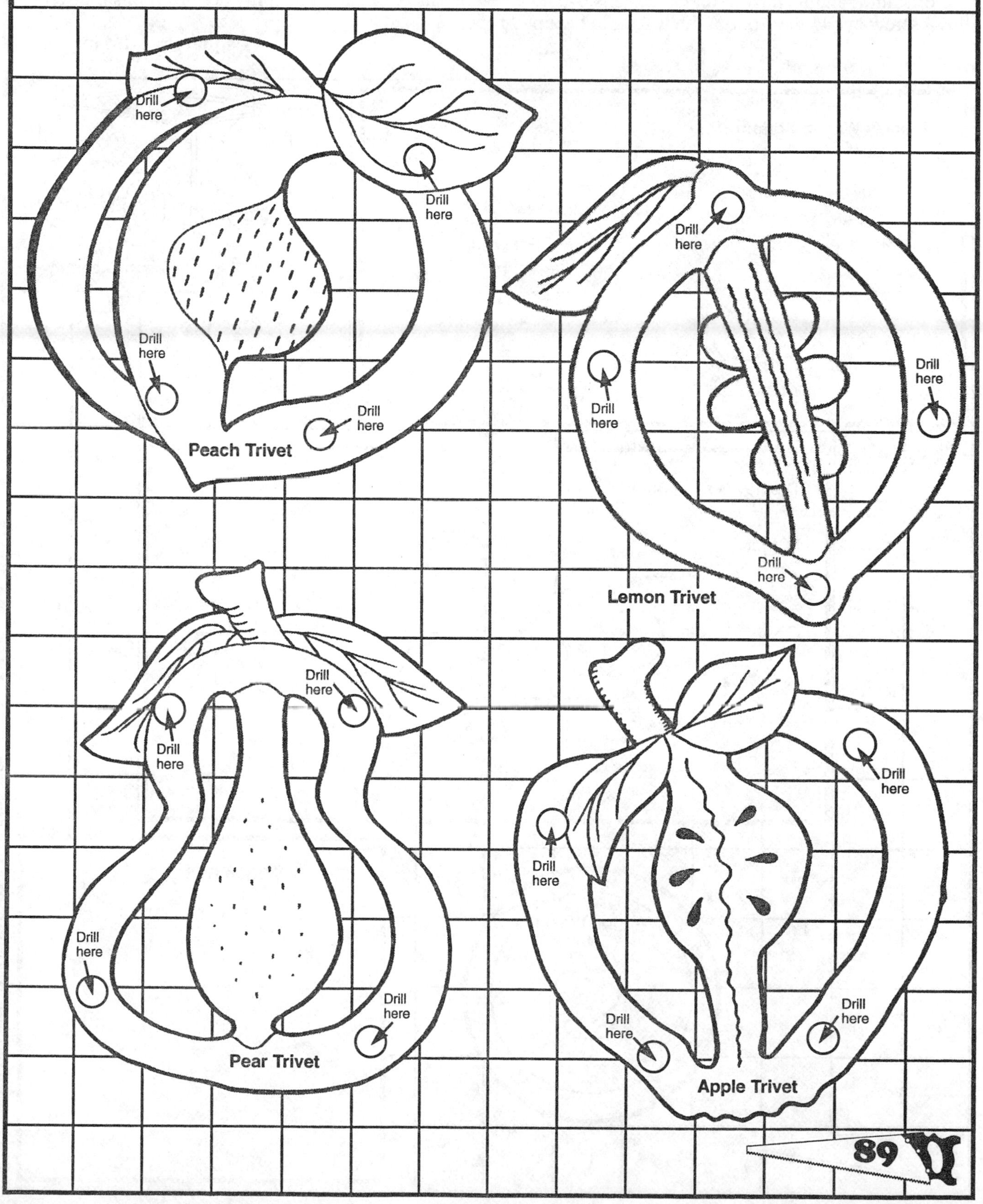

Small Display Wagon

This wagon can be just for looks, pose as a planter or used to hold collectibles. Cut two sides, two front/back pieces, one bottom and four wheels from 3/4" wood. Cut the middle heart out of the side pieces. Assemble with finishing nails using butt joints. Attach the wheels with screws. Paint with acrylics, or stain it and then paint on the designs. Apply several coats of brush-on or spray acrylic varnish. Insert a screw eye to the front of the wagon to tie a pull rope.

1 square = 1-1/4 inches

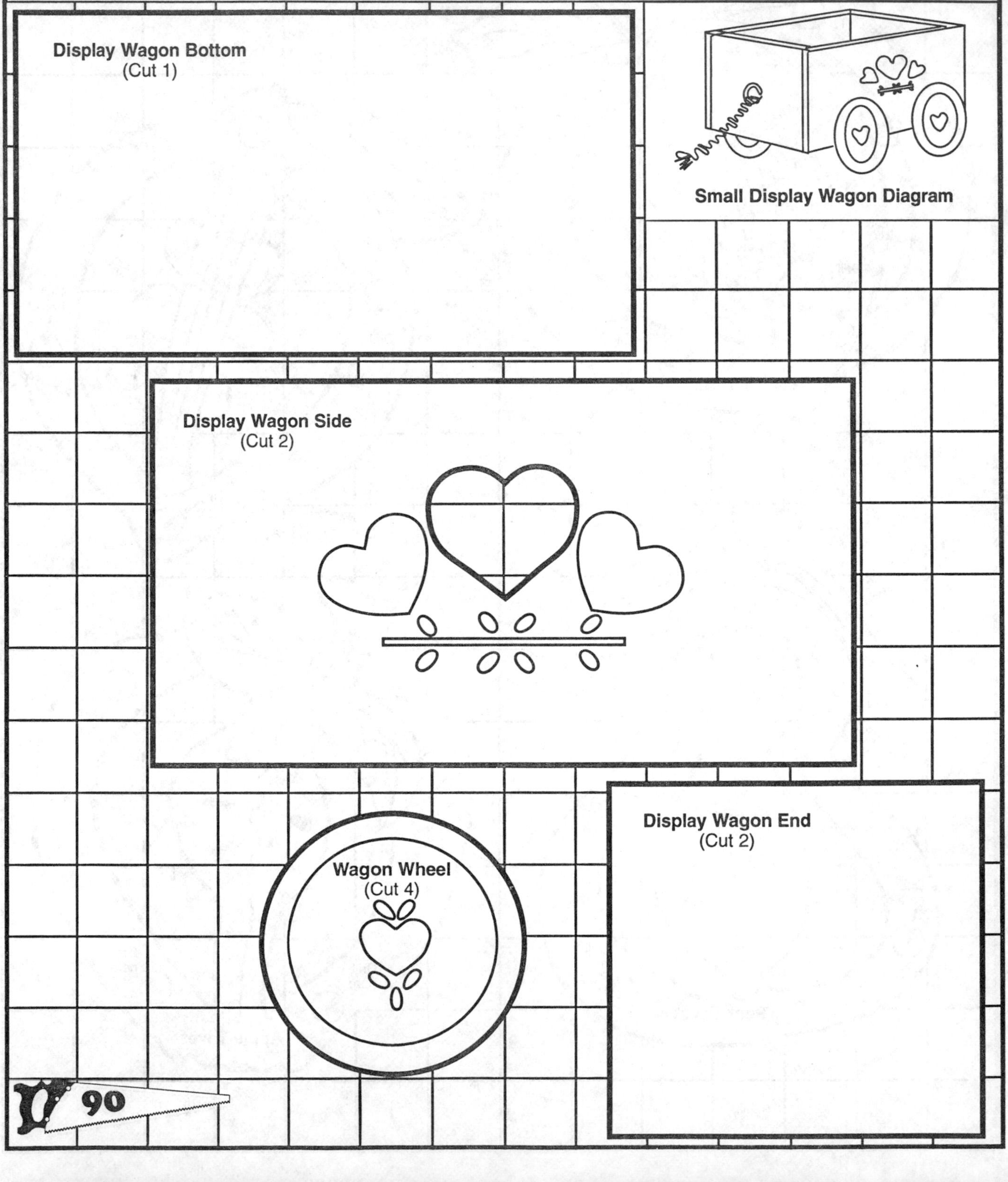

Little Helper Stool

Cut all of the pieces for this stool from 3/4" wood. Cut out the hearts on the side aprons and legs. Sand all of the pieces before assembly. Countersink wood screws and use glue for added strength. Plug all of the screw holes with dowel plugs. Stain or paint as desired. Apply a polyurethane sealer.

1 square = 1 inch

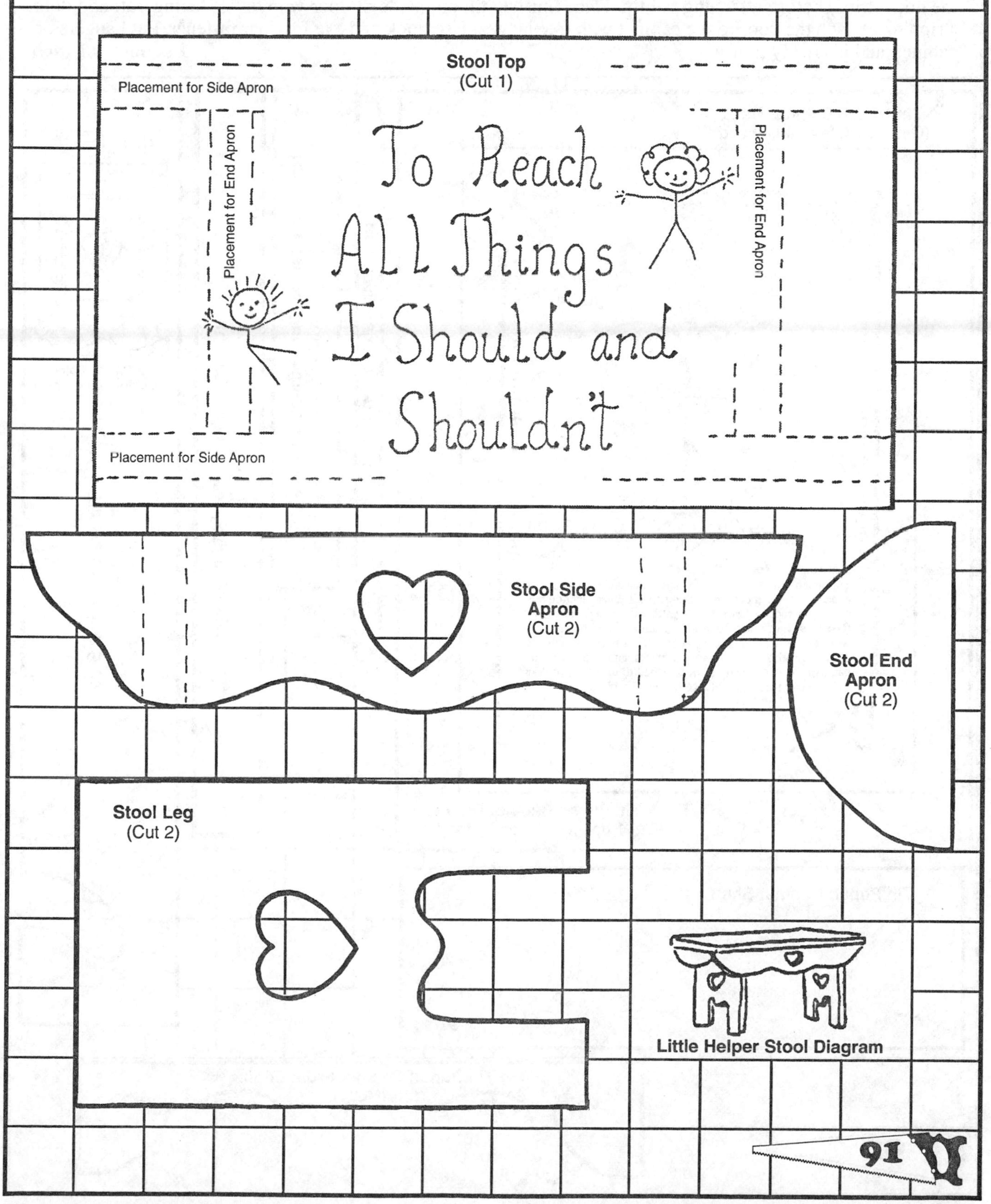

Tin Punch Spice Cabinet

Cut all pieces except the back from 1/2" wood. Using thin wood for the back will eliminate excessive weight on the wall. Assemble cabinet, attaching shelves to sides. (Top shelf will be the top of the cabinet.) Attach front edging and top trim (See diagram). Finish the tin punching using the instructions, and assemble the door. Use door sides and top, attach in corners with corrugated fasteners. Stain or paint entire cabinet (including the door strips) before attaching the tin. Place finished tin on inside of door with tin art facing out, add door stripping. Attach the door to the cabinet with free hinges. Use hook and eye for door fastener. Put hangers on cabinet, and it's ready to use.

1 square = 1 inch

Instructions for Tin Punch:
Tin punch may be done with a hammer and nail, or an ice pick. Draw punch pattern on thin paper. Center paper on precut tin and tape in place. Punch pattern through paper and tin (Use a stack of newspaper underneath to prevent damage to work area.) Remove paper pattern. If tin is bent or curved, place a towel over tin to prevent marks, and gently tap with hammer. Now it's ready to be attached to underside of door strips. Rough side should face inside of cabinet.

— CHAPTER EIGHT —

LETTERING

Fancy Lettering
1 square = 1 inch
or adjust size as needed

Letters and Signboards

Letters are provided on a grid so that you can enlarge them to the size you need to make your sign. Each square on the grid measures 1/2". Using this measurement as a guide, enlarge each letter on graph or tracing paper and cut from 1/4" exterior grade plywood, if using outdoors. Letters may be painted before attaching to the signboard to make painting easier. Stain or paint the signboard and coat with plenty of outdoor polyurethane to keep your sign from weathering.

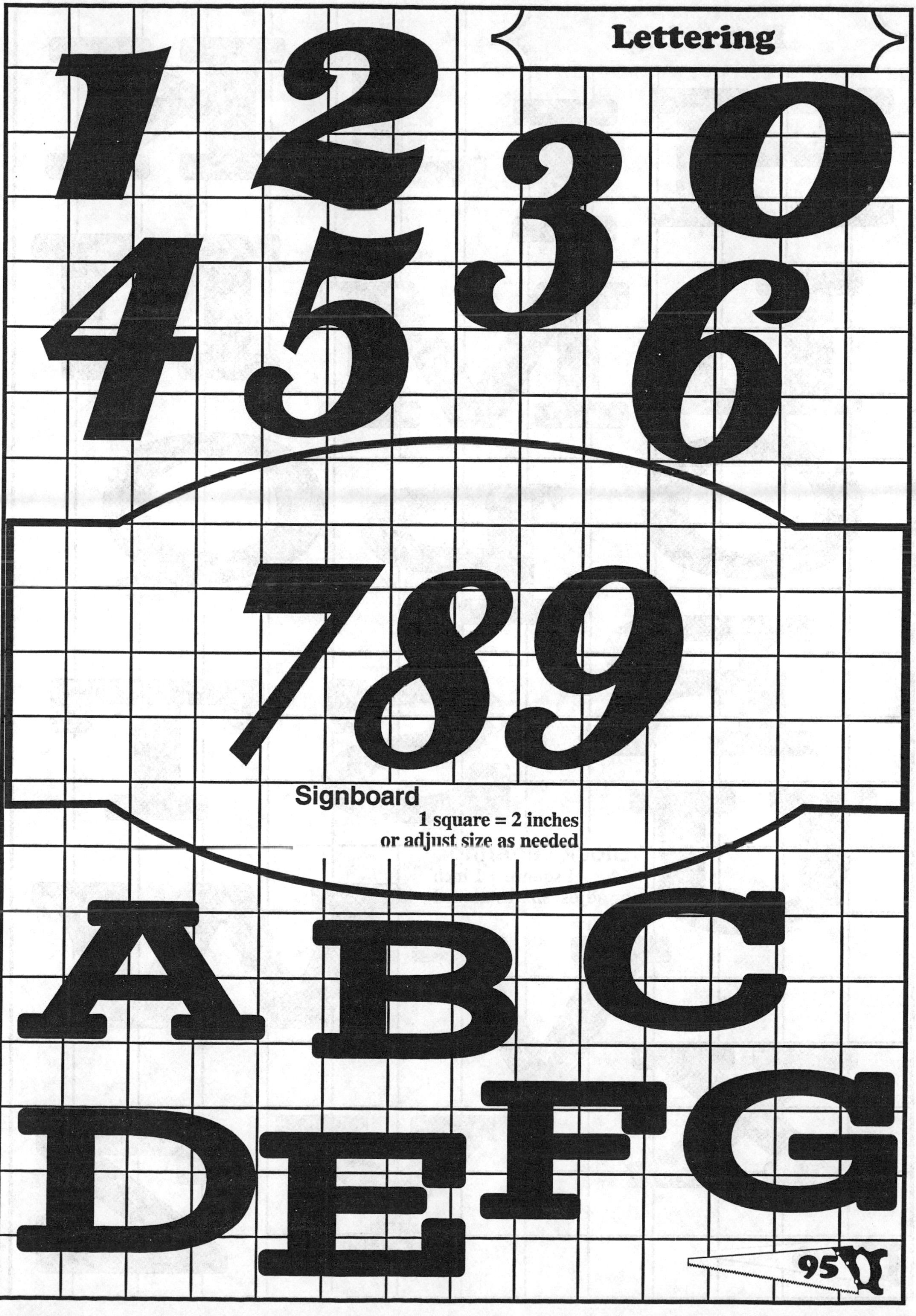
1 2 3 0
4 5 6
7 8 9
Signboard
1 square = 2 inches
or adjust size as needed
A B C
D E F G

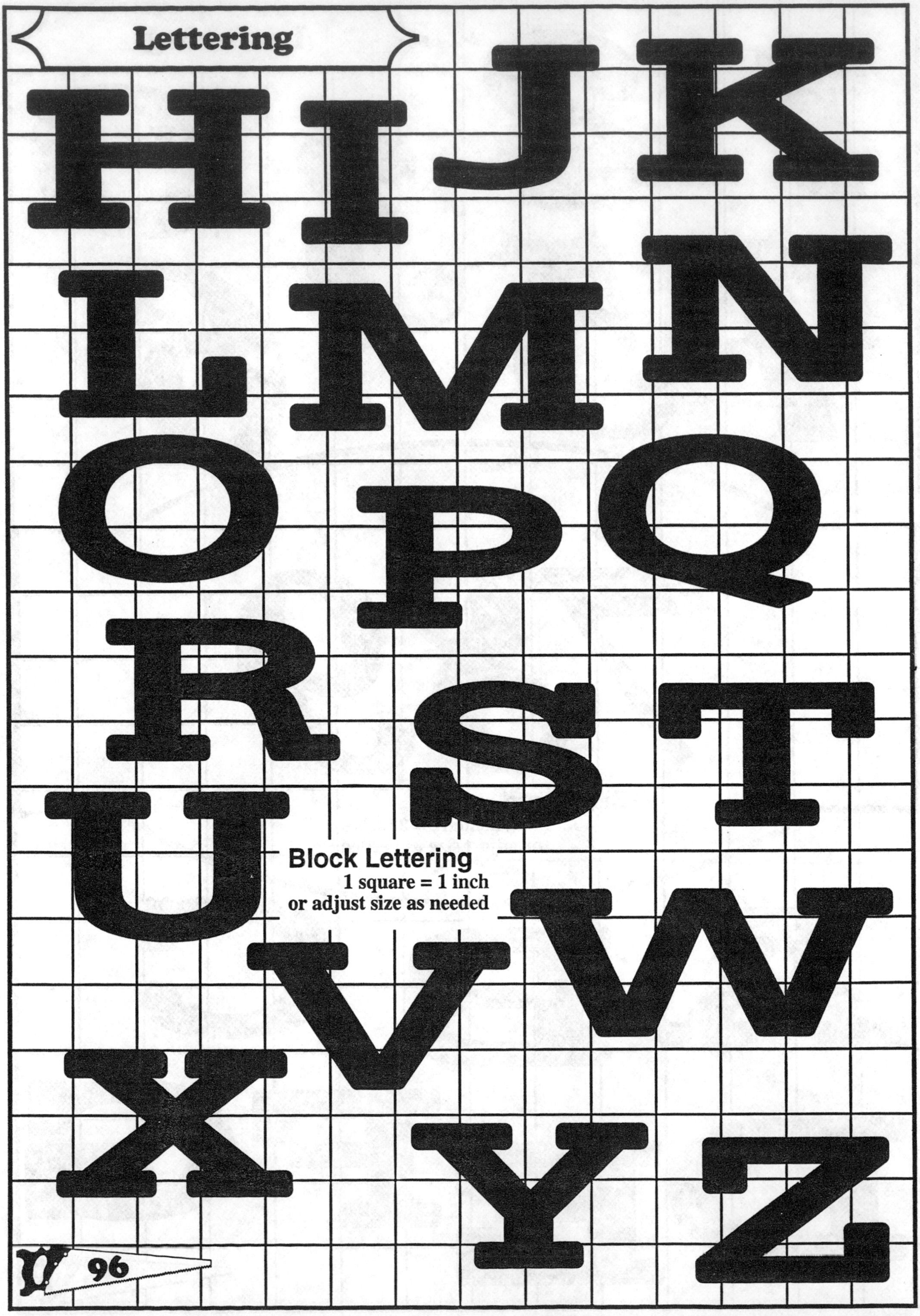

Block Lettering
1 square = 1 inch
or adjust size as needed

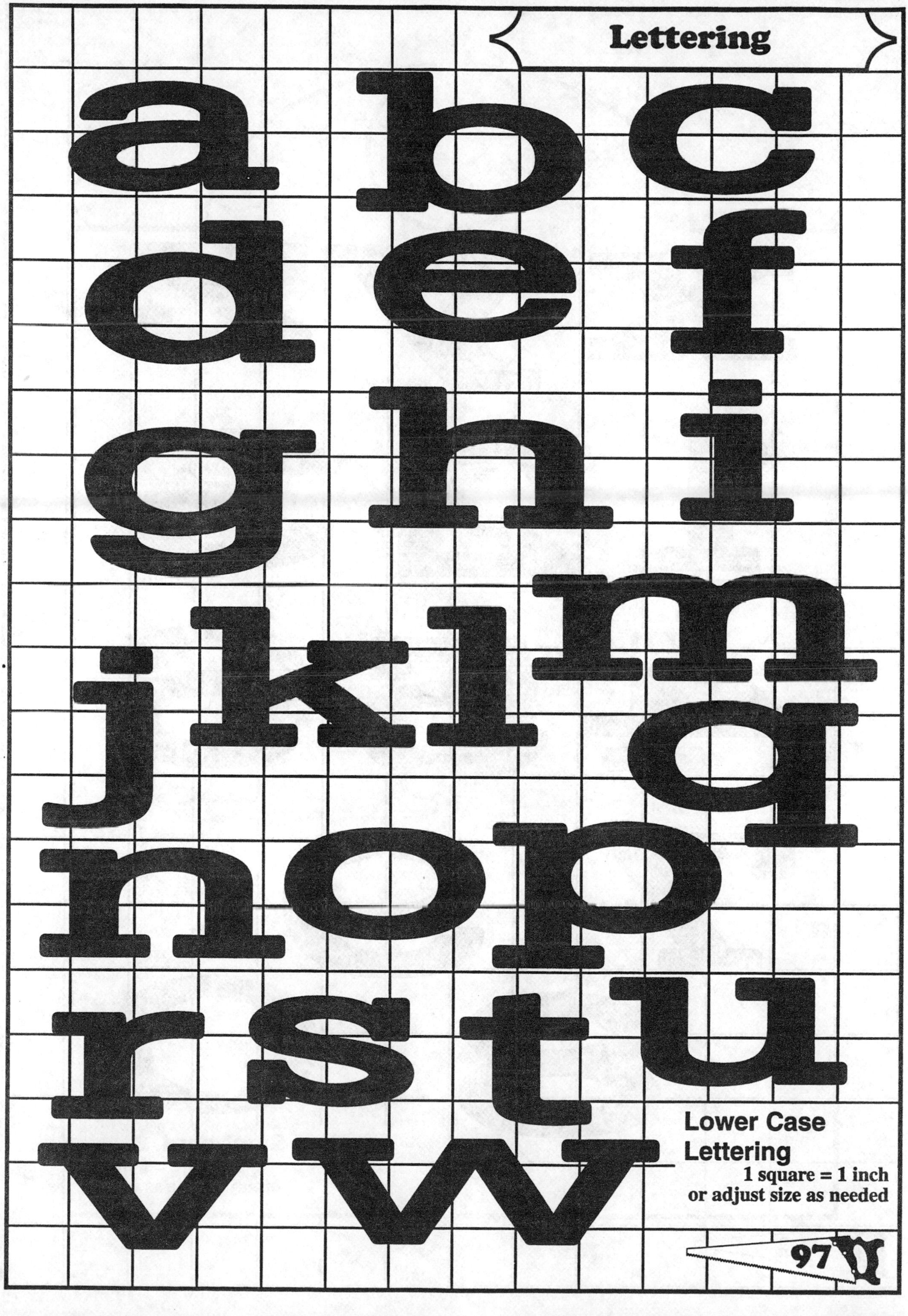

Lower Case Lettering

1 square = 1 inch
or adjust size as needed

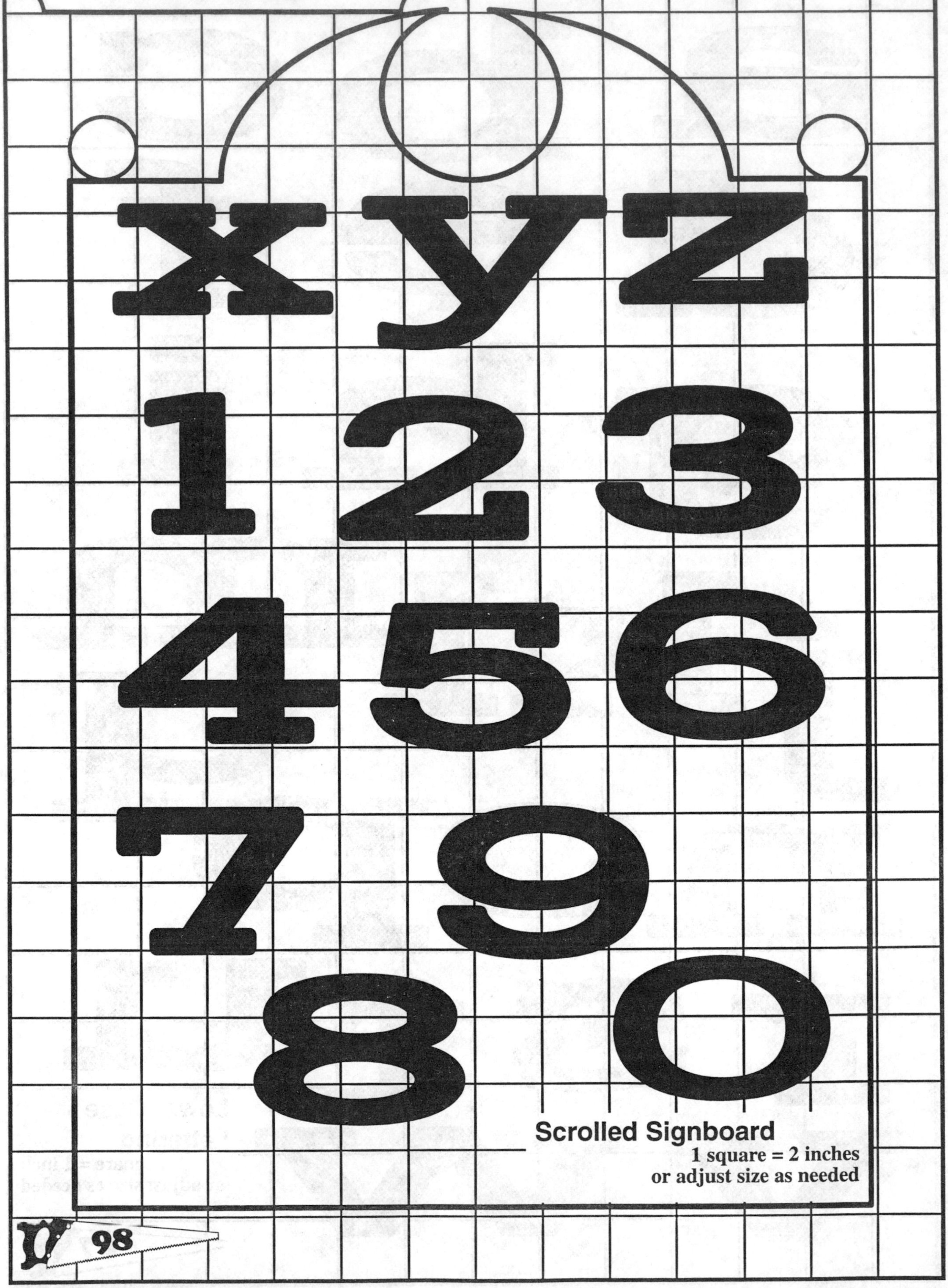

Scrolled Signboard
1 square = 2 inches
or adjust size as needed

Colonial Signboard

1 square = 2 inches
or adjust size as needed

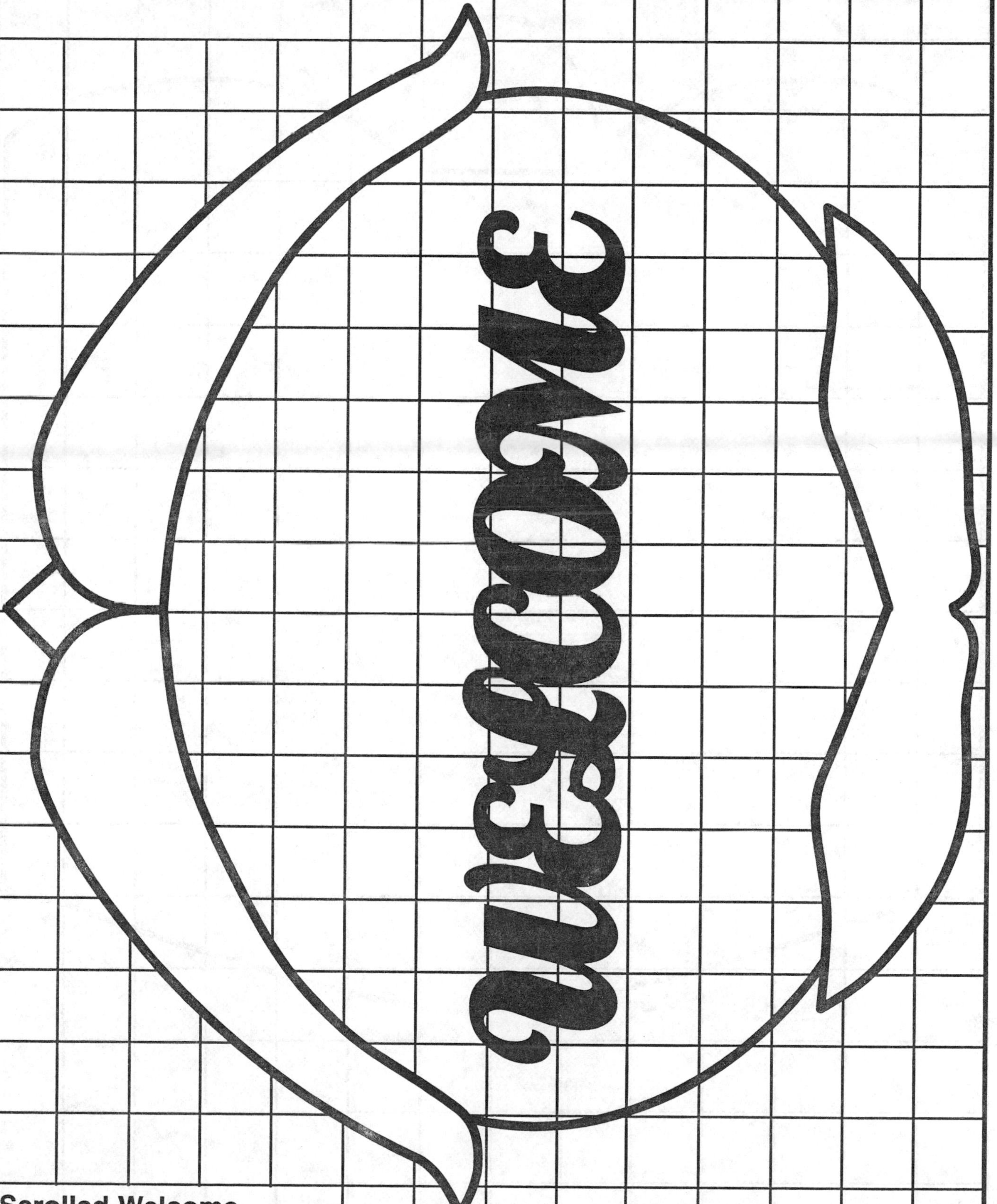

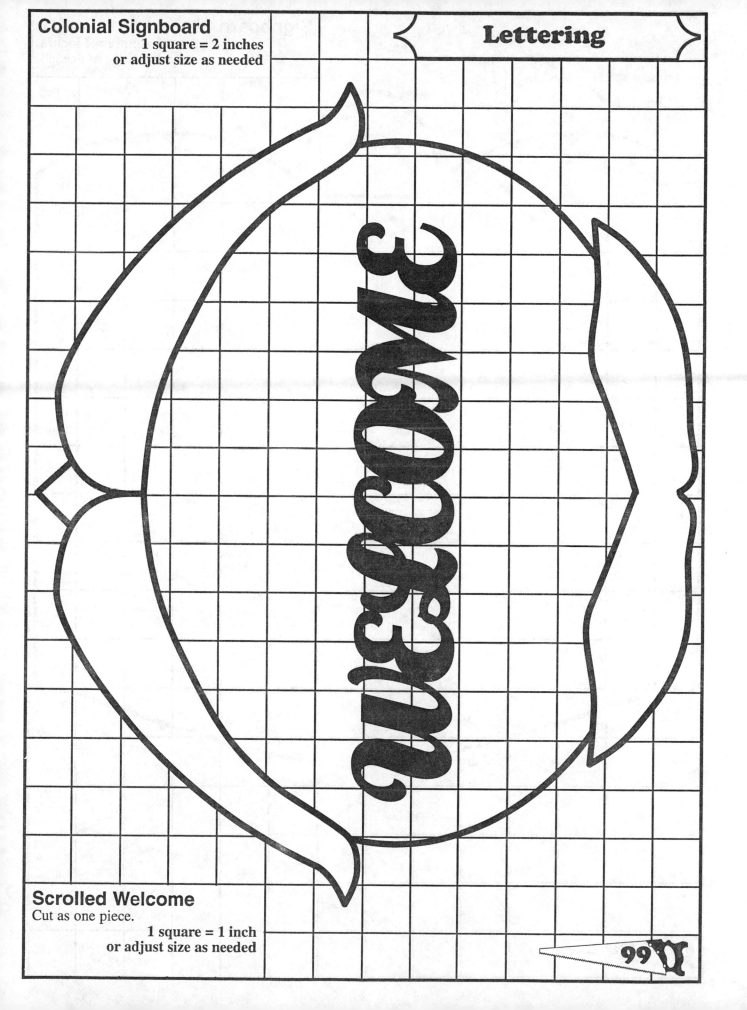

Scrolled Welcome

Cut as one piece.

1 square = 1 inch
or adjust size as needed

Lettering

Signboard

1 square = 2 inches
or adjust size as needed

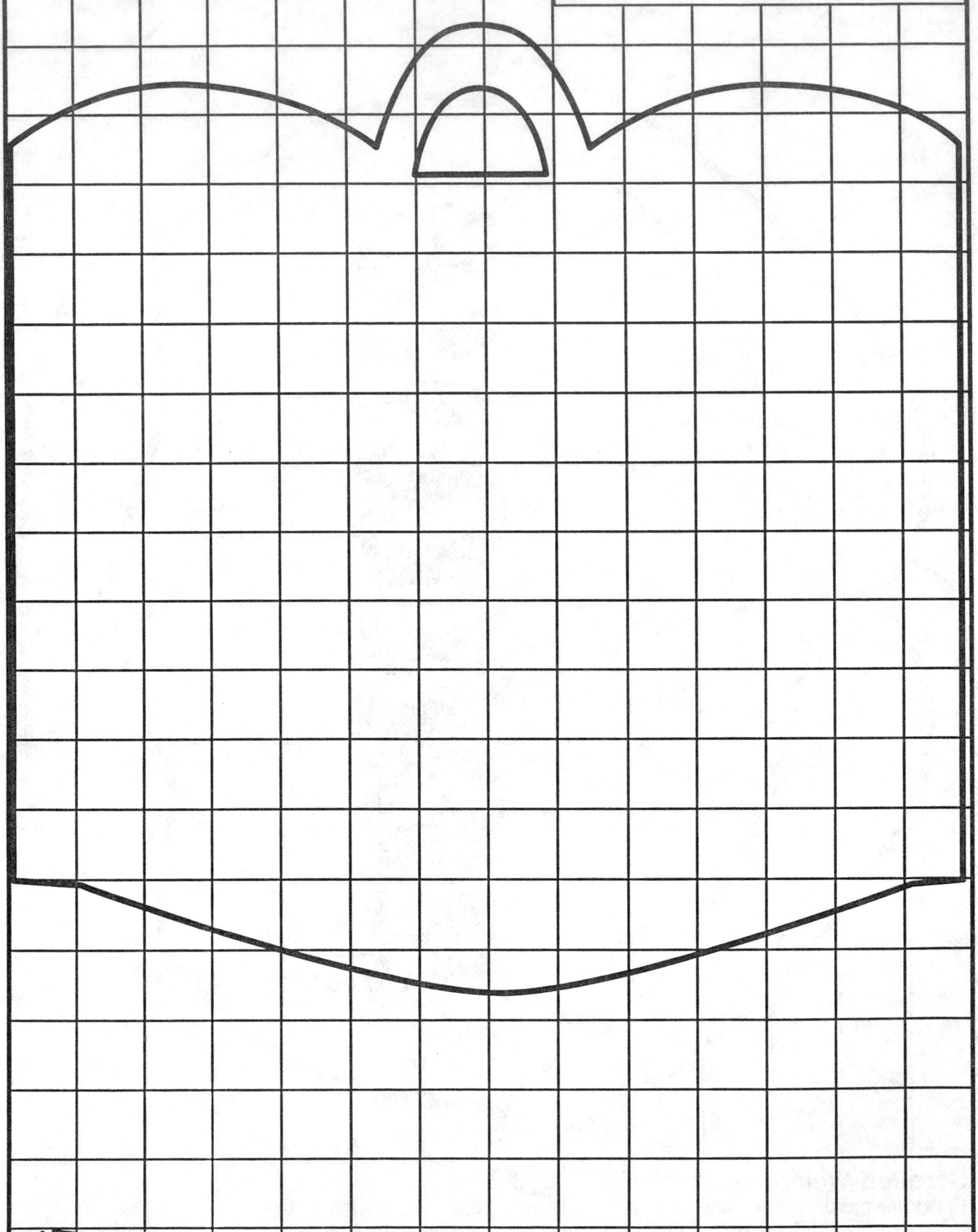

— CHAPTER NINE —

OUTDOOR PROJECTS

New Arrival Bunny

Cut this cute and clever baby announcement from 3/8" exterior grade plywood. Cut two stakes from a 1" x 2" length of wood which you will attach to the back of the finished design for insertion into the ground. Pre-drill the pattern and stakes in the areas indicated. Sand and attach the pieces with wood glue. Base coat the pattern. Paint with acrylic paints. Seal with several coats of outdoor grade polyurethane. Insert the stakes into the ground then attach the finished design with screws.

1 square = 2-3/4 inches

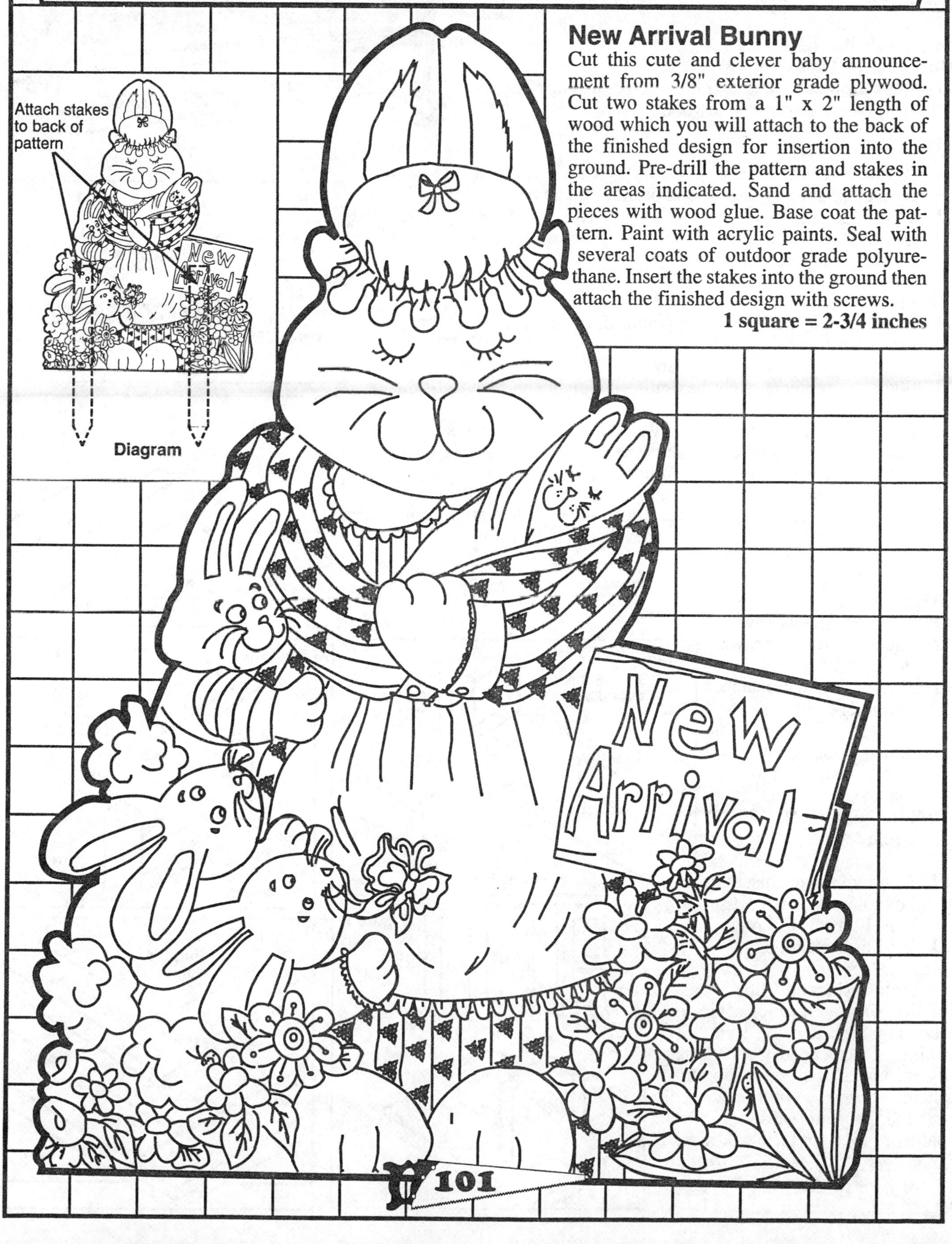

Wooden Glider Swing

Advanced skill level

Materials Needed

Base:

- ❑ 50 linear feet of pine 1" x 4", or an equivalent amount of 3/4" oak or other hardwood

Swing:

- ❑ 20 linear feet of pine 1" x 4" (or 1" x 3" if you can find it), or an equivalent amount of 3/4" oak or other hardwood
- ❑ Eight 8' lengths of pine 1" x 2", or equivalent 3/4" oak or hardwood (No waste allowance is included, so purchase longer 1" x 2"s if the ends are not perfect.)

Miscellaneous:

Note: All hardware should be galvanized, or made of brass, bronze, or stainless steel.

- ❑ Eight eyebolts with a shank length of 2"
- ❑ Eight flat washers, eight hex nuts, and eight cap nuts to fit the eyebolts
- ❑ 1-1/2" long flathead wood screws, and 2d finishing nails
- ❑ Four 8" lengths of heavy chain (be sure chain is strong enough to support the weight of several adults.)
- ❑ Eight connecting links (optional) at least as heavy as the chain
- ❑ Waterproof wood glue; wood filler; wood preservative (optional); Danish oil or other finishing materials of your choice; waterproofing wood sealer (optional)

Tools Needed

- ❑ Table or circular saw
- ❑ Saber, band or jig saw
- ❑ Power drill
- ❑ Bits: a bit that matches diameter of eyebolt shanks: pilot/countersink bit for wood screws; plug cutter attachment to match size of countersink bit (optional); 2-1/2" circle cutter attachment (optional)
- ❑ Hand mortise chisel, or keyhole saw, or mortise-chisel bit for drill press
- ❑ Pipe or bar clamps

This old-fashioned glider consists of two separate sections: the free-standing base and the swing. The swing is suspended from the base by means of four short lengths of chain. If you do not have room enough in your yard or on your patio or porch for the 5' x 2' x 2-1/2' basc, you can

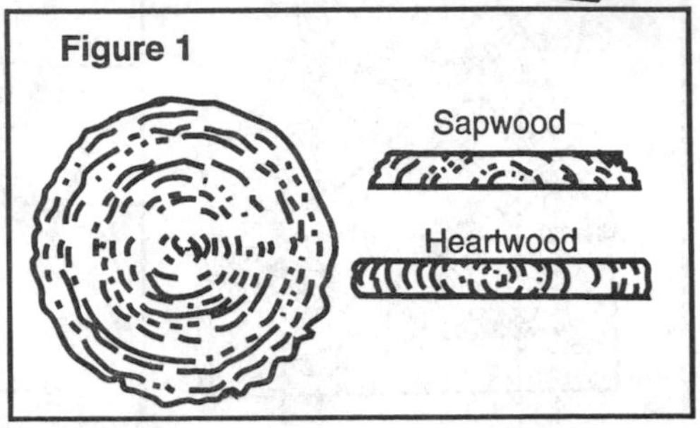

Figure 1

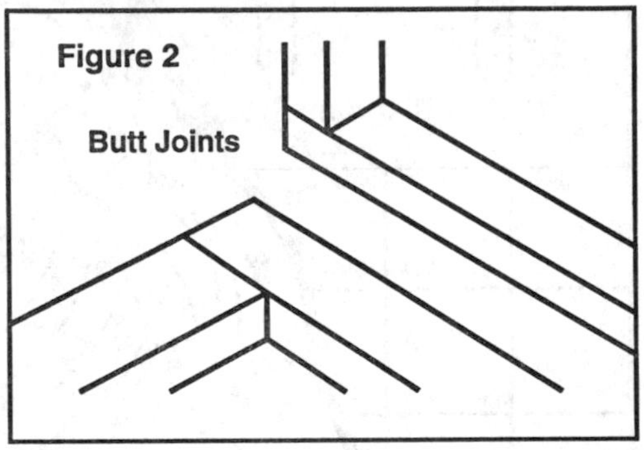

Figure 2

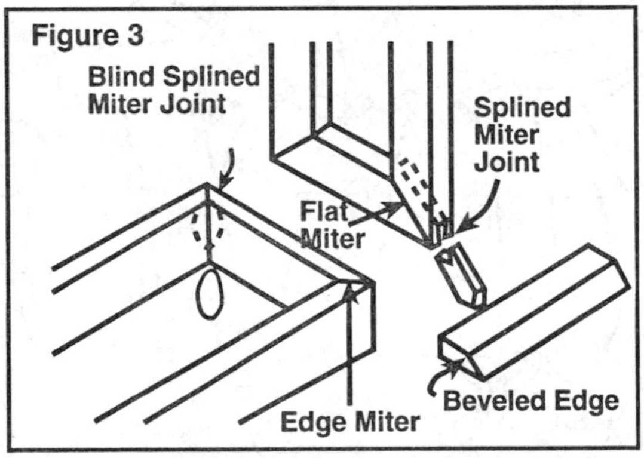

Figure 3

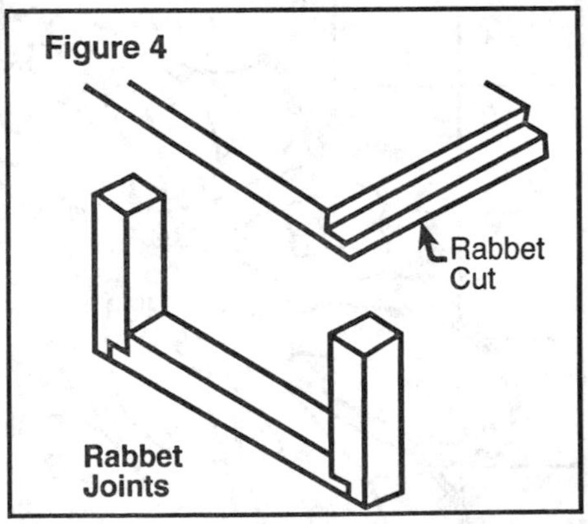

Figure 4

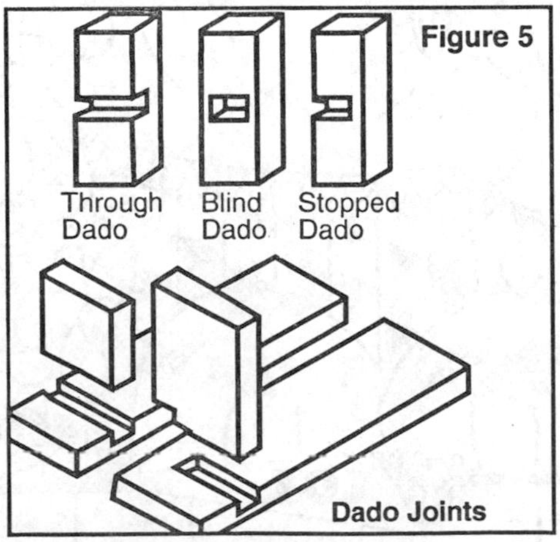

Figure 5

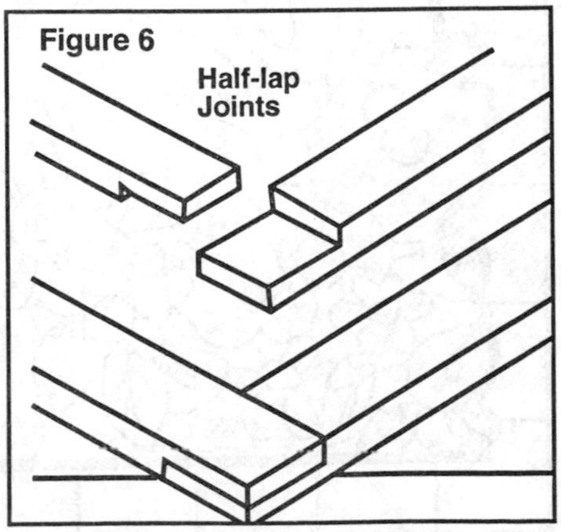

Figure 6

build the swing portion only, and hang it from your porch ceiling or from a friendly old tree.

Although this project carries an "advanced" skill rating, it really is not difficult to build. The trickiest part is cutting the interlocking joints of the base section.

We have divided the instructions into three main sections: (1) building the base, (2) building the swing, and (3) finishing and final assembly. For joints secured with screws, countersink the screws and cover the heads with plugs cut from matching stock. Recess all nails and cover with wood filler.

The Base

The base section is shown fully assembled in Figure I. It consists of two mirror image end sections, which are connected by three long braces. The pegged mortise-and-tenon joints allow you to disassemble the base for storage or transport. If you do not feel confident enough to cut the interlocking mortises and tenons, you can simply cut the braces shorter than specified, and permanently attach them to the end sections using glue and screws.

The instructions for the base are presented in two sections: (1) cutting the parts, and (2) assembly. We suggest that you read through the instructions before beginning work.

Cutting the Parts

1. Dimensions for the base parts are listed in this step. For the E, F, G, I, J, and Ks, use the patterns provided. All parts are cut from pine 1" x 4" or equivalent hardwood. We suggest that you begin by cutting the longest ones (the H and L braces), and work your way down to the smallest ones, so you'll be sure to get the most out of your wood stock. Label each part with its identifying code, for reference during assembly.

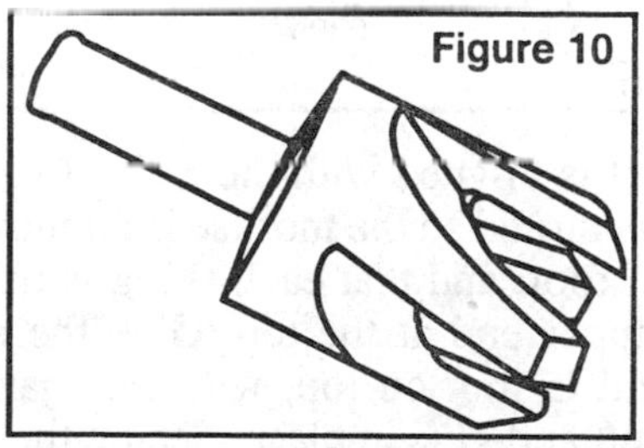
Figure 10

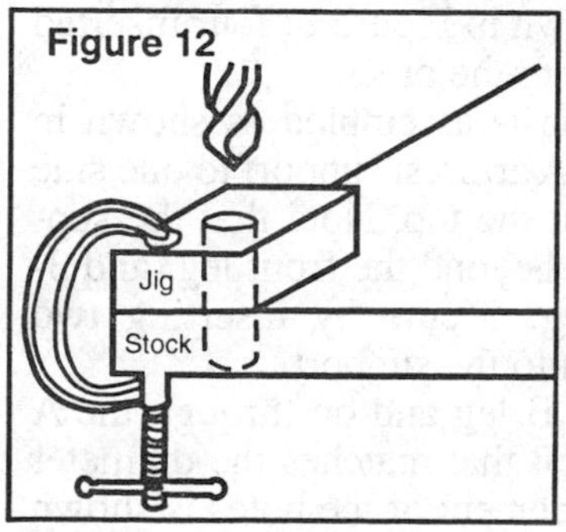

Figure 12

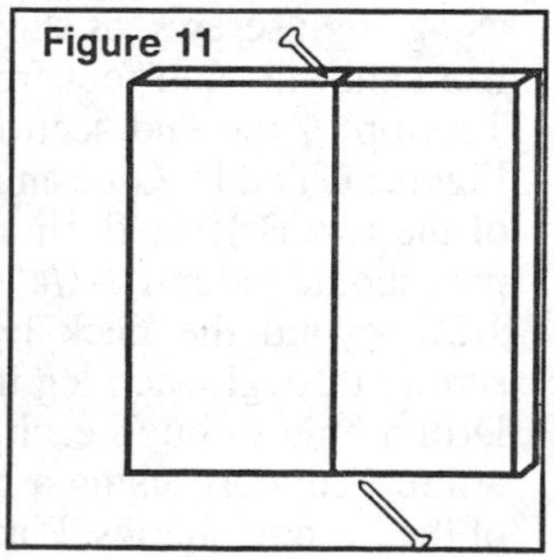
Figure 11

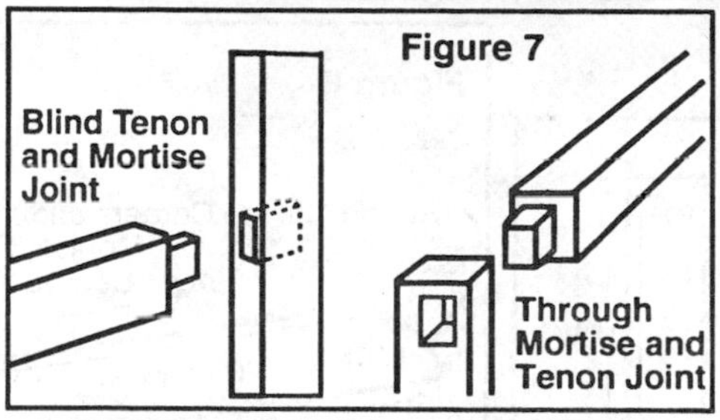

Figure 7

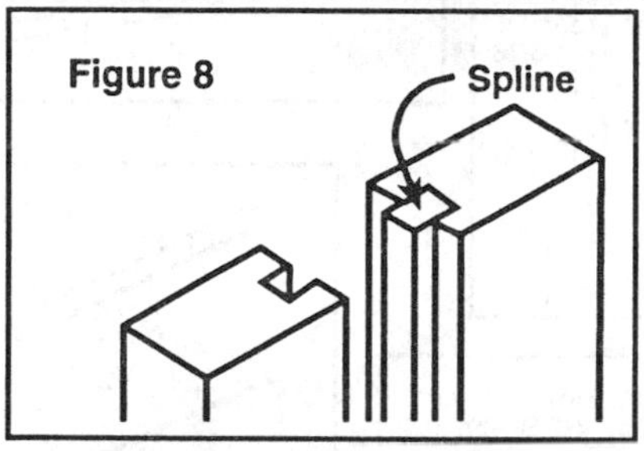

Figure 8

Figure 9

Code	Description	Dimensions	Quantity
A	Armrest Support	3-1/2" x 24"	2
B	Leg	3-1/2" x 24"	4
C	Foot	3-1/2" x 30"	4
D	Center Spacer	3-1/2" x 11"	2
E	Front Spacer	use pattern	2
F	Back spacer	use pattern	2
G	Armrest	use pattern	2
H	Lower Brace	3-1/2" x 62"	1
I	Peg	use pattern	6
J	Support Block	use pattern	2
K	Support Block	use pattern	2
L	Upper Brace	2-1/2" x 60"	2

2. Each B leg is mortised as shown in Figure A, to accommodate an upper brace tenon (see the assembly diagram, Figure I). Draw the outlines of the mortise on one of the B legs, referring to Figure A for size and placement. The mortise is centered between the long edges, but note that it is closer to one end than the other. Cut the mortise and mark the upper end of the B leg, so you won't get it upside down later on during assembly. Mortise each B leg in the same manner, using the first one as a pattern.
3. Each C foot is modified as shown in Figure B. (The mortise will accommodate the lower brace tenon, as shown in the assembly diagram, Figure 1.) You can use an E or F spacer as a pattern to round off the two top corners, being careful not to reduce the 30" length of the lower edge. Measure and mark the outlines of the mortise, referring to Figure B for size and placement. The mortise should be centered between the long upper and lower edges, but note that it is closer to one end than the other. Mark the front end of the C foot, as shown, for reference during assembly. Use the modified C foot as a guide to round off and mortise the three remaining C feet.
4. The D, E, and F spacers are used in the assembly of each foot (see Figures E

and F). Each D center spacer is mortised to match the C feet. The easiest way to get a good match is to align one set of spacers and B legs, as shown in Figure E, and place a C foot on top. Be sure that the marked front end of the foot is aligned with the E front spacer. Trace the outlines of the mortise in the foot onto the D spacer below. Mortise each D spacer in this manner.

5. We cut a recessed drinking-glass holder into each G armrest to help prevent spills when the swinging gets rambunctious. Placement of the circular holder is indicated on the armrest pattern. We used wood filler around the edge, because the plug was a little smaller than the opening. If you don't have a circle cutter, just drill through the armrest within the glass-holder outline indicated on the pattern; then use a saber, jig, or hand keyhole saw to cut along the circular outline. Rip or plane a piece of leftover 1" x 4" to a thickness of 1/4", and cut a 2-1/2" diameter circular piece from the reduced stock. Glue the plug into the hole in the armrest, flush with the bottom surface. Modify both G armrests in this manner. Note that the armrests will be mirror images of each other when they are attached to the end sections (see top-view detail diagram, Figure 1), so be sure to glue the glass-holder plugs flush with opposite surfaces of the two armrests.

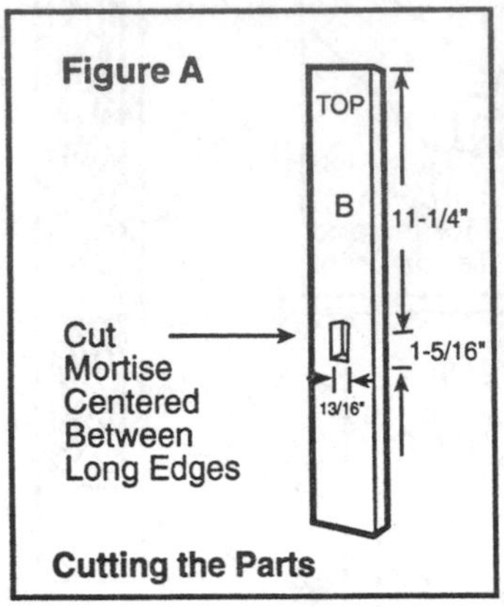

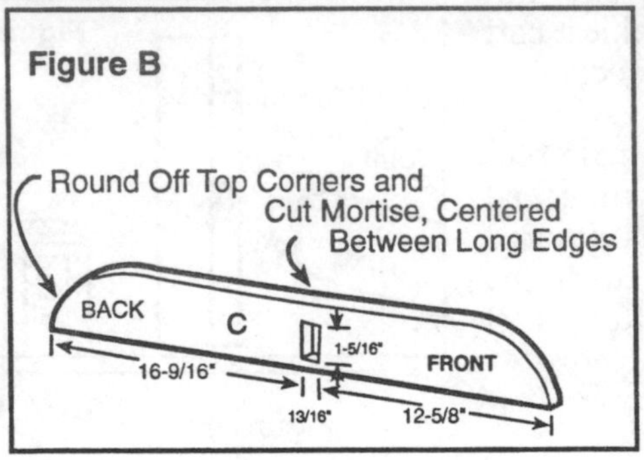

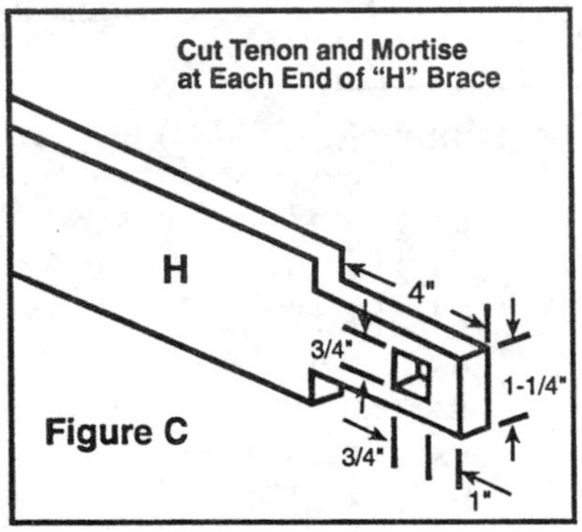

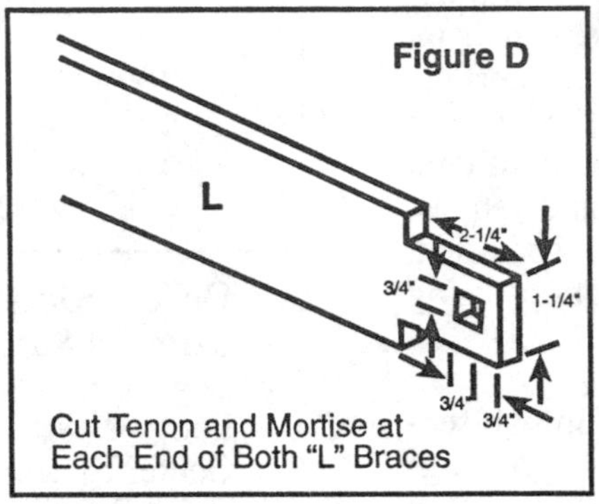

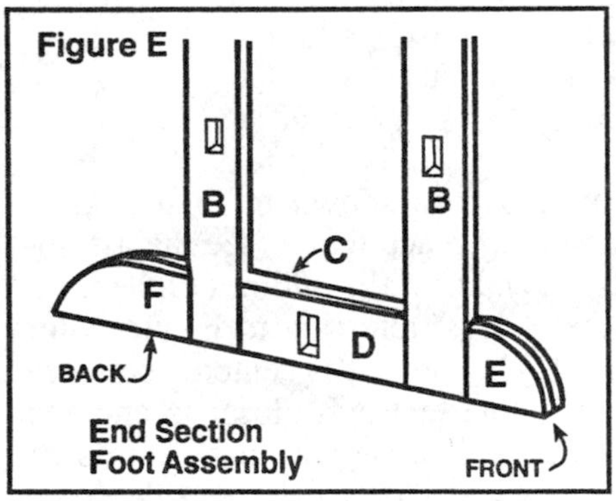

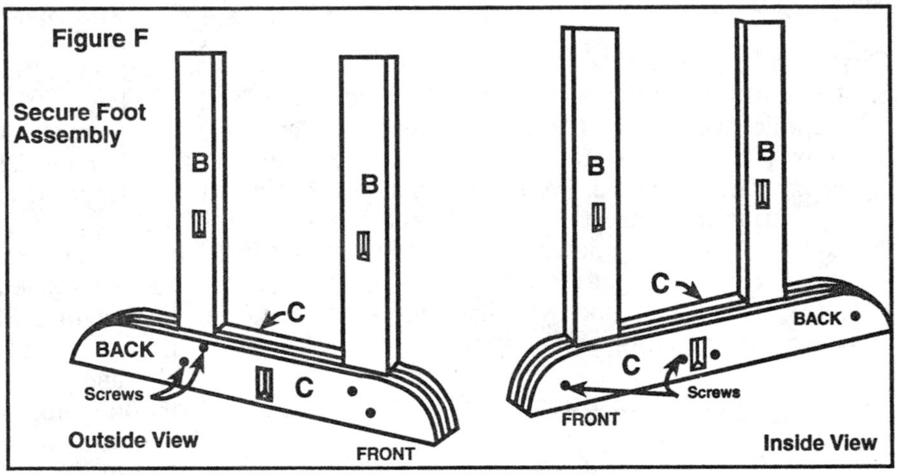

6. The H lower brace requires a tenon at each end, as shown in Figure C. Note that the tenon is mortised to accomodate a peg.
7. Both L upper braces require a tenon at each end, as shown in Figure D. Here again, each tenon is mortised to accommodate a peg, as shown.

Assembly

1. To begin assembling one end section (Figure E), place a C foot on a flat surface and arrange on top of it two B legs and a D, E, and F spacer, as shown. Notes: Be sure that the marked front end of the foot is aligned with the E front spacer; that the D spacer is turned so the mortise is aligned with the mortise in the foot; and that each B leg is turned with the marked upper end at the top. Glue the assembly. Place a second C foot on top, with the marked front end at the front, and glue in place. Secure the assembly using eight screws, as shown in Figure F: four inserted from one side and four from the other.
2. The top of the end section is assembled as shown in Figures G and H. Glue an A armrest support to one side of the two B legs, flush at the top. Note that the support should extend 2-1/4" beyond the front leg, and 3-1/2" beyond the back leg. Secure by inserting two screws through each leg into the support.
3. Drill a hole through each B leg and on through the A armrest support, using a bit that matches the diameter of the eyebolt shanks. Placement of the holes is shown in Figure G. We enlarged each hole at the leg end, to create a recess for the washer and hex nut. Insert an

eyebolt through each hole, from the armrest support side. Secure on the leg side using a washer, hex nut, and cap nut.

4. Add the G armrest and J and K decorative support blocks as shown in Figure H. Note that the straight edge of the armrest is flush with the outer surface of the A support. The armrest should extend just slightly beyond the support at the front end. Glue the assembly. Secure the armrest using two screws inserted into the A support. Secure each decorative support block using finishing nails.
5. Repeat the procedures described in Steps 1 through 4 to assemble a second end section. Note that it should be a mirror image of the first one, so place the A support on the opposite side of the legs, in relation to the front end of the foot assembly. The straight edge of the armrest will face the opposite direction also (see Figure I).
6. For the final assembly (Figure I), align the two end sections about 6 feet apart. Be sure that each one is turned as shown. Place the H lower brace and the two L upper braces between the end sections. Do not use glue in any of these joints, or you will not be able to disassemble the base. Insert the brace tenons through the respective mortises in the foot and legs of one end section, and then through the other end section. It may be necessary to sand the mortises slightly, to get the tenons to fit. Secure each joint with a peg, as shown.

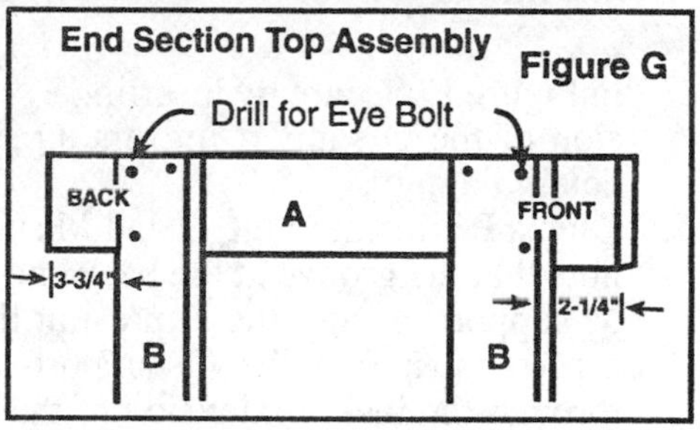

Figure G

Figure H
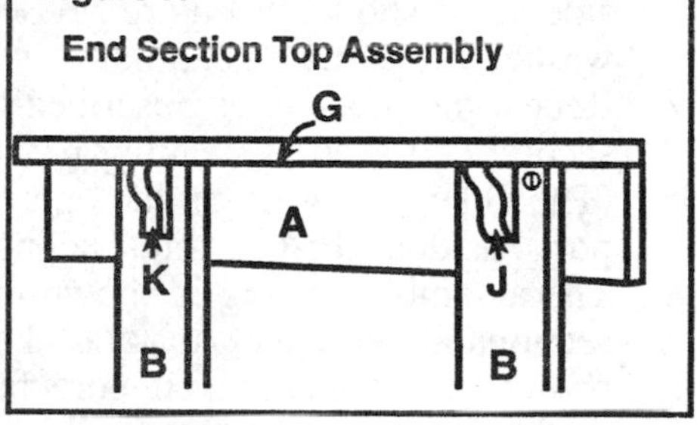

Figure I
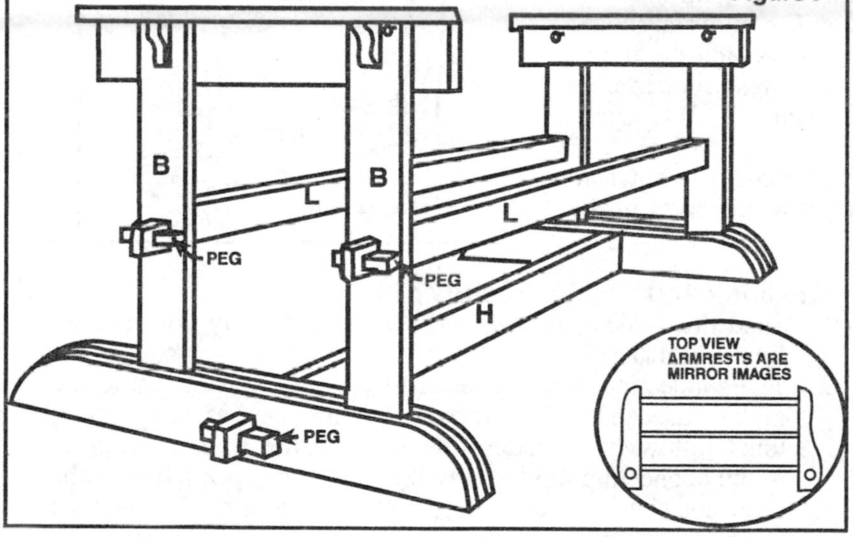

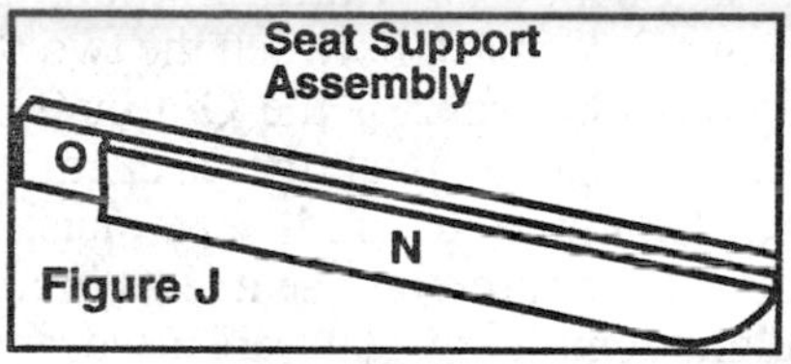

Figure J

Figure K
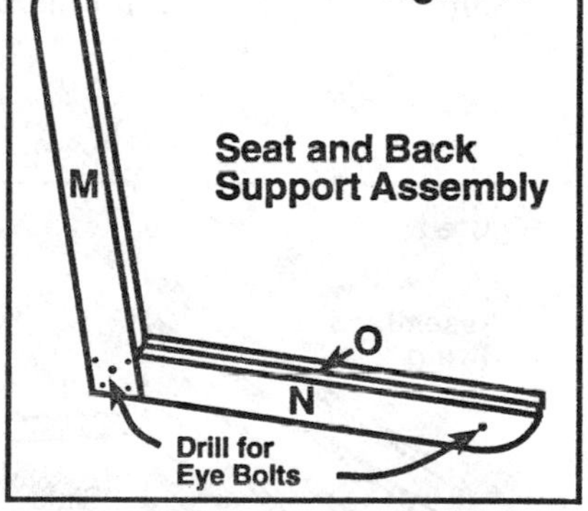

The Swing

The swing consists of two mirror image end sections (Figure M), connected by seat and back slats (Figure N).

Cutting the Parts

1. Cutting instructions for the swing end section parts are listed in this step. Patterns for all parts are provided on page 107. All parts are cut from pine 1" x 4" or equivalent hardwood. Label each part with its identifying code, for reference during assembly.

Code	Description	Dimensions	Quantity
M	Back Support	use pattern	2
N	Seat Support	use pattern	2
O	Seat Support	use pattern	2
P	Armrest	use pattern	2
Q	Armrest Support	use pattern	2

2. Cut 16 slats from pine 1" x 2" or equivalent hardwood, each 1-1/2" x 48".

Assembly

1. The seat support portion of one end section is shown in Figure J. Glue together one N and one O support, flush at the contoured front ends, as shown. Secure by inserting two screws through the O support into the N support. For future reference, the O support is on the inside surface of the end section.
2. Glue an M back support to the seat support assembly as shown in Figure K. Note that the assembly does not form a 90-degree angle, but rather a slightly wider one, so the back will tilt at a comfortable sitting angle. Insert four screws through the M support into the O support.
3. Drill two holes through the assembled seat and back supports where indicated in Figure K, using a bit that matches the diameter of the eyebolt shanks. Do not install the bolts just yet.
4. Glue a Q armrest support to the inside surface of the assembly, 6" from the front end, as shown

in Figure L. Secure by inserting a screw through the lower extension of the Q support into the O seat support, as shown in the detail diagram.

5. Glue a P armrest to the Q and M supports as shown in Figure M. note that the groove at the back end of the armrest fits around the M support. Secure the armrest at the front by inserting a single screw down into the Q support. At the back, insert a screw through the inside extension of the armrest into the M support.
6. Insert an eyebolt though each of the drilled holes, from the outside in, as shown in Figure M. Secure on the inside using a flat washer, hex nut, and cap nut.
7. Repeat the procedures described in steps 1 through 6 to build a second end section, making it a mirror image of the first one. (The O support goes on the opposite sides of the N and M supports, as does the Q armrest support.)
8. The assembled swing is shown in Figure N. Place the two end sections about 4 feet apart. Make sure they are both turned as shown, with the O seat supports facing center. Place a slat on top of the seat supports. Attach a second slat in the same manner, allowing a 3/4" space between the two slats. The third slat should butt against the front of the Q armrest supports, and the fourth slat should butt against the back of the armrest supports, as shown. Continue to add seat slats, allowing a 3/4" space between. There are eight seat slats in all.
9. The eight remaining slats are used as back slats, as shown in Figure N. They are attached to the upright M supports in the same manner as you did the seat slats.

Figure L

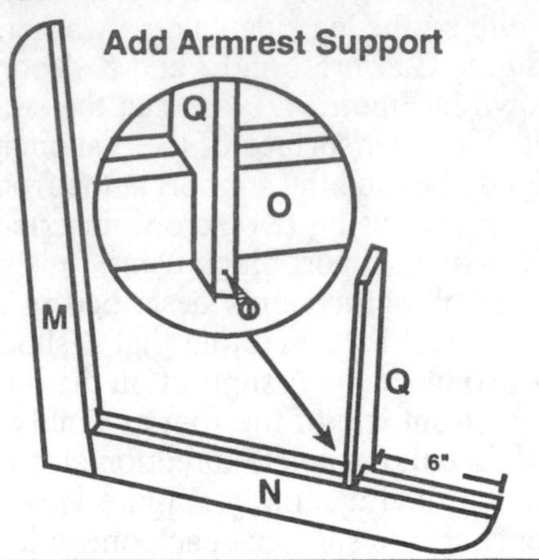

Figure M

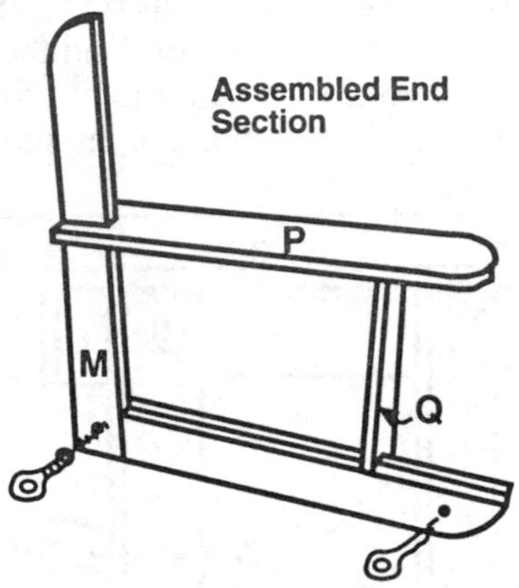

Figure N

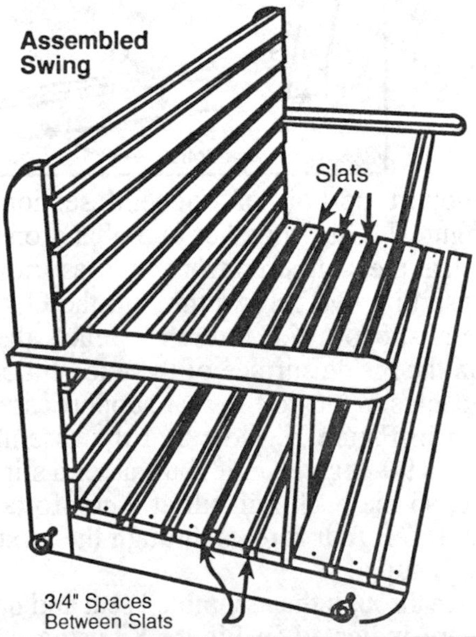

Finishing and Final Assembly

1. Sand the assembled base and swing, and apply your chosen finishing materials.
2. The connecting links are used to join the four chains to the glider base and swing. If you did not purchase connecting links, follow the procedures described in this step, but in place of the connecting links you will have to pry open a link of the chain itself, to connect it to the eyebolt. Join an 8" length of chain to each of the eyebolts on the base section. Secure the opposite end of each chain to the corresponding eyebolt on the swing. Notes: Be sure that the front of the swing faces the same direction as the front ends of the base armrests and feet. It may be necessary to adjust the swing, by attaching the connecting links to higher links of the chains, to get the swing to sit level and high enough above the upper braces of the base.
3. If you built the swing to be hung from your porch ceiling or a tree, you will need quite a bit more chain. The amount will depend, of course, on the height of the ceiling or branch. For each side of the swing, measure from the desired height of the top of the armrest to the ceiling or branch, and add about 3 more feet to form an inverted V-shape at the bottom. If the swing will be hung from a tree, you may wish to wrap the chain around the branch instead of inserting hangers into it. If so, add a bit more to accommodate the circumference of the branch. In addition to the chain, you'll need a total of eight connecting links (optional) and two heavy-duty hangers to join the chains to the ceiling. Many hardware and home centers carry packaged porch swing chain that's already assembled in the proper configuration.

1 square = 1-1/4 inches

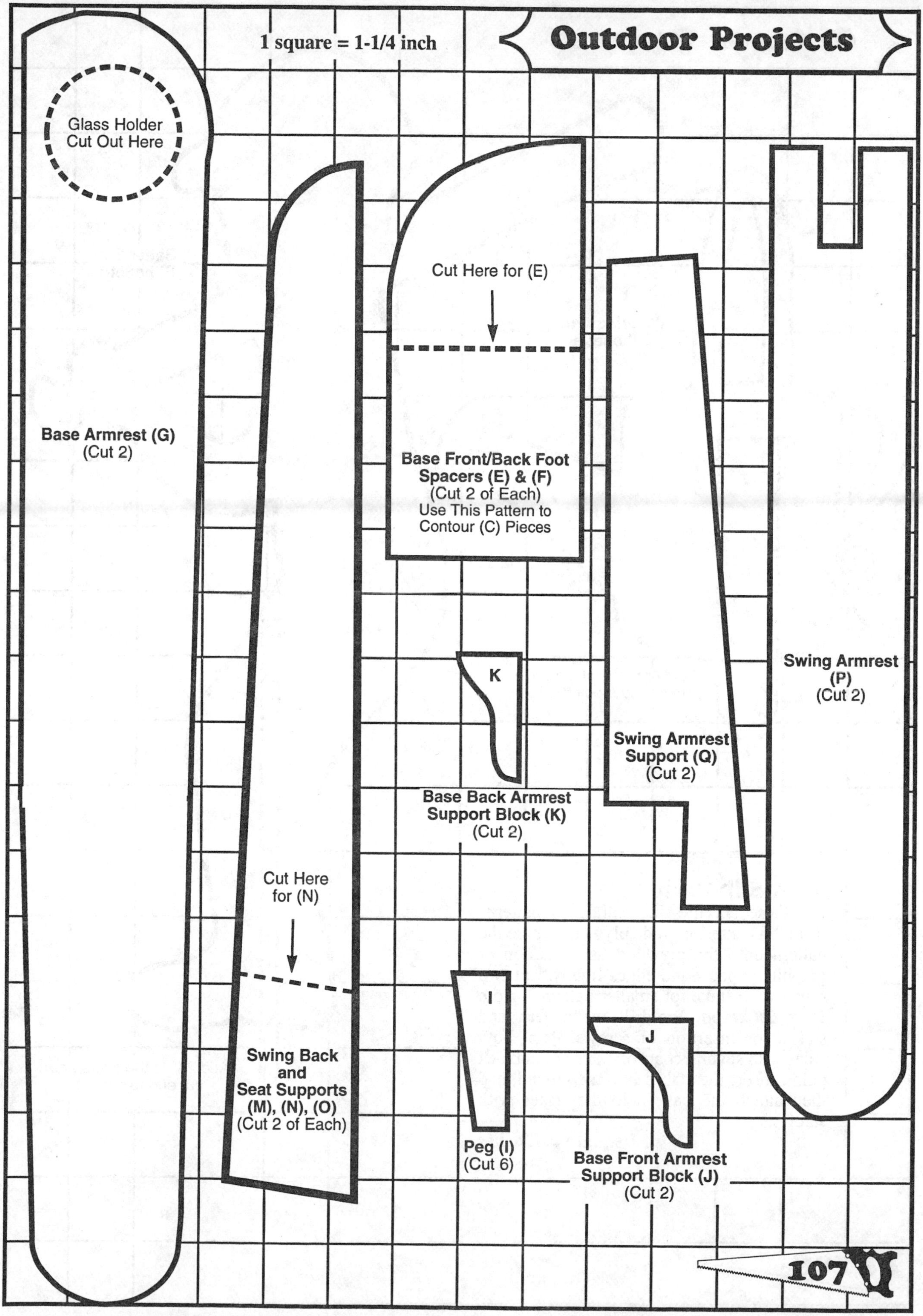
1 square = 1-1/4 inch
Glass Holder Cut Out Here
Base Armrest (G) (Cut 2)
Cut Here for (N)
Swing Back and Seat Supports (M), (N), (O) (Cut 2 of Each)
Cut Here for (E)
Base Front/Back Foot Spacers (E) & (F) (Cut 2 of Each) Use This Pattern to Contour (C) Pieces
K
Base Back Armrest Support Block (K) (Cut 2)
I
Peg (I) (Cut 6)
J
Base Front Armrest Support Block (J) (Cut 2)
Swing Armrest Support (Q) (Cut 2)
Swing Armrest (P) (Cut 2)

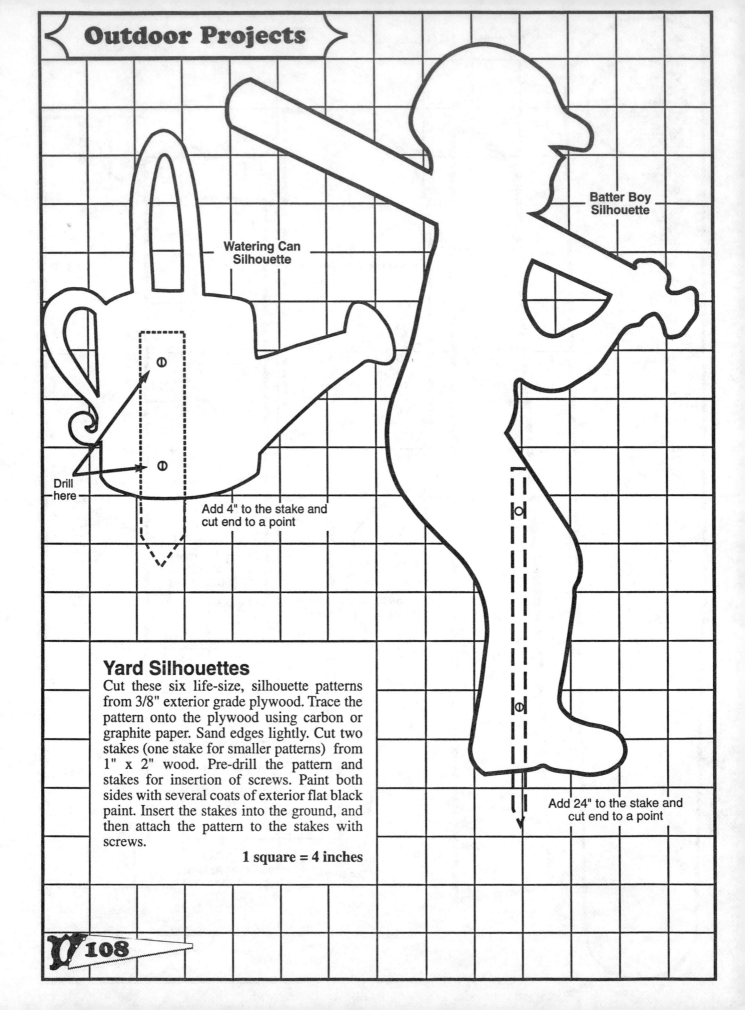

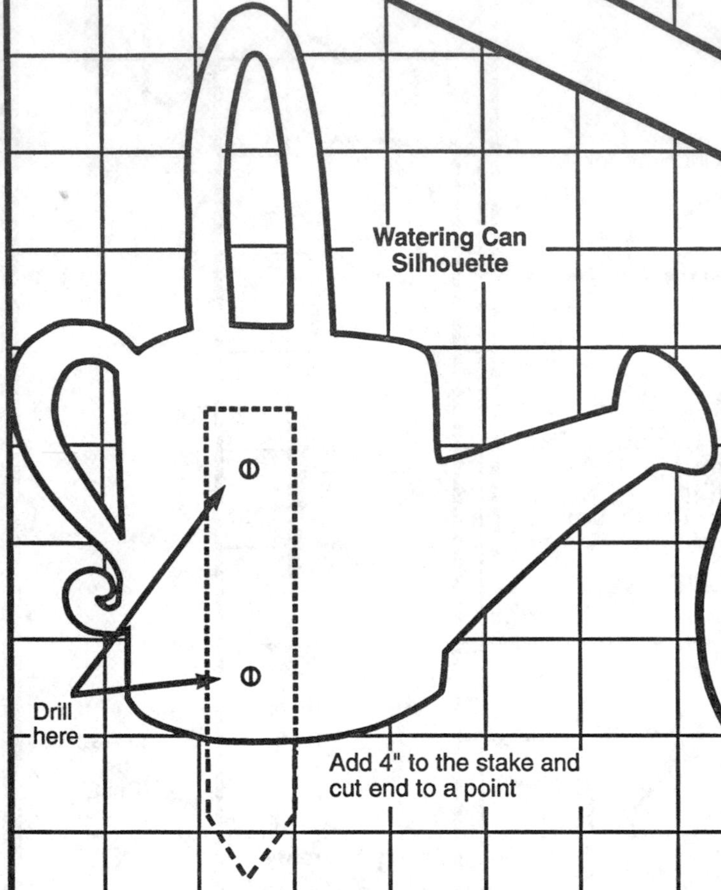

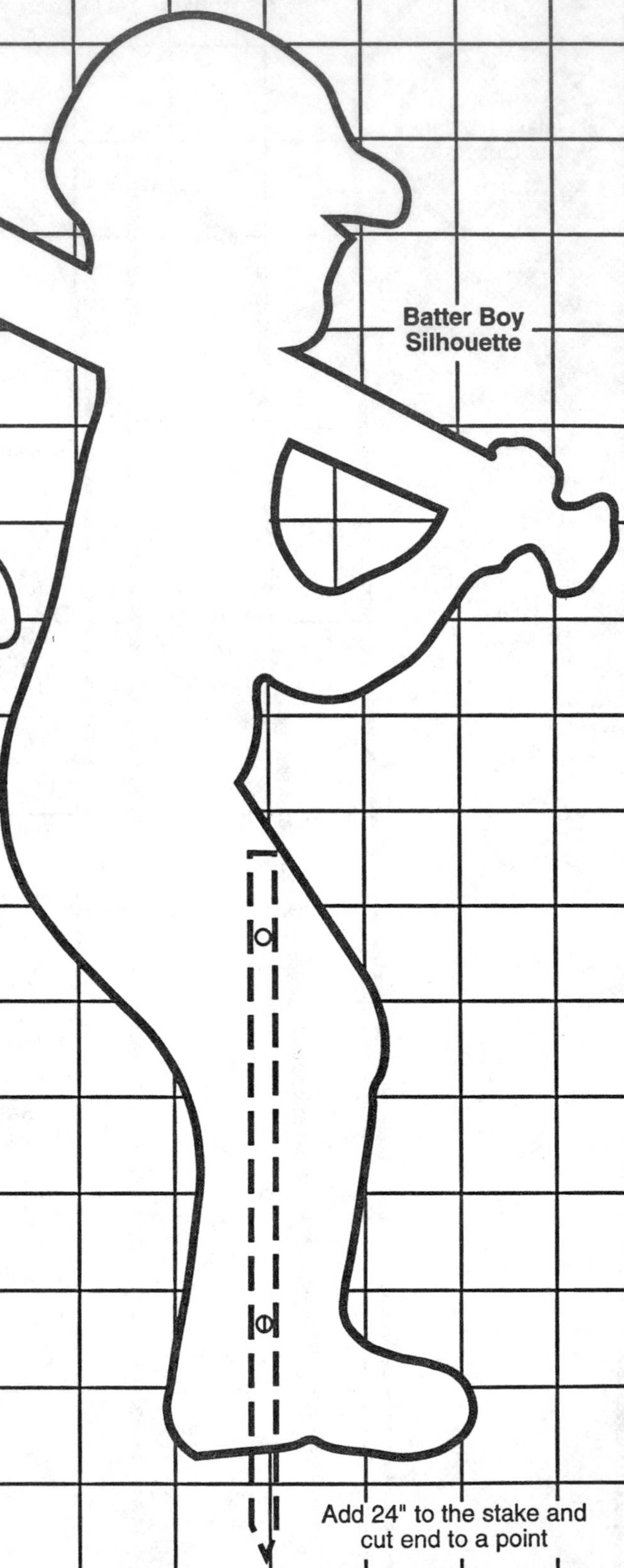

Yard Silhouettes

Cut these six life-size, silhouette patterns from 3/8" exterior grade plywood. Trace the pattern onto the plywood using carbon or graphite paper. Sand edges lightly. Cut two stakes (one stake for smaller patterns) from 1" x 2" wood. Pre-drill the pattern and stakes for insertion of screws. Paint both sides with several coats of exterior flat black paint. Insert the stakes into the ground, and then attach the pattern to the stakes with screws.

1 square = 4 inches

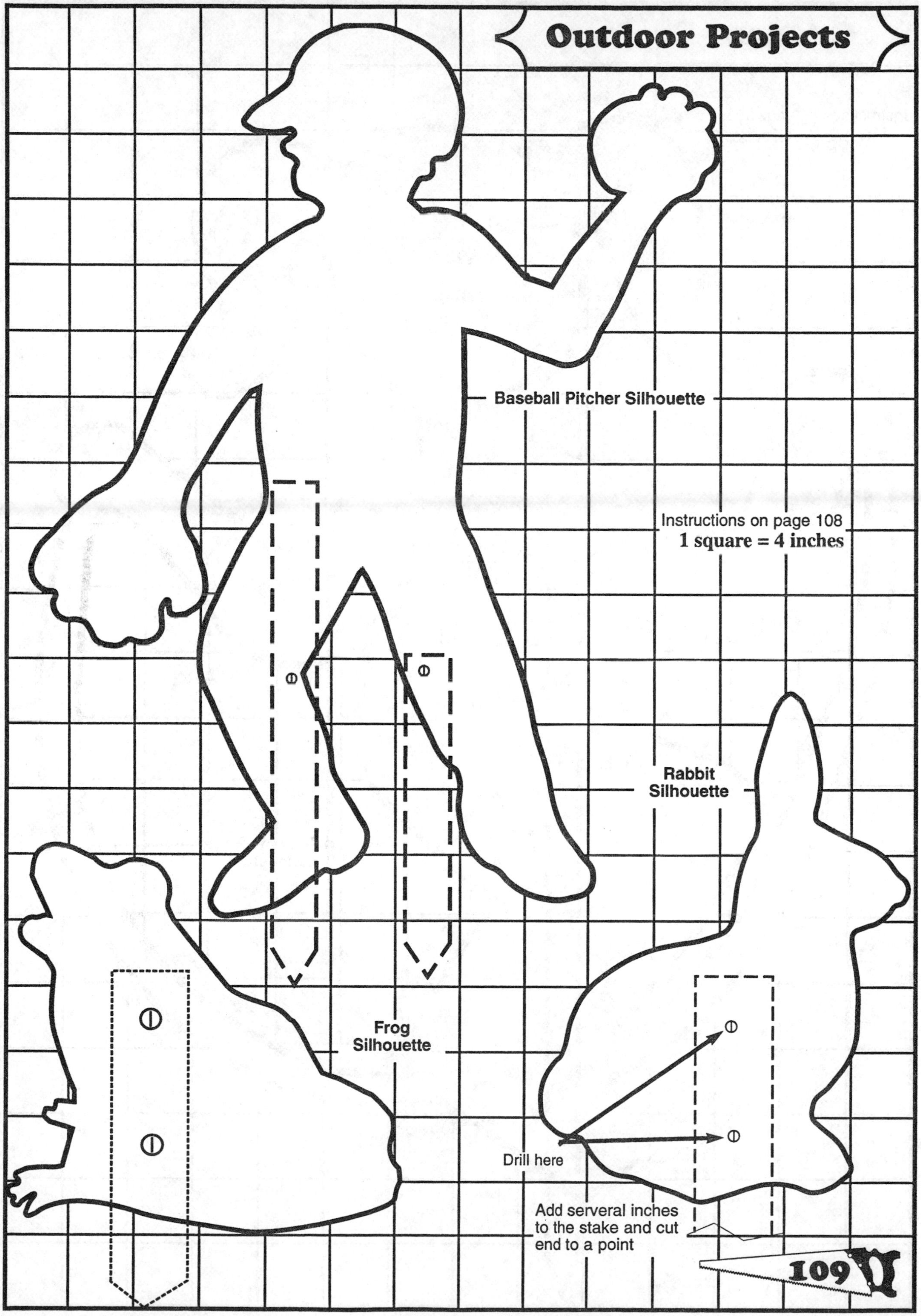
Baseball Pitcher Silhouette
Instructions on page 108
1 square = 4 inches
Rabbit Silhouette
Frog Silhouette
Drill here
Add serveral inches to the stake and cut end to a point

Instructions on page 108

1 square = 4 inches

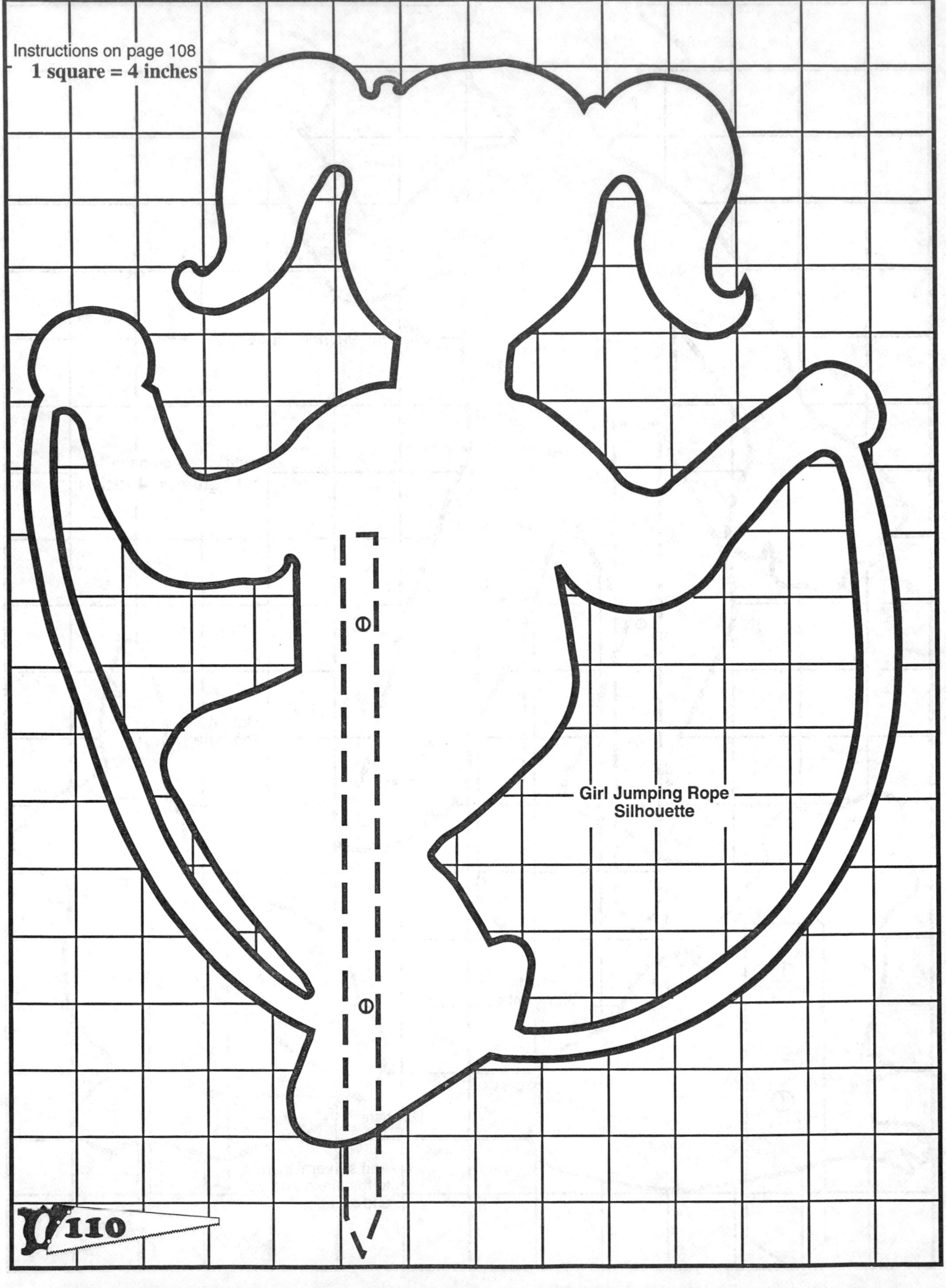

Swan Planter

Cut two swan sides, one bottom and two front/back pieces from 1/2" exterior grade plywood. Assemble the pieces with galvanized nails. Paint with several coats of acrylic paint. Seal with several coats of exterior grade varnish.

1 square = 1-1/4 inches

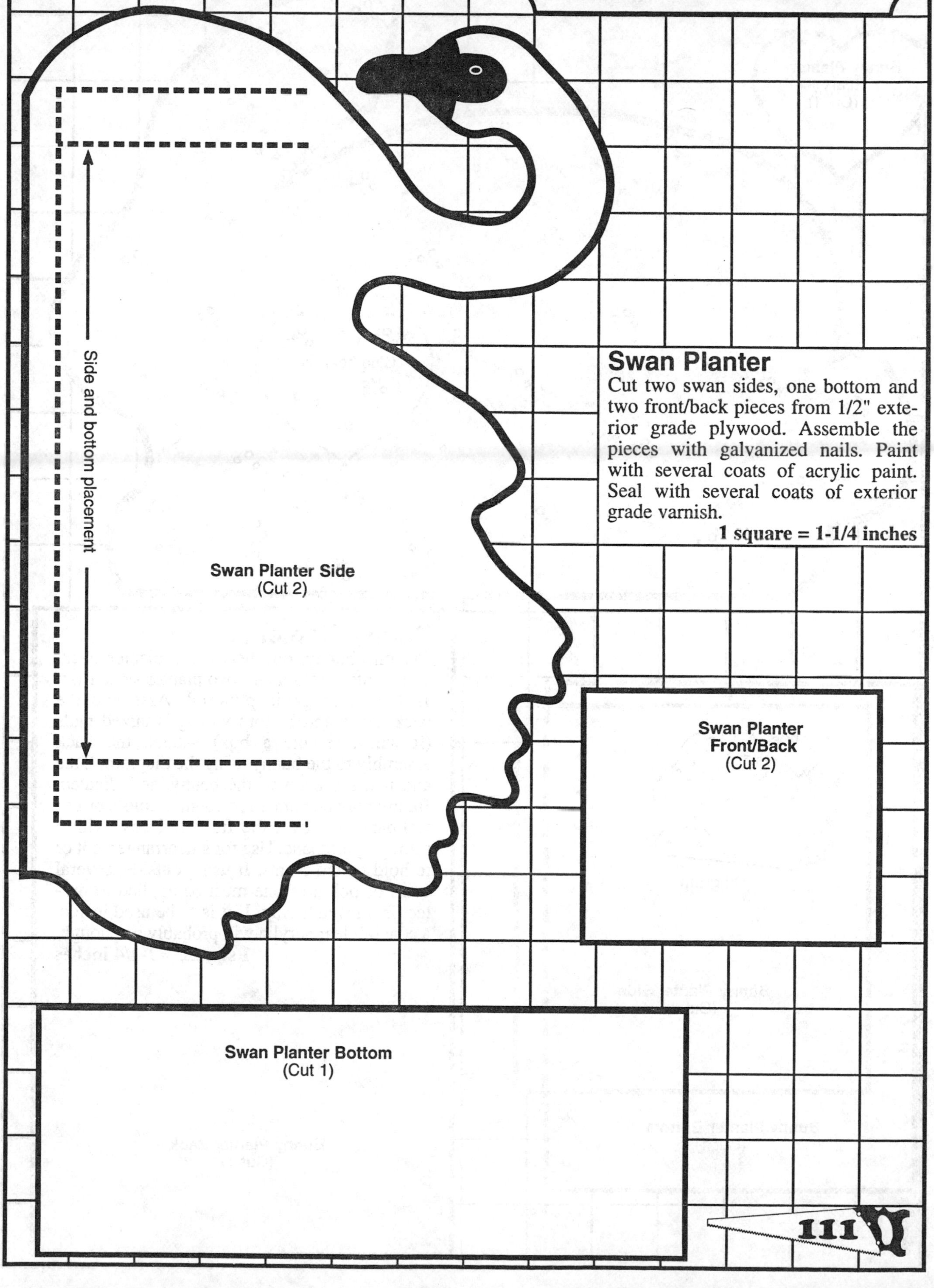

Bunny Planter
Heart
(Cut 1)

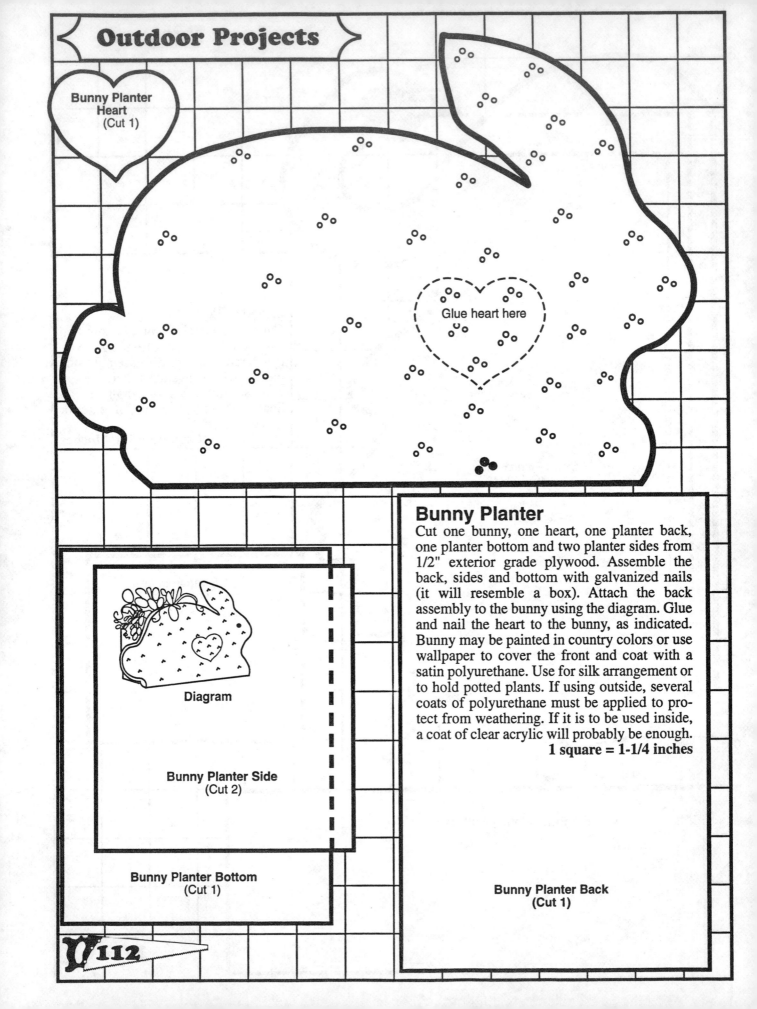

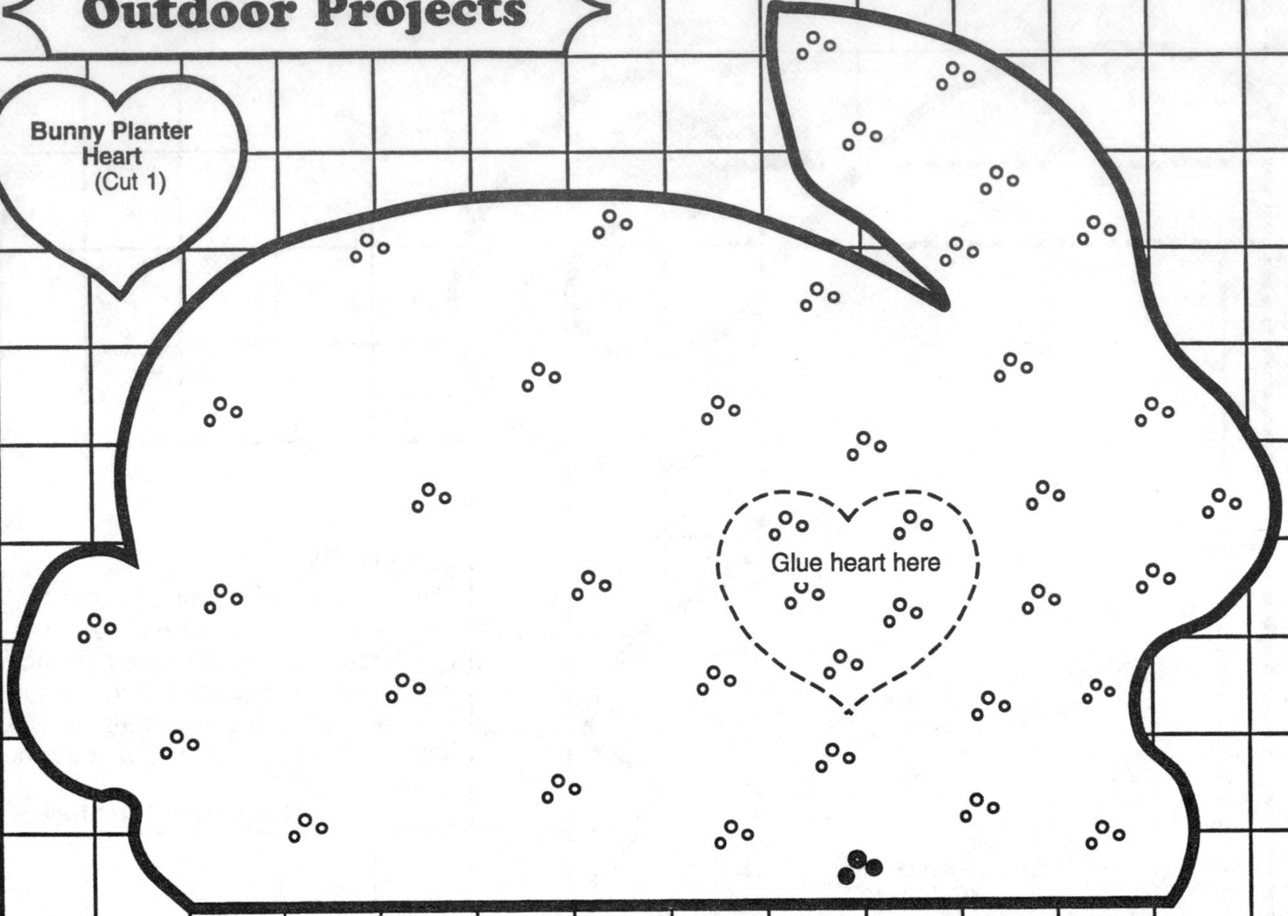

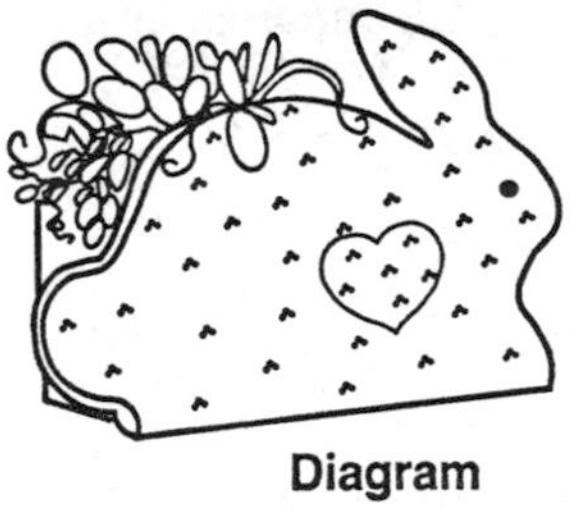

Diagram

Bunny Planter Side
(Cut 2)

Bunny Planter Bottom
(Cut 1)

Bunny Planter

Cut one bunny, one heart, one planter back, one planter bottom and two planter sides from 1/2" exterior grade plywood. Assemble the back, sides and bottom with galvanized nails (it will resemble a box). Attach the back assembly to the bunny using the diagram. Glue and nail the heart to the bunny, as indicated. Bunny may be painted in country colors or use wallpaper to cover the front and coat with a satin polyurethane. Use for silk arrangement or to hold potted plants. If using outside, several coats of polyurethane must be applied to protect from weathering. If it is to be used inside, a coat of clear acrylic will probably be enough.

1 square = 1-1/4 inches

Bunny Planter Back
(Cut 1)

Clubhouse Doghouse

Tools Needed:
Table saw
Jig saw
Router with panel cutting bit
Hammer
Paint brushes
Utility knife

Wood Needed:

Qty:	Size	Notes
1	1/2" x 4' x 8'	Plywood
1	1/2" x 4' x 8'	Vertical plywood siding
4	2" x 4" x 8'	Pressure treated wood
	OR	
8	2" x 2" x 8'	Pressure treated wood

Miscellaneous Materials:
5# 16d. coated nails
1# 6d. galvanized spiral siding nails
5# 3/4" roofing nails
1 roll 10# felt
1 square shingles
1 gallon exterior paint or stain

Optional Material:
Three 1" x 4" x 8' pine ripped in half for trim.
Two 1-1/2" x 4' x 8' styrofoam for insulation
30" x 42" carpet for floor
1/2 gallon trim paint

Directions for dog house assembly

1. Using 16d. nails, assemble corner braces (A) to floor joist (C). Nail floor joist (B) to previous assembly. Next nail middle floor joist (C) to center of side joists (B).
2. Cut out of 1/2" plywood a 24" x 36" rectangle. On all four corners cut out a square of 1-1/2" x 1-1/2". Nail to floor with 6d. galvanized spiral nails.
3. Next attach upper support (J) to corner braces (A). Then use last two front/rear support (C) as in Figure 2.
4. Find middle supports (E) and nail in center of the sides. Then the middle supports (E) will be used to make the door as shown in Figure 1.
5. Assemble roof supports (F) to frame of house at front and rear walls only.
6. Cut out siding to approximate sizes of walls, NOT cutting out for the door. Attach one piece at a time with 6d. galvanized nails starting with the left side and working clockwise. Note: Use a router with a panel cutting bit to trim the siding (after each panel is nailed to the frame) to exact size of the frame. Continue same action with other three sides. Also use router to cut front door opening.
   *At this time, if insulation or carpet options are desired: Cut insulation to size and using appropriate glue, secure in place. The carpet is secured at this time using staples. Insulation may also be used under floor. Cut styrofoam with a table or circular saw.
7. Find ridge (H) and attach to roof supports (F) leaving 4" on both front and rear overhang. Nail two rafters (G) in center of ridge (H) and to upper support (J). Next, attach roof nailers (I) (directly above upper support (J) to previously assembled rafters (G) and to roof supports (F). Finally attach last four rafters (G) to ends of roof nailers (I) and to ridge (H). *If insulation was used previously, now is the time to put it in the roof. Cut styrofoam to size, glue on edges and install.
8. Cut plywood to size (M) for roof and attach both sides. Roll felt on to roof leaving an overhang all around. Use roofing nails to hold corners down. Nail shingles onto roof per instructions on package. Trim felt with utility knife.
9. If desired, attach trim boards to corners, around door, and around overhang with 6d. galvanized spiral nails.
10. Paint walls and trim with exterior grade paint.

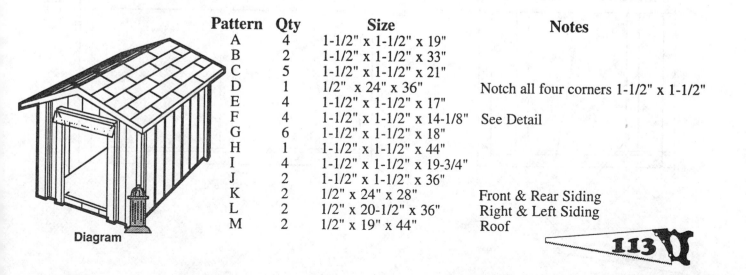

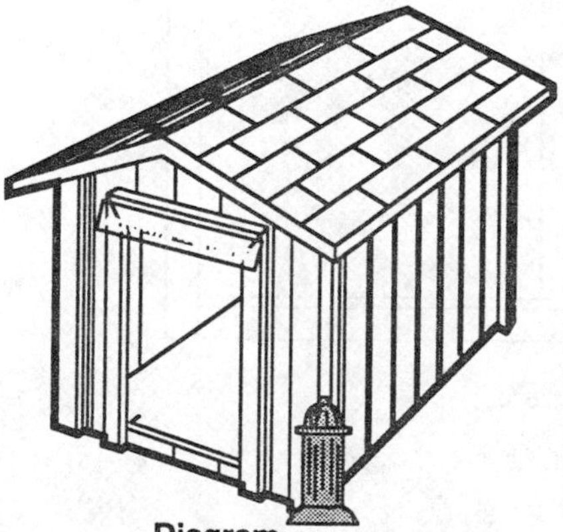

Diagram

Pattern	Qty	Size	Notes
A	4	1-1/2" x 1-1/2" x 19"	
B	2	1-1/2" x 1-1/2" x 33"	
C	5	1-1/2" x 1-1/2" x 21"	
D	1	1/2" x 24" x 36"	Notch all four corners 1-1/2" x 1-1/2"
E	4	1-1/2" x 1-1/2" x 17"	
F	4	1-1/2" x 1-1/2" x 14-1/8"	See Detail
G	6	1-1/2" x 1-1/2" x 18"	
H	1	1-1/2" x 1-1/2" x 44"	
I	4	1-1/2" x 1-1/2" x 19-3/4"	
J	2	1-1/2" x 1-1/2" x 36"	
K	2	1/2" x 24" x 28"	Front & Rear Siding
L	2	1/2" x 20-1/2" x 36"	Right & Left Siding
M	2	1/2" x 19" x 44"	Roof

Figure 1

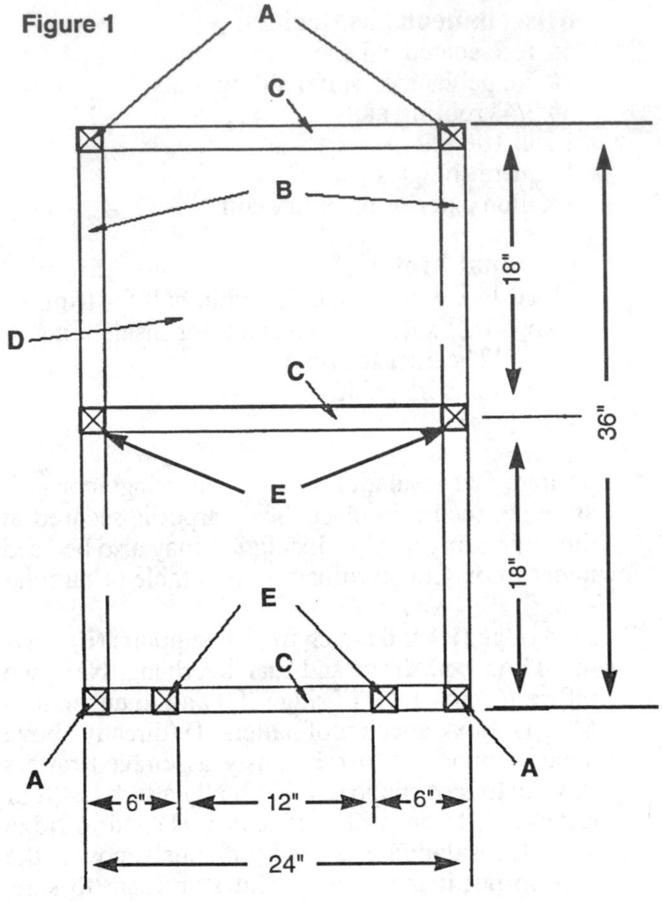

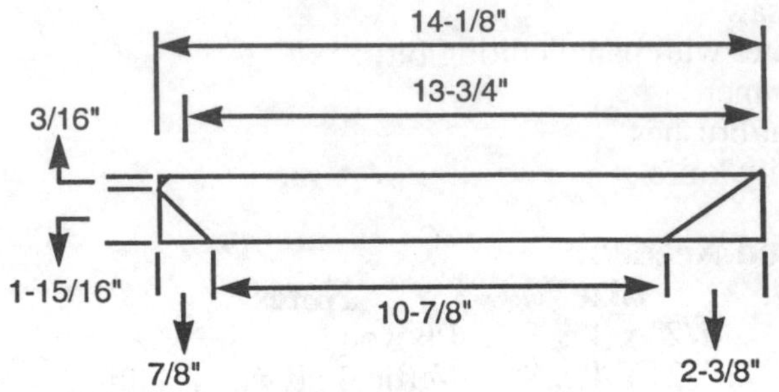

Detail Pattern Piece (F)

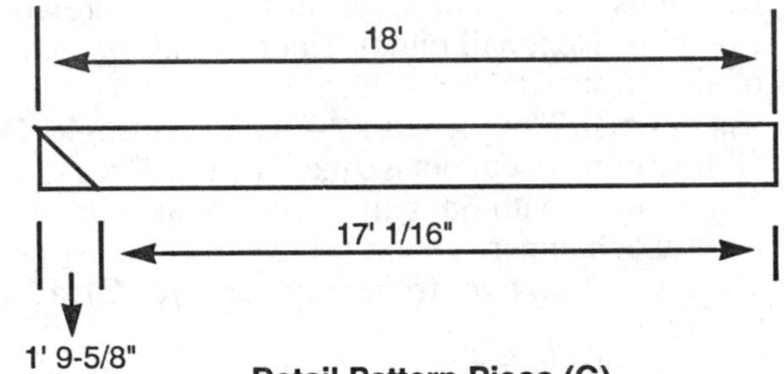

Detail Pattern Piece (G)

Figure 2

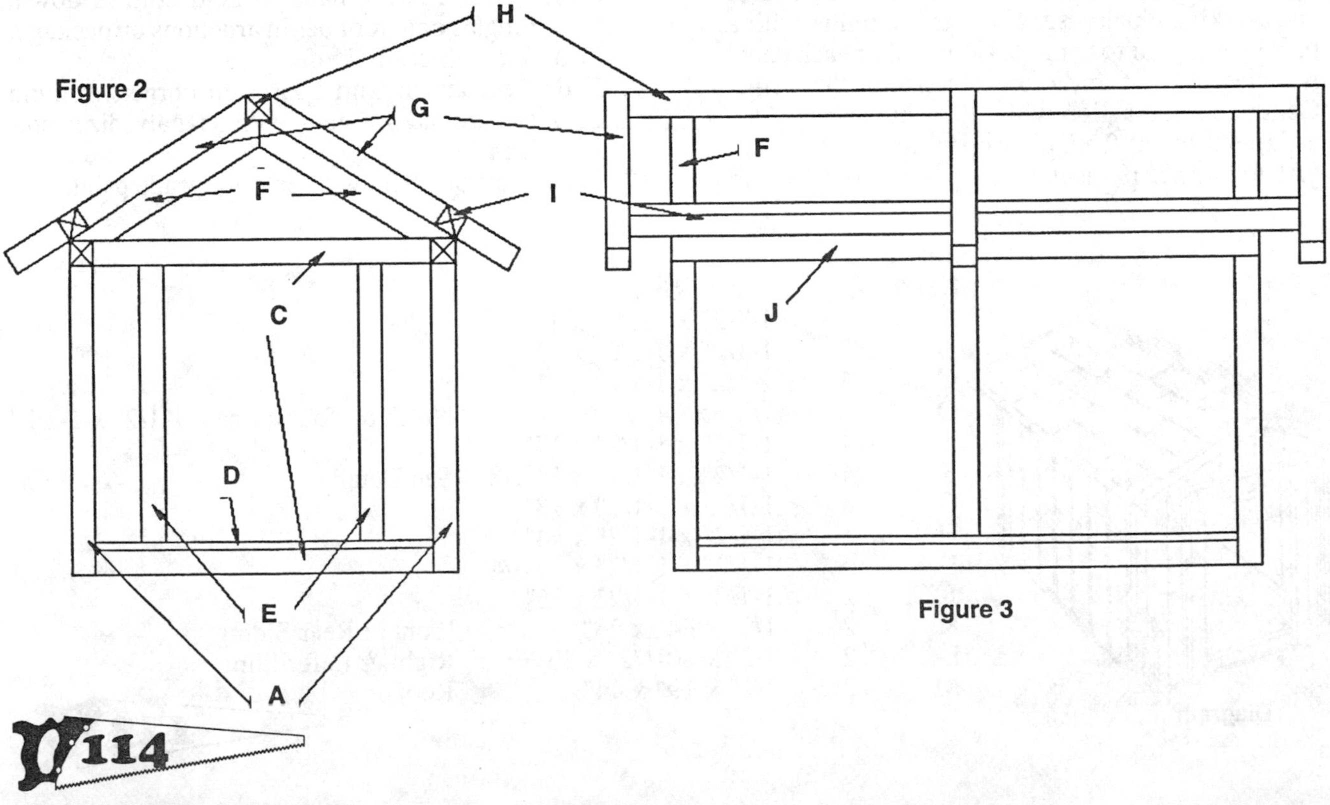

Figure 3

— CHAPTER TEN —

PEG RACKS & SHELVES

Primitive, Amish Mini-Clothes Wall Rack

Use this rack for the Amish hang-able clothing. Cut 1 rack out of 1" wood, stain and coat with clear acrylic. Using headless finishing nails, drive in at an angle where indicated by an "X". Cut out each piece of clothing from 1/4" wood and finish in grays and dark colors. Accent with white. Hang on the rack for a unique wall decoration.

1 square = 1 inch

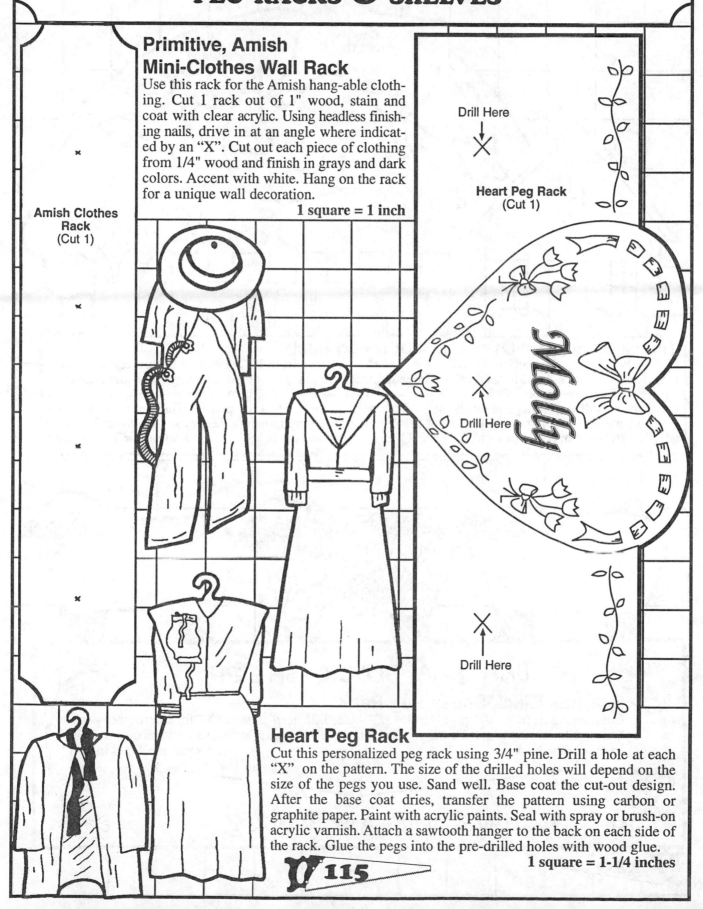

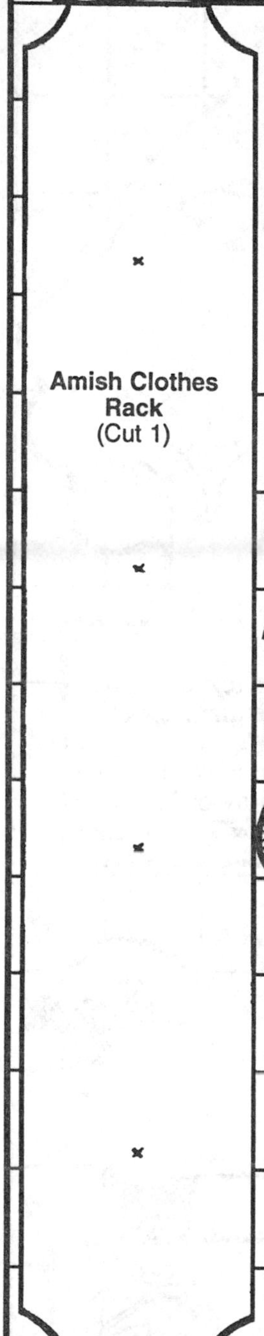

Heart Peg Rack

Cut this personalized peg rack using 3/4" pine. Drill a hole at each "X" on the pattern. The size of the drilled holes will depend on the size of the pegs you use. Sand well. Base coat the cut-out design. After the base coat dries, transfer the pattern using carbon or graphite paper. Paint with acrylic paints. Seal with spray or brush-on acrylic varnish. Attach a sawtooth hanger to the back on each side of the rack. Glue the pegs into the pre-drilled holes with wood glue.

1 square = 1-1/4 inches

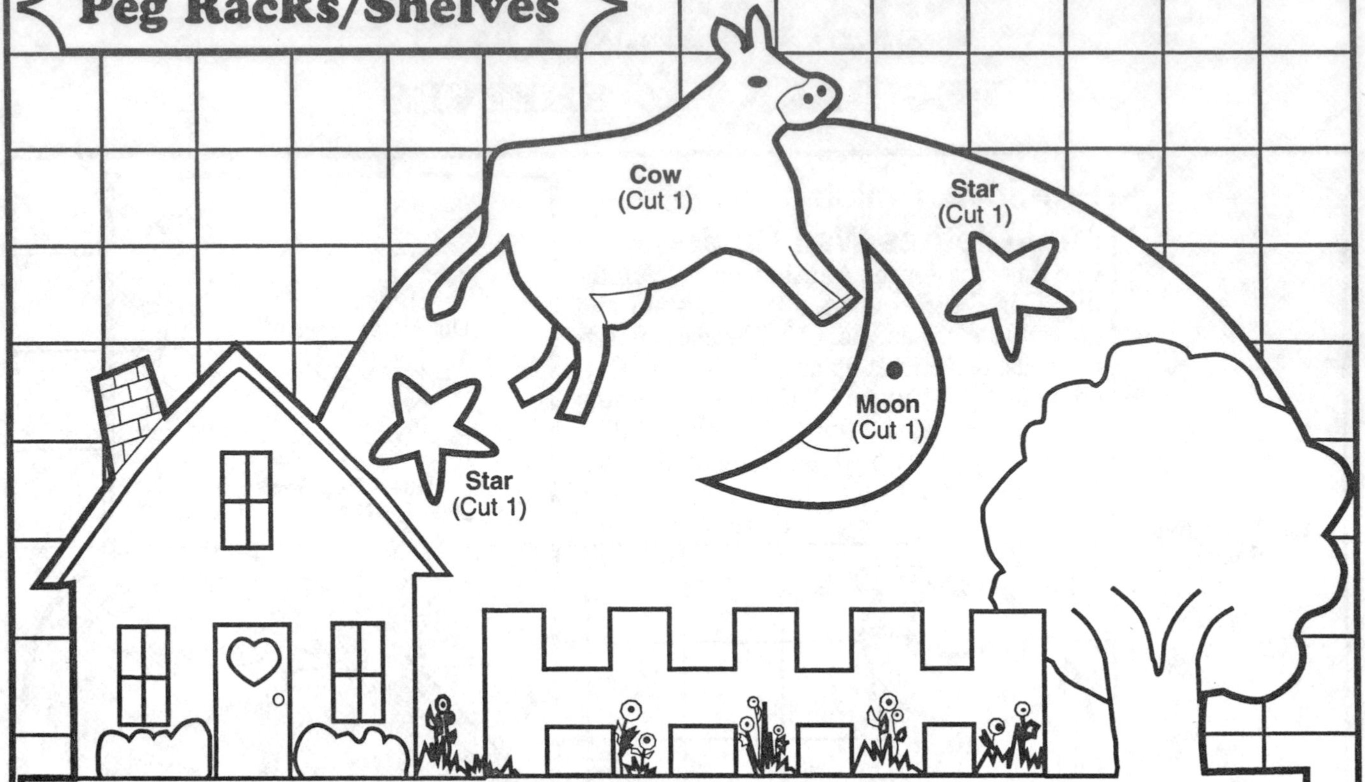

The Cow Jumped Over The Moon Peg Rack

Use the heavier lines as cutting lines. Cut the cow, stars & moon from 1/4" plywood. Cut the rest of the pattern from 3/4" stock. Drill holes on the rack as indicated for placement of shaker pegs. The diameter of

X ← Drill here → X ← Drill here → X

the holes you drill will depend on the size of the pegs you use. Sand the pieces. Glue the cow, stars and moon to the back with yellow glue. Paint the peg rack with acrylic paints. Seal with a spray or brush-on acrylic varnish. Attach a hanger to the back. Glue the pegs into the holes. **1 square = 1-1/4 inches**

BAA BAA BLACK SHEEP

Baa-Baa Black Sheep Peg Rack

Cut the pattern from 3/4" pine. Drill a 1/2" hole, 1/2" deep at each "X" for insertion of pegs. Sand well. Paint with acrylic paints. Seal with an acrylic spray or brush-on varnish. Attach a hanger to the back. **1 square = 1-1/4 inches**

X X X

Drill here

HAVE YOU ANY WOOL?

Decorative Miniature Barn Shadow Box

This is ideal for displaying miniatures, especially animals. Cut out each piece from 1/4" wood and assemble using the diagram as a guide. There are 14 pieces in this pattern. Transfer the design onto the front and sides using tracing or graphite paper. Assemble the shelves as shown and glue together. Insert the shelves into the shadow box and glue in place. Paint or stain and seal with clear acrylic or polyurethane.

1 square = 1-1/2 inches

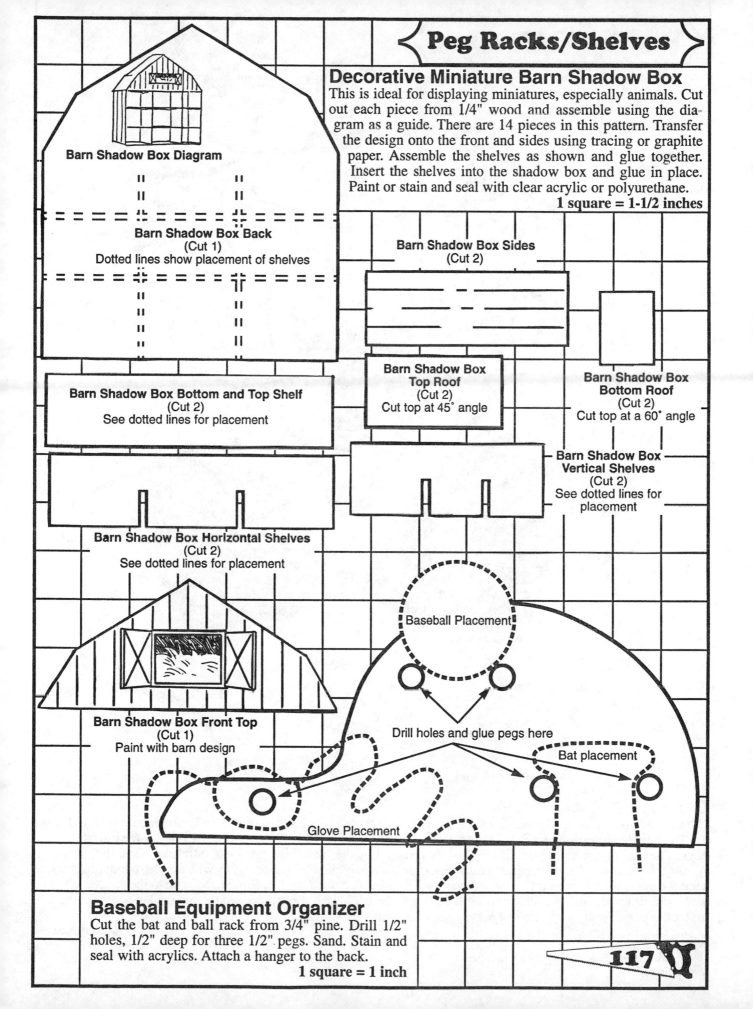

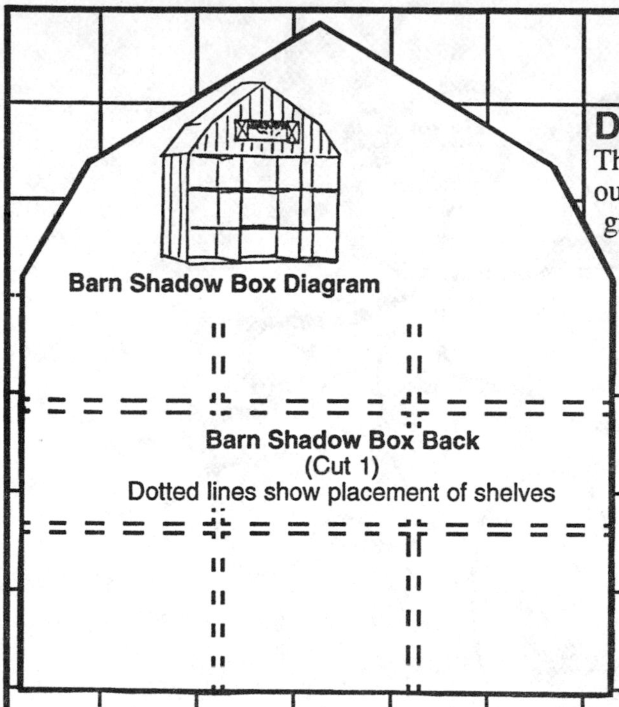

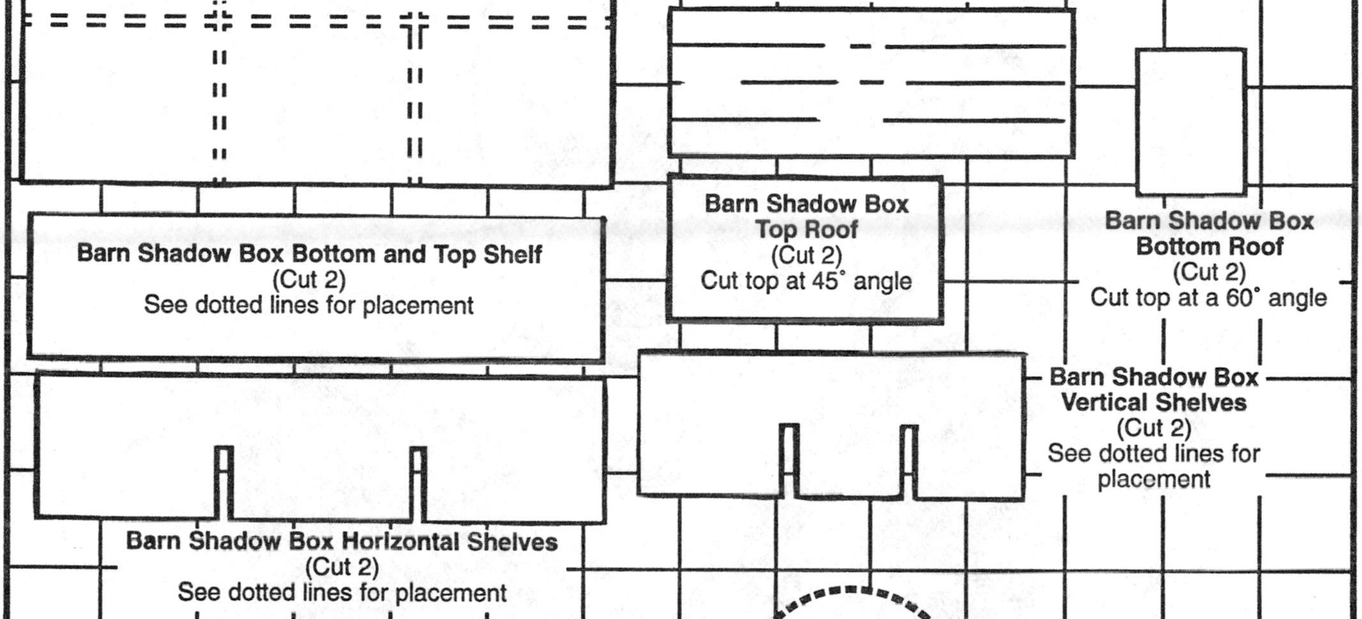

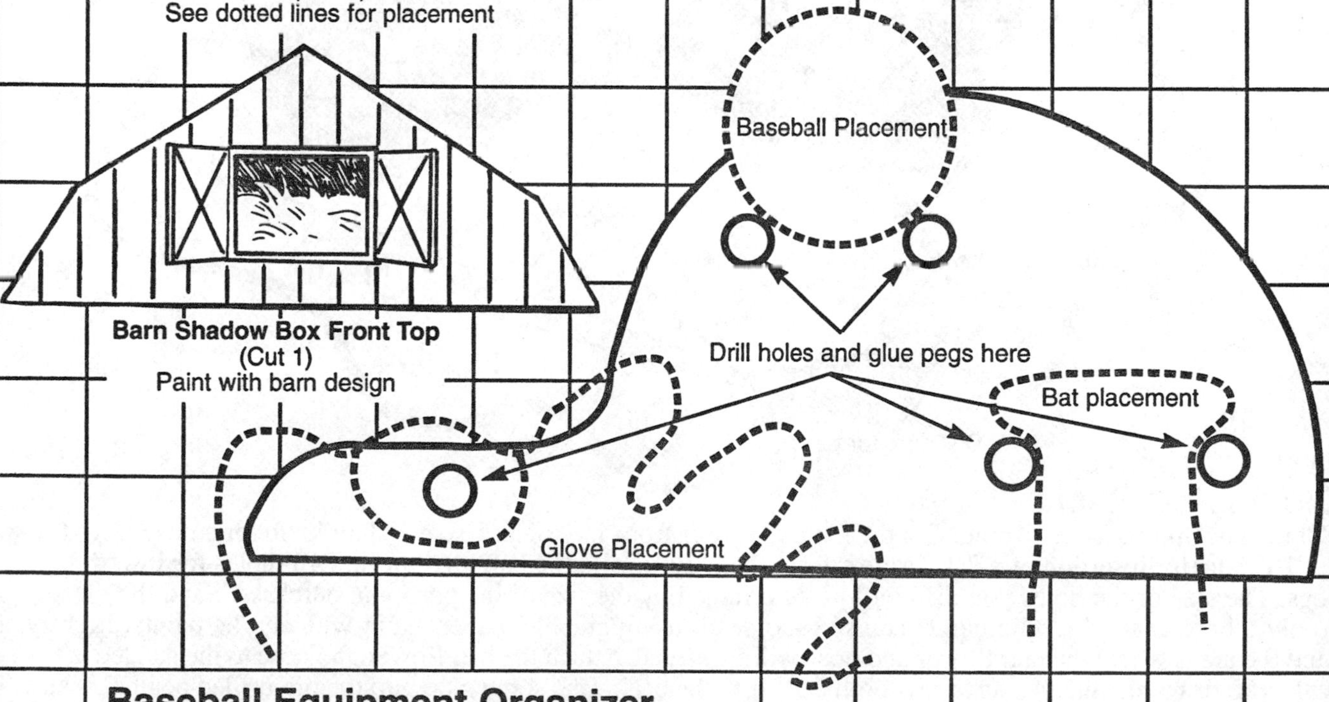

Baseball Equipment Organizer

Cut the bat and ball rack from 3/4" pine. Drill 1/2" holes, 1/2" deep for three 1/2" pegs. Sand. Stain and seal with acrylics. Attach a hanger to the back.

1 square = 1 inch

Clown Peg Rack

Cut the back piece from 1" pine. Cut the hat and flower from 1/2" pine. Use a 1" ball knob for a nose. Pre-drill a 3/16" hole for insertion of a 3/16" screw from the back to hold the ball knob nose. Drill holes for insertion of pegs. The size of the holes you drill will be determined by the size of the pegs you purchase. Sand the pieces. Apply a base coat of acrylic paint. Transfer the detail using graphite paper. Paint with acrylic paints. Lightly sand the areas where the hat, flower and nose will be placed. Attach the hat, flower and nose to the sanded areas with craft or wood glue. Attach a sawtooth hanger to the back. Dab some glue into the pre-drilled peg holes and insert the pegs. Apply two coats of acrylic spray or brush-on varnish.

Actual Size

Mini What-Not Cabinet

Cut all pieces from 1/8" wood. Pieces include one back, two sides, one top, two shelves, one bottom, two doors, one bottom front facing and four door braces. Assemble with wood glue. Sand and then stain or paint with acrylic paints. Doors should be glued open at a 45° angle or small hinges could be used so they will open and close.

1 square = 3/4 inch

Mini What-Not Cabinet Diagram

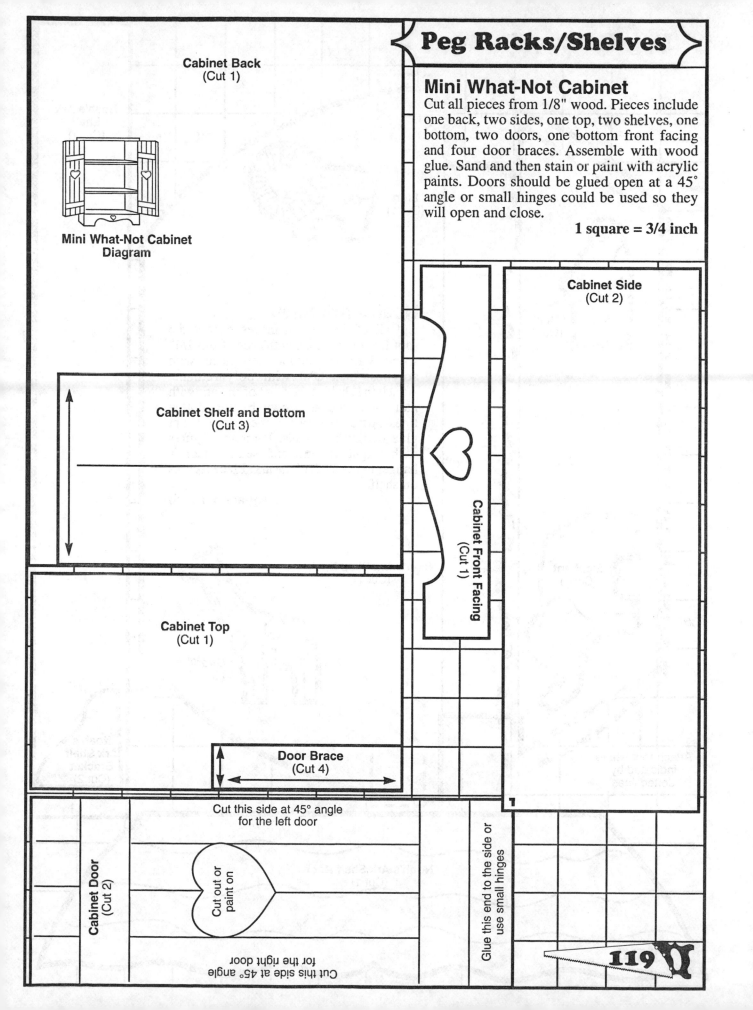

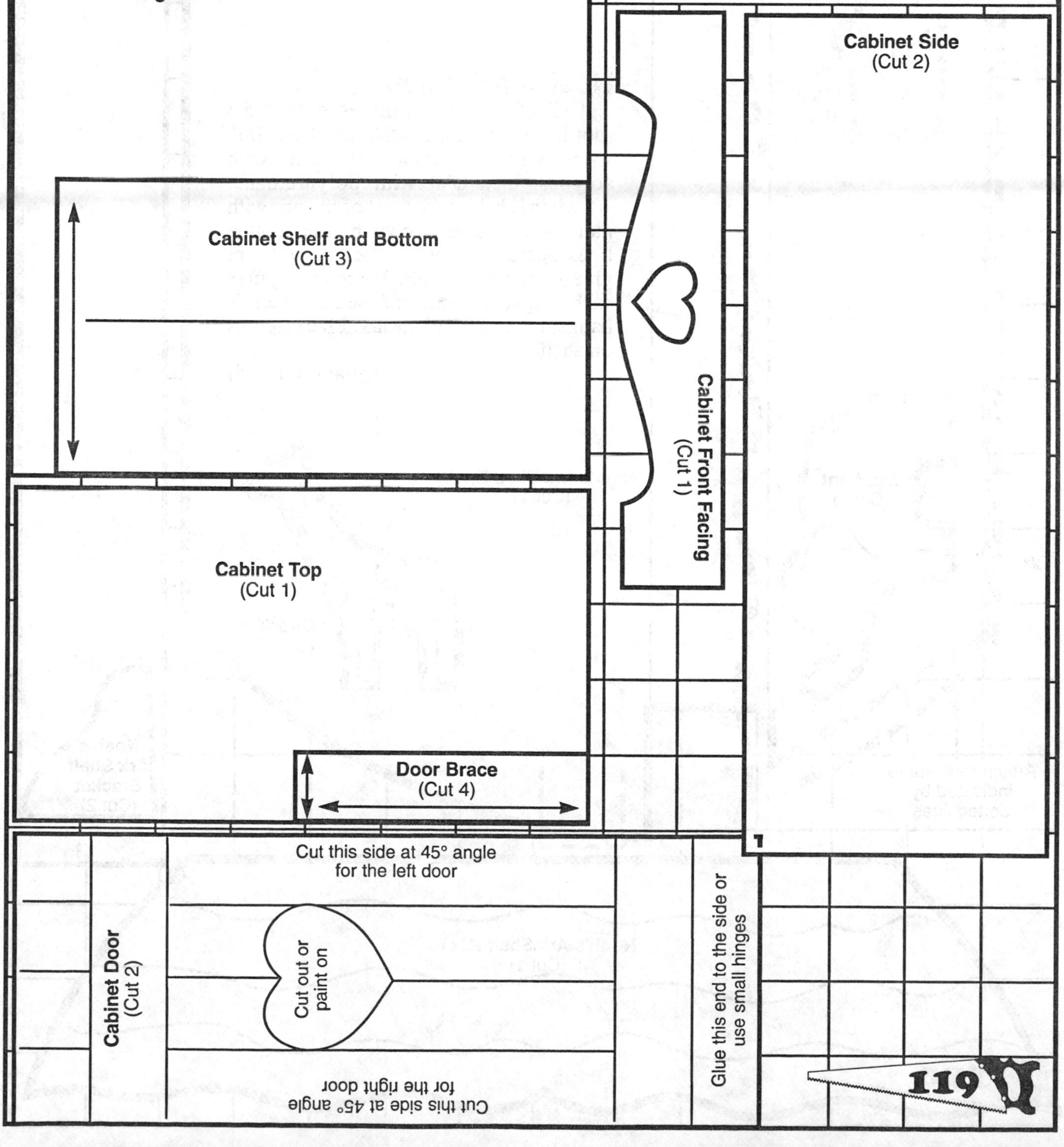

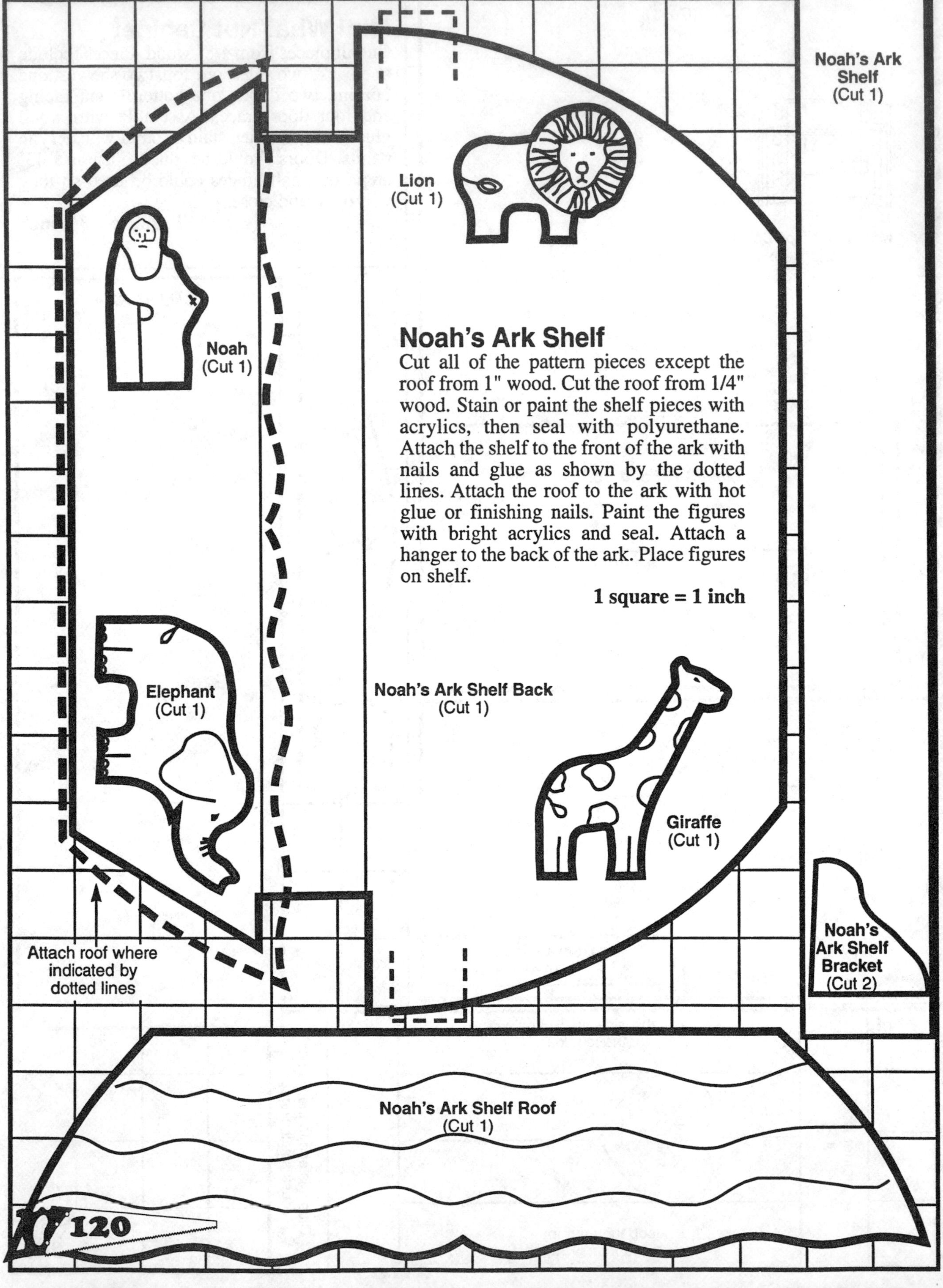

Noah's Ark Shelf

Cut all of the pattern pieces except the roof from 1" wood. Cut the roof from 1/4" wood. Stain or paint the shelf pieces with acrylics, then seal with polyurethane. Attach the shelf to the front of the ark with nails and glue as shown by the dotted lines. Attach the roof to the ark with hot glue or finishing nails. Paint the figures with bright acrylics and seal. Attach a hanger to the back of the ark. Place figures on shelf.

1 square = 1 inch

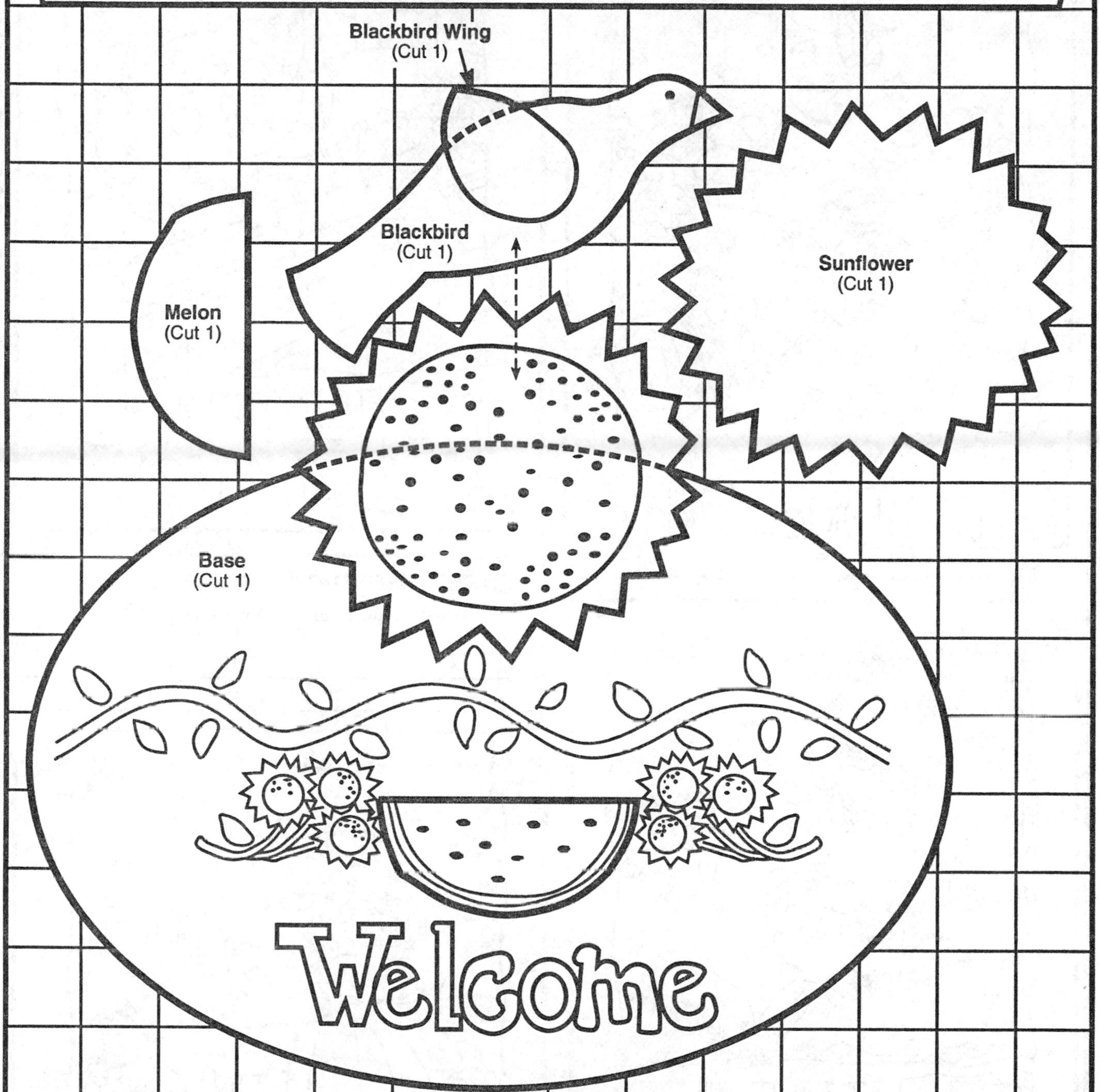

Summertime Welcome Sign

Decorations of summer's pleasures abound on this plaque. Cut one plaque base, one sunflower and one blackbird body from 3/4" pine. Cut one blackbird wing and one watermelon slice from 1/4" plywood. Sand all of the pieces. Drill a 1/4" hole in the sunflower top and blackbird bottom for a 2" length of dowel. Attach the pieces to the base with wood glue and finishing nails. Paint with acrylic paints. Seal with an acrylic spray or brush-on varnish.

1 square = 2 inches

Nursery Rhyme Plaques

Follow basic plaque directions on page 124.

1 square = 1-1/2 inches

Nursery Rhyme Plaques

Follow basic plaque directions on page 124.

1 square = 1-1/2 inches

Plaque Directions

Even though plaques are not complicated projects, they are a favorite among beginning woodworkers, painters and younger woodworking enthusiasts. Unless otherwise indicated, cut each plaque from 1/2" wood. Edges may be sanded or routed to produce a decorative edging. Transfer the design onto the wood with graphite paper and paint using acrylics. Coat with polyurethane or spray with a matt finishing spray to protect the artwork. Attach picture hanger to back. Plaques are one of the most appreciated gifts given by woodworkers.

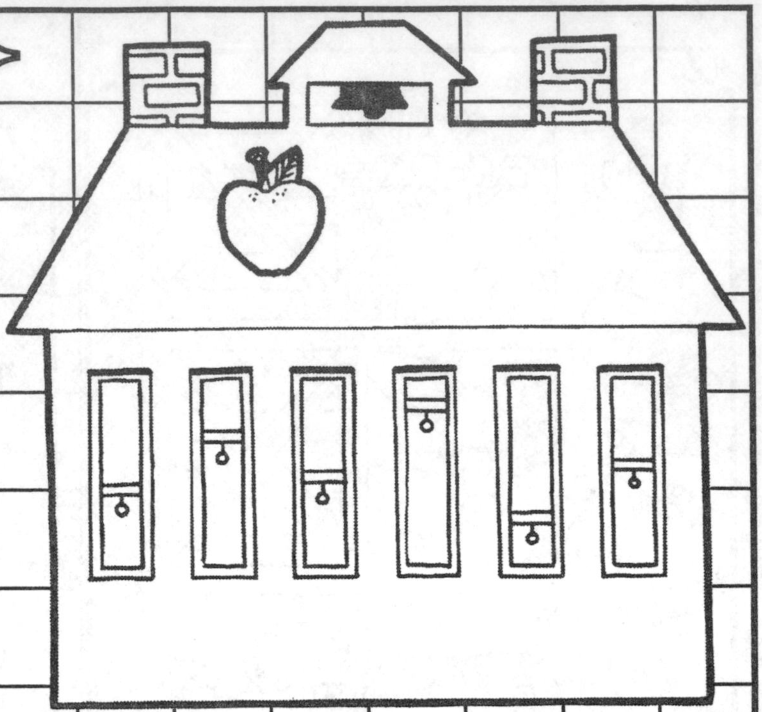

Schoolhouse Plaque

Follow basic plaque directions, above left. Cut apple from 1/4" wood.

1 square = 2 inches

Amish Cow Plaque or Peg Rack

Follow basic plaque directions, above left. A cup hook may be added, if desired as indicated by an X.

1 square = 2 inches

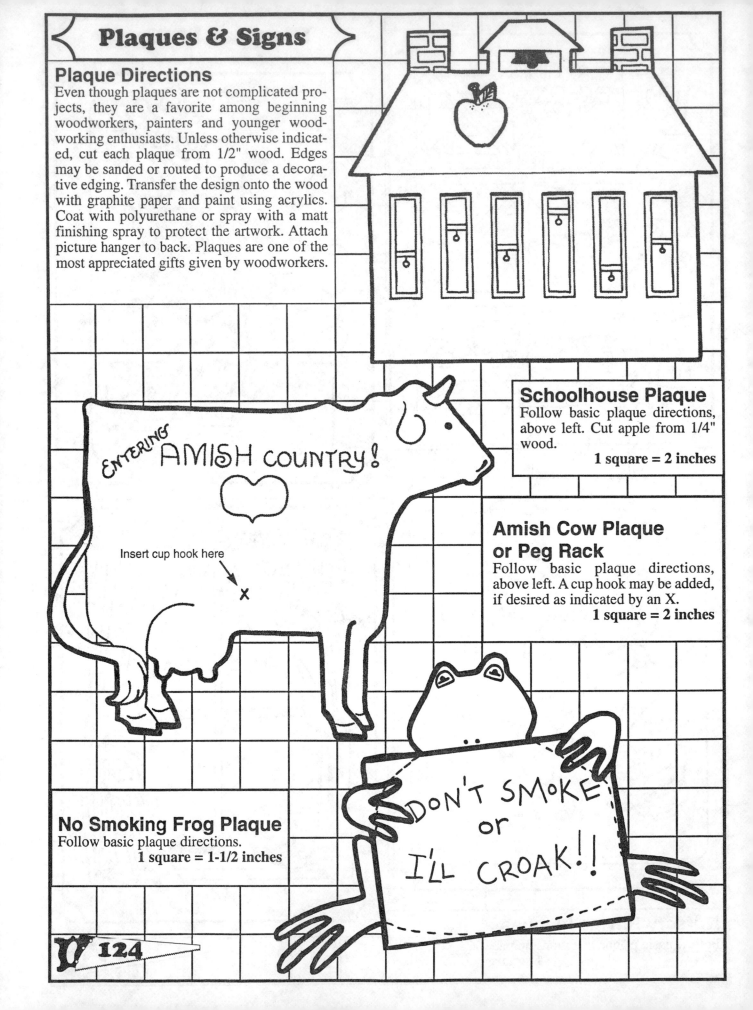

No Smoking Frog Plaque

Follow basic plaque directions.

1 square = 1-1/2 inches

Ahoy! Sailboat Plaque

Follow basic plaque directions on page 124.

1 square = 2 inches

Old Fisherman Plaque

Follow basic plaque directions on page 124.

1 square = 2 inches

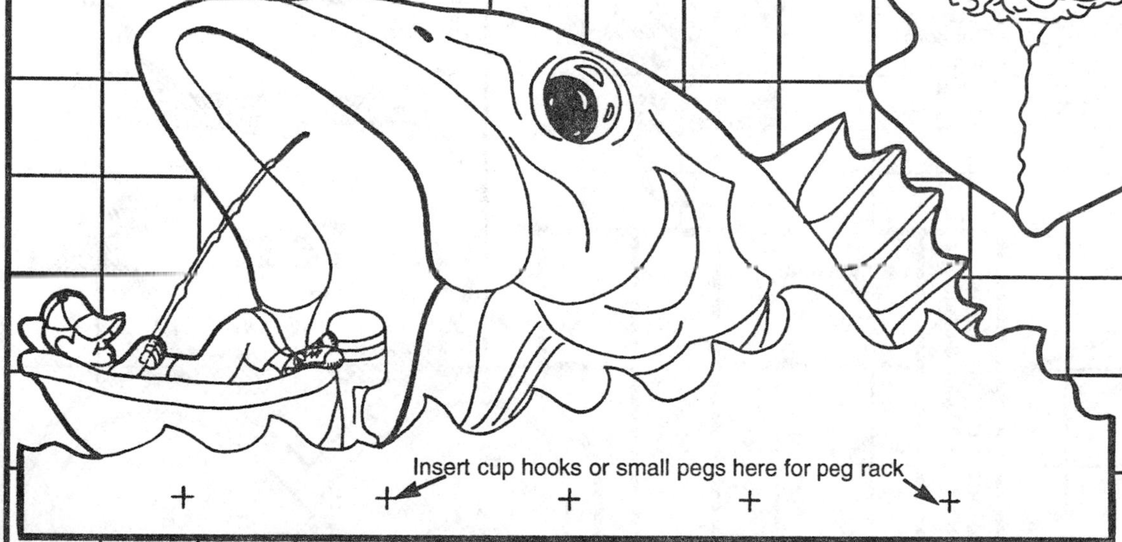

Fisherman's Dream Plaque or Peg Rack

Cut plaque from 1/2" wood. Sand edges until smooth. Transfer the design onto the wood with graphite paper and paint using acrylics. The finished plaque may be coated with polyurethane or sprayed with a matt finishing spray to protect the artwork. On finished plaque, use a picture hanger on the back to hang onto the wall, or drill a small hole into the center, back to hang on a nail. Use cup hooks or small pegs, if desired where indicated by an X to make this a peg rack.

1 square = 2 inches

Scarecrow Picket Fence Welcome

Trace the blackbird's wing, corn hanging from the scarecrow's arm and "Welcome" onto 1/4" wood, then cut out. Trace and cut the rest of the pieces from 3/4" wood. Cut two vertical fence pieces and three horizontal pieces. Use yellow glue and finishing nails to attach the scarecrow and sunflower to the fence. Paint with acrylics. Coat with polyurethane and hang on the front door to greet visitors.

1 square = 2 inches

Scarecrow Picket Fence Diagram

Sheep Family Plaque

This plaque is designed for one cut, but you must adjust the number of sheep according to the size of your family. (For two family members, only trace two sheep, heart and top hanger.) Drill a hole as indicated by the X to hang. Makes a great front door plaque. Paint with acrylics and coat with outdoor polyurethane.

1 square = 1-1/2 inches

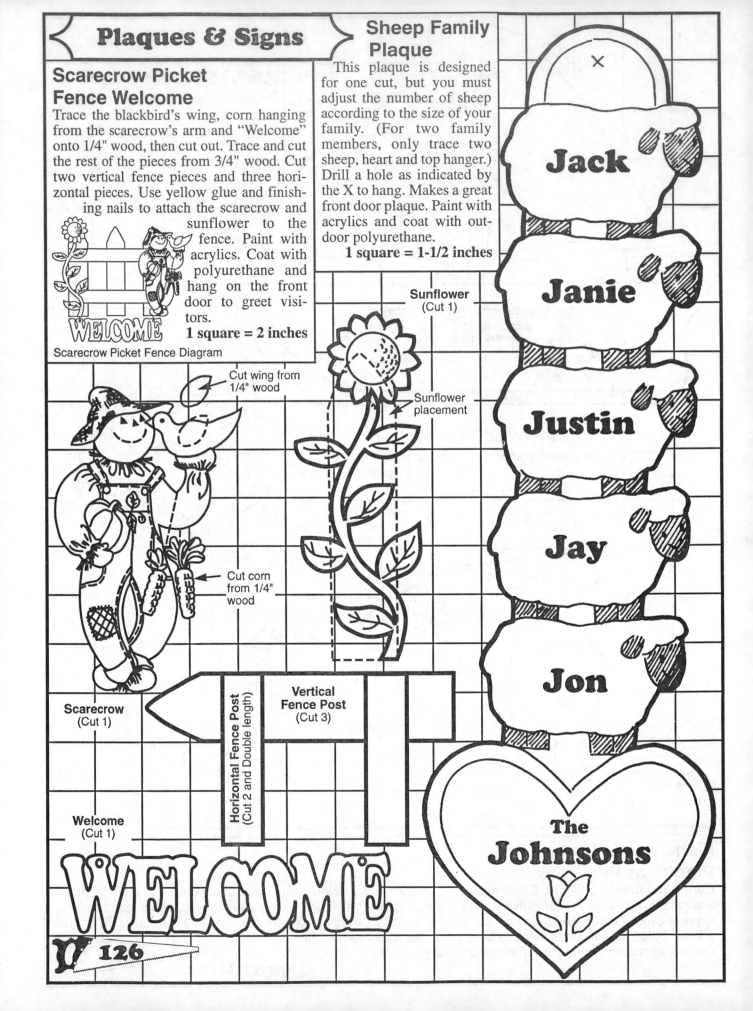

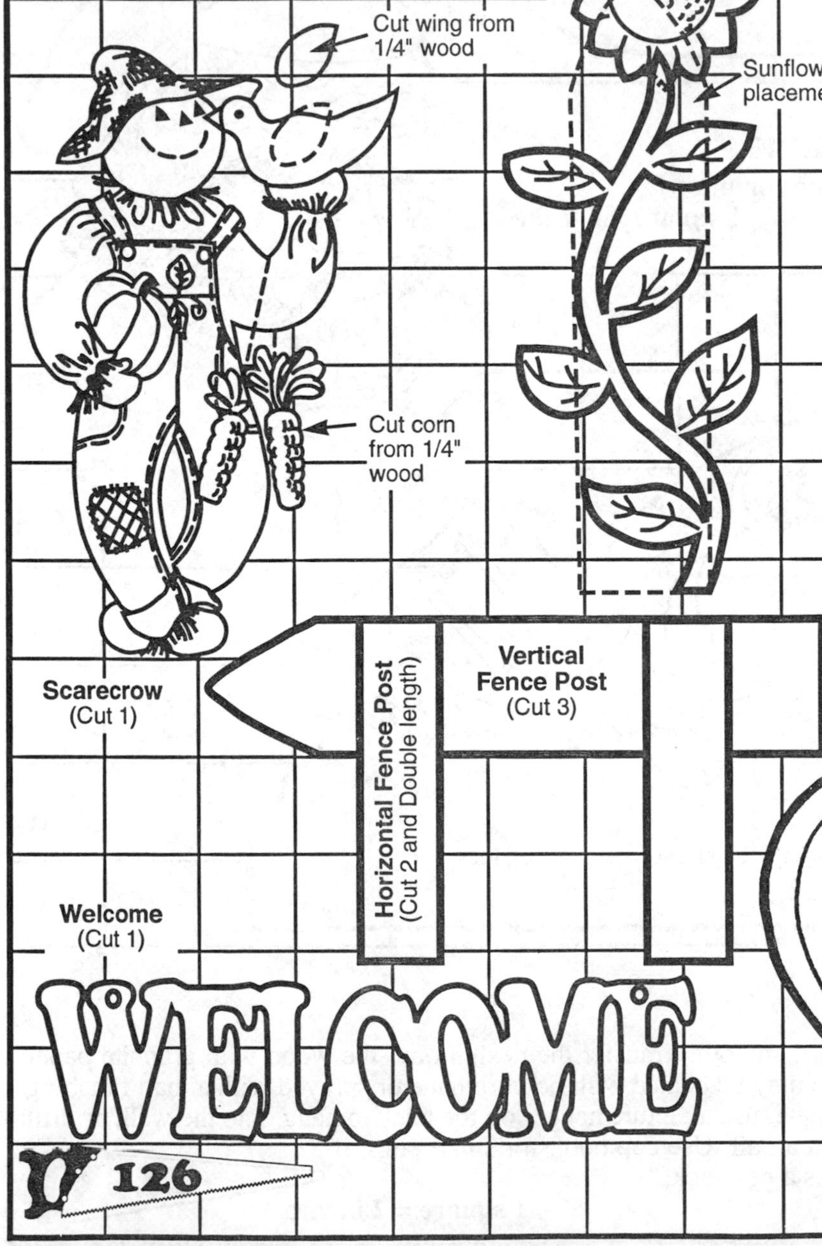

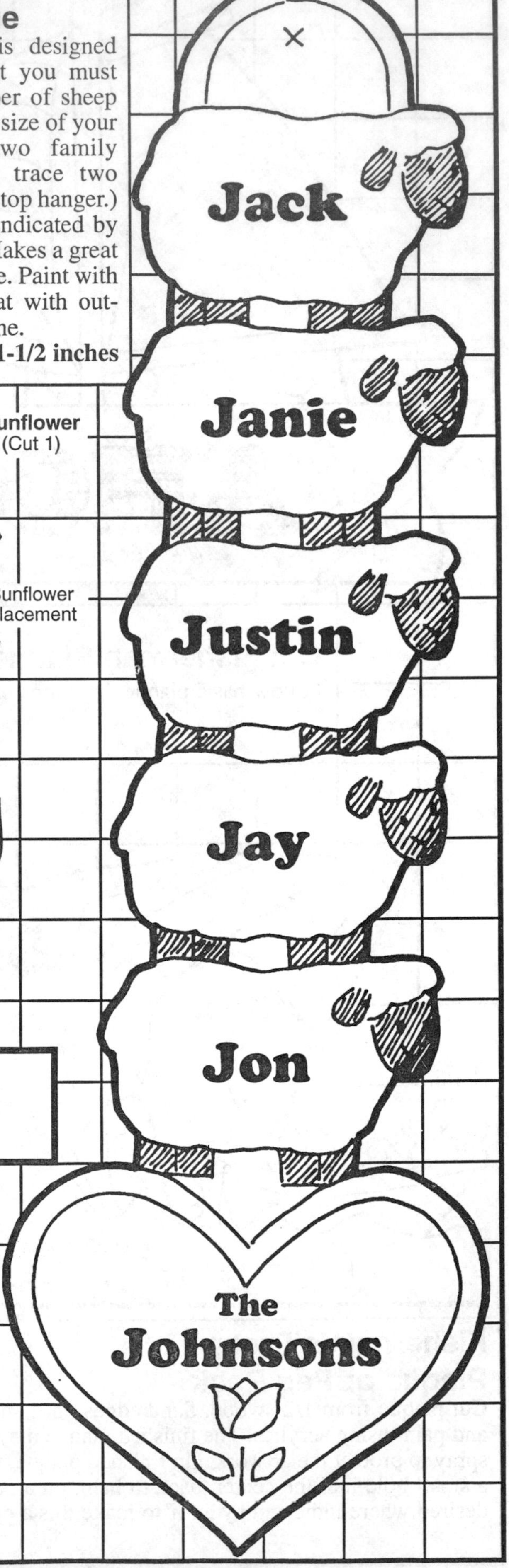

Gecko Welcome Peg Rack

Cut the back from 1/2" wood. Cut the gecko from 1/4" wood. Drill a hole at the place marked with an X for a shaker peg. Sand and glue the gecko to the back. Paint and seal with acrylics. Attach a hanger to the back.

1 square = 3/4 inch

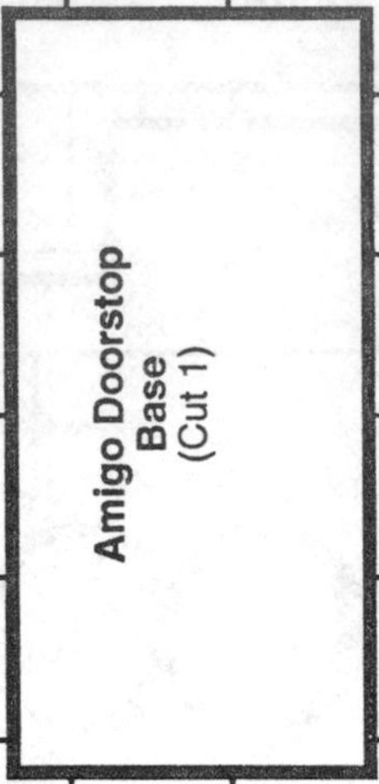

Adobe Bookends or Doorstop

1 square = 3 inches
Adjust size for Bookends

Amigo Bookends or Doorstop

1 square = 3 inches
Adjust size for Bookends

Door Stops

Cut door stop from 1" wood. Cut the base from 1/2" wood and taper along one end to enable it to fit under a door. Attach the base to the back with countersunk wood screws. Sand, paint and seal.

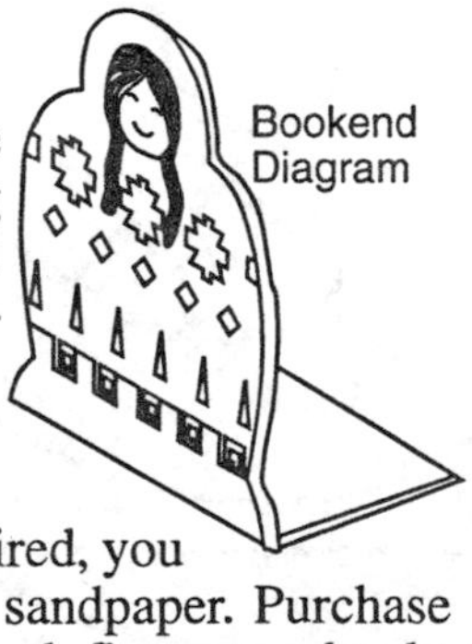

Bookends

Cut two bookends from 1" wood. If desired, you may round the edges using a rasp and sandpaper. Purchase metal bookends and centre and attach each figure to a bookend using epoxy glue and screws, if needed. Sand, paint and seal. **Note:** The enlargement of the pattern will depend on the size of the purchased bookend. We only give a general recommendation. Measure your bookends before cutting for optimum satisfaction.

Indian Bookends or Doorstop

1 square = 3 inches
Adjust size for Bookends

Southwestern Clock

This clock is designed to hang on the wall but will sit alone if cut from thick wood. Cut one from at least 3/4" wood. Drill a hole for the clock assembly which must be purchased from a craft shop or ordered through the mail. If desired, make a wooden box frame for the clock assembly and attach to the back. Paint the numbers on as shown or use numbers purchased with a clock assembly. Transfer the pattern using graphite paper and paint with acrylics. Coat with clear acrylic beforc adding the clock assembly. See page 15 for order information.

1 square = 3 inches

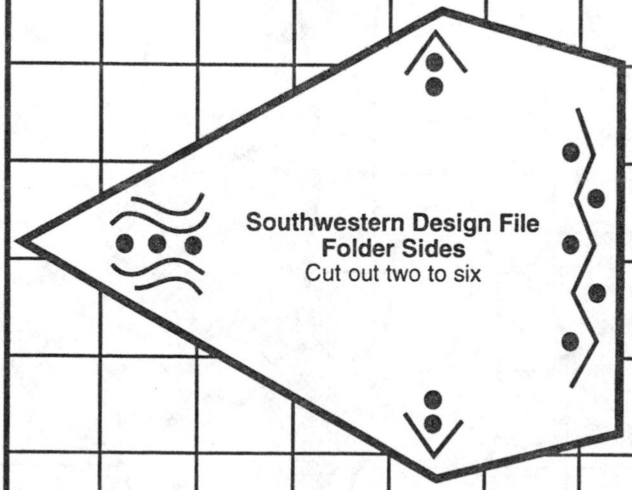

Southwestern Design File Folder Bottom Spacer
Cut out and place between each side piece.

Southwestern Design File Folder Holder

Cut two to six side pieces depending on how many sections you desire. Finish and assemble using diagram.

1 square = 3 inches

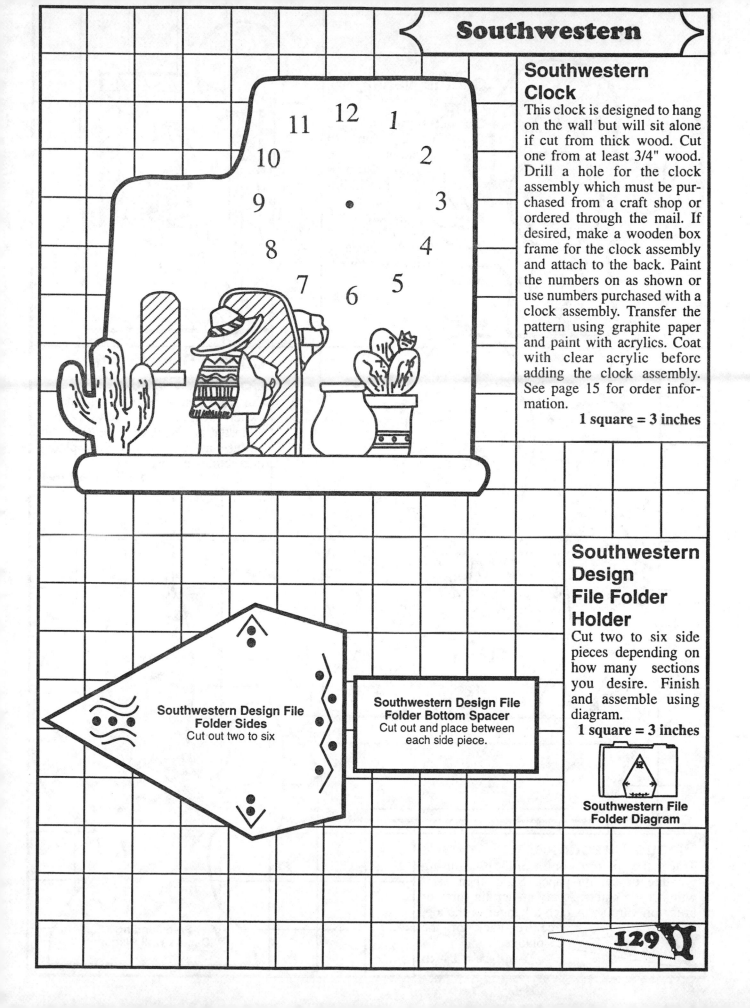

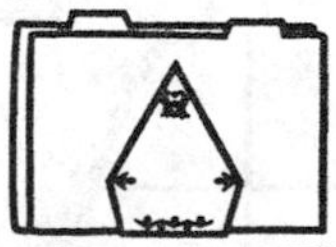

Southwestern File Folder Diagram

Southwestern

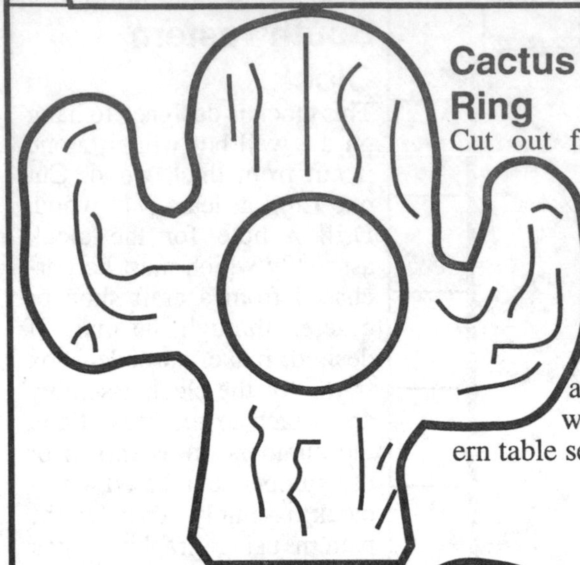

Cactus Napkin Ring

Cut out from 3/4" pine (don't forget to cut out the hole to insert napkin) and finish as shown on both sides. Coat with clear acrylic and enjoy with a southwestern table setting.

Actual Size

Coyote Switchplate Cover or Plaque

Cut from thin wood. Cut out hole for switch. Drill holes for screws. Paint as indicated and coat with clear acrylic. To use as a plaque, follow plaque instructions below.

1 square = 1 inch

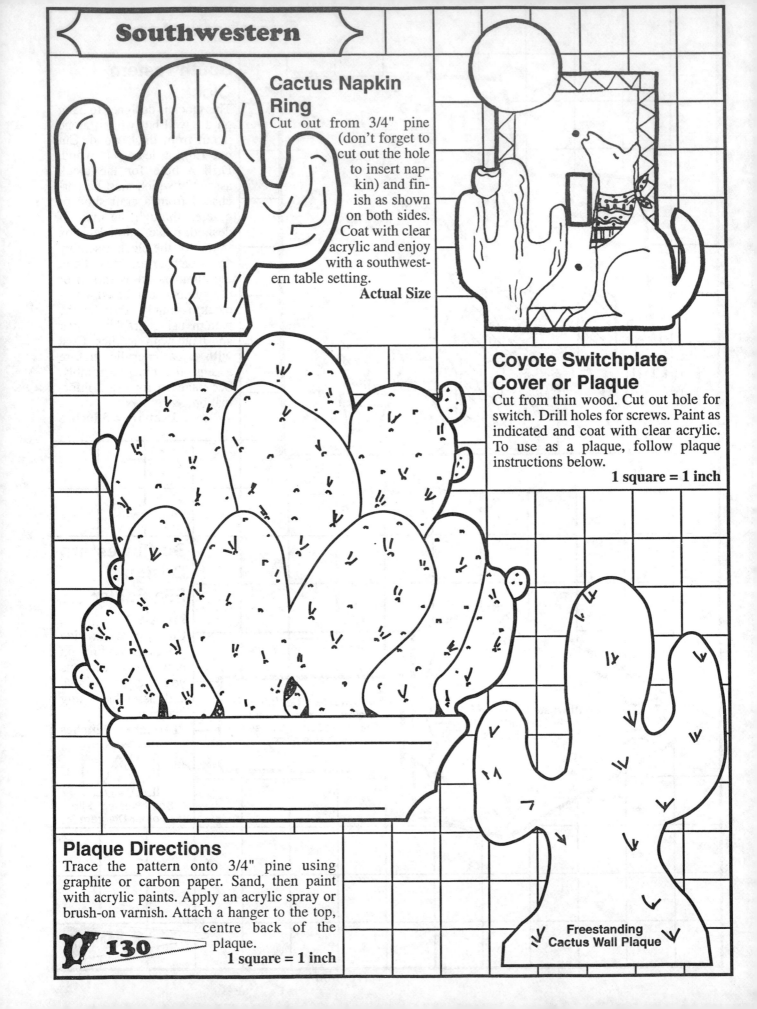

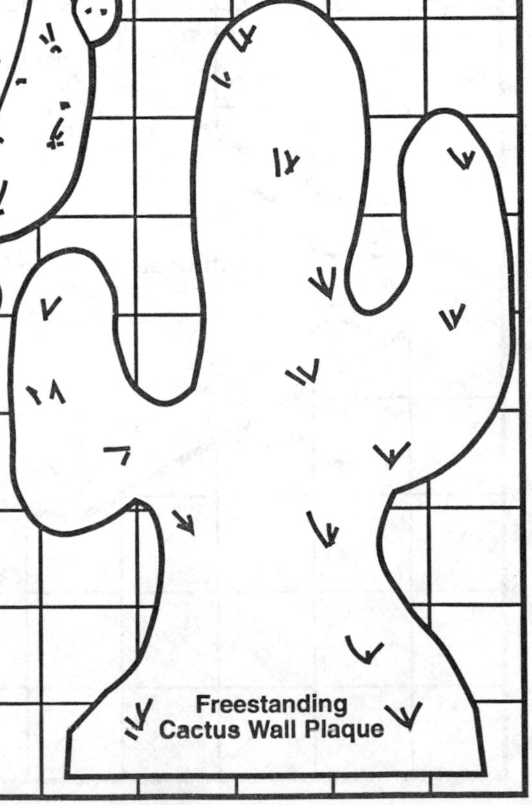

Freestanding Cactus Wall Plaque

Plaque Directions

Trace the pattern onto 3/4" pine using graphite or carbon paper. Sand, then paint with acrylic paints. Apply an acrylic spray or brush-on varnish. Attach a hanger to the top, centre back of the plaque.

1 square = 1 inch

Southwestern Cactus Shelf

Cut all shelf pieces from 1/2" wood. Cut one back, two braces and one shelf top piece. Cut a piece 19-1/4" x 7-1/2" (pattern not shown) for the shelf top piece. The shelf top may be routed around the outside edge, if desired. The cactus is an inside cut. Assemble all of the pieces using wood glue and screws. Paint using southwestern colours or stain. Seal with acrylic sealer.

1 square = 2 inches

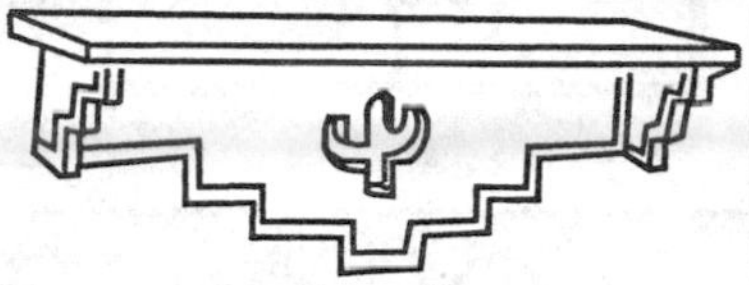

Southwestern Cactus Shelf Diagram

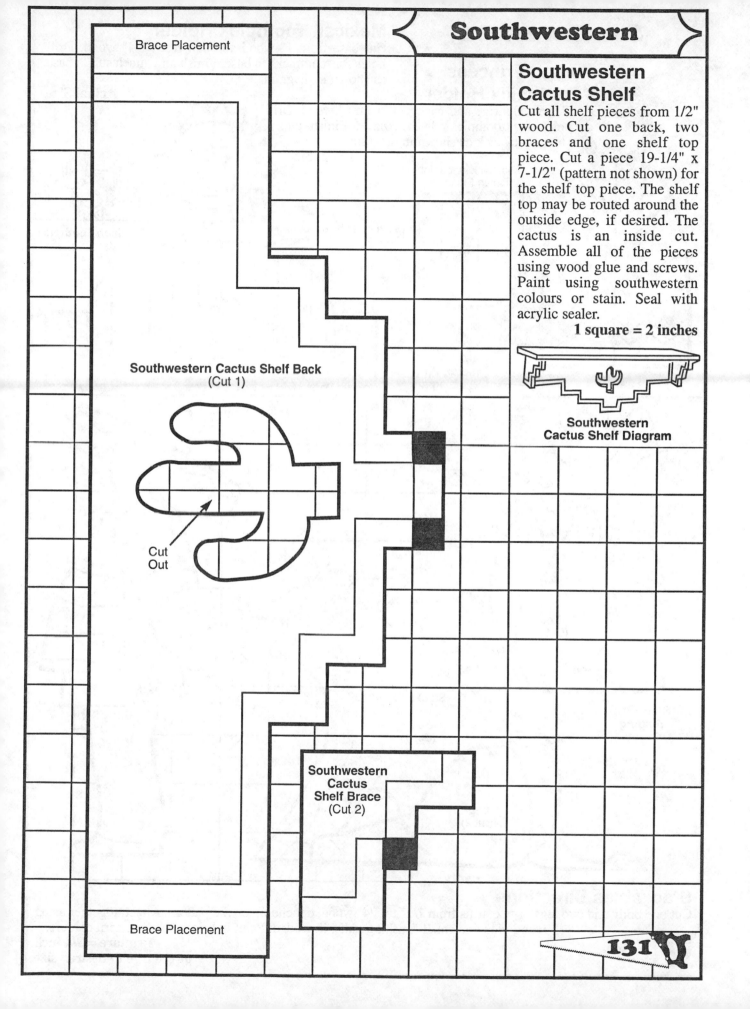

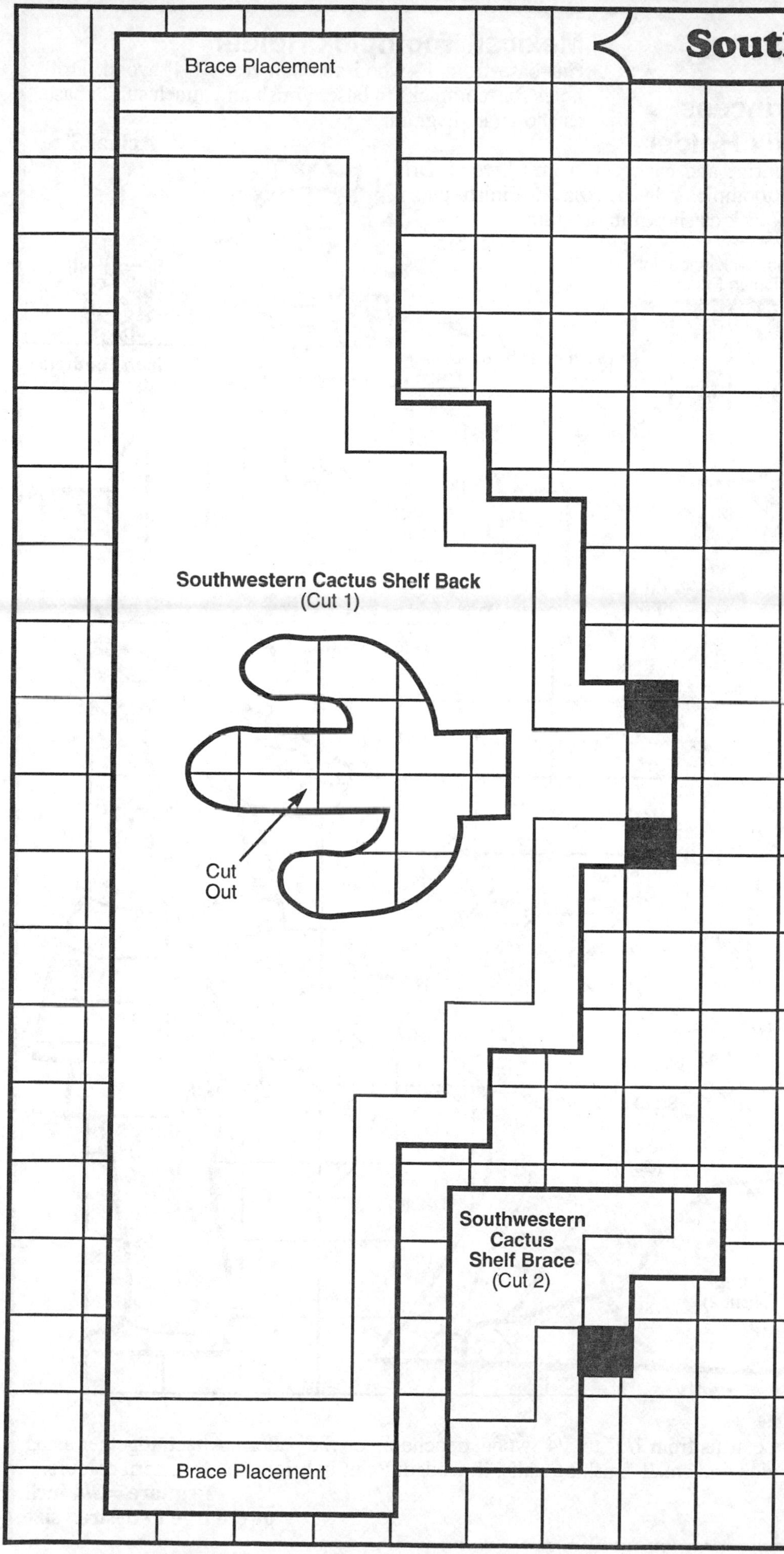

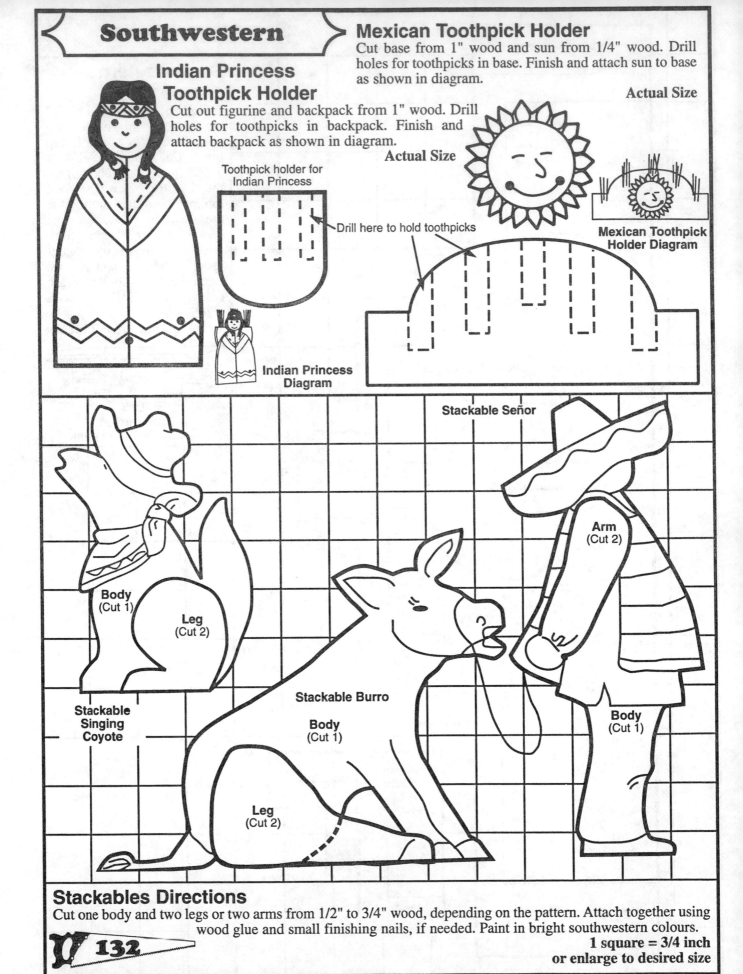

Southwestern

Indian Princess Toothpick Holder

Cut out figurine and backpack from 1" wood. Drill holes for toothpicks in backpack. Finish and attach backpack as shown in diagram.

Actual Size

Toothpick holder for Indian Princess

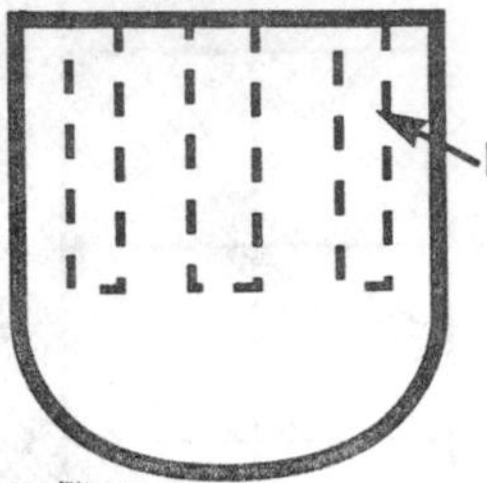

Drill here to hold toothpicks

Indian Princess Diagram

Mexican Toothpick Holder

Cut base from 1" wood and sun from 1/4" wood. Drill holes for toothpicks in base. Finish and attach sun to base as shown in diagram.

Actual Size

Mexican Toothpick Holder Diagram

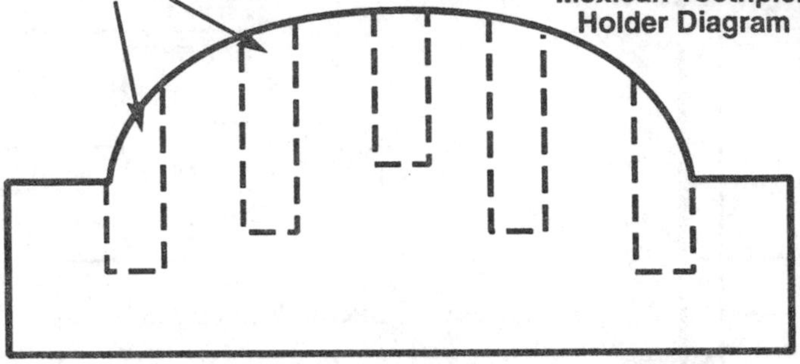

Stackables Directions

Cut one body and two legs or two arms from 1/2" to 3/4" wood, depending on the pattern. Attach together using wood glue and small finishing nails, if needed. Paint in bright southwestern colours.

1 square = 3/4 inch or enlarge to desired size

3-D Coyote Peg Rack

Cut the back of the peg rack and moon from 1/2" wood. Cut the remaining pieces from 1/4" wood, and paint. Assemble all of the pieces with glue. Drill a hole in the places marked with an X for placement of shaker pegs. Seal with acrylic sealer.

1 square = 2 inches

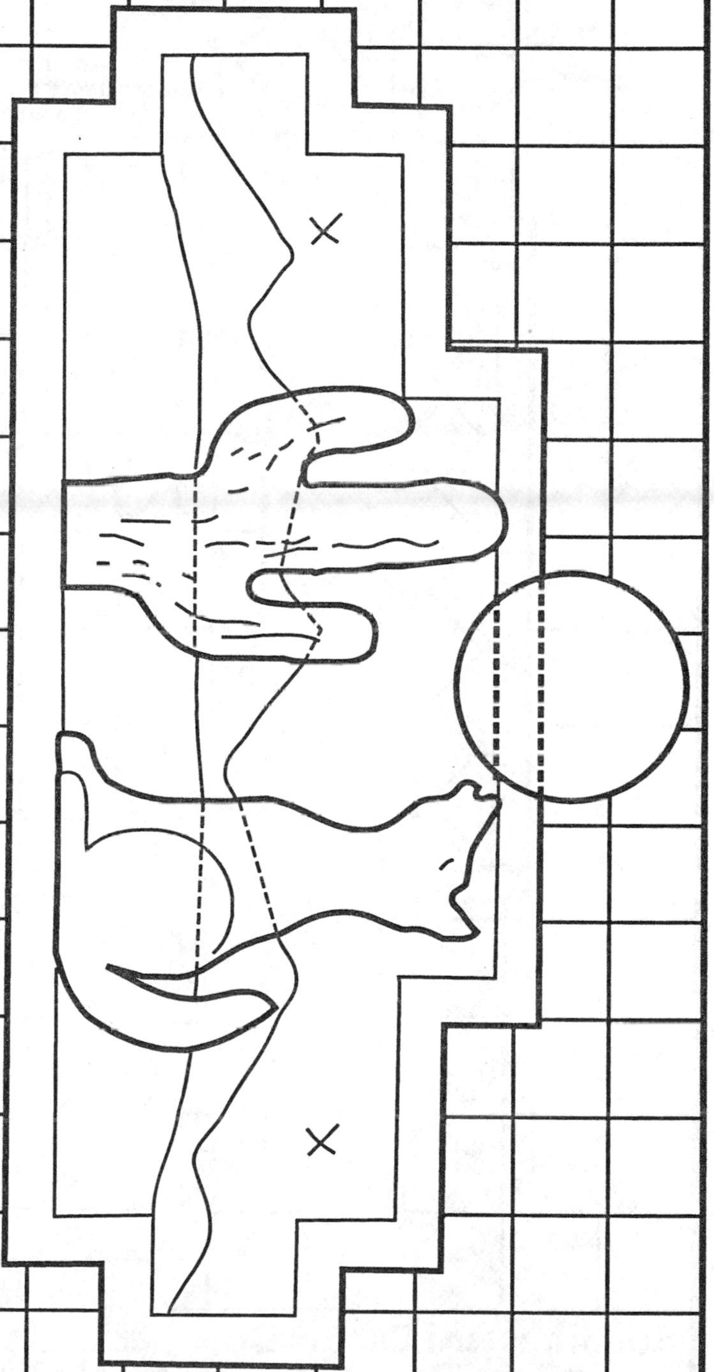

Stackable Señorita

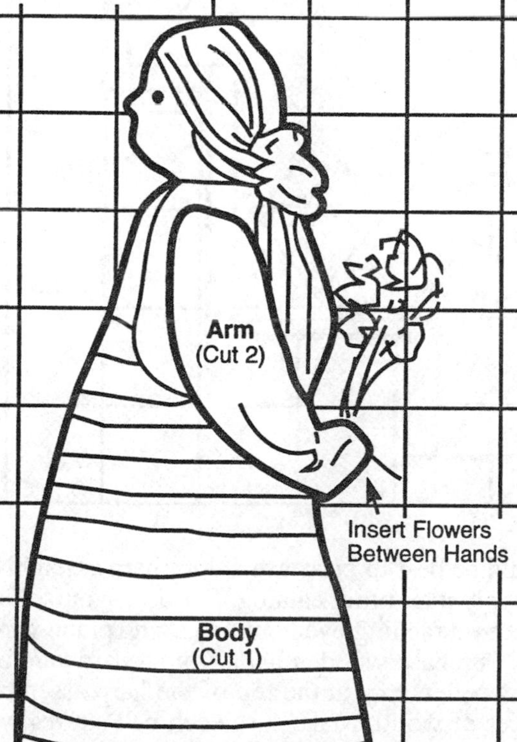

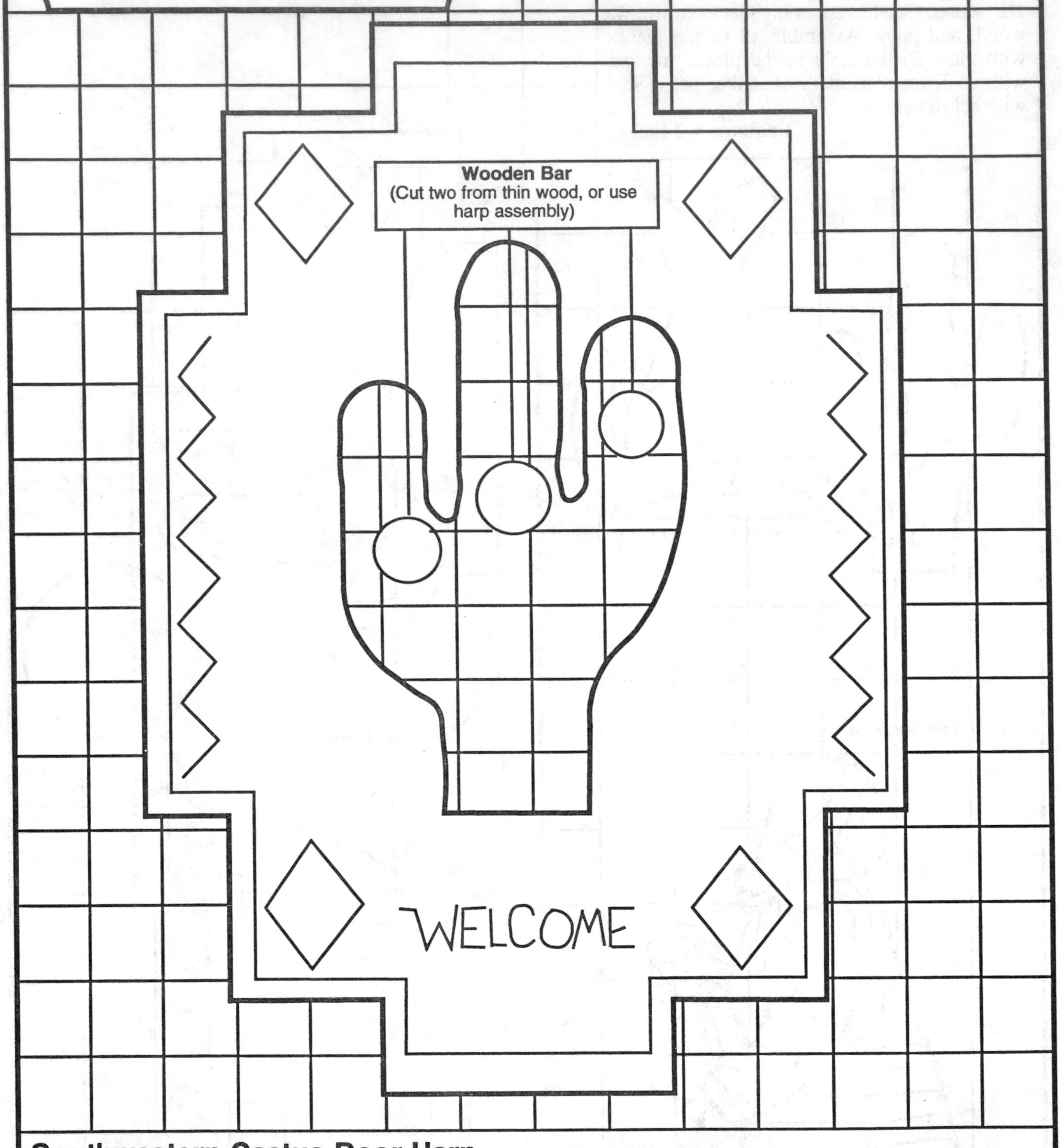

Southwestern Cactus Door Harp

Cut from 1" pine. This door harp does not need a back. It would be best to purchase a door harp assembly from a hardware store, craft store, or order from a woodworker's supply mail order catalog. For do-it-yourselfers: the quality will not necessarily be the same but you may assemble by attaching eye hooks to string piano wire. You could also purchase guitar strings and posts to mount strings. Purchase wooden balls from a hardware or DIY store. String balls on fishing line. Attach by cutting two thin wooden bars at the top of the harp assembly and glue together, clamping the fishing line between the two pieces of wood. Make sure each ball strikes wires to make a musical sound. Hang on door so that when the door is opened and closed, the harp will play.

1 square = 1 inch

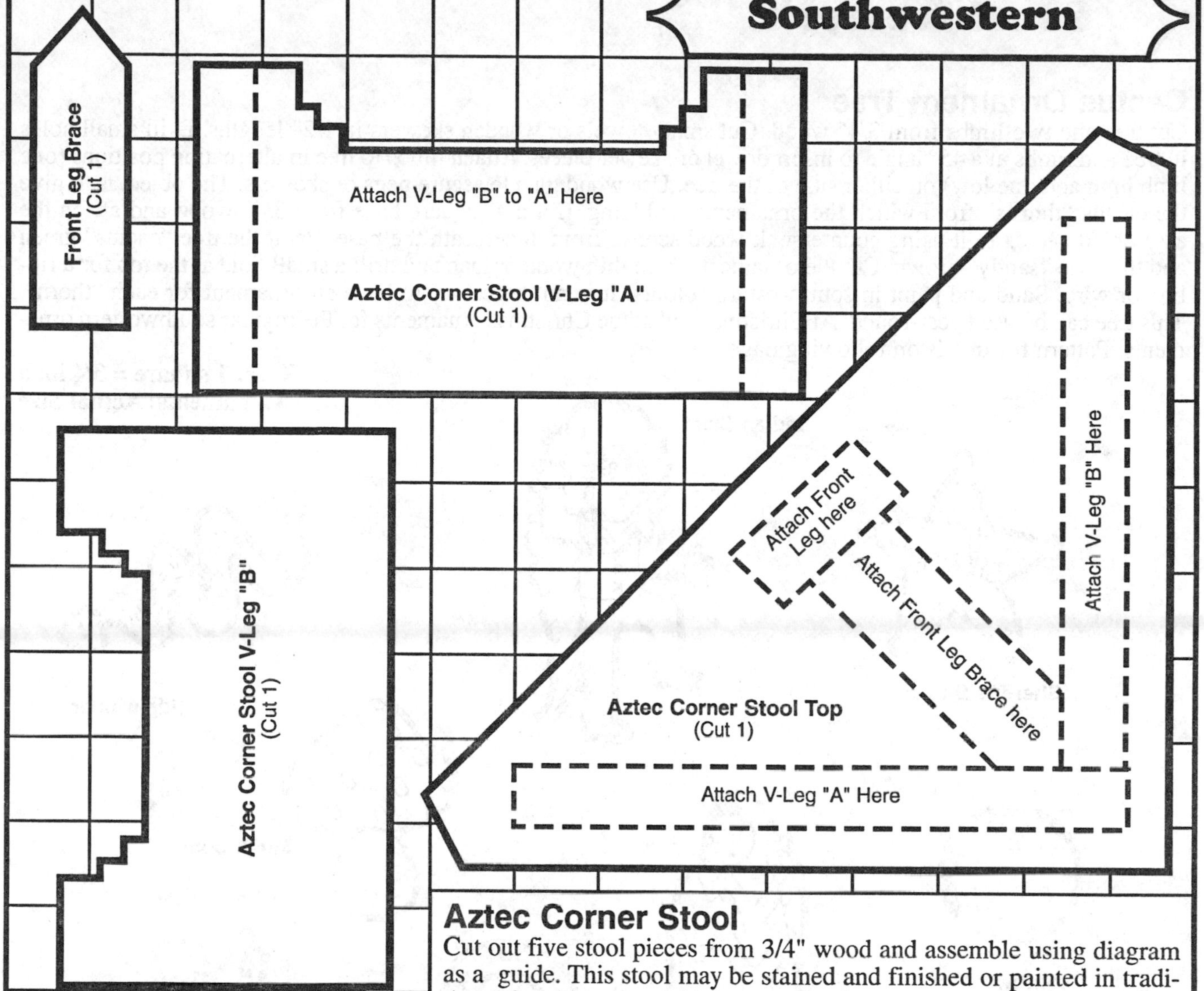

Aztec Corner Stool

Cut out five stool pieces from 3/4" wood and assemble using diagram as a guide. This stool may be stained and finished or painted in traditional Southwestern colours.

1 square = 3 inches

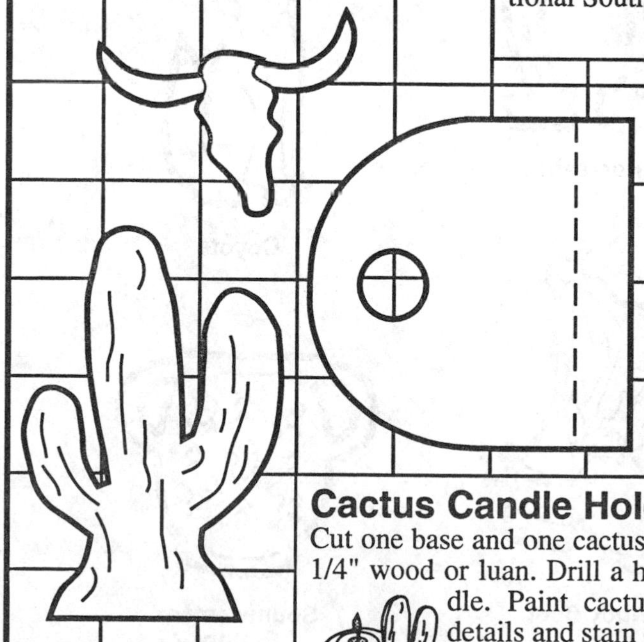

Aztec Corner Stool Diagram

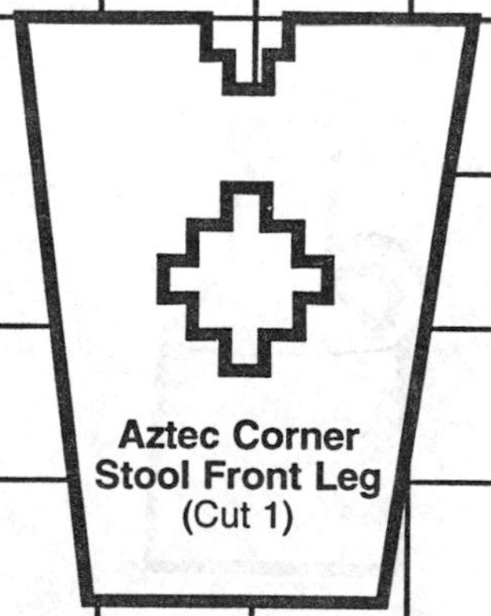

Cactus Candle Holder

Cut one base and one cactus from 1/2" wood. Cut a skull from 1/4" wood or luan. Drill a hole, as indicated for a votive candle. Paint cactus green, skull white with black details and stain or paint the base brown. Coat with clear acrylic.

1 square = 3/4 inch

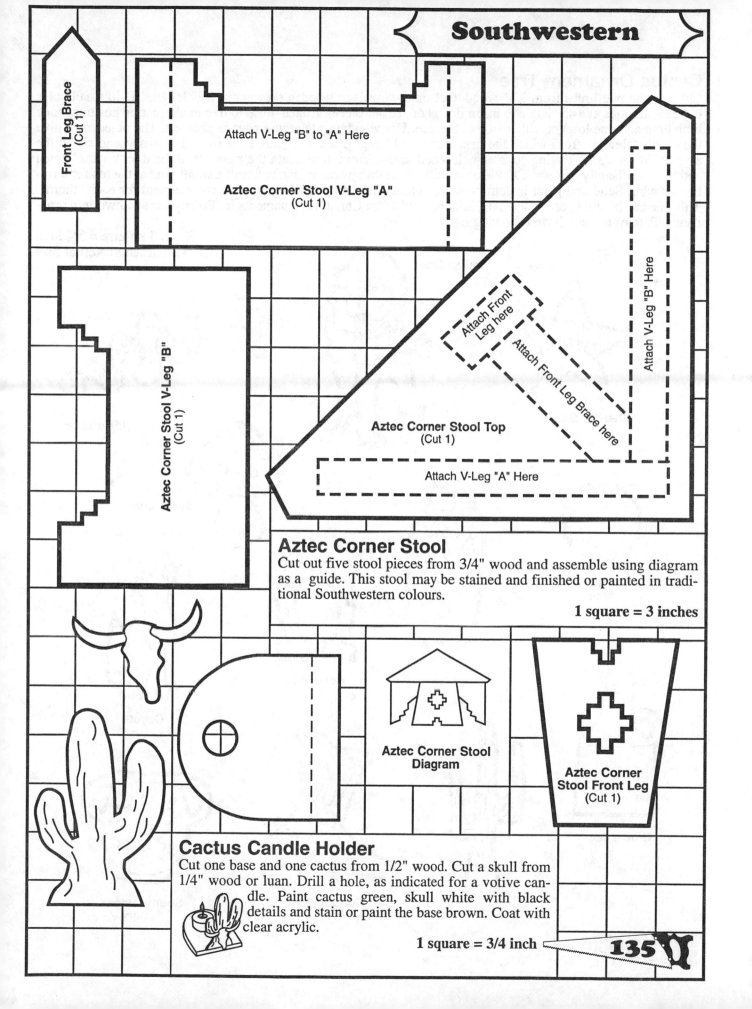

Cactus Ornament Tree

Cut tree and two limbs from 3/4" wood. Cut small dowels or wooden skewers in 1/2" lengths. Drill small holes in tree and limbs at a 45° angle to insert dowel or skewer pieces. Attach limbs to tree in alternating positions (one limb high and one low) on either side of the tree. Use wood glue to secure pegs or skewers. The object is to give the cactus "thorns" from which the ornaments will hang. Cut a 4" square base from 3/4" wood and attach the assembled cactus to it using countersunk wood screws from underneath the base. Paint the tree "cactus" green and the base "sandy" brown. Cut the ornaments from thin wood or luan and drill a small hole at the top for a ribbon or wire. Sand and paint in southwestern colours. It is not necessary to have an ornament for each "thorn." This tree can be used year-round. At Christmas, substitue Christmas ornaments for the regular southwestern ornaments. Pattern for tree is on following page.

Tree: 1 square = 3/4 inch
Ornaments: Actual Size

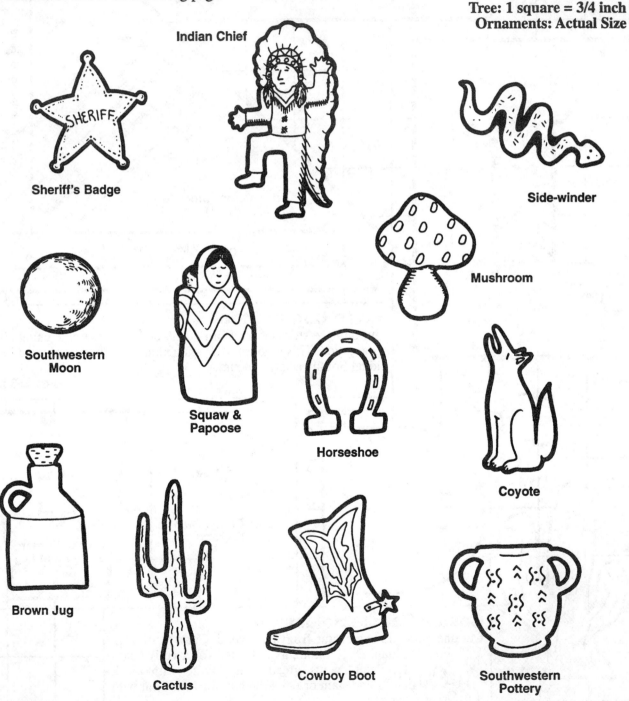

Indian Chief

Sheriff's Badge

Side-winder

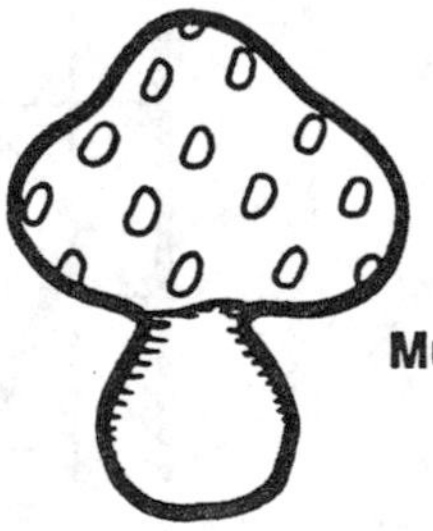

Mushroom

Southwestern Moon

Squaw & Papoose

Horseshoe

Coyote

Brown Jug

Cactus

Cowboy Boot

Southwestern Pottery

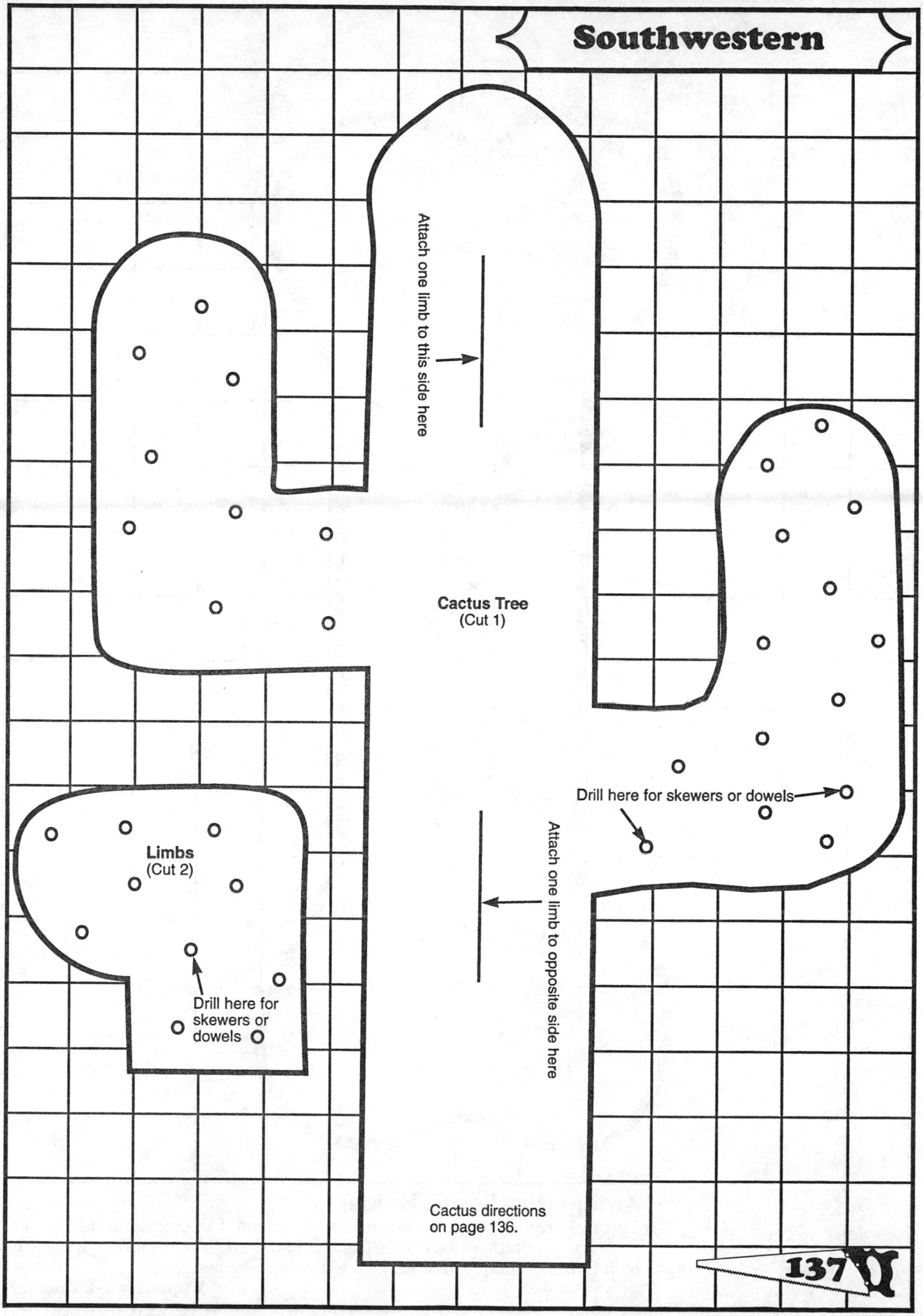
Attach one limb to this side here
Cactus Tree
(Cut 1)
Drill here for skewers or dowels
Limbs
(Cut 2)
Drill here for skewers or dowels
Attach one limb to opposite side here
Cactus directions on page 136.

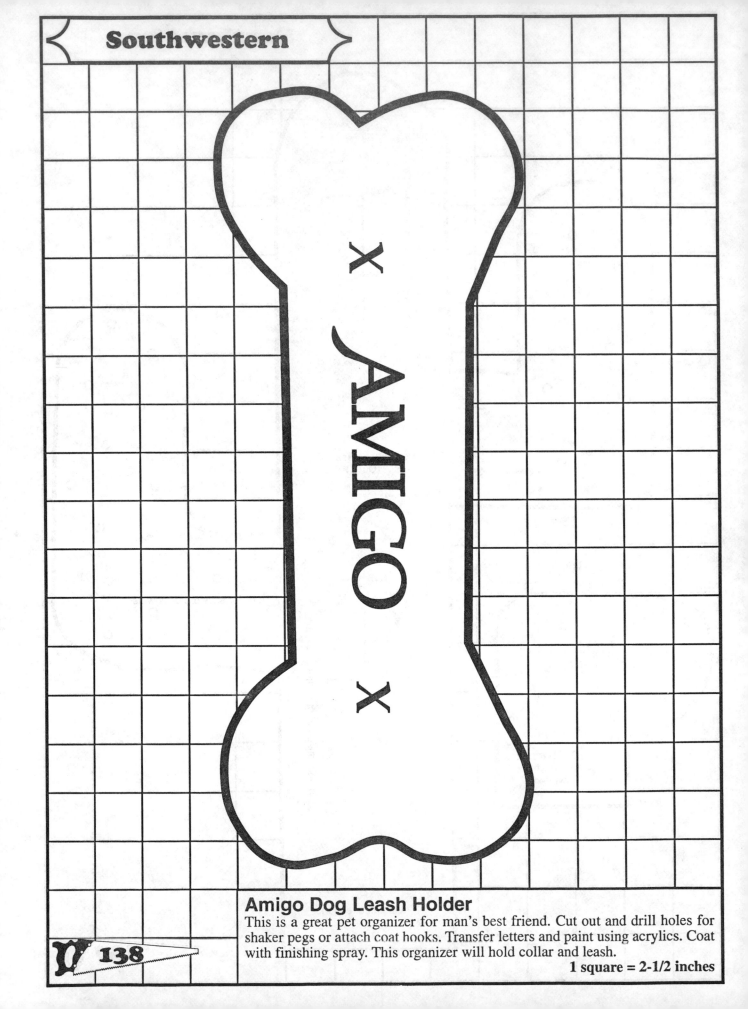

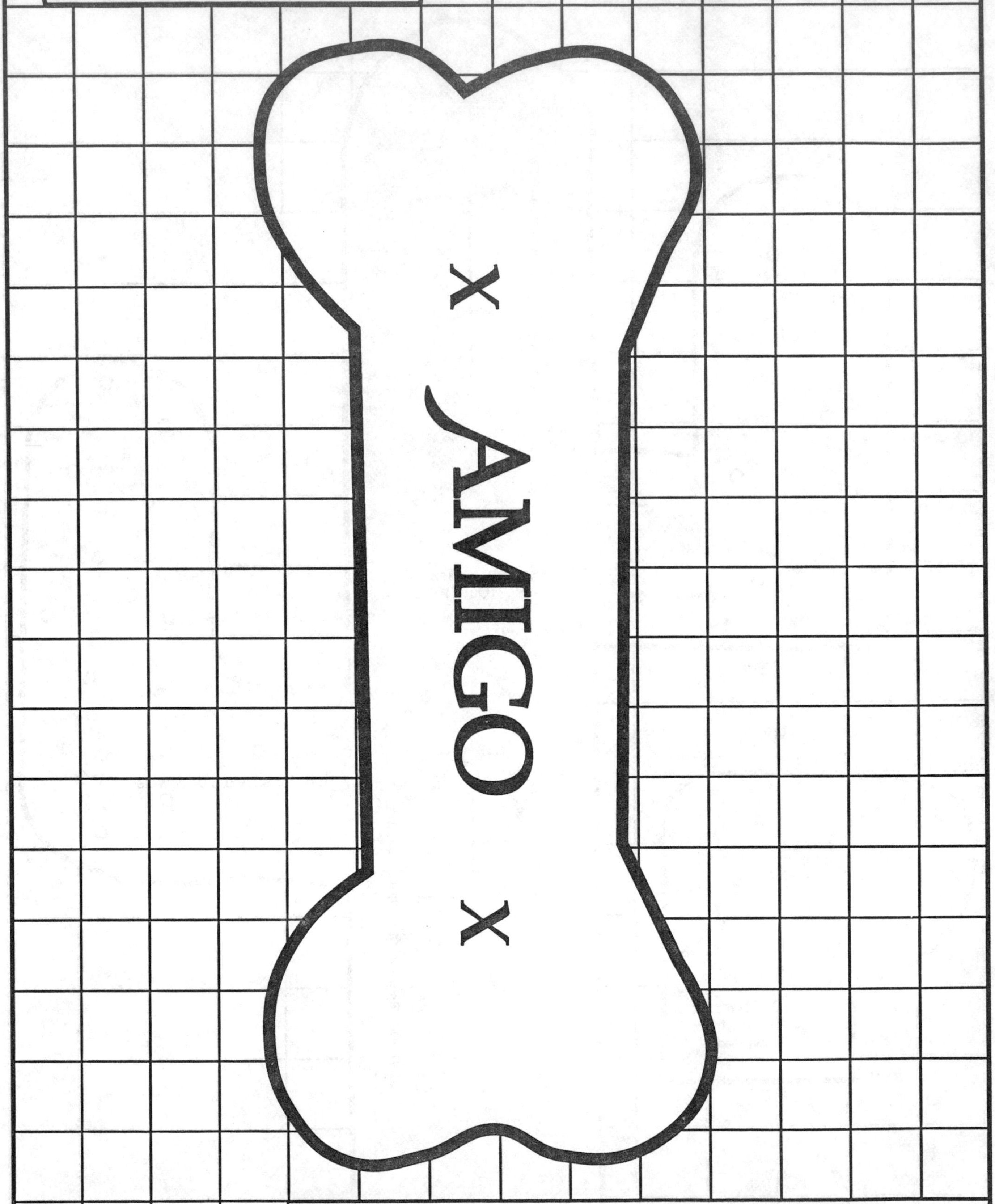

Amigo Dog Leash Holder

This is a great pet organizer for man's best friend. Cut out and drill holes for shaker pegs or attach coat hooks. Transfer letters and paint using acrylics. Coat with finishing spray. This organizer will hold collar and leash.

1 square = 2-1/2 inches

— CHAPTER THIRTEEN —

TOYS & GAMES

Cat Picture Puzzle

Cut two pieces of 3/4" wood the size of the entire picture. One piece will be the frame, the other will be the puzzle. Take the top piece and transfer the puzzle design onto the wood using tracing or graphite paper. First, cut out the strips on the sides for a frame. Next cut out individual pieces. Attach the strips to the outside of the base. Paint the entire piece. Make sure that the bottom and top of the base are painted. The frame would look nice if painted a contrasting color or white. Make sure, when painting, that the puzzle pieces are painted separately. If they are painted while connected, the paint could possibly cause them to stick together.

1 square = 1-1/4 inches

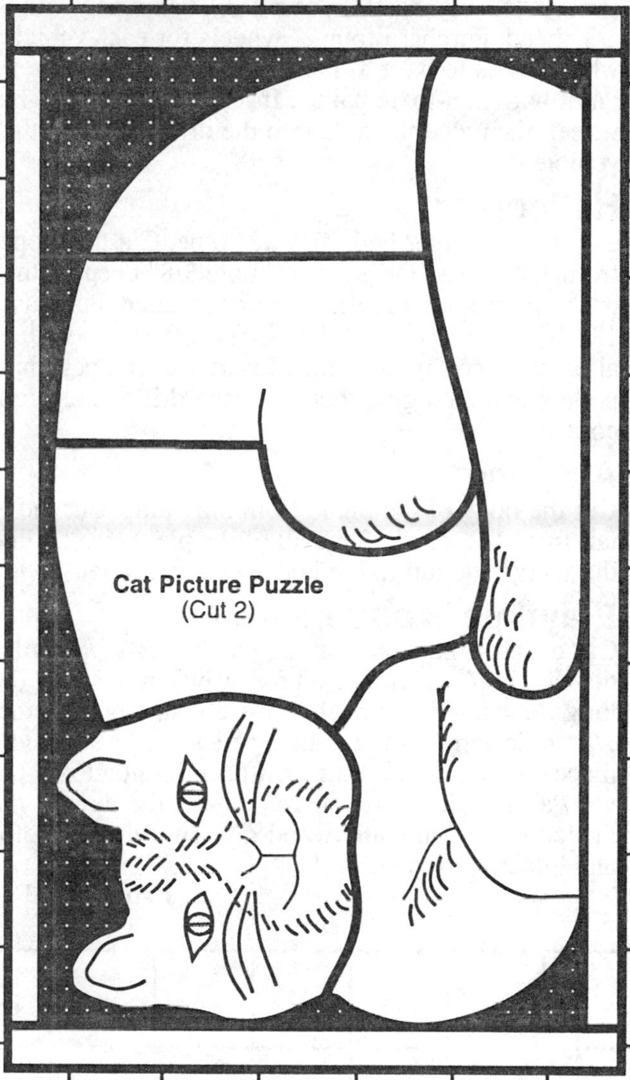

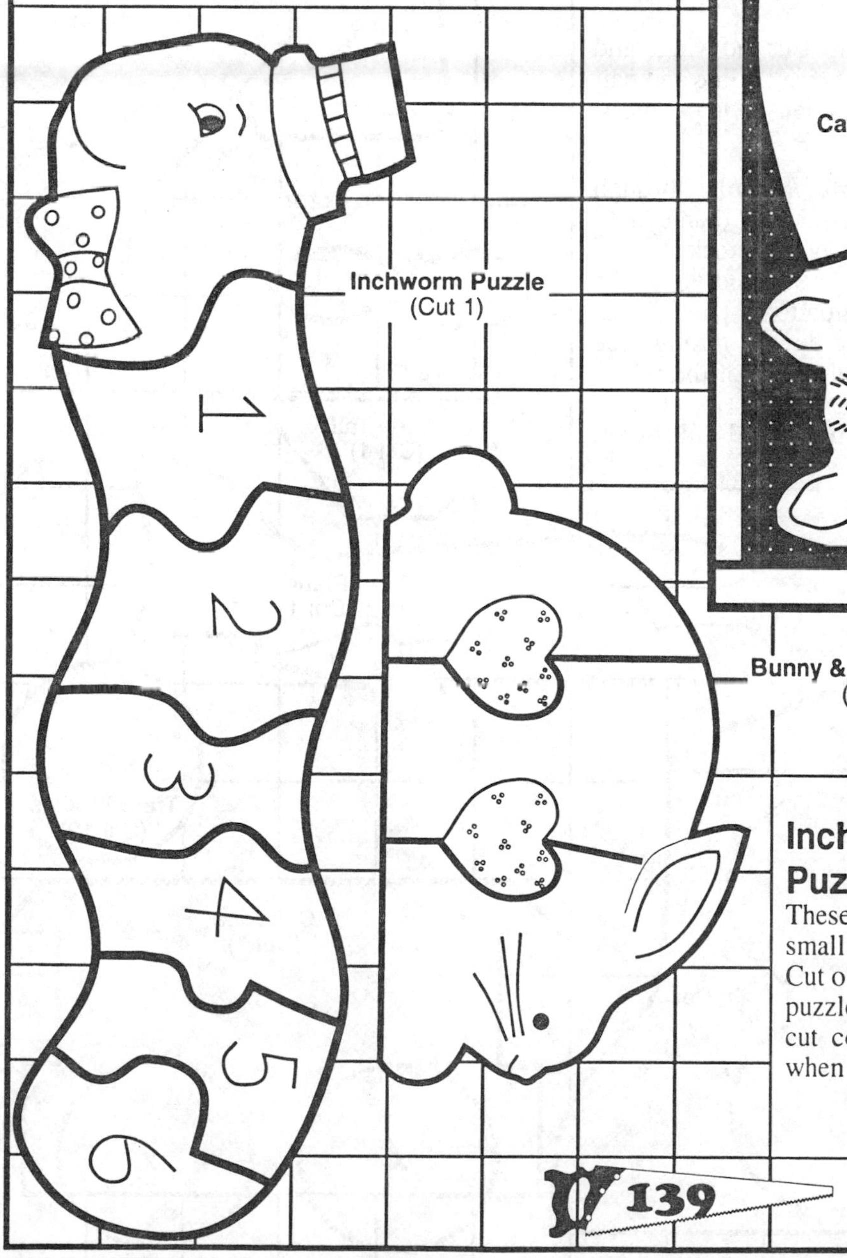

Inchworm and Bunny & Hearts Puzzles

These puzzles make great learning tools for small children. Cut all pieces from 3/4" wood. Cut out and finish the same way that the other puzzle is cut except that there is no frame. If cut correctly, these puzzles will sit upright when assembled, amazing younger children.

1 square = 1-1/4 inches

Truck, Van and Car

(These patterns are found on page 141)
Cut each of the toys from 2" pine. Drill a 7/32" hole 1/2" deep at each "X" for insertion of a 1-3/8" axle peg with a 3/8" head. Purchase four 2" wheels for each vehicle (the wheels need to have 1/4" holes.) Sand the toys well. Paint with non-toxic paints. Insert the axle through the wheel, then glue the axle into the drilled hole in the vehicle.

Helicopter

Cut the helicopter body from 2" pine. Cut the propellers from 1/2" stock. Drill a 5/32" hole 3/8" deep on the top of the helicopter and the side as indicated. Purchase two 13/16" axle pegs. Sand the pieces well. Paint with several coats of non-toxic paints. Insert the axle pegs into the propellers and then glue them into the drilled holes on the helicopter.

Airplane

Cut the body of the plane from 3/4" pine. Cut the wings and tail from 1/2" stock. Sand all of the pieces well. Glue and nail the wings and tail to the body. Paint with non-toxic paints.

Playtime Wooden Train

Cut each of the cars from 2" stock. Drill 3/8" holes through the cars in places indicated for insertion of a 3/8" diameter 4" long dowel. Cut 4 wheels for each car from 1" stock. Drill a 3/8" hole through the center of each wheel. Sand all of the pieces until smooth. Paint with bright, non-toxic paints. Seal with an acrylic spray varnish. Insert the dowels through the drilled cars. Dab some wood glue into the hole of the wheel and attach it to the dowel.

1 square = 1-1/4 inches

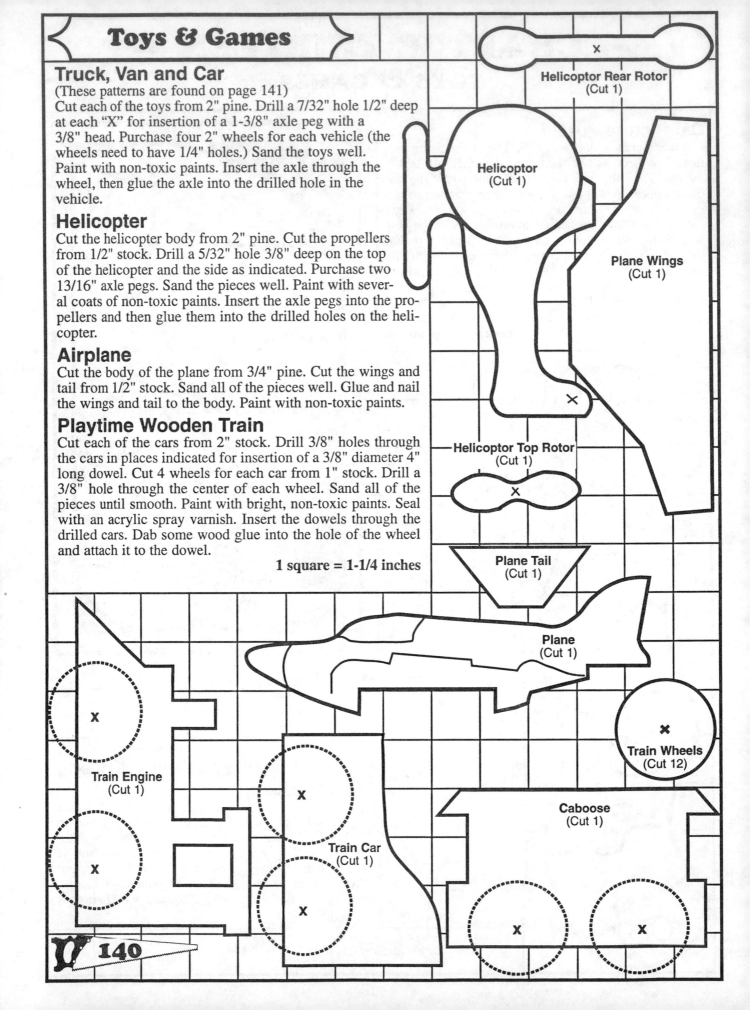

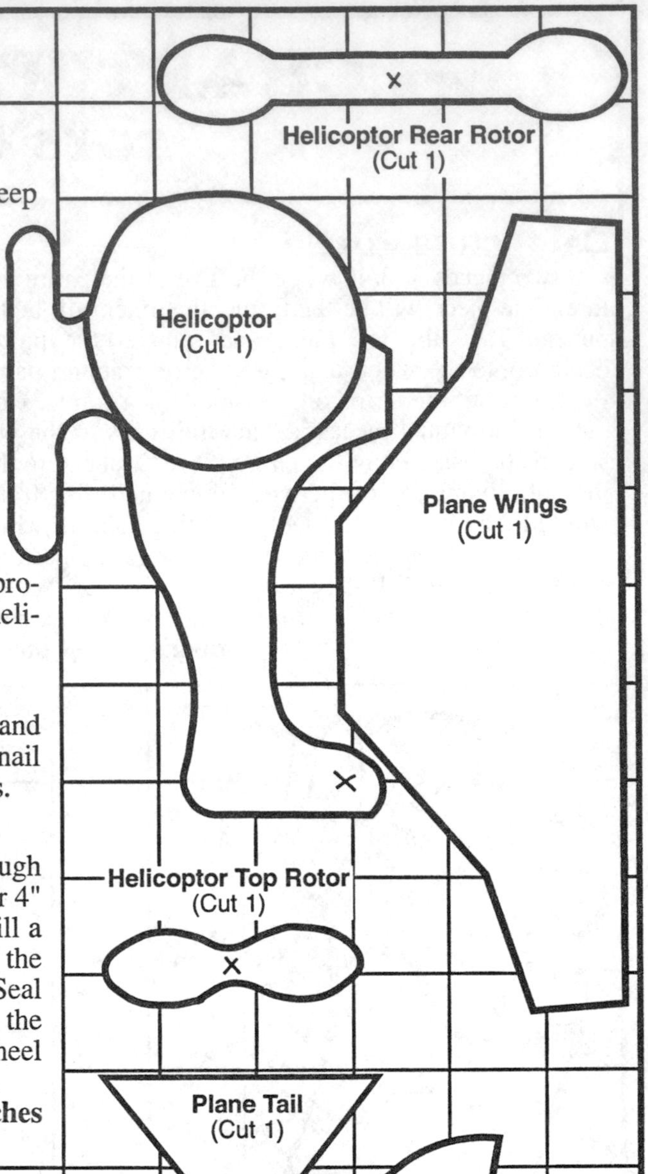

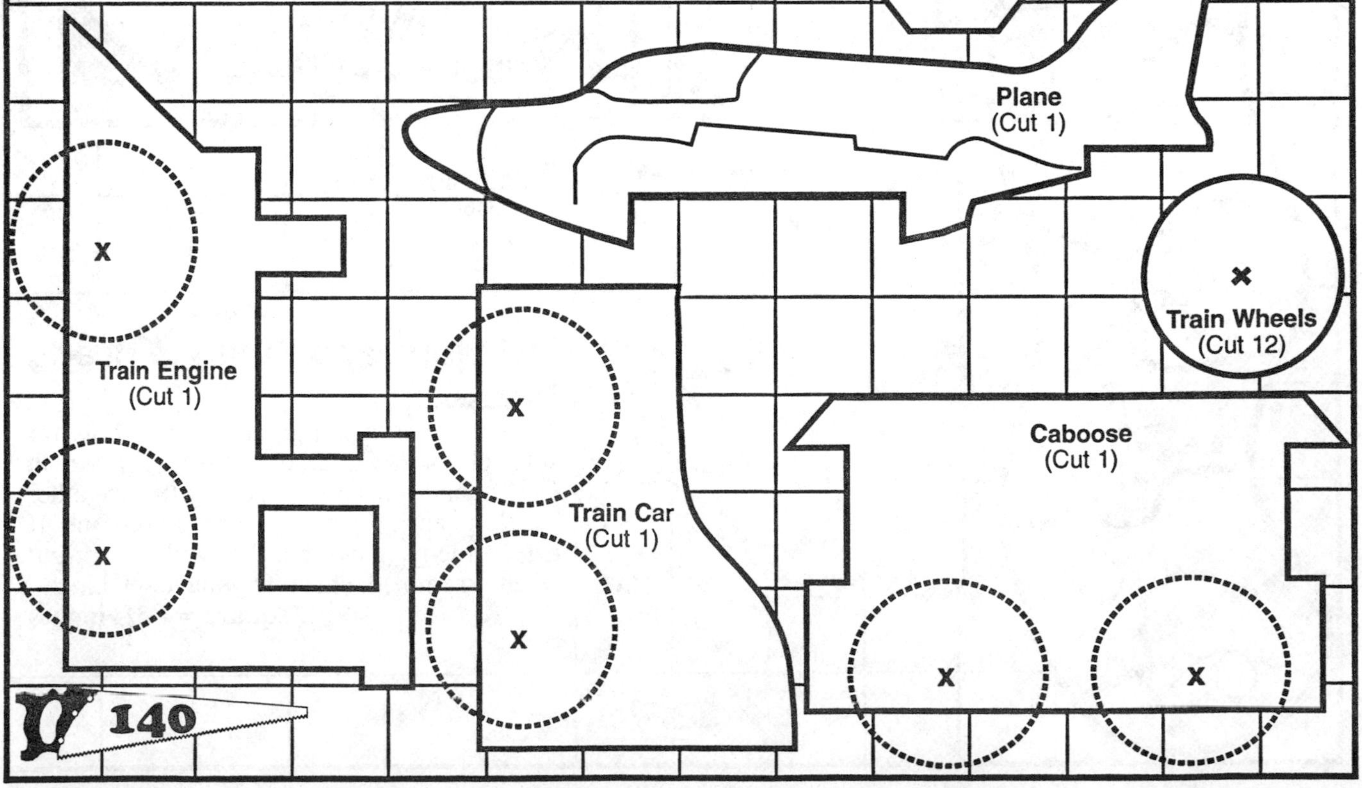

Bug Observatory

Cut one side A, one side B and one bottom. Cut out a hole for the door. Purchase a cork larger than 2-1/2" for the door on side B. Assemble using the diagram. Staple fine screen wire to the sides and top. Screw eye hook as shown to the top of the side pieces. Tie a rope handle between the eye hooks. Choose one of the motifs for Side A, as shown. Paint and coat with polyurethane.

1 square = 1-1/4 inches

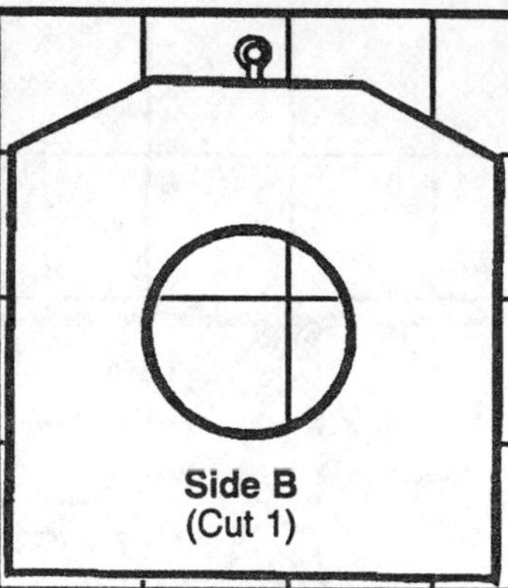

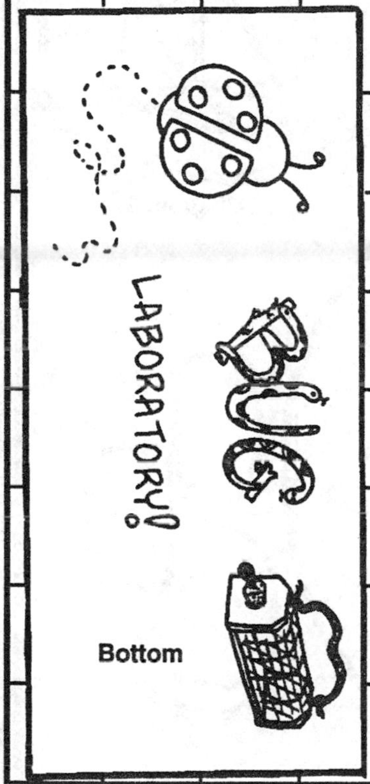

Homestead Puzzle

Cut two 10" x 10" pieces from 1/4" wood. One piece is the back. Trace the bold lines of the puzzle on the second piece of wood and cut each puzzle piece out. After cutting, glue the outside strips to form a tray for the puzzle. Paint the designs on all the individual puzzle pieces (making sure not to stick the puzzle pieces together with paint). Paint the tray with a dark color. It would look nice to paint the inside of the tray.

1 square = 1 inch

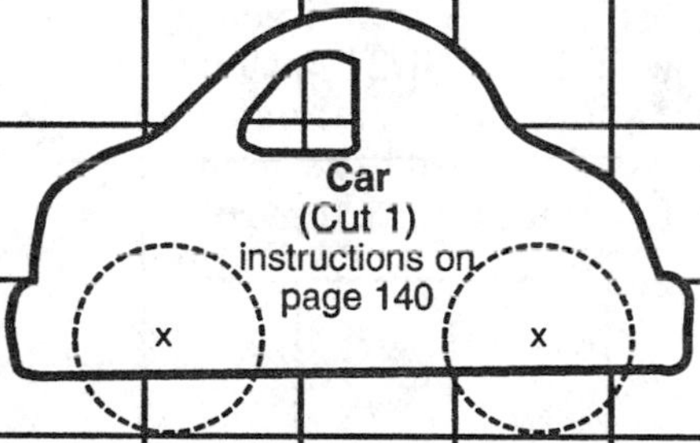

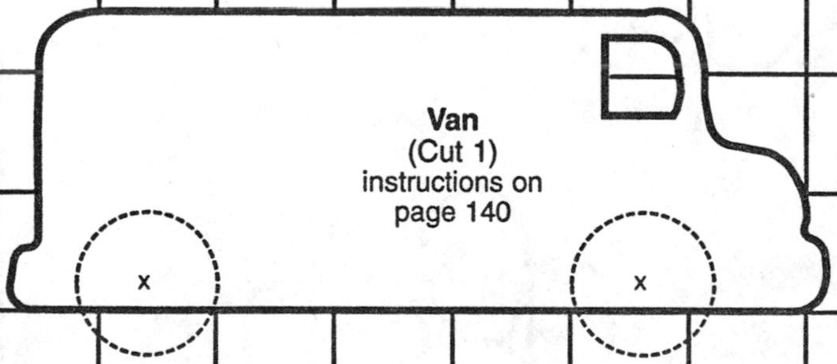

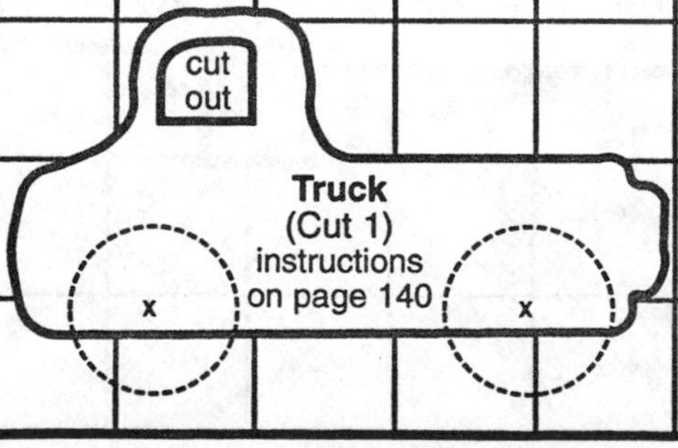

Wheels for Wooden Toys

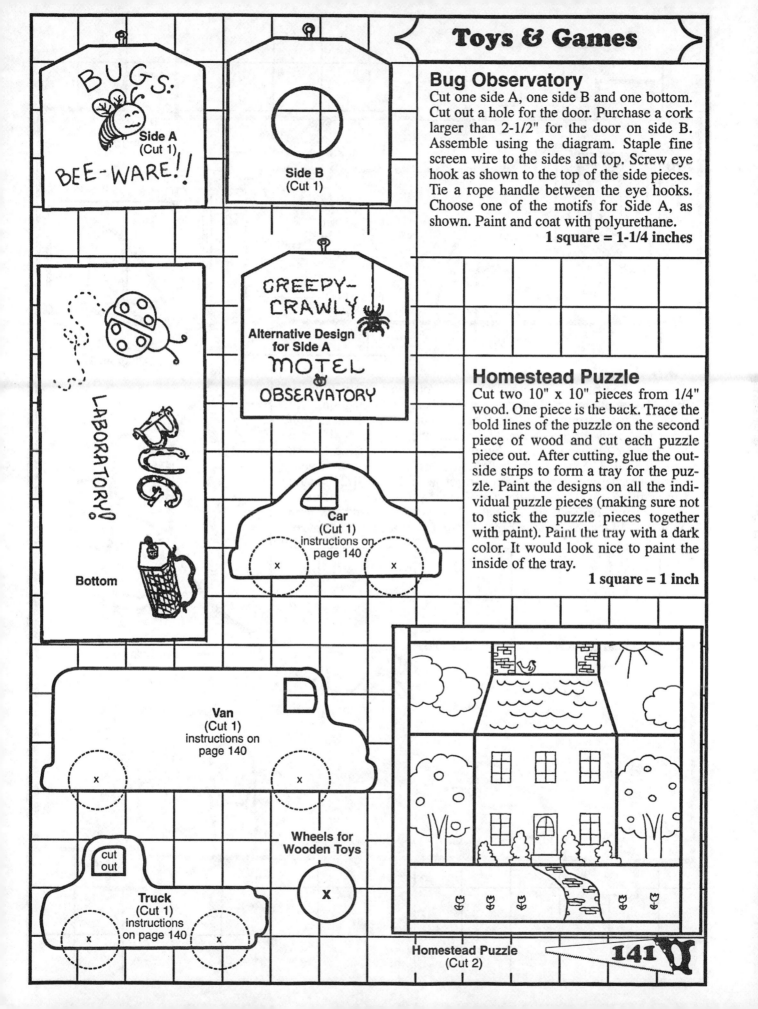

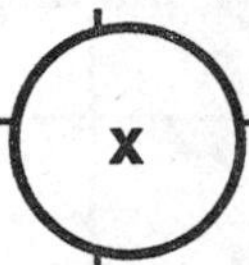

Homestead Puzzle
(Cut 2)

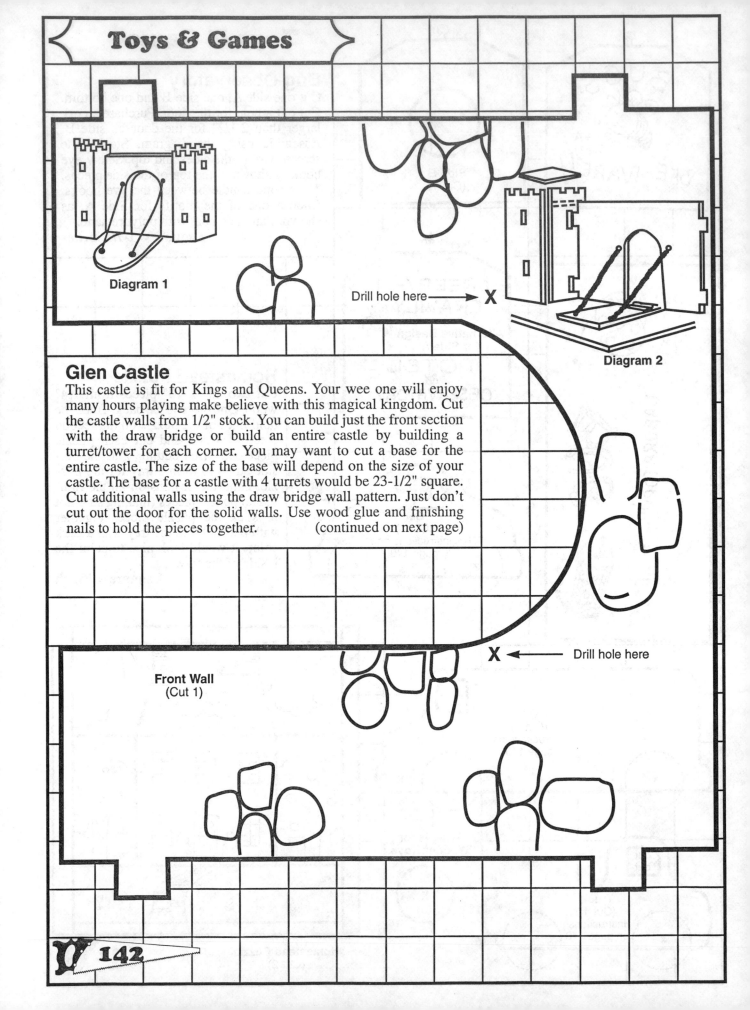

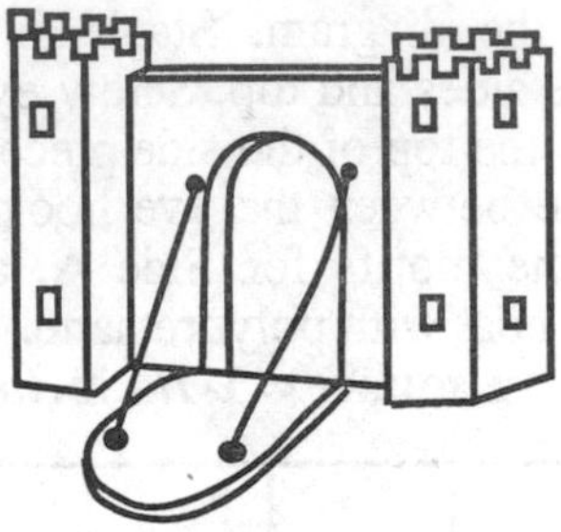

Diagram 1

Diagram 2

Glen Castle

This castle is fit for Kings and Queens. Your wee one will enjoy many hours playing make believe with this magical kingdom. Cut the castle walls from 1/2" stock. You can build just the front section with the draw bridge or build an entire castle by building a turret/tower for each corner. You may want to cut a base for the entire castle. The size of the base will depend on the size of your castle. The base for a castle with 4 turrets would be 23-1/2" square. Cut additional walls using the draw bridge wall pattern. Just don't cut out the door for the solid walls. Use wood glue and finishing nails to hold the pieces together. (continued on next page)

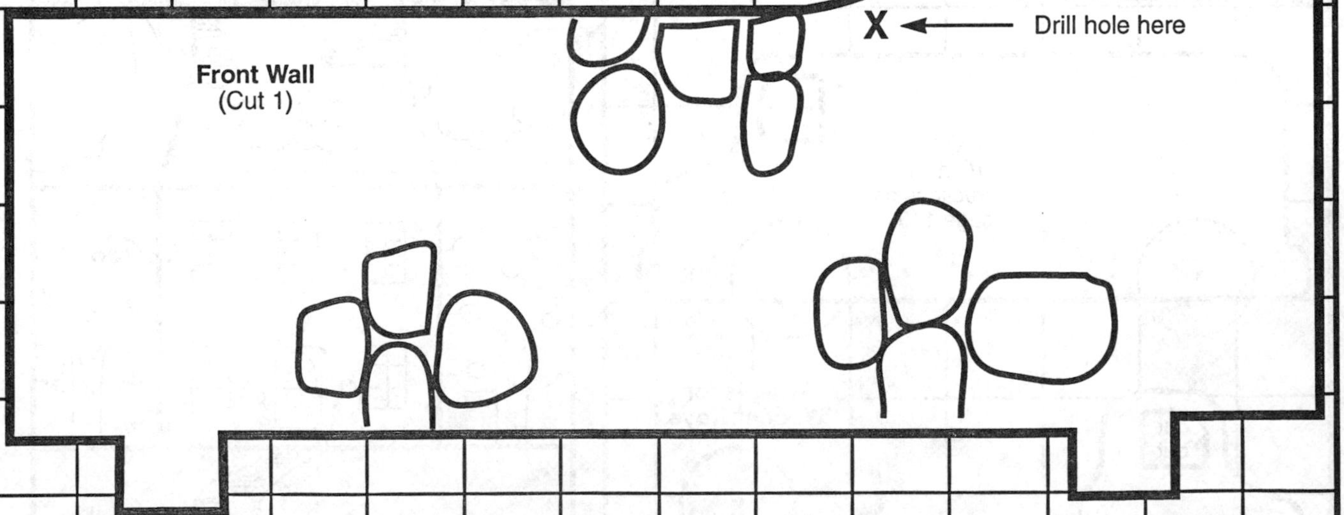

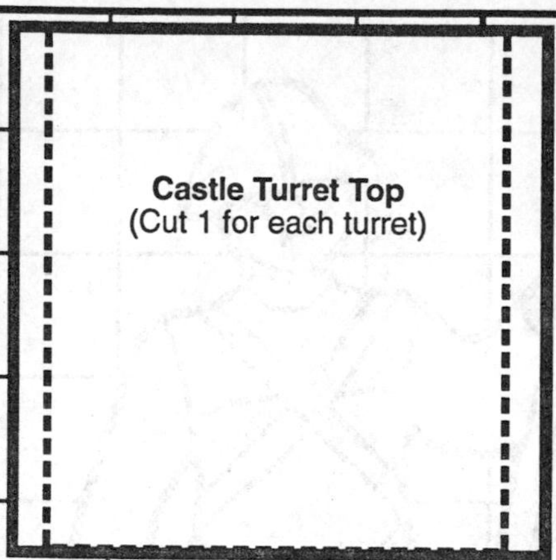

A pattern for the draw bridge is not given. Cut a draw bridge which is 1/2" x 7" x 10" and attach with very thin chain or strong rope at places marked with an X on the castle front. The chain or rope needed to open and close the drawbridge should be about 14" long. Cut one for each side. Drill small holes into the front castle wall, large enough to enable the chain or rope to pass through. Attach two small cup hooks on the back of the wall, one inch from the holes you have drilled. This will allow you to hook the extra length of chain on it or to wind the rope around it when the draw bridge is pulled closed. Attach the draw bridge to the base with a small piano hinge. Sand, then paint with acrylic paints and seal with an acrylic varnish. Cut the figures out of 1" stock. Figures are intended to stand alone. Paint them in jeweled or muted colors.

1 square = 3/4 inch

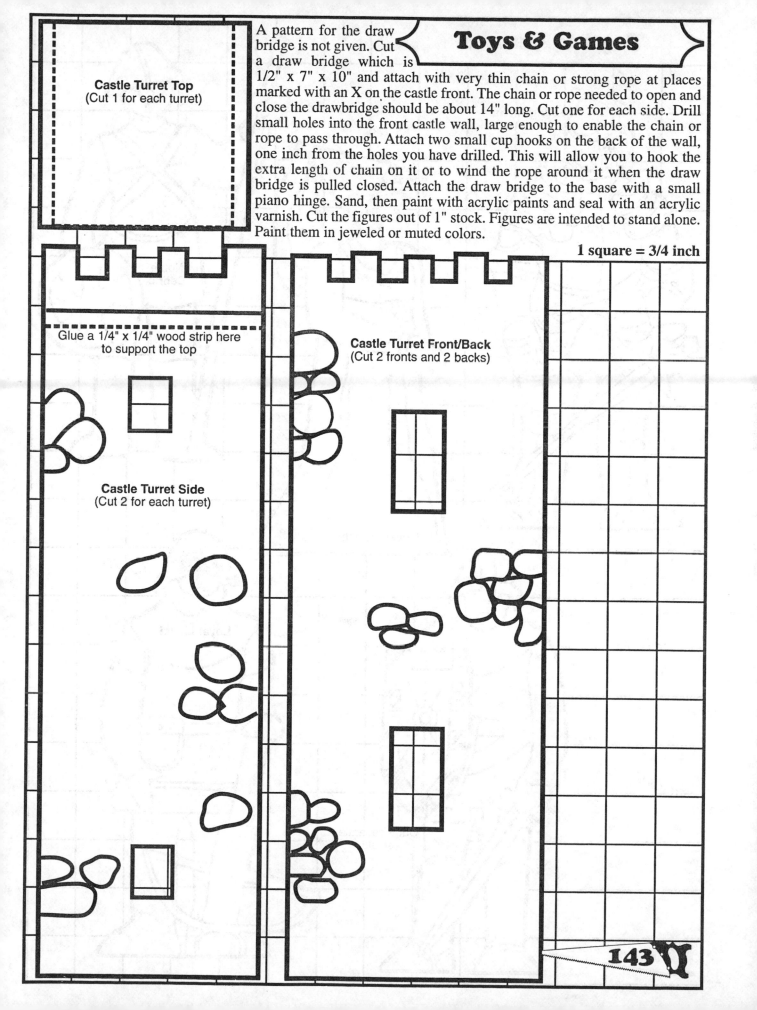

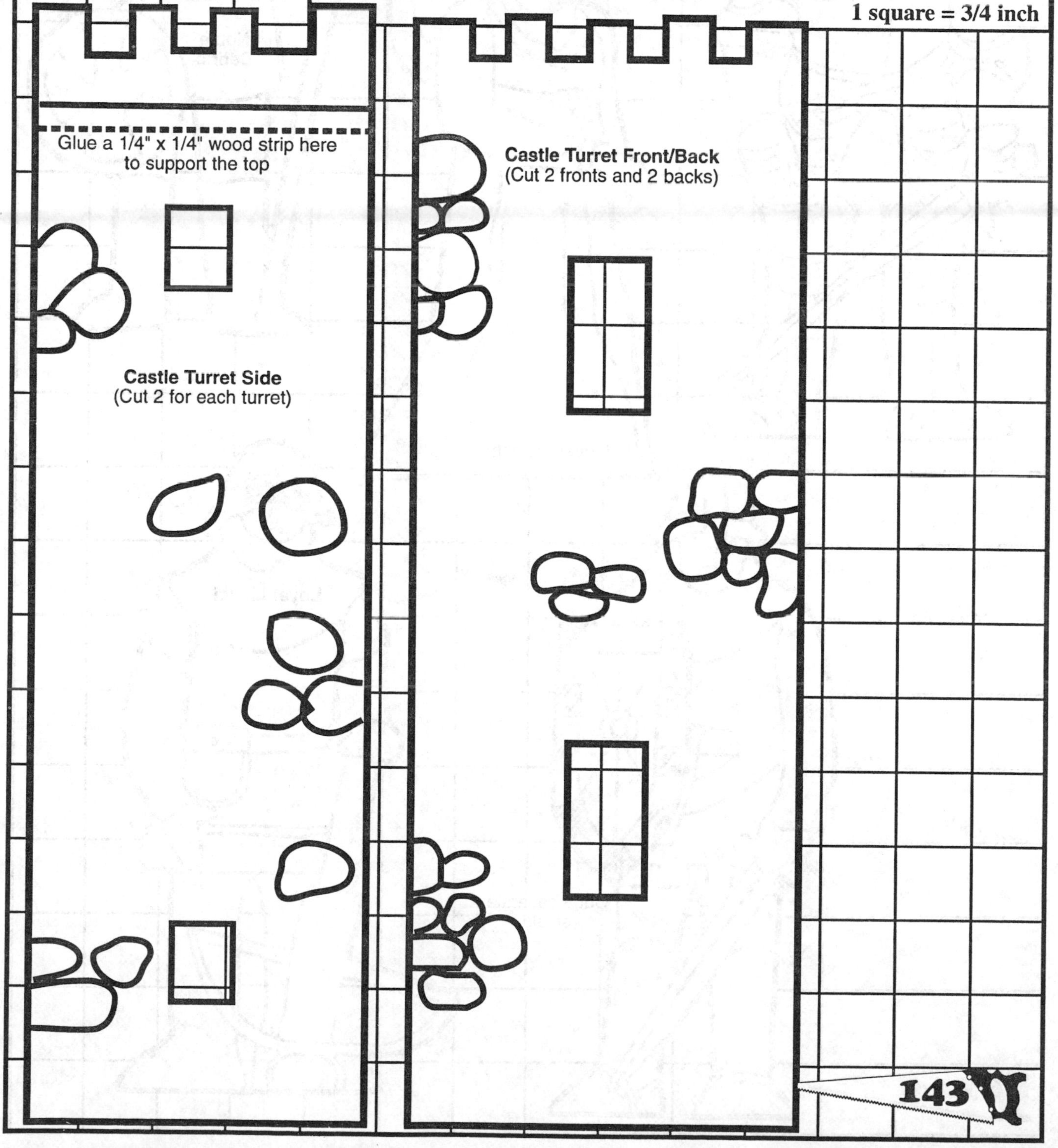

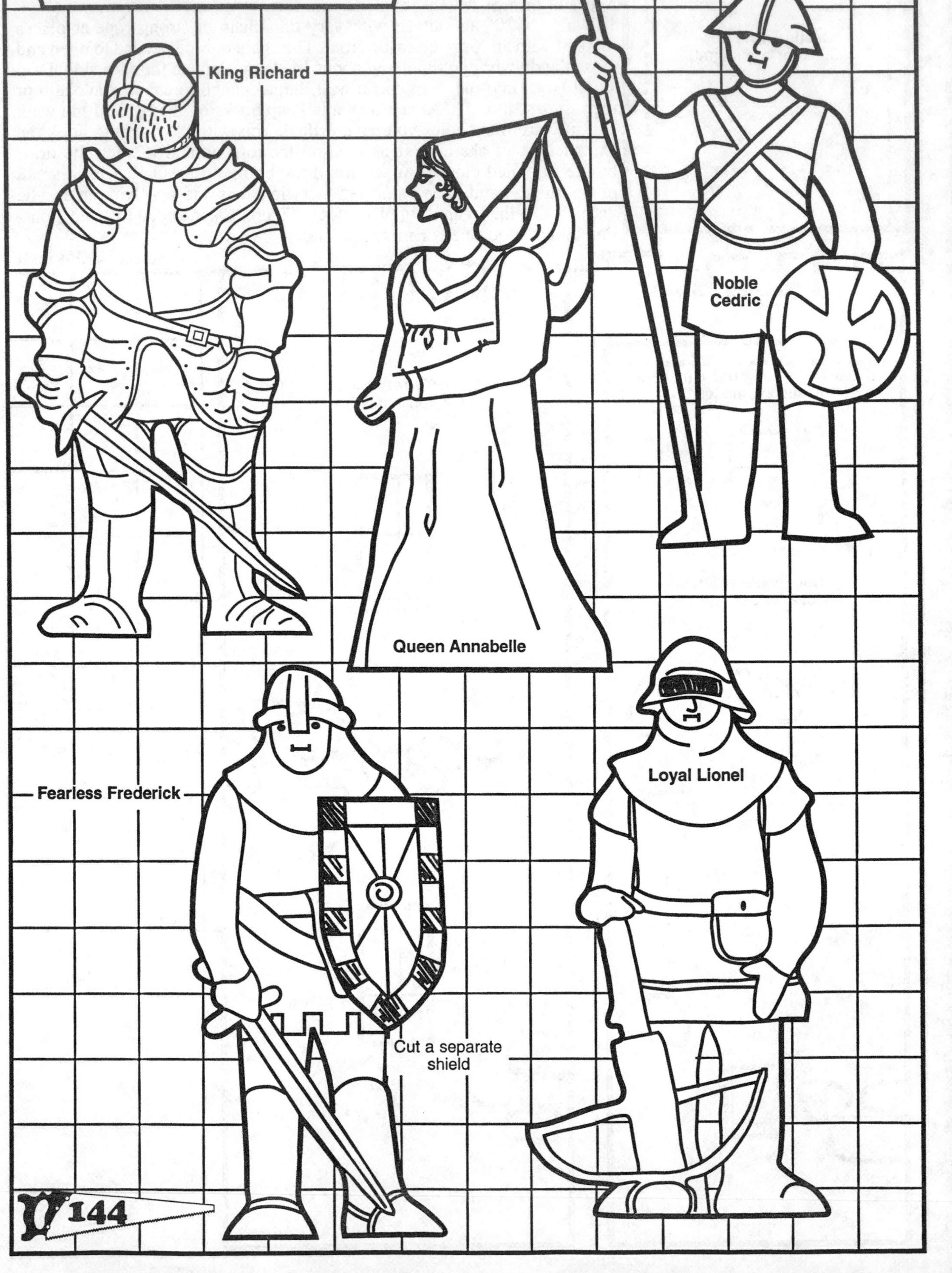
King Richard
Queen Annabelle
Noble Cedric
Fearless Frederick
Loyal Lionel
Cut a separate shield

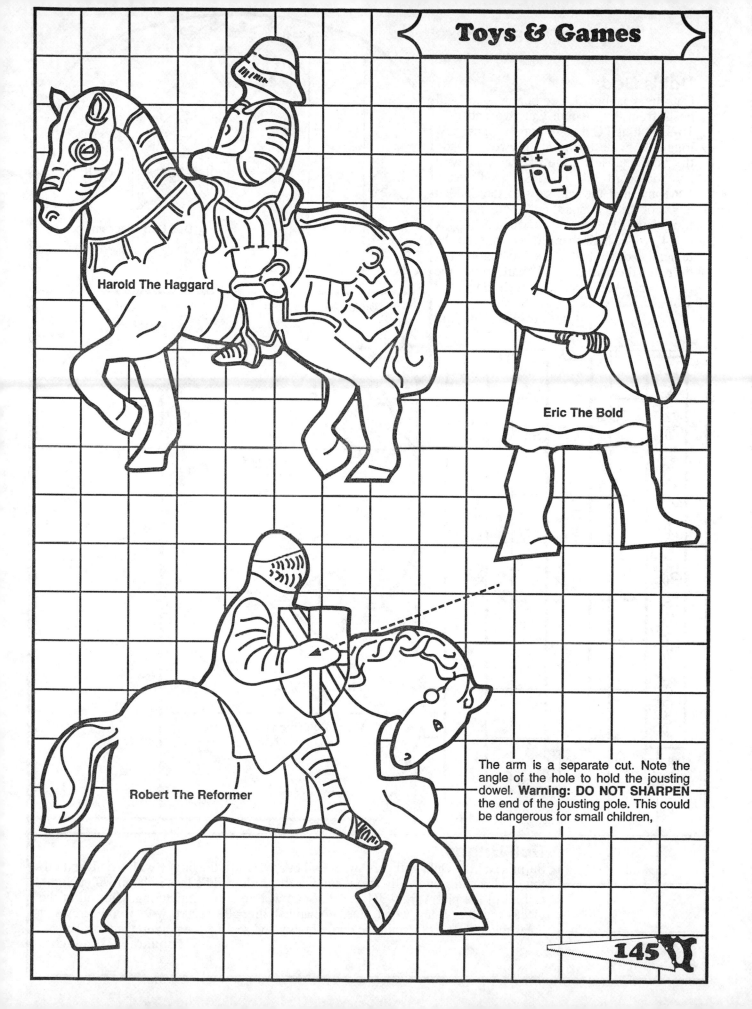

The arm is a separate cut. Note the angle of the hole to hold the jousting dowel. **Warning: DO NOT SHARPEN** the end of the jousting pole. This could be dangerous for small children,

Doll's Bed

Cut the headboard, footboard, slats and posts from 3/4" wood. Cut two end rails 16-3/8" long. Cut a bottom support 15" long x 9" wide from 1/4" plywood. Dado the bottom inside edge of the headboard and footboard 3/4" x 1-1/8" x 3/4" deep. Glue and nail the end rails to the dadoed edges of the headboard and footboard. Cut four slats from 1/4" stock, 10-1/2" long x 1-1/4" wide. Nail them to the rails on the underside of the bed. Place the bottom support into the bed. Glue a 1" ball knob to the top of each bed post. Sand well. Paint and seal using acrylics.

1 square = 1-1/4 inches

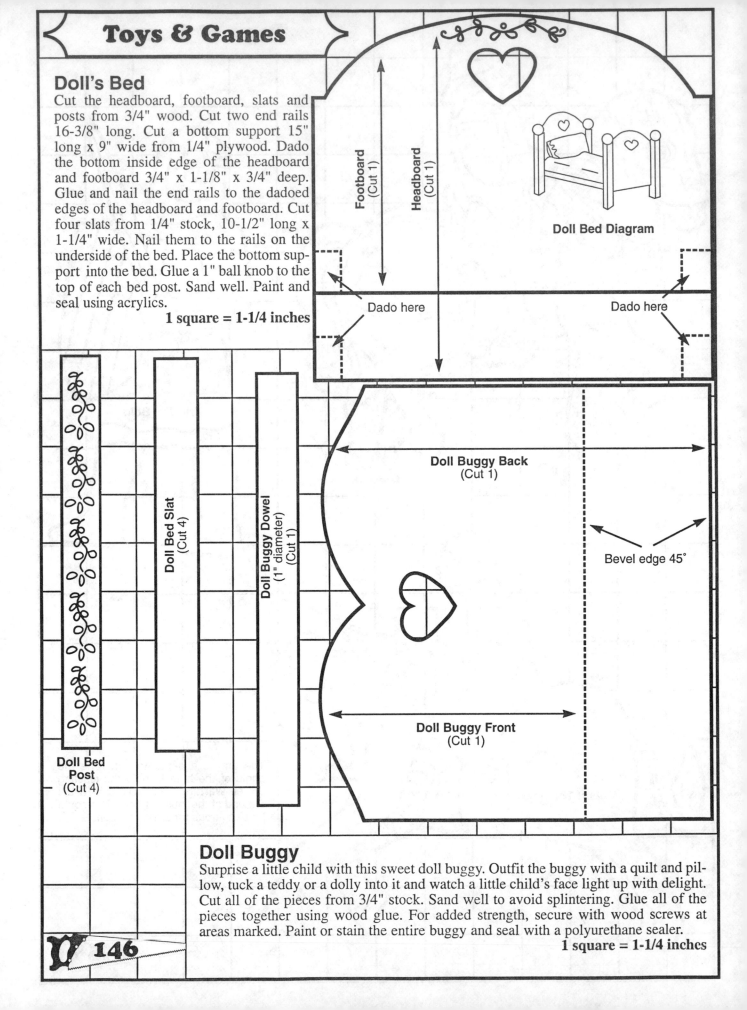

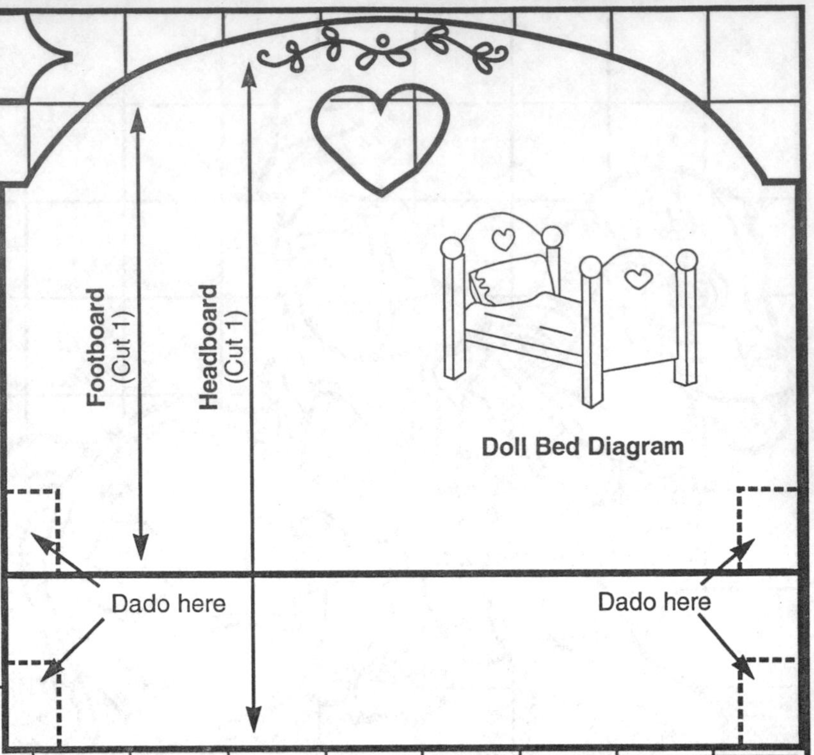

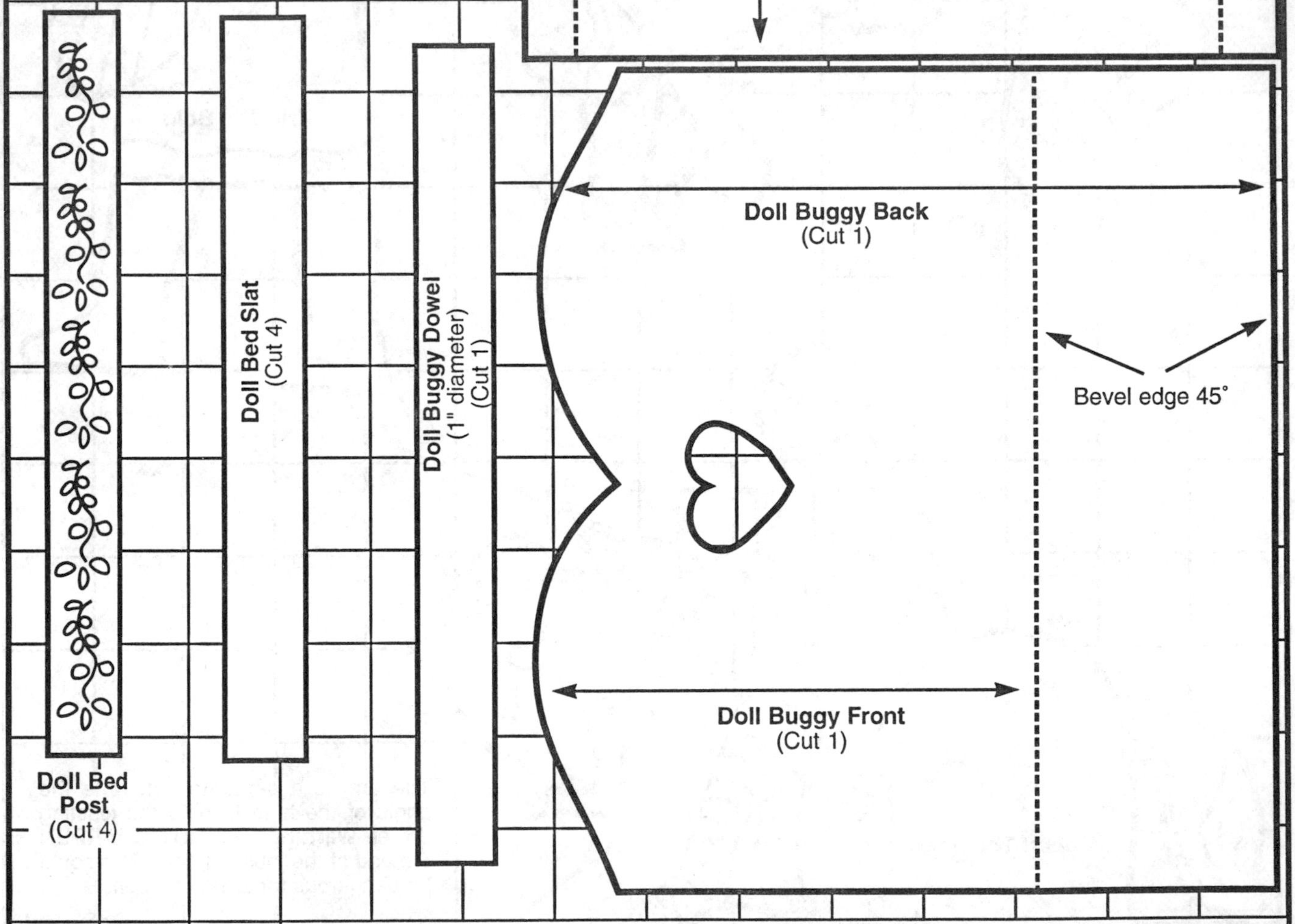

Doll Buggy

Surprise a little child with this sweet doll buggy. Outfit the buggy with a quilt and pillow, tuck a teddy or a dolly into it and watch a little child's face light up with delight. Cut all of the pieces from 3/4" stock. Sand well to avoid splintering. Glue all of the pieces together using wood glue. For added strength, secure with wood screws at areas marked. Paint or stain the entire buggy and seal with a polyurethane sealer.

1 square = 1-1/4 inches

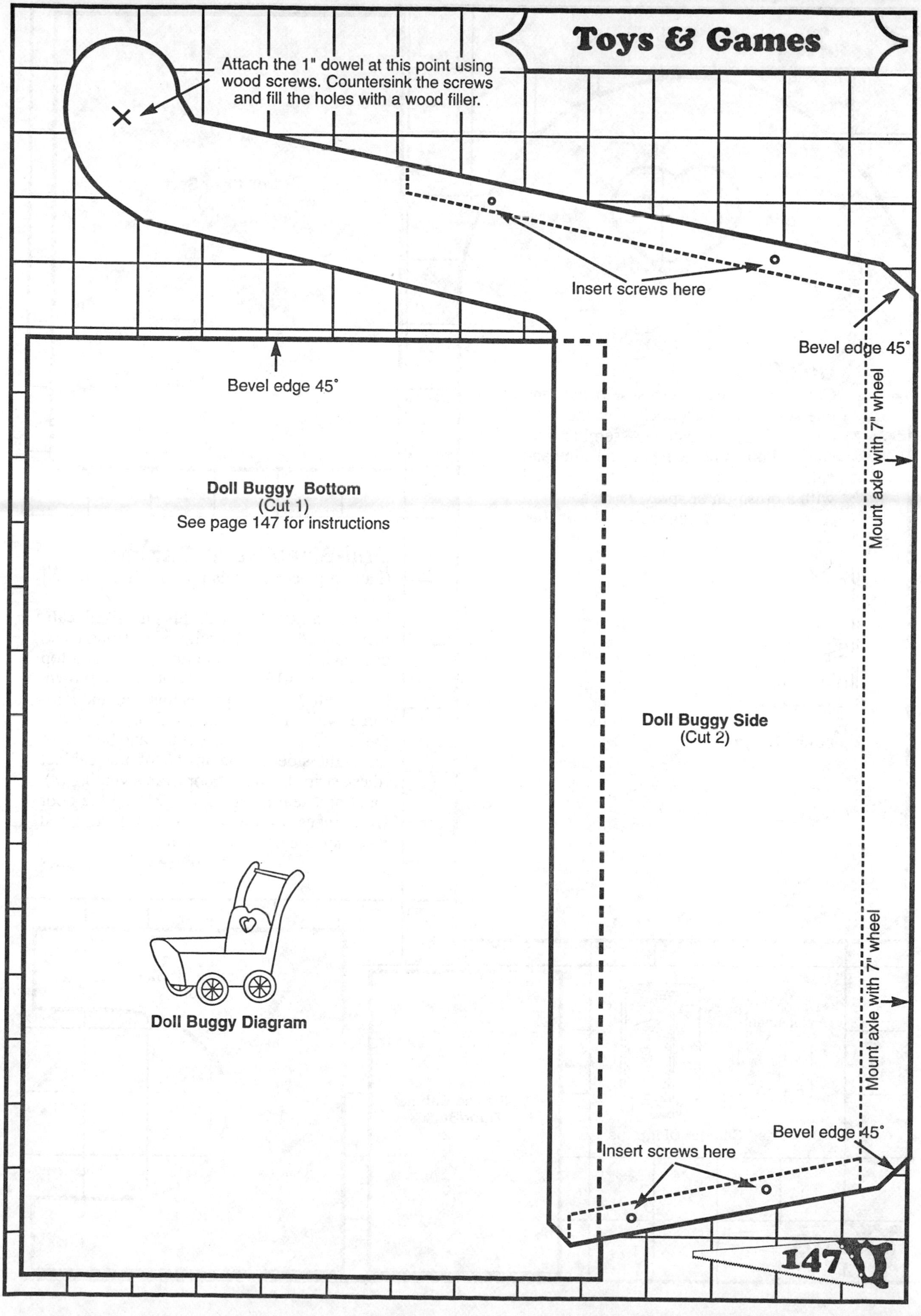
Attach the 1" dowel at this point using wood screws. Countersink the screws and fill the holes with a wood filler.
Insert screws here
Bevel edge 45˚
Bevel edge 45˚
Mount axle with 7" wheel
Doll Buggy Bottom
(Cut 1)
See page 147 for instructions
Doll Buggy Side
(Cut 2)
Mount axle with 7" wheel
Bevel edge 45˚
Insert screws here

Doll Buggy Diagram

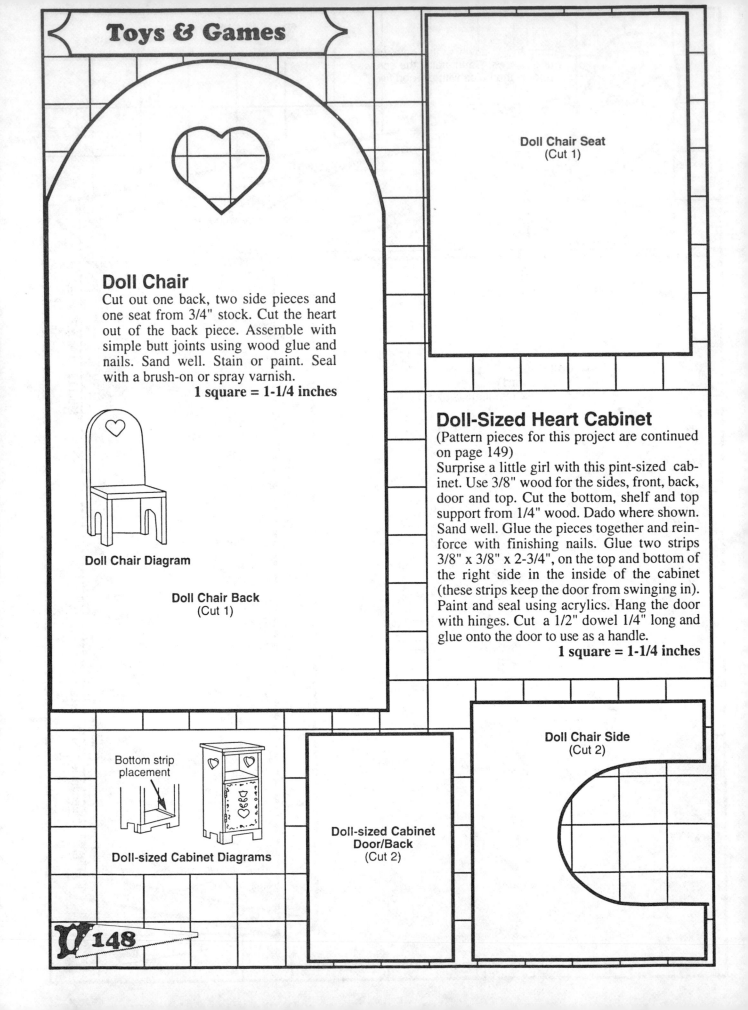

Doll Chair Seat
(Cut 1)

Doll Chair

Cut out one back, two side pieces and one seat from 3/4" stock. Cut the heart out of the back piece. Assemble with simple butt joints using wood glue and nails. Sand well. Stain or paint. Seal with a brush-on or spray varnish.

1 square = 1-1/4 inches

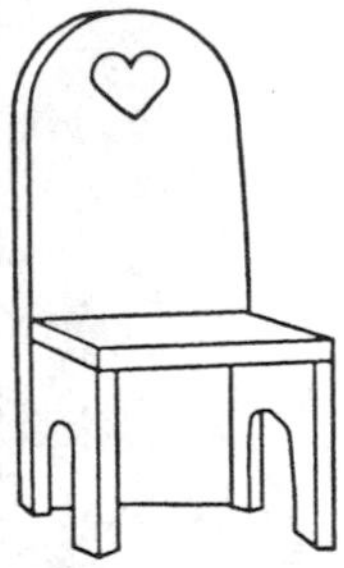

Doll Chair Diagram

Doll Chair Back
(Cut 1)

Doll-Sized Heart Cabinet

(Pattern pieces for this project are continued on page 149)

Surprise a little girl with this pint-sized cabinet. Use 3/8" wood for the sides, front, back, door and top. Cut the bottom, shelf and top support from 1/4" wood. Dado where shown. Sand well. Glue the pieces together and reinforce with finishing nails. Glue two strips 3/8" x 3/8" x 2-3/4", on the top and bottom of the right side in the inside of the cabinet (these strips keep the door from swinging in). Paint and seal using acrylics. Hang the door with hinges. Cut a 1/2" dowel 1/4" long and glue onto the door to use as a handle.

1 square = 1-1/4 inches

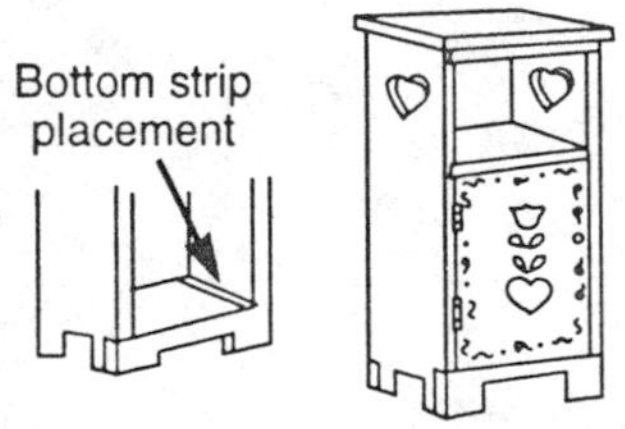

Doll-sized Cabinet Diagrams

Doll-sized Cabinet Door/Back
(Cut 2)

Doll Chair Side
(Cut 2)

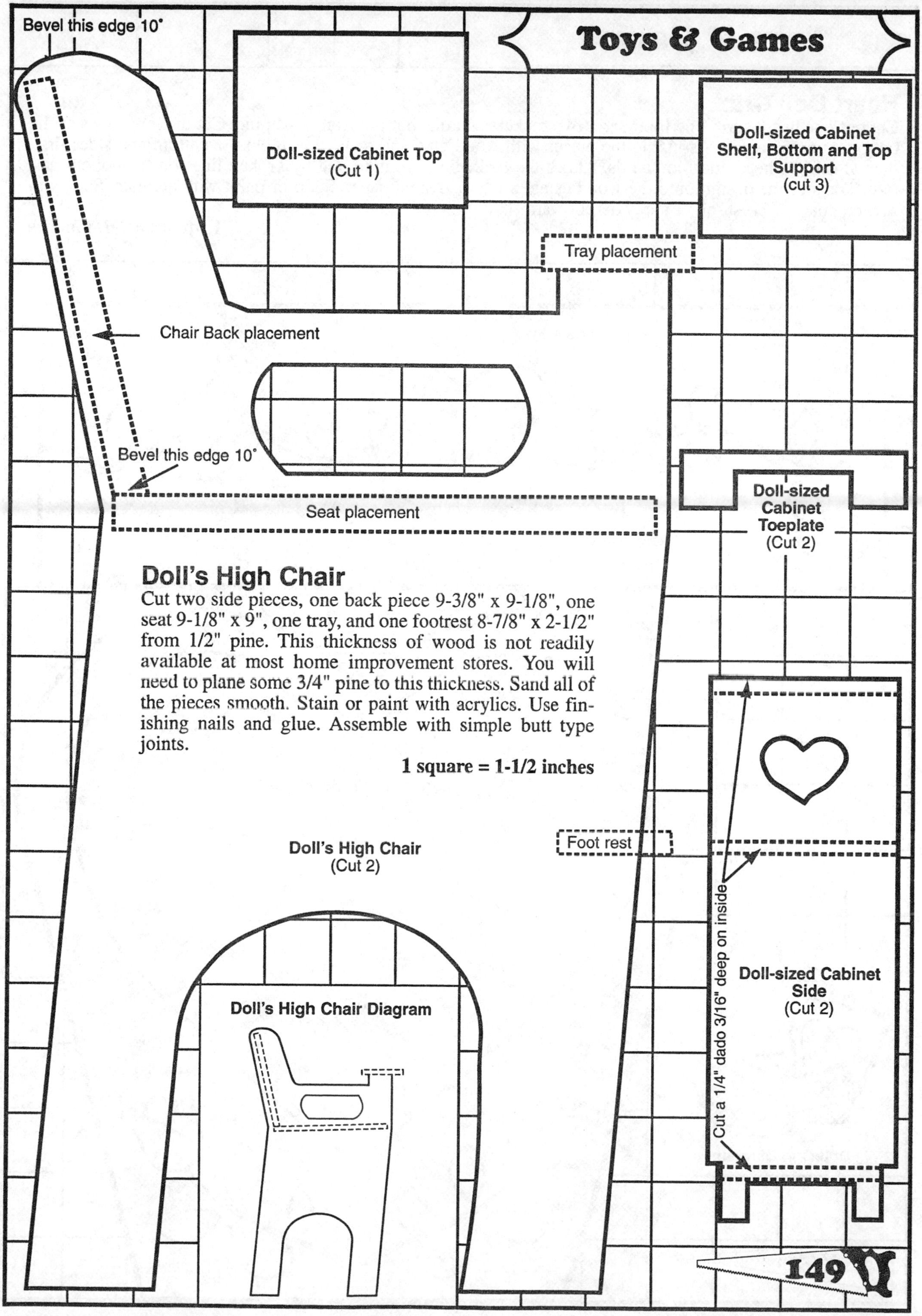

Doll's High Chair

Cut two side pieces, one back piece 9-3/8" x 9-1/8", one seat 9-1/8" x 9", one tray, and one footrest 8-7/8" x 2-1/2" from 1/2" pine. This thickness of wood is not readily available at most home improvement stores. You will need to plane some 3/4" pine to this thickness. Sand all of the pieces smooth. Stain or paint with acrylics. Use finishing nails and glue. Assemble with simple butt type joints.

1 square = 1-1/2 inches

Heart Doll Crib

Cut out one headboard, one footboard, two rockers and one bottom from 3/4" pine. Cut the long sides of the bottom at a 15° angle. Assemble the pieces with wood glue and nails. Assemble the bottom and sides first, then attach the head and footboards. Attach the rockers where indicated by broken lines on the bottom pattern. Transfer the design onto the wood using graph or tracing paper. Stain or paint with acrylics. Seal with several coats of brush-on or spray acrylic varnish.

1 square = 1-1/4 inches

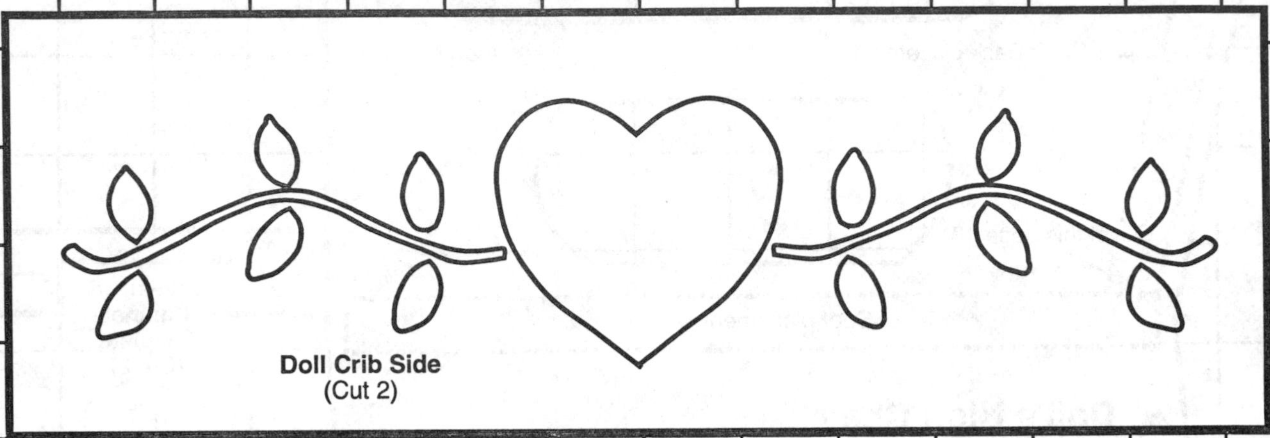

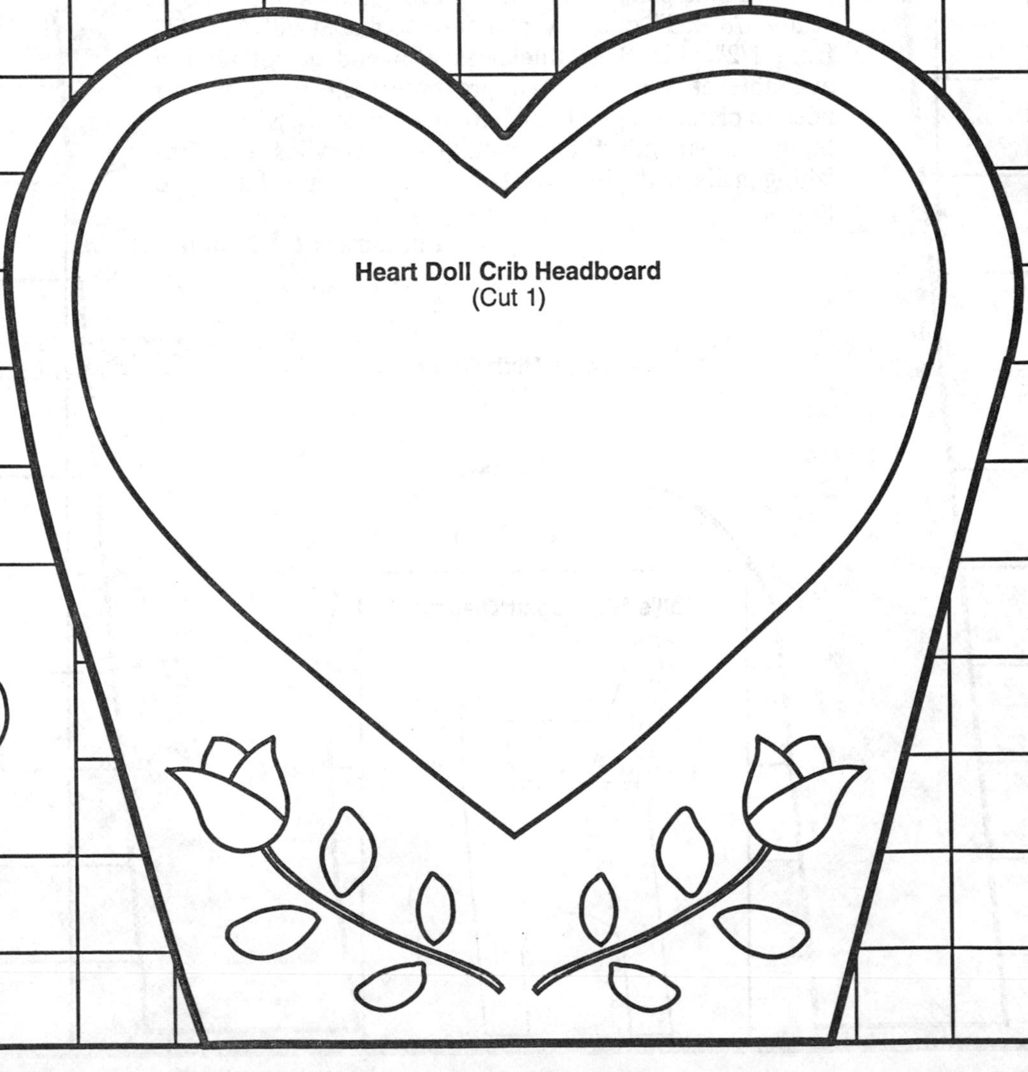

Doll Crib Diagram

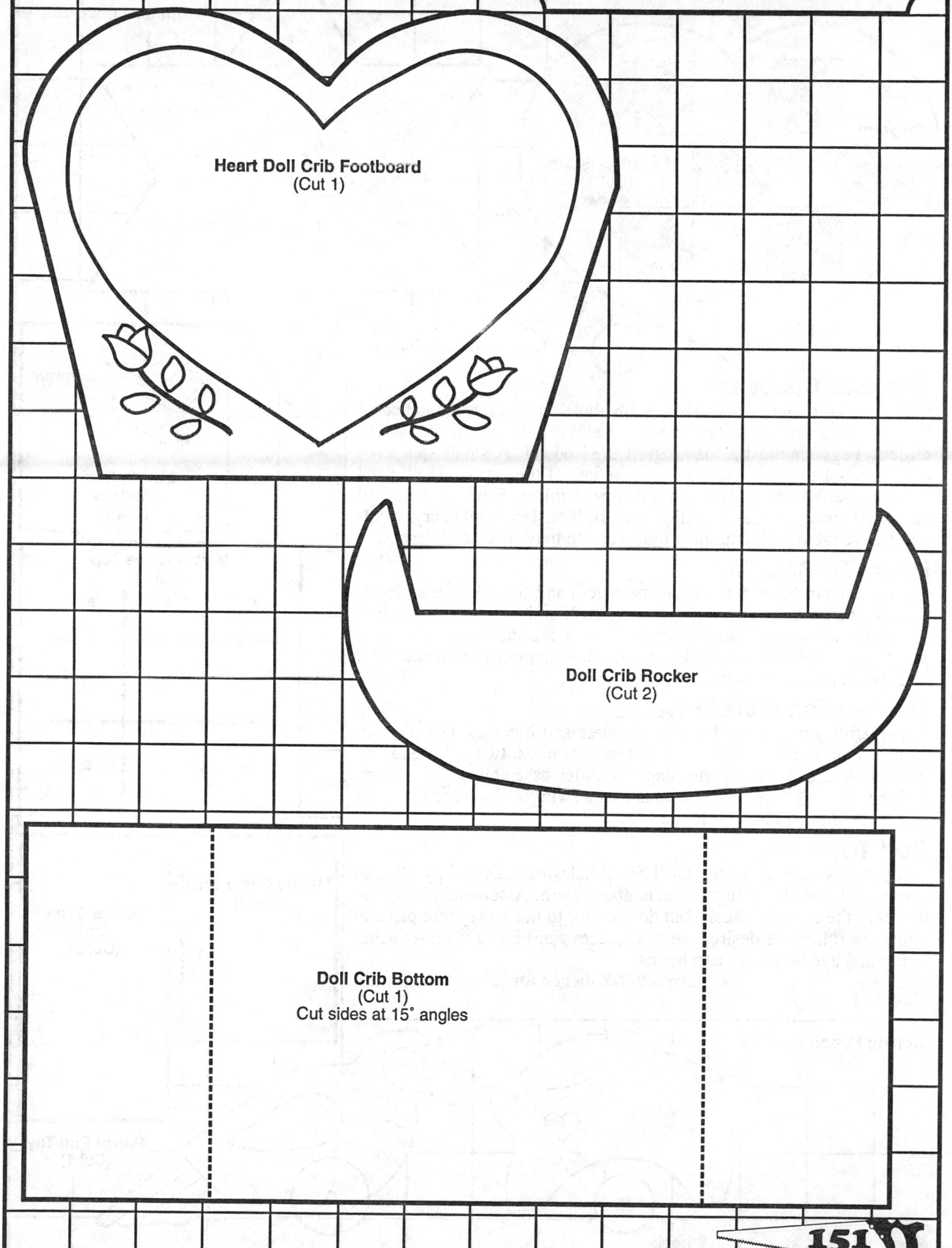
Heart Doll Crib Footboard
(Cut 1)
Doll Crib Rocker
(Cut 2)
Doll Crib Bottom
(Cut 1)
Cut sides at 15° angles

Toys & Games

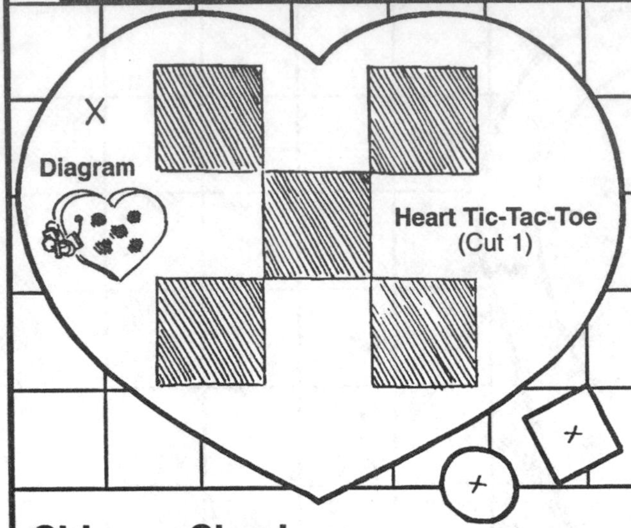

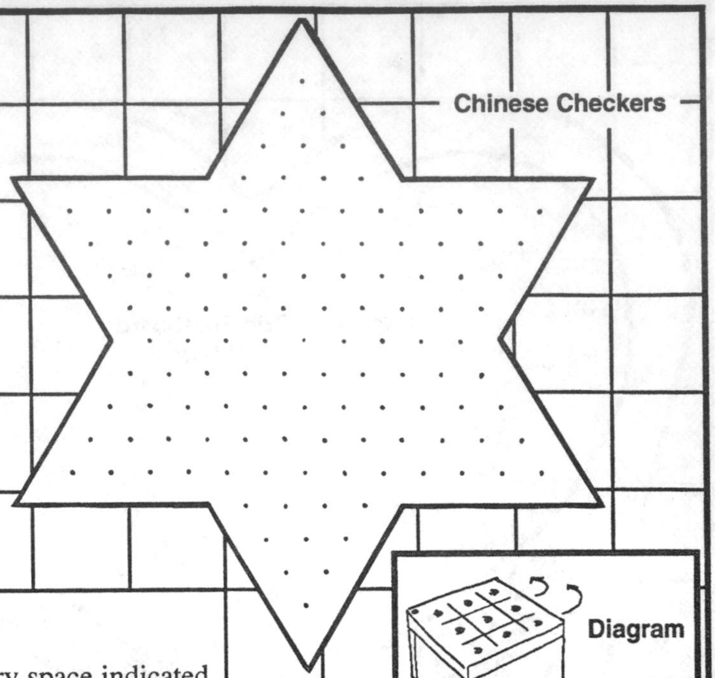

Chinese Checkers

Cut board from 3/4" wood. Drill a 3/8" hole on every space indicated by a dot. It is very important to space holes evenly, just as the pattern directs. Pegs should be made from 3/8" dowel. A small sphere or design may be purchased to glue to the end of the peg. You will need 60 pegs that will be finished in 6 different colors. Paint 10 white, 10 black, 10 green, 10 red, 10 yellow and 10 blue. Use bright acrylic colors. Leave the board natural. A light varnish may be used if desired.

Heart Tic-Tac-Toe

Cut out 1 heart base, 5 square game pieces and 5 circle game pieces. Drill a hole in the heart as indicated by an X and drill holes in each of the 10 game pieces. Transfer pattern onto heart and finish all pieces. We suggest country colors. Hang the playing pieces from the heart with twine as shown in the diagram.

Tic-Tac-Toe Marble Game

This marble game is great fun for children and it comes with it's own storage compartment. Cut out one top, two ends, two sides and one bottom. Assemble using the diagram. After assembling the bottom, drill a hole in the top and side to use as a swinging hinge to close the top. Store the marbles inside the box.

Pull Toys

Cut patterns from 1" wood. Drill 5/16" holes as indicated by "X"s to insert 1/4" dowels through wheels and pattern. Assemble, gluing the dowel to the outside wheels, but do not glue to the center base piece to allow for rolling. If desired, several pieces can be tied together using string and eye hooks, or cup hooks.

1 square = 2-1/2 inches for all of these games

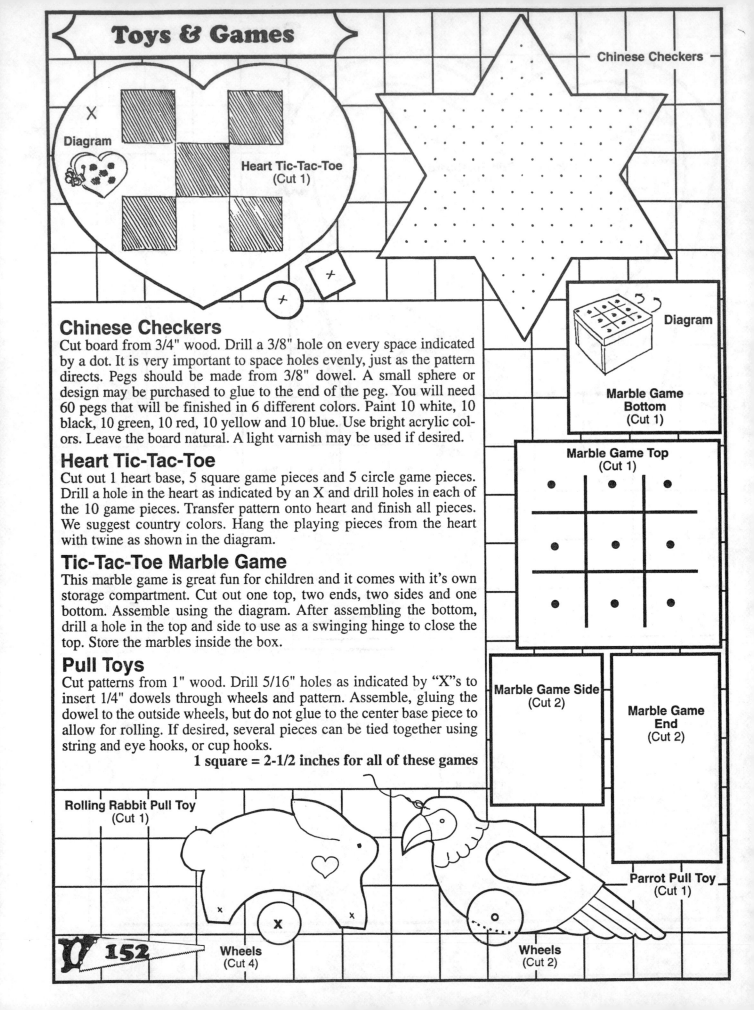

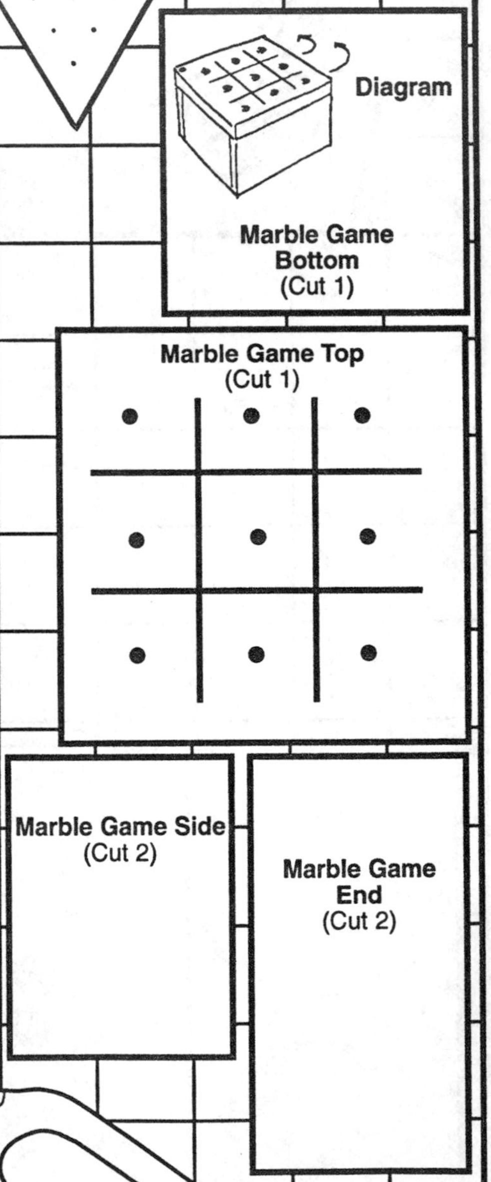

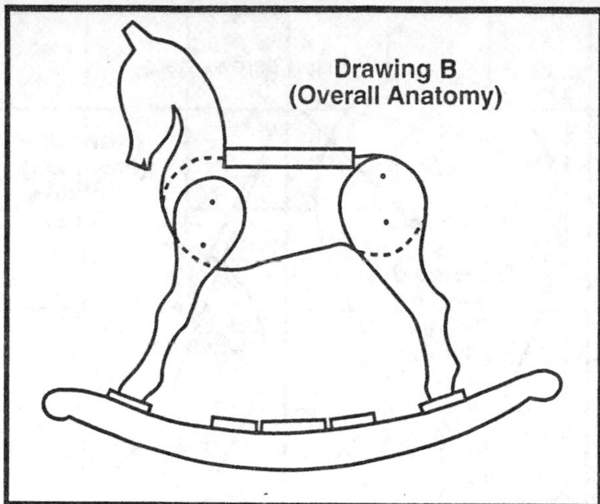

Giant Rocking Horse

This rocking horse will provide hours of entertainment for young and old alike if you heed the following cautions:

- Check all components for splits and cracks
- Use a 1/4" round-over router bit on all exposed edges
- Sand all surfaces to remove any splinters

The most critical pieces in the rocking horse are the rockers. These two pieces should be cut out at the same time. Clamp the two pieces of wood together before cutting the full rockers and keep them clamped until the bottom and top surfaces have been sanded. Test the rockers as a unit to ensure a smooth rocking action.

We have found the most durable wood for this project to be yellow pine. It totals about 14 feet of 2" x 12", 5-1/2 feet of 1" x 4", 2 feet of 2" x 6", 2 feet of 2' x 8" and 16 feet of 1" x 6".

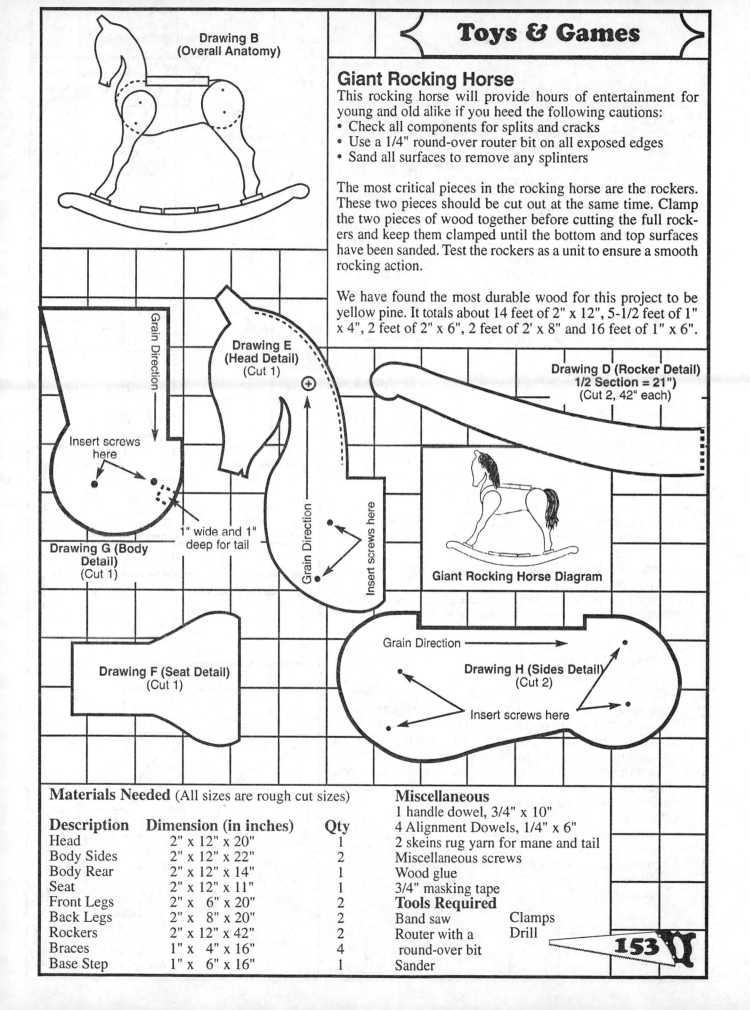

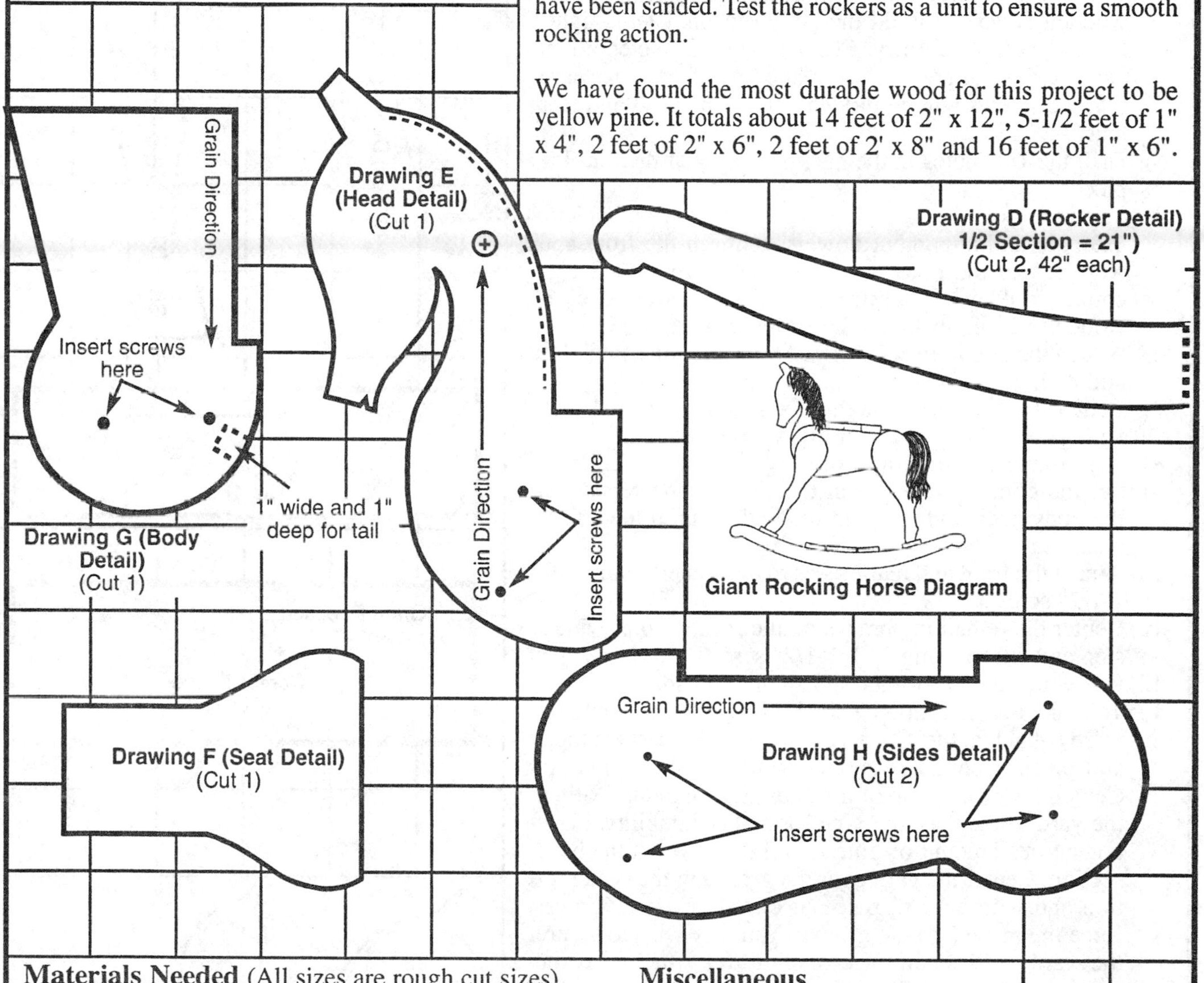

Materials Needed (All sizes are rough cut sizes)

Description	Dimension (in inches)	Qty
Head	2" x 12" x 20"	1
Body Sides	2" x 12" x 22"	2
Body Rear	2" x 12" x 14"	1
Seat	2" x 12" x 11"	1
Front Legs	2" x 6" x 20"	2
Back Legs	2" x 8" x 20"	2
Rockers	2" x 12" x 42"	2
Braces	1" x 4" x 16"	4
Base Step	1" x 6" x 16"	1

Miscellaneous

1 handle dowel, 3/4" x 10"
4 Alignment Dowels, 1/4" x 6"
2 skeins rug yarn for mane and tail
Miscellaneous screws
Wood glue
3/4" masking tape

Tools Required

Band saw
Router with a round-over bit
Sander
Clamps
Drill

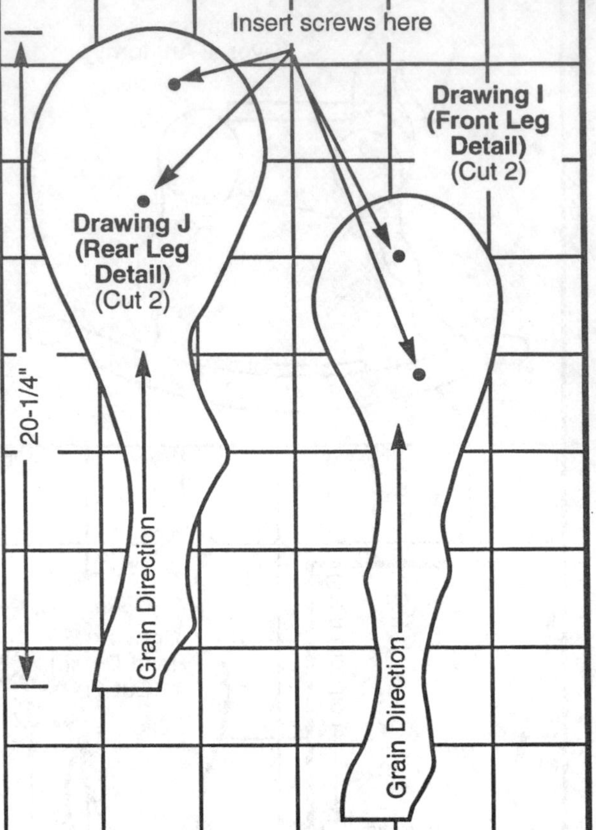

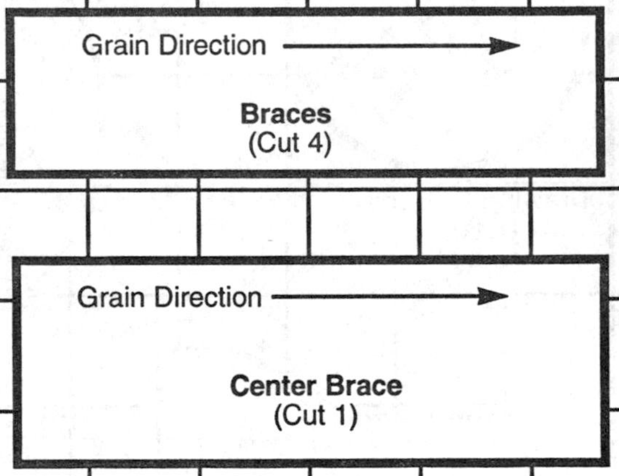

Assembly Instructions

Make scale drawings of all pieces. Trace onto wood. Position all pattern pieces to avoid any unusually rough spots or knots. Cut out all pieces, using the round-over router bit on exposed edges. Sand each piece until smooth.

1) Use 1/4" veining bit to rout the 1/4" x 3/8" groove in the head for the mane. See Drawing A.
2) Drill 1/4" holes completely through the head, the two body sides and the body rear.
3) Fit all these parts together to make sure they are properly cut and drilled. When complete, use glue and 1/4" wooden dowels to build the body section. Clamp tightly until completely dry. See Drawing C. Note: When using screws to help hold the body together, make sure that the screws will be hidden behind the front and rear legs.
4) Drill the 1/4" holes in the back side only of the four leg pieces.
5) Test fit legs to the assembled body and when complete, use glue and alignment dowels to attach the front and rear legs to the body section. Note: Two #10, 2-1/2" countersunk wood screws in each leg, covered by a wooden button, make the horse much more stable.
6) Attach the seat to the completed body section using glue and #10, 2" screws.
7) Center the front feet onto a 1" x 4" x 12" brace. Attach with glue and a #10, 2" screw in each foot.
8) Repeat above instruction for the back feet.
9) Set the completed body on the rockers and reposition the body back and forth on the rockers until the unit is balanced.
10) Attach the front and rear braces to the rockers using #10, 1-1/2" screws.
11) Center the remaining braces on the rockers to provide a step and attach using #10, 1-1/2" screws.
12) Use your favorite primer and stain to finish.
13) To make mane: Unloop a skein of rug yarn and cut into three equal lengths. Cut a 12" strip of 3/4" masking tape, and place it on a flat surface with the sticky side up. Center the yarn on top of the entire length of tape. Stitch the yarn to the masking tape for added durability. Place a generous amount of glue into the groove on the head section. Center the yarn over the groove in the head section and with a small piece of dowel or a screwdriver force the mane into the groove. You may wish to secure the yarn with small pieces of dowel which may be removed when the glue is dry.
14) To make the tail: Fold one skein of yarn in half. Cut one strand of yarn and wrap to about 1" up the folded end. Pour glue into the 1" hole on the body rear. Using a screwdriver or dowel force this end into the hole. Using a 10 penny common nail, drive the nail directly into the center of the tail.

1 square = 3 inches

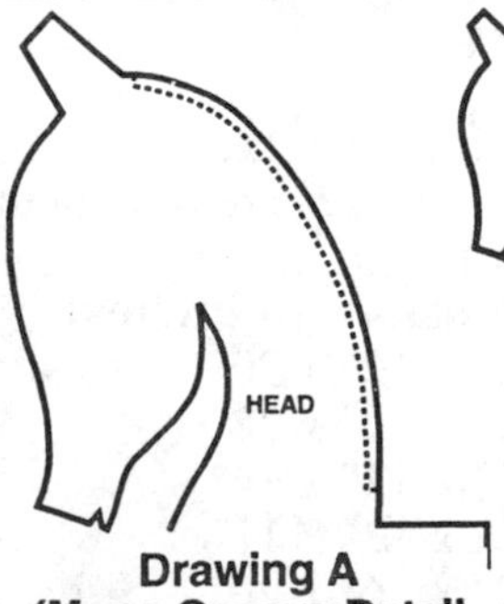

Drawing A
(Mane Groove Detail

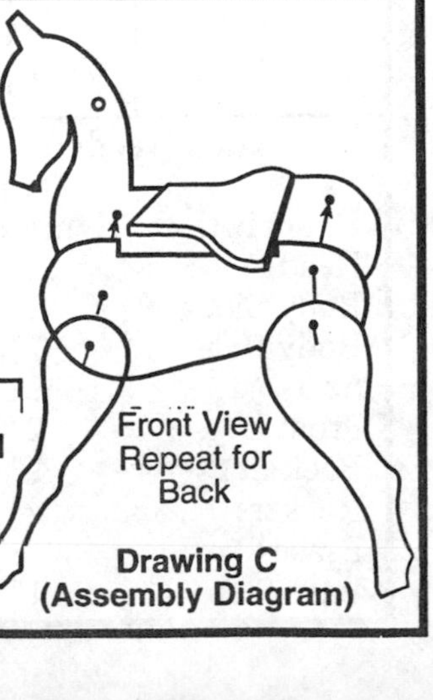

Drawing C
(Assembly Diagram)

— CHAPTER FOURTEEN —

WALL & SHELF BRACKETS

Decorative Shelf and Corner Brackets

These brackets can be very simple (stained or painted) or various techniques (such as woodcarving and wood burning) may be used by the more experienced woodcrafter for almost any result you desire. Cut all brackets from 3/4" or 1/2" wood. Cut one back for each bracket at the centre lines and use wood screws to attach to the wall. Some designs require inside cuts and others may require dowels.

1 square = 1 inch

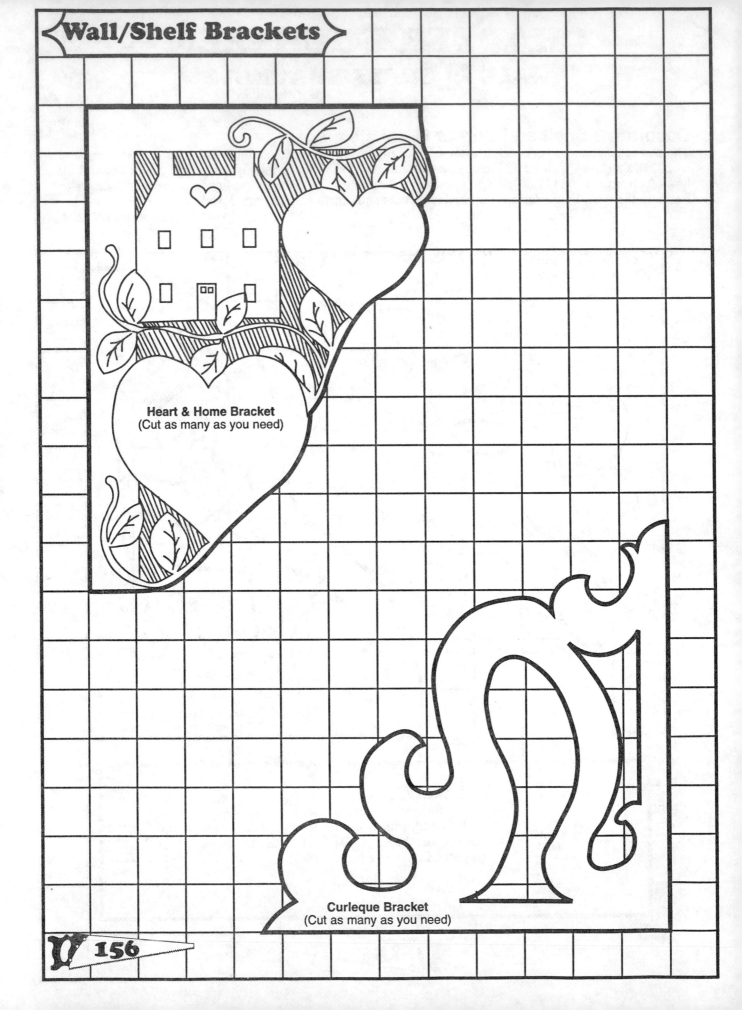

Wall/Shelf Brackets

Heart & Home Bracket
(Cut as many as you need)

Curleque Bracket
(Cut as many as you need)

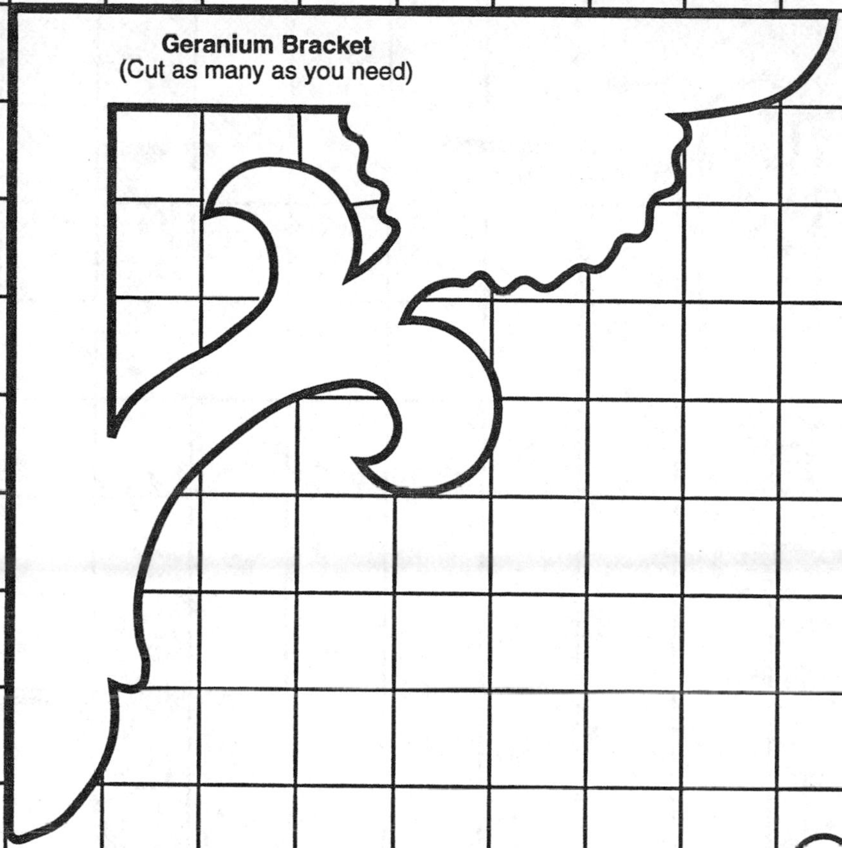

Dowels & Beads Bracket

This pattern calls for three 1/4" dowels and seven 1/2" beads. (Cut dowels long enough to go through bracket and glue the bead on the end of the dowel.) Cut one bracket and drill holes for dowels in top and bottom of brackets. Insert dowels through beads as indicated. Glue the beads to the end of the dowels. Glue a bead to the end of the bracket (as shown), if desired.

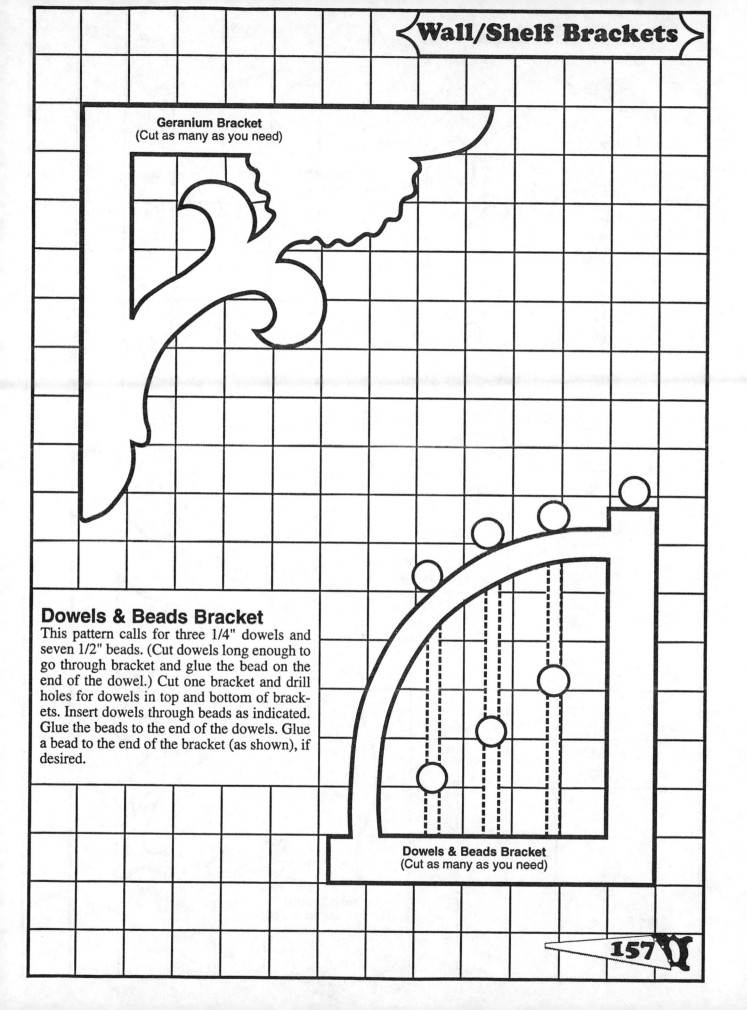

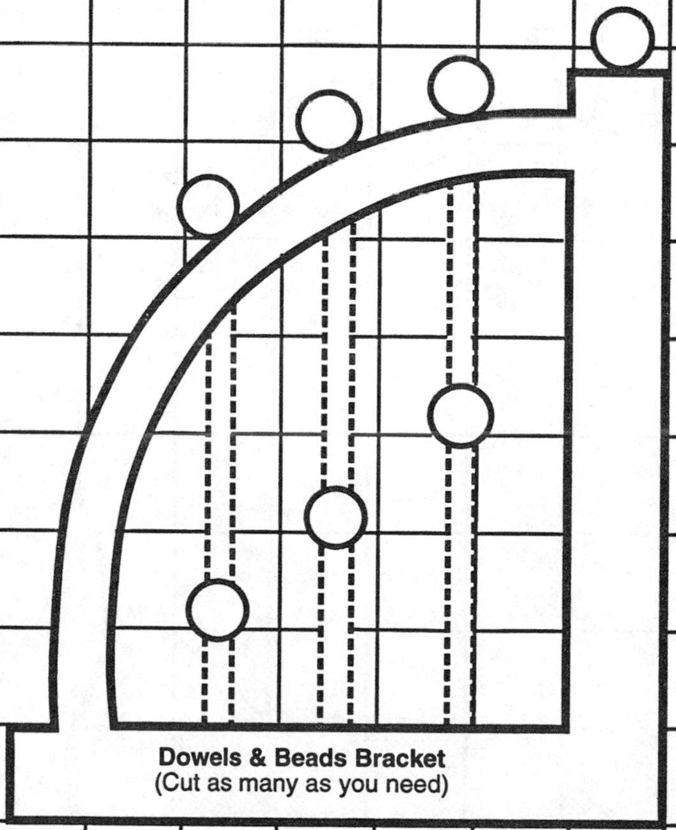

Wall/Shelf Brackets

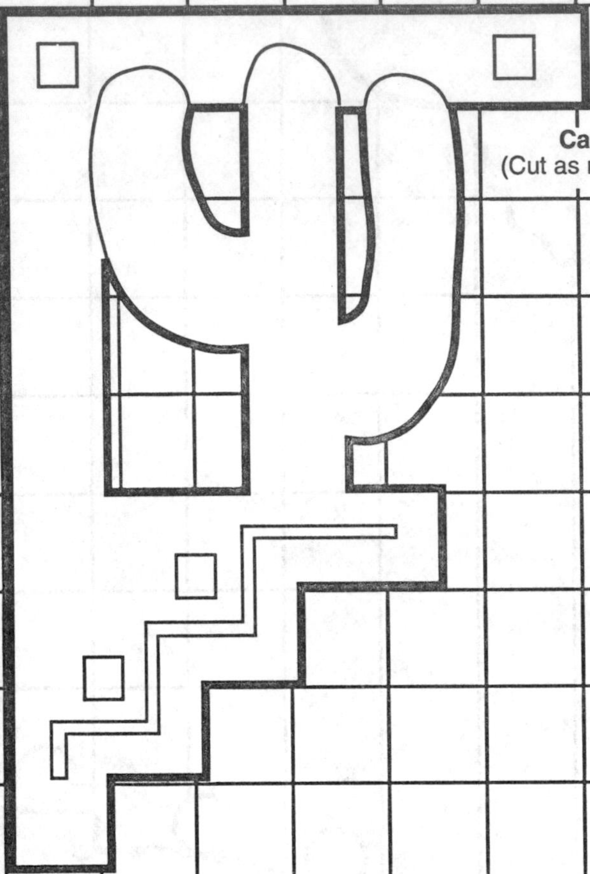

Cactus Bracket
(Cut as many as you need)

Tulip Bracket
(Cut as many as you need)

— INDEX —

Index